About the Authors

Roger Palmer MBA, PhD, DipM, FCIM, MILT, ARAgS is a faculty member at Henley Management College, and was formerly with Cranfield School of Management. He has held positions as marketing director and chief executive in both the business-to-business goods and consumer services sectors, and remains active as a consultant with a portfolio of business and not-for-profit clients. He has published several books and numerous academic journal articles, and has taught graduate and executive education programs around the world. He is a Visiting Professor at the Brisbane Graduate School of Business, and a regular visitor to Australia and New Zealand, where he usually manages to find the time to experience the wine industry from a consumer perspective.

Juanita Cockton Chartered Marketer, MA, Dip.BA, DipM, MCIM, LIPD has run her own business successfully for eighteen years and works with organizations on training and development programmes to create a marketing orientation and for organizational change. She has worked on in-company management development programs and has coached and mentored managers to develop and implement business and marketing plans. She is a Course Director for the Chartered Institute of Marketing (CIM) on its Senior Management Postgraduate Diploma Course, and has been a Senior Examiner for CIM. She has worked with the Chartered Institute of Personnel and Development (CIPD) as a consultant and tutor, and has been a guest speaker at the CIPD Human Resource Development (HRD) conference.

Graham Cooper Chartered Marketer, BSc, MSc, DipM, FCIM is a lecturer at the University of Central England in Birmingham and a Visiting Lecturer at Kingston Business School, Thames Valley University and the Oxford College of Marketing. He has spent many years in industry as a marketer, and acts as a business strategy consultant in areas such as defence, IT, education, marine and aerospace.

Contents

Introduction

Marketing is fundamental to an organization; every commercial or not-for-profit organization has customers and stakeholders. In turn, their association with the organization as client, consumer or somebody who experiences its service will influence their desire to repurchase or return, and also their perceptions, which they may well use to influence others. Yet in recent years marketing has had a bad press, and many in the profession would argue that it is not sufficiently well represented at senior management and board level. Perhaps one of the reasons for this is not a lack of marketing knowledge, but a less than sufficient ability on behalf of marketers to turn their knowledge and understanding into things that will make a positive difference to organizations and their customers. So this is not a book about marketing, but rather a book about the managerial skills, expertise and knowledge that we believe are necessary to be not just an effective *marketer* but also an effective *manager* as well.

The authors all have substantial and senior level commercial experience, as well as being involved with students and managers in their roles as educators and consultants. All of the authors have been or are examiners with the Chartered Institute of Marketing (www.cim.co.uk), and bring this insight and understanding to their work. They are all acutely aware of the sometimes radical differences between theory and practice, and the challenges that can face well-trained but potentially inexperienced marketers in the sometimes tough, political and unforgiving world of business.

The target market for this book is therefore the qualified but perhaps less experienced manager, somebody who has good knowledge and understanding of the functional skills of marketing – whilst these are touched upon in this book there is an implicit assumption that the principles of marketing are understood – but who needs wider managerial insight. A recent job advertisement in *The Economist* for a client manager was from a very well-known, blue-chip organization, and asked for applications from people with good first degrees from prestigious universities, deep understanding of the business area concerned, and several years of work experience as well as being fluent in Russian and possibly other Eastern European languages – all for what seemed a remarkably modest salary. So managers these days need more than functional skills; these need to be complemented by managerial capability and other attributes, such as language skills or specific experience, in order to be successful in an ever more competitive employment market. This book will also be useful to established managers who recognize the need to refresh and challenge their own experience, as well as for students who are studying for professional qualifications as they attempt to build on their academic skills and kickstart their careers.

The book is divided into three major sections, with chapters contributing to each of these. This is outlined in Figure I.1.

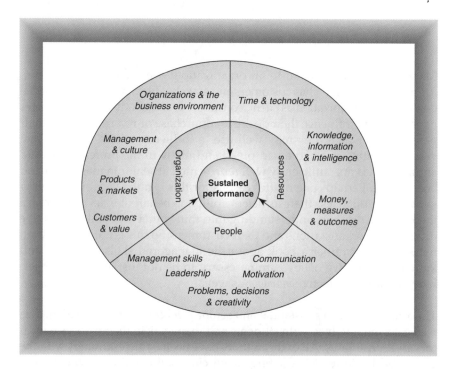

**Figure I.1
Structure of
the book**

There are three main themes – organization, people and resources. Each of these main areas is broken down into a series of chapters which discuss these topics in more detail. Each of the chapters is designed to give insight into the subject area, and to discuss relevant tools and techniques. There are checklists, vignettes and short case studies designed to help managers understand practical application. One of the problems with a book is that it contains content but in order to be relevant also needs context – and of course each manager has a slightly different problem to cope with. We hope that the design and presentation of the book will stimulate thinking, support marketing knowledge and provide resources which will help managers to deal with the problems they face. One of the things that we know from previous research is that managers are unlikely to read this or any other book from the first page to the last. Hence readers can skim the chapters and dip in and out to obtain the information they need, and the book is written in such a way as to provide checklists, summaries and accessible takeaway for the reader in a hurry.

Finally, we would like to offer our thanks to and acknowledge the support and assistance of a number of friends and colleagues, including Professor Cliff Bowman of the Cranfield School of Management; Professor Paul Millier of EM Lyon, whose ideas on marketing and management stimulated our own; Professor Richard Brookes of the University of Auckland, a lateral thinker who always brings fresh, applied insights; and Roger Singer, for allowing us to use information from his website (www.market-modelling.co.uk). Finally, our thanks to Tim Goodfellow, our editor at Elsevier/Butterworth-Heinemann, whose enthusiasm provided us with such staunch support from when the idea for this book first emerged.

Roger Palmer, Henley Management College
Juanita Cockton, The Marketing Studio
Graham Cooper, University of Central England

Part I Organization

1 Customers and value

Introduction

As will be discussed in Chapter 2, products and their relationship to markets is central to our thinking. Managing products in markets and measuring the outcomes in terms of market share and perhaps customer satisfaction are almost unquestioned in the minds of many marketers. However, the dramatic and dynamic changes that are occurring in marketplaces have led to the role of marketing, and the contribution that it makes to business success, being questioned. It seemed in the boom times of the 1980s that marketing was enjoying something of a renaissance, but from then on its role has been increasingly in doubt.

The concept of relationship marketing provided a much greater focus on customers and other stakeholders rather than on products, features and benefits. This put the emphasis on longer-term, mutually profitable relationships, but one criticism of relationship marketing has been the absence of tools and techniques that enable managers to 'do' relationship marketing, and differentiate this from transaction marketing. Recognizing that the purpose of the business is to deliver value to shareholders and other stakeholders in the business, the ability to link marketing activity to the financial objectives of the organization is seen as an important one (see Chapter 12). A leading thinker, the late Peter Doyle (Doyle, 2000), wrote a book called *Value Based Marketing*, which has sparked much discussion and debate on this topic. This chapter will investigate some of the issues surrounding this area and present some concepts, tools and techniques to enable managers to address the issues more comprehensively.

The 4Ps – adequate but insufficient

The principles of marketing emerged as a consumer-focused, brand-orientated topic area characterized in the 1950s and 1960s by the acronym '4Ps'. Just as few of us would prefer to drive a car, watch a television or use a telephone made in the 1950s and 1960s, so we also have to question the validity of this original concept half a century later. Inevitably there has been enormous change in business and society, and those factors fundamental to change have been identified (Brookes and Palmer, 2004) by some recent research:

- *Increasing emphasis on service aspects of products* – it is increasingly difficult to compete on the basis of product features. Some products, such as mobile phones, now contain such a bewildering array of features that simple and straightforward phones are being sold as differentiated. Service has become a major source of differentiation and, in many developed economies, a critical aspect of marketing.

- *Financial accountability, loyalty and value management* – marketing is invariably seen as a cost rather than an investment, and marketers have to recognize the need to justify their actions in financial terms and demonstrate the contribution to profitability.

- *Increased retailing power and 'systemic' relationships* – the largest company in the world, Wal-Mart, is a retailer. Retailers, and other network builders and managers such as Toyota, have both the capability and the power to reach back to their suppliers in order to integrate systems and business processes.

- *Organizational transformation and new organizational structures* – organizations have changed in response to changes in the business environment, such as increasing consumer power, the increasing importance of service, demands for value and the trend towards globalization. Decision-making has moved from the top of the hierarchy to the front line in order to increase responsiveness, and organizations both cooperate and compete in a complex network of relationships.

- *Interactive media and mass communication* – before the Internet and the proliferation of media, mass communication was almost as simple as buying an advertising slot in the commercial break of a popular soap opera. Media of all kinds have proliferated – TV and radio channels, numerous niche newspapers and magazines, and of course the Internet – together with the changes in behaviour that this has brought about.

The media explosion

In the UK in 2006, it was estimated that there are:

- 739 radio stations
- 479 television stations
- 1680 magazines
- 1491 newspapers
- 4389 UK media brands on line

and that the average manager

- receives 99 emails a day
- spends 11.3 hours a week on the Internet.

(Source: Craig Hanna, e-consultancy)

Against this backdrop we have also seen a change in the value of the customer. When markets were buoyant and expanding, the conventional 4Ps or transactional style of marketing was a well-developed means of entering and gaining markets. As markets became more mature, gaining new customers became more expensive and the strategic value of current customers increased.

Increasingly, the battle is now not just for market share as the driver of volume. The drive for share combined with takeovers and rationalization has led to a position where many companies now enjoy the economies of scale and experience that have accrued in the industry; technology and its application is common amongst competitors.

The battle has developed from market share to market space as companies utilize their inherent resources and capabilities, the skills with which they utilize their resources, to drive their businesses forward. At the forefront of this are those retailers such as Tesco and Carrefour who, as well as battling for market dominance and leading the charge in the Chinese and east European markets, are also building on their skills and capabilities to diversify into new markets. Tesco, for example, is the largest Internet retailer in Europe, as well as having substantial interests in financial services and insurance, clothes and petrol retailing, and further expansion into household goods, pharmacies and optician services.

As the Chief Executive of Tesco, Sir Terry Leahy, said in a media interview in January 2004:

> We have only got 5% of the non-food market in Britain, we've only got 6% of the convenience market and we have only got 2–3% of the banking market … In all those examples we could be much bigger.

So competition is based not just on market share but also on share of customer spend. Hence the focus has moved from supplying products and services to understanding the value of the customer to the organization and how the company can in turn provide better value to that customer in order to capture an ever higher share of the customer's spend.

It is currently said that the only asset the company has is the ability to earn an income stream now and in the future from its customer base. Those customers are becoming more vociferous and harder to please, but, at least intuitively, many managers recognize the need to compete not just for share of the market but also for share of wallet – the proportion of the customer's total spend that they can capture.

The demanding customer

The case of the Ford Pinto is iconic in the history of consumerism. In 1968, Ford in the US started development of a small saloon car to be rushed into production to compete with Japanese cars that were beginning to eat into the market. Due to a design flaw, the fuel tank was much more prone to rupture in the event of a rear-end collision. The spillage and burning of fuel led to a much higher incidence of death and serious injury when these vehicles were involved in road accidents. It later emerged that the vehicle could have been easily modified at a cost of just a few dollars per car. Ford decided against this on the basis of a cost–benefit analysis that weighed the cost of the modification against financial calculation of the benefit of lives saved and injuries not incurred. There was outrage that such a value could be placed on human life, and that for only a few dollars per car so much death, pain and injury could have been avoided.

In developed economies, consumers have power and are not afraid to use it. Greenpeace took on and then defeated Shell, one of the largest companies in the world, concerning the issue of the disposal of the Brent Spar oil rig – a redundant oil rig that Shell planned to sink in a deep trench in the north Atlantic. Greenpeace mobilized its forces, arguing that this was environmentally unsound, and Shell eventually backed down.

The Internet has enabled not just organizations but also individuals with a grudge or complaints to air their concerns. Individuals can even develop their own websites, and whilst smaller sites may flower and then die, others, such as www.mcspotlight.org, have developed from a single issue – a legal case involving protesters and the McDonald's chain – into a sophisticated protest site directed at multinational companies. Another example is the disaffected customer of United Airlines in the USA who started a website – www.untied.com – and presented the pages in a parody of the United corporate style. Legal action by United and subsequent press publicity rapidly propelled the site to the ranks of the most visited, receiving hundreds of thousands of hits a day. If you enter 'United Airlines' into Google, this site usually appears third in the search list. More considered organization is provided by websites such as www.notgoodenough.org, an Australian website where individual consumers can air their grievances.

However, such protests and consumer engagement is not confined to sophisticated, developed markets. In China, *tuangou* (or team buying) is being used to exercise consumer muscle and drive down prices. Specialist websites such as www.teambuy.com.cn have quickly evolved to increase buyer power and coordinate consumer action. One tactic is for a coordinated group of buyers simply to arrive unannounced at a store and demand a high level of discount on the products they intend to purchase. Increasingly, the price on the ticket is seen as simply an invitation to start negotiation.

The Internet has redressed the balance of power between large corporations and individual consumers who are increasingly willing to engage – and win.

(Sources: *The Economist*, numerous websites)

Recognizing the shifts that have occurred in marketplaces, we have also seen a reorientation of the concept of marketing from a functionally orientated focus on managing products and the product range, with an emphasis on new product development and an escalating list of features and benefits for each new product, to a revised emphasis on the role of the customer in terms of relationship marketing. However, the business imperative is for profitability, and an understanding of value is important to marketers in helping them to relate more closely to the objectives of the business. This evolution in approach is demonstrated in Figure 1.1.

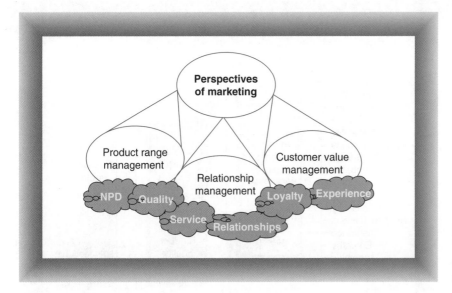

Figure 1.1
The changing emphasis of marketing

Figure 1.1 demonstrates some of the concepts that are linked together by these various perspectives of marketing. Three of these – quality, satisfaction and loyalty – are discussed here in a little more depth.

Quality

Japanese manufacturing industries taught Western economies a lesson with regard to quality. The 1980s saw a major commitment to quality through the auspices of the technique referred to as TQM – total quality management – which was useful, but not sufficient. Quality was seen to be associated with manufacturing but not with other aspects of the business, and in particular service quality. Here, the service quality model with its identification of service gaps provided a framework by which service could be managed. The framework is based around five dimensions of service quality, as shown in Table 1.1.

Table 1.1
Dimensions of service quality

Servqual dimension	Description
Reliability	Ability to perform the promised service dependably and accurately
Responsiveness	Willingness to help customers and provide prompt service
Assurance	Employees' knowledge and courtesy, and their ability to inspire trust and confidence
Empathy	Caring, individualized attention given to customers
Tangibles	Appearance of physical facilities, equipment, personnel and written materials
Source: Zeithaml and Bitner (2003)	

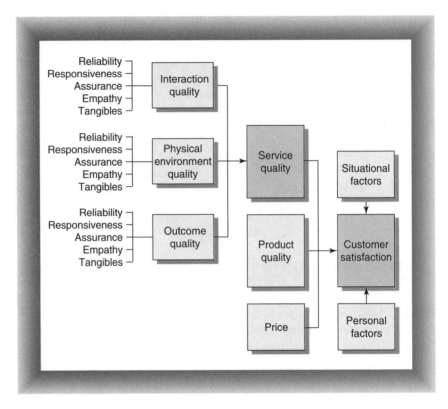

Figure 1.2
The SERVQUAL
model (Source:
Zeithaml and Bitner,
2003)

These are integrated into a framework known as the SERVQUAL model
(Figure 1.2).

This model allows the essentially intangible nature of service and the
maintenance of service standards to be deconstructed into a number of
specific areas that can be identified and managed. These are known as the
service quality gaps, of which there are five; the first gap represents a cul-
mination of the other four:

● *Gap 1 – expected service versus perceived service gap.* This represents the
  overall expectation of service by a customer compared to his or her perception of the service actually received. If the perceived service received
  does not meet expectations, then the opportunity exists to address the
  service gaps which combine to deliver the perceived service.

● *Gap 2 – consumer expectations versus management perceptions.* This gap
  occurs because of the lack of correct understanding by the management
  team of what the consumer actually expects, unfiltered by the management's own perceptions and interpretations.

● *Gap 3 – management perceptions versus service quality specifications.* The
  understanding of the required service then has to be translated into a
  specification that defines the level of service to be delivered. An inappropriate specification can cause this gap. The specification is sometimes
  referred to as a service blueprint.

- *Gap 4 – service quality specifications versus service delivery.* If the actual delivery of the service does not meet the specification, then this fourth gap will arise. As part of its service specification, a well-known chain of conference centres specifies that a bottle of wine and will be placed in the tutors hotel room – a gesture very much appreciated by the tutor concerned!

- *Gap 5 – service delivery versus external communications.* If service standards are communicated directly by advertising and promotion, or indirectly by word-of-mouth or experience, then this sets a level of expectation in the mind of the customer. If expectations are raised only to be disappointed, this is a significant failure and expensive waste of effort.

Satisfaction

There is a widespread belief and almost unquestioned assumption that customer satisfaction is linked to the propensity for customers to repurchase the product – in other words, customer satisfaction creates loyalty. Satisfaction has been the focus of considerable research, and this shows that it is only when satisfaction is at very high levels that this links to loyalty and repurchase.

Few would argue that customer satisfaction is an unreasonable goal. However, in itself this does not guarantee loyalty, although it does predispose customers to be loyal. From the customers' perspective, they would no doubt expect to be satisfied with their purchase, but this simply meets expectations and does not necessarily motivate them to purchase further products or services.

Measuring customer satisfaction

J D Power and Associates is an international marketing information and research company, well-known and respected for its authoritative reports in the area of customer satisfaction. Originally employed in the automotive sector it now works in a wide range of industries, including health care, consumer electronics and telecommunications.

Its recent research demonstrates that such automotive brands as Lexus, Skoda and Honda deliver the highest levels of customer satisfaction. Yet none of these brands necessarily has the highest level of market share, despite the undoubted satisfaction expressed by their customers. It may be that individual customers are loyal and time and again will repurchase their favoured products, but car buyers on the whole are known for their promiscuous behaviour.

Satisfaction is not the only component of the buying decision and, as Jones and Sasser (1995) note, customers are prone to defection 'whenever these customers have choices and feel free to make a choice'. So while satisfaction, underpinned by quality, is a necessary component of the offering, it does not necessarily correlate with loyalty and repurchase.

(Source: http://www.jdpower.com/default.aspx)

Loyalty

The idea of loyalty can be interpreted in a number of different ways. The outcome of loyalty from a business perspective is repurchase and/or an increased level of purchase. However, this could be achieved from several different perspectives:

- *Behavioural.* The act of repurchase may be due to a number of factors – perhaps loyalty, where the customer has a preference for the product, or simply through habitual buying behaviour or the lack of alternatives.

- *Attitudinal.* Repurchase is driven by underlying emotions which are expressed as preference for the brand, product or service despite the opportunities posed by alternative and substitute products.

Behavioural and attitudinal loyalty

Many smokers regularly purchase the same brand of cigarettes, although blind taste tests demonstrate that different brands cannot be distinguished. Indeed, the product itself detracts from the ability to taste differences.

It is late on a Saturday evening and a smoker realizes that he has run out of cigarettes. He gets in the car and goes to an all-night convenience store, but the store doesn't happen to have the smoker's particular favourite brand in stock. What is the smoker to do? Drive to the next retail outlet, which could be another 10 or 15 minutes away and even then not have the preferred brand in stock, or simply buy the next best alternative?

The answers to these questions help to distinguish between behavioural and attitudinal loyalty.

Similarly, research demonstrates that many 'loyalty cards' do not necessarily generate attitudinal loyalty, but that consumers make a trade-off between the benefits enjoyed in terms of discounts or free offers against the alternatives that are available.

In the minds of many managers, loyalty is usually associated with some form of emotional commitment. It is therefore difficult to determine loyalty simply by examining purchasing behaviour. Oliver (1999) takes this discussion a stage further and considers loyalty in four different phases:

1. *Cognitive* – a preference is expressed for the product or service.

2. *Affective* – an underlying emotional preference.

3. *Conative* – a desire to repurchase.

4. *Action* – deliberate action and choice to achieve a repurchase.

So loyalty is composed of both behavioural and attitudinal characteristics. Whilst repurchase rates can be ascertained and behavioural loyalty influenced in a number of different ways (for example, by loyalty cards, sampling, sequentially dated discount coupons, discounts for large and repeat purchases, etc.), understanding and managing attitudinal loyalty is more challenging. Reichheld (2003) suggests that in addition to measuring repurchase managers should also consider the likelihood of a customer recommending an organization's product or service to another customer. The willingness to recommend can be seen as a measure of the level of attitudinal customer loyalty.

Customer satisfaction can be considered as a measure of current performance, and the propensity of customers to recommend a product or service to other potential customers can be one guide to the future value of customers.

Indeed, the argument now goes further in that it is not just important to manage the physical product and the intangible aspects of service, but also to go further and manage the entire customer experience. It may be that every aspect of a flight is satisfactory, but the lasting memory is the time taken for the baggage to arrive and the difficult journey from the airport to the office or home. By managing all aspects of the customer experience – whether a flight, owning and running a car or taking a course at a university – the levels of satisfaction, loyalty and advocacy can be improved.

Understanding value

The argument is that customers are now a scarce commodity, and as a consequence they have a greater strategic value. Businesses need not only to gain customers but also to retain them having won them. The underlying arguments concern not just exchange of products and services, but the value that is created and divided between supplier and customer. This section will explore some of the concepts and arguments surrounding the understanding of value.

Value to the customer

Accountants can tell us all about costs and profits, but the expert on value is the customer. The value of the product to the customer can be considered in two parts:

1. *Economic value* – otherwise known as 'value in use'. This refers not just to the initial purchase price but also to wider areas such as switching costs, training and installation costs, ongoing costs of maintenance, depreciation and end-of-life disposal costs. By relating economic value in use to the requirements of the customer, a higher price can often be justified.

2. *Perceived value* – qualitative aspects of the product such as the brand, previous experience and reputation can all add to perceived value. Whilst products may be functionally similar, the customer may perceive one as superior to the other. Ford, a classic mid-range brand of car, has been unsuccessful in competing in the executive/luxury area of the market.

When paying executive car prices, BMW, Mercedes, Lexus and other upmarket brands are the products of choice. Ford has now acquired brands such as Volvo, Jaguar and Lincoln in order to appeal to this attractive market sector.

Value is about much more than price, and the exchange is about more than a product. The customer value equation gives a more comprehensive overview in terms of the benefits received against the sacrifices made by the customer (Figure 1.3).

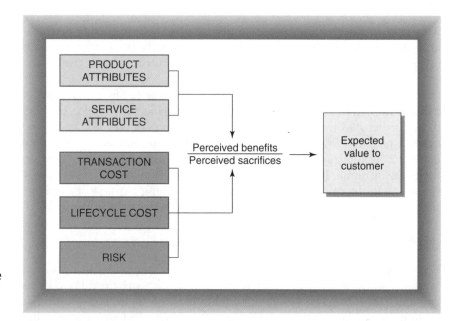

Figure 1.3
The customer value equation (Source: Neumann, 1995)

Value of the customer

Work at the Harvard Business School in conjunction with Bain and Company, a consulting firm, generated some powerful and influential data that suggests that retained customers are disproportionately more valuable to the firm. As Figure 1.4. suggests, reducing the rate at which customers are lost (the defection rate) leads to an increase in the average customer lifetime. As a consequence, the income stream for the customer is extended and therefore the total revenue captured is increased. Figure 1.4 suggests some attractive figures in terms of the percentage increase in customer value; even if a manager doesn't quite know what it means, which manager would not like to see an increase in customer value of anywhere from 30 to 85 percent?

A few words of explanation are necessary here:

- *Net Present Value of the profit stream*. The profit stream refers to the anticipated income adjusted for the time-based value of money. Just as we earn interest on a sum of money invested now, so we have to apply the opposite of interest – a discount – to anticipated revenues in order that we can compare them on a like-for-like basis. Hence customer lifetime

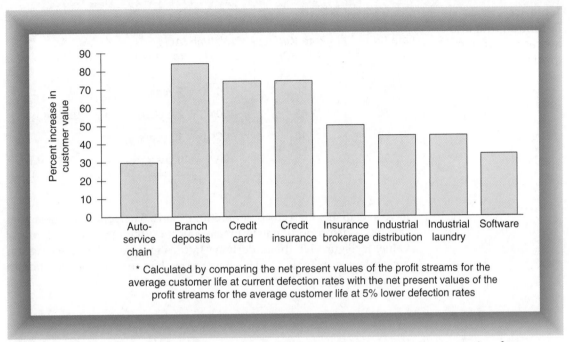

* Calculated by comparing the net present values of the profit streams for the
average customer life at current defection rates with the net present values of the
profit streams for the average customer life at 5% lower defection rates

Figure 1.4   Profit impact of a 5 percentage points increase in customer retention for
selected businesses (Source: Reichheld and Sasser, 1990)

value is often expressed in terms of NPV (net present value). Defining
quite what is meant by 'profit' is also a large area for debate which will
be discussed shortly.

* *Customer lifetime and customer value.* There is not a straight-line relationship between these two factors, as Figure 1.5 demonstrates. If we already

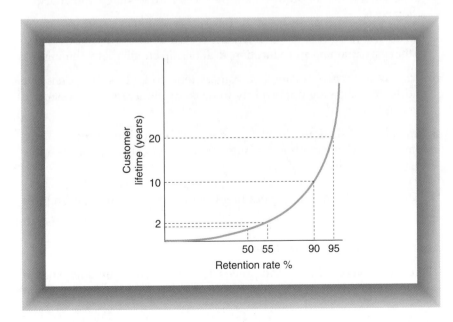

Figure 1.5
Retention rate and
average customer
lifetime

Table 1.2
Retention rate and
average customer
lifetime

Retention Rate (RR)	Defection Rate (DR) (100–RR)	Average Customer Lifetime (ACL) (Total customers/DR)	Increase in ACL for a 5% lower DR
50	50	100/50 = 2 years	
55	45	100/45 = 2.2 years	+10% ACL
90	10	100/10 = 10 years	
95	5	100/5 = 20 years	+100% ACL

have a relatively high customer lifetime, then a 5 percent lower defection rate has a disproportionately greater effect on the increase in customer value. In Figure 1.5, the underlying figures represented in the diagram are explained in Table 1.2. This helps to explain some of the variation in the increase in customer value noted in Figure 1.4.

Why retained customers are valuable

The arguments to explain why retained customers are more valuable can be explained by six factors (Buchanan and Gillies, 1990):

1. *Offset acquisition costs* – the cost of acquiring a customer is relatively high compared to maintenance. The longer the life of a customer, then, the better the value obtained from the investment in acquisition.

2. *Increased volume* – as the volume of products currently supplied increases, more customer volume for that category of product is captured.

3. *Incremental sales* – as an established supplier, there is the opportunity to range sell additional products and services with lower customer acquisition costs.

4. *Reduced maintenance costs* – maintenance costs themselves decline over time as the cost of training and education, relationship building, etc., diminishes.

5. *Price management* – retained customers tend to be less price-sensitive and there is also the opportunity to resist or moderate the pressure to decrease prices.

6. *Referrals* – satisfied and loyal customers can act to refer additional customers. Word-of-mouth is not only persuasive; it also represents a low cost of acquisition.

See Chapter 12 for a more accounting-oriented discussion regarding this topic.

Creating value for customers

There are some convincing and powerful reasons why companies should seek to retain customers for longer. However, if we turn the argument around we can ask the question, why would customers want to stay with the current supplier? One of the reasons might be that the supplier offers higher value than alternatives. Understanding how that value might be configured and supplied is the subject of this section; shortly we will also consider which types of customers should be the focus of value-added attention. As Treacy and Wiersema (1995) note in the subtitle of their book *The Discipline of Market Leaders*, 'choose your customers, narrow your focus, dominate your market'. Not all customers value the same things in the same way, and hence we need to match what customers find valuable with our capability to deliver.

In essence, Treacy and Wiersema proposed a series of value disciplines. Each of these disciplines delivers different kinds of value to meet the needs of different types of customers. They defined these as:

- *Operational Excellence* – a highly efficient business model that drives down costs, improves service but perhaps does not excel in any one of these characteristics. When taken together, it adds up to a best value deal. The exponential growth of low-cost airlines demonstrates that whilst customer service and convenience may not be ideal, or the airlines offer the greatest travel experience, when taken together with the low price and opportunity to visit otherwise unaffordable places this adds up to high-value to the customer.

- *Product Leadership* – value is delivered by producing class-leading products and highly valued brands. Korean car manufacturer Hyundai was at one time noted for rather dreary, dismal cars with a modest reputation for reliability. With attention to detail, a focus on quality and keen pricing, sales of their cars in key markets such as the USA have increased significantly, supported by Hyundai's class-leading 10-year/100 000-mile powertrain warranty. Staying within the automotive sector, many experienced motorcyclists would suggest that the Harley Davidson is not class-leading in terms of performance and road-holding, yet the power of the brand is very persuasive. HOGs (members of the Harley owners group) flocked to rallies in 2003 to celebrate the hundredth anniversary of the brand. In the services sector, eBay has provided a marketplace around the world – the largest online car-boot and garage sale!

- *Customer Intimacy* – from a deep and insightful understanding of requirements, customers are offered not just products but also solutions that add value to the client's business and build long-term relationships. For example, a manufacturer of fragrances doesn't just provide perfumes to include in things such as bathroom and cleaning products, but also has a product development unit that develops a complete portfolio of products, including packaging and sales support material, to present to their large retailer clients.

Brookes and Palmer (2004) built on this and the work of Christopher (1996) to present a more comprehensive framework in which the implications for managers of adopting a value stance can be understood (Table 1.3).

Table 1.3   Value stance and managerial implications

	Product and brand focus	*Customer focus*	*Network efficiency*
Basis of competition	Develop loyalty and repeat purchase	Improve value offering	Improve channel coverage
Product velocity			
Focus	Brand development	Service and quality	Responsiveness
Low cost to serve			
Product differentiation	Features and benefits	Value-in-use	Service enhancement
Route to profit	Brand premium	Increase and retain value	Reduce costs below umbrella of price
Promotion	Awareness, involvement with brand Broadcast	Communicate value proposition Narrowcast	Presence/dominance to purchaser via channels
Service	Routinized	Customized	Class leading
Route to market	Differentiate by channel	Channel neutral	Ubiquitous
Processes	Supporting	Enhancing	Transforming

Adapted from Brookes and Palmer (2004)

Of course this is not to say that we do not strive to be good or excellent in everything that we do, but if we are truly to differentiate, be distinctive and offer high levels of value then we have to be clear as to the nature of the value that we offer and implement to achieve the desired results. This has sometimes quite fundamental implications for our business, affecting not just the operational issues but also the underlying culture, attitudes and values. If we consider this in terms of the processes (supporting, enhancing, transforming) discussed in Table 1.3, implementation involves not only different ways of doing things but also more fundamental and different ways of thinking about and running a business. This is illustrated by Table 1.4.

Managing the value of customers

In this section we shall consider how customers can be managed for lifetime value. A word of warning is appropriate here. We are marketers and not accountants, and hence are not primarily concerned with the precision of the figures as long as they are sufficiently accurate for decision-making purposes. We subscribe to the view that it is better to be approximately right and get on with managing the business, rather than worrying about an infinite level of detail which prevents us from making progress. Hence we present

Table 1.4   Relating value stance to process and implementation

Value stance and processes	Characteristics
REINFORCE	• Competitive
	• Gain power and advantage
	• Capture value
Example:	*Unilever*
Value stance: Product and brand focus	Stated policy is to rationalize and focus on major brands, increase spend behind each brand, reinforce position in the market.
ENHANCE	• Cooperative
	• Create advantage
	• Increase value
	• Role of resources
Example:	*Apple*
Value stance: Customer focus	Create value in the market, actively seek to change and adapt relationships in order to create value. Combine resources to create new product and service experiences.
TRANSFORM	• Cooperative
	• Gain advantage, counteract power
	• Create mutual value, prevent value destruction
	• Synergistic resource combination
Example:	Merger of *Carrefour* and *Promodes* (see Hendrickson *et al.*, 2001)
Value stance: Network efficiency	These two French companies, both retailers, chose to merge in order to combat the perceived threat of Wal-Mart's continued expansion. The merged businesses have market leadership in a number of South American, European and Far Eastern countries. The merger created the second largest retailer in the world.

some 'crafty cook', practice-based ideas to stimulate your own thinking on this important topic, which is investigated in more detail in Chapter 12.

Customer profitability

Many accounting and marketing reporting systems are organized in such a way that they report profitability by geography, sales team, product line or some similar permutation. If a company does report profitability by customer, this is often at sales revenue or possibly gross margin/contribution level. It is unusual for companies to establish a profit and loss account by customer whereby otherwise unallocated costs, such as sales and marketing and distribution, are allocated to each account. It is more typical for such costs to be 'marmaladed' – that is to say, spread or averaged evenly across each customer. However, customers want and require different levels of service, and hence this creates different costs; understanding is lost by the averaging of costs across accounts. Establishing a system to understand net customer profitability can lead to considerable insight.

As this example illustrates, the way that we consider costs and allocate them to customers can affect the way that we understand their value.

For this example, the customer base of a market research company was analysed. Of the 157 accounts, 10 were determined as having both high margin and high volume. Clearly, these most valuable accounts are the ones that should receive particular focus and attention. Looking at two of those accounts (Table 1.5) shows that at the level of *revenue* customer A appears more attractive than customer B, but when all the costs that are incurred by the customers are allocated then customer B is nearly three times more profitable than customer A at the level of *contribution margin*, as it is referred to in this case. As this is a service business there are very few raw material costs as such, and the direct costs essentially represent executive time allocated to each customer. Customer A also required a higher level of sales servicing.

Table 1.5
Customer profitability analysis (Sharna *et al.*, 2001)

	Customer A ($K)	Customer B ($K)
Revenue	203.3	156.0
Direct costs	174.9	113.1
Selling costs	14.2	3.1
Contribution margin	14.2	39.7
% of Revenue	7.0	25.0

One such company that has developed a customer profitability tool is a Japanese manufacturer of air-conditioning systems, operating throughout Europe. It supplies heating, ventilation and air-conditioning components and equipment to its distributors. The company has identified its most important clients and has established a process whereby it can estimate customer profitability by means of a customer profit-and-loss account. An example of this is shown in Table 1.6. As actual figures are used, the company is not named.

The costs were estimated on the basis of what actually causes or creates the cost. This concept is known as *activity-based costing*. If we look at the example in Table 1.6, field sales costs are estimated at €6840, calculated on the basis of 57 sales visits at a cost of €120 per visit. Other costs may be more accurately identified, such as the cost of discounts. However, the general principle of this approach to management accounting is that the cost of gathering the data should not exceed its value. Providing the data

	€	Example
Sales value	962582	**962582**
Cost of sales	635650	
Gross margin	326931	**326931**
Discounts	38503	
Advertising and promotion spend	14300	
Administration costs	53281	
Field sales cost	6840	
Total costs	112924	**112924**
Operating profit		**214007**

Table 1.6
Individual customer profit-and-loss account

is sufficiently accurate for decision-making purposes, and is not misleading, then it is fit for purpose.

The company also established a series of critical success factors that were scored on a 1 to 5 scale. Each distributor could then be mapped on a matrix of CSFs on one axis, and customer operating profits on the other. Monthly revenue against the annual target was also expressed in a graphical format, and this gave the management team a simple but powerful set of tools for comparison purposes and to manage their most important customers. Chapter 12 presents a more formal tool, the balanced scorecard, that performs a similar function.

Customer lifetime value

The concept of managing customer value is an appealing one, but as soon as we start to consider the practical application of this concept it becomes a little more problematic. When we are calculating the future income stream, which of the following should this refer to?

- *Sales revenue* – at the gross level, or after being adjusted for discounts or rebates? Sales people would typically think of customers in terms of their revenue.

- *Gross margin or contribution* – when we relate this to the profit-and-loss account, this equates to sales revenue less the cost of goods sold. However, it does not account for significant costs that may be incurred but are not directly allocated or capable of being allocated at the product level.

- *Net customer profitability* – calculated after allocating costs which can be related to customers who have caused them to be incurred.

The more detailed (approximately) the figure that we can arrive at, then the more appropriate it is likely to be for our purposes. Hence, net customer profitability as calculated in the example above could be suitable for this purpose.

Gupta and Lehmann (2005) provide a simple tool to help in calculating the lifetime value of the customer. In doing this, they make three assumptions:

1. Profit margins remain constant over the life of the customer.

2. The retention rate for customers stays constant over time.

3. Customer lifetime value is estimated over an infinite horizon.

They demonstrate that whilst changing these assumptions does influence customer lifetime value, it is a simple and straightforward approach that follows our dictum of being sufficiently simple yet fit for purpose. As they say in their book, '{it}does not require large amounts of data, is simple to understand and use for decision-making purposes, and yet provides a good approximation of more detailed and data intensive methods'. The formula they propose is noted in Figure 1.6.

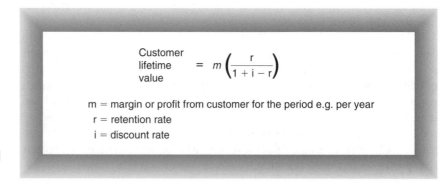

$$\text{Customer lifetime value} = m \left(\frac{r}{1 + i - r} \right)$$

m = margin or profit from customer for the period e.g. per year
r = retention rate
i = discount rate

Figure 1.6
Simplified CLV
formula (Gupta and
Lehmann, 2005)

The discount rate should be set to reflect the level of risk associated with the security of the future income stream; typically, discount rates would be in the range of 8–16 percent. Using this formula, the lifetime value of a customer is typically between one and five times m. The most important factor influencing lifetime customer value is the retention rate.

Calculating the lifetime value of customers helps us to think in a different way about their value to the business, and to consider the relative costs of customer acquisition and retention. It seems an almost axiomatic and unquestioned assumption that (apparently) it costs five times more to gain a customer than it does to keep one. However, this is a generalization, and by generating company-relevant data this can be tested and sensible management choices made.

Customer acquisition and retention

An insight into lifetime customer profitability may well encourage a different perspective on the investment that is required to gain and then retain a customer. There is a large assumption here that businesses do actually consider their marketing investments as activities which are designed to either acquire or retain customers. However, if the company is attempting to engender customer loyalty by some form of relationship marketing activity, then considering marketing spend in a different way could give a useful perspective. As we have seen when considering customer profitability, it is all too easy to average out costs and lose the clarity and insight that detail lends.

For many organizations, one of the largest investments in customer acquisition is represented by the sales force. The role of sales is to gain and maintain customers, but it is rare for the cost of customer acquisition and the targeting of sales resource against not just quantity but quality of customers to be actively driven by an understanding of acquisition and retention costs, as an investment in the future income stream represented by customer lifetime value.

To assist in gaining clarity in this area, two activities are worthwhile:

1. *Salesforce efficiency and effectiveness analysis*. The cost of the sales team can be reasonably accurately estimated. Allowing for administrative time, sales training, meetings, holidays, etc., the time available for customer visits can be estimated. This is then further subdivided into time invested in managing relationships with current customers, and that committed to prospecting for new customers. Netting off the number of accounts gives the figure for net account gain. Reviewing this against sales costs then gives the cost per account gain. When conducting exercises of this nature, it is invariably interesting and occasionally surprising for managers to discover:

   - the amount of time invested in servicing current customers

   - the (sometimes low) rate of net account gain

   - the cost per account gain

   - the rate at which accounts are turned over (customer churn).

2. *Marketing spend analysis*. The marketing budget is reviewed in order to determine investments in customer acquisition and customer retention. Often marketing activities are not conceived with these metrics specifically in mind, but it is surprising how a new perspective can help in refocusing attention. For example, trade shows are a common feature of business-to-business marketing, but what is their purpose? Often answers include such things as meeting customers, managing relationships, showcasing new products, initiating contact with new customers and maintaining a presence in the market. If objectives can be defined in this way, then appropriate measures can be put in place to determine the cost effectiveness of the event.

By utilizing the data gained from the salesforce and marketing spend analyses, it is possible to develop (at least sufficiently accurately for decision-making purposes) a good insight into the cost of customer acquisition and retention against the value of the customers concerned. Managers should then start to ask some hard questions about the use of resources against the return being made.

Typical problems that often arise include:

- the overservicing of current customers

- excessive price flexibility to gain what are actually unprofitable new customers

- imbalance between short- and long-term actions

- lack of clear definition of objectives and results for the often significant investments made in marketing and sales support activities.

The customer portfolio

The Boston matrix is a well tried and understood tool that assists in managing the product portfolio. The discussion in this and other chapters proposes that value is generated by customers rather than products, and hence an understanding of the value drivers in the portfolio can help us in making better marketing decisions. The customer strategy matrix gives some guidance (Figure 1.7).

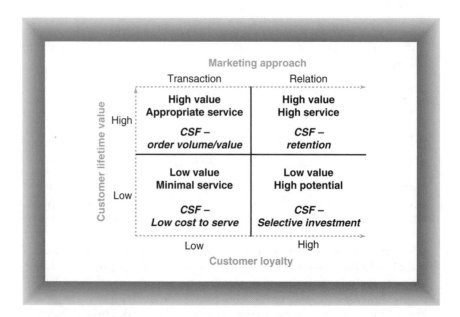

Figure 1.7
Customer strategy matrix

The matrix suggests that the marketing approach should be adapted to the characteristics of the customer, taking into account customer lifetime value (CLV) and also some understanding of customer needs. Critical success factors (CSFs) can also be determined and used to develop measures of performance. Some customers do not need or want a relationship, but they can be just as valuable as those who do although they need to be treated in a different way. A few brief comments on each of the four boxes of the matrix follow:

- *High value, high service* – these are likely to be our most valuable customers who take time to grow and develop into this box of the matrix; the critical success factor here is that these customers should, as far as possible, never be lost. The value of these customers more than justifies the high level of service that they often require.

- *High value, appropriate service* – these customers are significantly large, and are invariably aware of their purchasing power. They will drive a hard deal, and it is important that senior and experienced salespeople, skilled in the art of negotiation, work with such customers. They are deal-focused, but their size alone makes them attractive. The measure of success here is the volume and value of the orders gained.

- *Low value, high potential* – some of these customers have the potential to be our long-term and large customers in the future. We need to take a long-term view of the investment required, and selectively invest in those customers that we believe have the potential to grow with our support in the future. A relatively small investment at this stage may well lead to a disproportionately high return. Our skill in selecting future winners and managing our investment in them is critical.

- *Low value, minimal service* – virtually every market has a proportion of customers who are price-driven and relatively small buyers. Whilst the volume and revenue from such buyers may be useful, it is essential not to over-invest valuable marketing resources in this quadrant. A critical success factor here will be the ability to reach this market at low cost with a suitably attractive offer. Often price-led, the market can be used to tactically manage the volume/margin equation, with appropriate price-led offers when capacity or resource is surplus.

The overall approach to the profitable management of the customer and market interface is summarized in a framework loosely based on the work of Best (2005); see Figure 1.8.

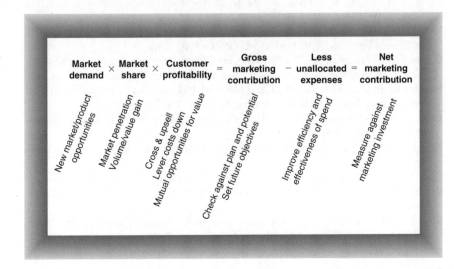

Figure 1.8
Summary of customer/market strategy

The management of customer profitability as part of an overall relationship management strategy depends on:

- *Identifying profitable customers* – identify profitable customers in order to select those to whom particular attention should be paid and who represent the highest and most secure potential income stream for the company.

- *Customer profitability* – develop a method which is contextually relevant and appropriate to the particular circumstances of the company and enables customer profitability to be sensibly estimated without excessive cost and complication.

- *Calculating CLV* – use the understanding of customers to develop insight into the future revenue streams for the company. The risk associated with each customer can be adjusted by means of the discount rate, but the calculation is most sensitive to variations in retention rate.

- *Developing marketing programs* – using the understanding of the differing types of customers, different programs and measures can be developed for each customer group.

- *Managing resource allocation* – the sales resource and marketing budget are scarce resources, and they should be allocated against a clear understanding of how they will generate current and future returns. Suitable measures of performance should be developed and objectives set for staff involved.

References

Best, R.J. (2005). *Market-Based Management: Strategies For Growing Customer Value And Profitability*, Upper Saddle River, NJ: Pearson Prentice Hall.

Brookes, R.W. and Palmer, R.A. (2004). *The New Global Marketing Reality*, Basingstoke: Palgrave Macmillan.

Buchanan, R.W. and Gillies C.S. (1990). Value managed relationships: the key to customer retention and profitability. *European Management Journal*, **8(4)**, 523–525.

Christopher, M. (1996). From brand values to customer values, *Journal of Marketing Practice*, **2(1)**, 55–66.

Doyle, P. (2000). *Value-Based Marketing: Marketing Strategies for Corporate Growth and Shareholder Value*. Chichester: John Wiley & Sons Inc.

Gupta, S. and Lehmann, D. (2005). *Managing Customers as Investments: The Strategic Value of Customers in the Long Run*, Upper Saddle River, NJ: Pearson Education.

Hendrickson, M., Heffernan, W.D. and Howard, P.H. (2001). Consolidation in food retailing and dairy. *British Food Journal*, **103(10)**, 715–728.

Jones, T.O. and Sasser, W.E. (1995). Why satisfied customers defect. *Harvard Business Review*, **73**, 88–100.

Neumann, E. (1995). *Creating Customer Value*. Cincinnati, OH: Thompson Executive Press.

Oliver, R.L. (1999). Whence consumer loyalty? *Journal of Marketing*, **63**, 33–34.

Reichheld, F.F. (2003). The one number you need to grow. *Harvard Business Review*, **81**, 46–54.

Reichheld, F.F. (1996). *The Loyalty Effect: The Hidden Forces Behind Growth, Profits, and Lasting Value*. Boston MA: Harvard Business School Press.

Reichheld, F.F. and Sasser, W.E. (1990). Zero defections: quality comes to services. *Harvard Business Review*, **Sep/Oct**, 105–111.

Sharma, A., Krishnan, R. and Grewal, D. (2001). Value creation in markets – a critical area for focus in business to business markets. *Industrial Marketing Management*, **30(4),** 391–402.

Treacy, M. and Wiersema, F. (1995). *The Discipline of Market Leaders: Choose Your Customers, Narrow Your Focus, Dominate Your Market*. London: HarperCollins.

Zeithaml, V.A. and Bitner, M.J. (2003). *Services Marketing: Integrating Customer Focus Across The Firm*. London: McGraw-Hill.

2 Products and markets

Introduction

Classically, the concept of marketing revolves around the 4Ps – Product, Price, Promotion and Place. This is sometimes enhanced to include some additional Ps – people processes, physical evidence, proactive customer service, etc. Yet, as we have seen, since the development of this original framework markets have changed dramatically and the role of marketing is seen as much more strategic and cross-functional. However, some things don't change, and the product or service remains at the core of the exchange process. This chapter will refer to the change in the perspective of marketing and its role in the organization, and illustrate and enhance this by discussing concepts and, more particularly, tools and techniques for functional marketing management.

The nature of markets

As an economist, Kay (2003) takes a singularly pithy view of what is required for a market to operate. In essence, this revolves around agreed procedures or laws relating to the nature of contracts and the ownership of property. For a market to operate, the legitimate right of the seller to pass ownership to the buyer, and for that exchange to be recognized and enforceable, is fundamental. Of course, for markets to operate satisfactorily, often more than these basics are required. However, many owners of the copyright to music, software and branded luxury goods, for example, would regard contract and property rights as a significant step forward – as a walk round a street market in Shanghai, Bangkok or any other home of counterfeit products would testify.

Imagine you are walking down a street and a well-dressed woman comes up to you holding in her hand a small, thin roll of paper not much bigger than a cigarette. She tells you that it is actually a £10 note, and she would be prepared to sell it to you for £9 but won't allow you to unroll or even touch the paper before you pay for it. What would you do? Take an immediate profit or keep on walking? Experiments suggest that most people would forego the profit opportunity, fearing the greater risk of losing £9. Trust and commitment are also essential to the operation of markets, and that can be demonstrated in many different ways – the trusted nature of the brand, an impressive confidence-enhancing building such as a bank or hotel, the use of warranties and guarantees, after-sales service and, particularly in business-to-business markets, the importance of reputation.

One definition of a market is that it is composed of closely substitutable needs. I may buy a television, but my need is for information and entertainment in the evening. This need could be fulfilled in many other ways – going to the cinema or theatre, reading a newspaper, listening to music, or even talking to my partner perhaps over a glass of wine. The mistake that many organizations make is at this fundamental level, failing to define the marketplace. Many managers feel comfortable in defining their markets in terms of what their products are, yet customers buy products not because of what they are but because of what they do. Essentially, products are problem-solving devices with features that deliver benefits to the customer. This is exemplified in a recent article published by the Harvard Business School:

> Marketers have lost the forest for the trees, focusing too much on creating products for narrow demographic segments rather than satisfying needs. Customers want to 'hire' a product to do a job, or, as legendary Harvard Business School marketing professor Theodore Levitt put it, 'People don't want to buy a quarter-inch drill. They want a quarter-inch hole!'
>
> With Levitt's words as a rallying cry, a recent *Harvard Business Review* article, 'Marketing Malpractice: The Cause and the Cure', argues that the marketer's task is to understand the job the customer wants to get done, and design products and brands that fill that need.
>
> (Christensen *et al.*, 2005)

Defining the market

Jack Welsh, the former chief executive of the American giant General Electric, was famous for saying that GE would be number one or number two in every market that it served. This is not unreasonable, as there is plenty of evidence to suggest that the leader in a market has substantially improved returns compared to followers. However, he was given cause to think when in discussion with an army officer, who commented that it was all too easy to be number one or number two if it was you that defined the market. The consequence of this comment was to cause General Electric to redefine its aeroengine business and transition from simply selling capital goods to extend into the maintenance and repair of the engines once installed.

Defining the market in which we participate is not just sophisticated wordsmithing, but is important because it defines our perspective of competitors, market growth and development, and market size and segmentation. Markets are places where buyers and sellers meet to exchange goods of value. Hence as sellers we only see part of the equation, and a sensible way to address market definition is from the point of view of the buyer. If markets are composed of closely substitutable needs, then we can start to define the market and thus our competitors by asking our customers what other products and services they would purchase were ours not available. In this way we can arrive at a market/customer-based definition of the market rather than a product/seller view. As with the example of General Electric, we can further extend our understanding of the market by considering the additional products and services that we could potentially provide.

Following this market-based definition, we can start to understand that for one sector of the market the sale of theatre tickets might compete in the same market as restaurants when fulfilling the need for relaxation and entertainment. For a younger age profile, alcopops compete with recreational drugs to fulfill the need for a different type of experience. Ultimately, our definition of the market is an artificial one, and it could be argued that in fact we serve 100 percent of the market to which we are best suited. An important part of the marketing process is continual environmental scanning to question and reappraise the focus and direction of the organization.

Market space

This introduces us to the idea of market space; the extent to which we define our current market is to define existing market space. Within our market space we compete with other suppliers of goods and services; sometimes we win and sometimes we lose in the battle for market share. In today's highly competitive markets this becomes ever more ruthless as margins and profitability are relentlessly squeezed. How much more attractive, then, to create new market space and occupy the territory revealed. This can be done principally in two ways:

1. *Market innovation* – to extend current market space.

2. *Invention and new product development* – to create new market space.

The concept of market space is discussed by Kim and Mauborgne (1999), but Bowman (1994, 1998) provides the perceived use value (PUV) tool which helps in making tangible this concept, in principle similar to the strategy canvas tool (Kim and Mauborgne, 2002).

Market innovation

The use of Bowman's tool builds on the principle that different elements of the marketing mix can attract different prices due to differing levels of price sensitivity, hence they are of different value to the buyer. This is illustrated in Figure 2.1.

This begs the question, how can these factors of differing value and price sensitivity be elicited? In this case we can tap into the intuitive knowledge that managers have of their products and markets; this is best achieved in a workshop with a team of managers. Working from a customer perspective, the process is:

1. Brainstorm the factors that are of value to customers – what attracts them and convinces them to purchase our product.

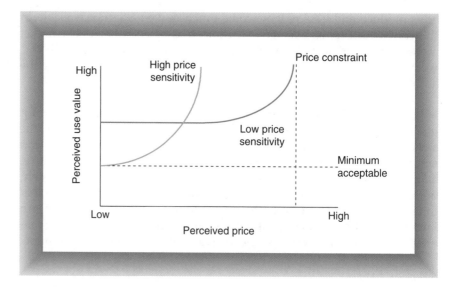

Figure 2.1
Price and perceived
use value

2. Reduce the list of factors to a manageable number of the most important – typically around half a dozen.

3. Of the factors elicited, score them on a 1–5 scale for both our product and those of our competitors for each value dimension.

4. Map the scores to produce a PUV profile.

Figure 2.2 shows a profile for three different types of cars – a typical family saloon, an Italian sports car and a class of vehicle known as an MPV (multiple purpose vehicle) or people mover. Each of these vehicles is rated on a number of perceived and tangible value dimensions.

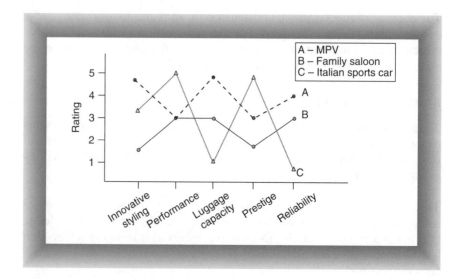

Figure 2.2
PUV profile for
three motor cars

What the profile illustrates is the opportunity to occupy market space – the gap left in the profile by competitors. Many industries have a tendency towards competitive convergence as competitors become more concerned about matching each other's offering, losing sight of the needs of the customer. This gives the opportunity to move into market space and 'zig' when everybody else is 'zagging'.

There are numerous examples of this, such as the airline that allows smoking on its flights to and from Japan – which is a nation of committed smokers. The business travellers overnight hotel, Formula 1, offers what travellers want – a comfortable bed, cleanliness, easy check in/out and proximity to a major route – and no more. The company concerned makes a return on capital employed of up to double that of some of its competitors, who still leave a chocolate on the pillow and hairs in the bath.

The Body Shop is an often quoted example. Rather than following the industry practice of high prices, prestigious sales outlets, expensive packaging and pseudoscientific potions and lotions, it offers high-quality, fairly priced, straightforward products, and social and environmental responsibility. In Figure 2.2, the MPV itself was a significant and previously unconsidered innovation. The PUV tool illustrates and applies a core marketing concept – differentiation.

Segmentation

Segmentation is a critical task for marketers, and is the primary means whereby we can gain a unique insight and understanding of the marketplace and at the same time generate competitive advantage. If we have a better and different understanding of the marketplace, then the rationale for our subsequent marketing activities is not clear to our competitors. They may copy what we do, but not understand why we do it. This 'complex ambiguity' can assist in maintaining our advantage.

In principle, segmentation is easy to understand. We attempt to divide our marketplace into groups of customers that are as similar as possible to each other, but as different as possible from other groups. If these groups are identifiable, accessible and commercially significant to us, then we can reasonably call them segments. If we do our job well, then sustainable competitive advantage results. Hence, segmentation is a fundamental and strategic aspect of marketing. Underlying the principle is the notion that different types of customers need different things. Some may require high levels of technical service and others guaranteed and reliable product or service delivery, while there will always be a segment that is driven by price. The latter segment, though, is often overestimated, as price can always be given as a superficial reason for not purchasing and often masks deeper needs.

Needs-based segmentation is one of the main ways, and some would argue the only and most important way, in which markets can be segmented. It may well be that a segment also has some other useful defining characteristic by which it may be identified. Such segments can be thought of in terms of characteristics and buying behaviour, and these may in turn be used to discriminate between customers in the wider marketplace. Hence we may identify that families with young children purchase large amounts of breakfast cereals. By targeting customers that have these characteristics, then we may identify more opportunities for sales. People who have retired from full-time work may be encouraged to shop at less busy times by the added incentive of a small discount. By understanding the drivers of buying behaviour, more sales and better service may result.

Although originally a consumer concept, segmentation is also widely used in business-to-business markets. Whilst the idea is widely accepted and is a subject of many market research studies, in practice it is often poorly implemented and managers find it difficult and confusing. The reasons for this have been suggested (Palmer and Millier, 2004) as follows:

● *Context dependent* – the principle is easy to understand, the practice within the circumstances of the specific company and market are often more difficult. The textbook explanations just don't seem to work in certain circumstances.

● *Multiple interactions* – the customer base and competitors in the marketplace together with the product range are all flexible and dynamic. There are additional constraints as to what may be desirable versus what is actually feasible. Understanding and managing the complex interaction of issues in order to come up with a solution can be very challenging.

● *Difficult and demanding* – the principle of segmentation is well understood, but in practice many marketers may have little direct experience or expertise in undertaking and subsequently implementing the results of segmentation studies.

● *Implementation* – the purpose of segmentation is to create competitive advantage, and this is critically dependent upon implementing the results of the segmentation study in practice. This can often prove difficult, as at a fundamental level this requires change. It may be difficult to convince managers to commit different resources in different ways, particularly if the perceived risk outweighs the promise of future returns.

New product development

The product lifecycle is a concept that is conventionally used to understand how products can be managed from introduction through to deletion. A significant problem with new product development is the 'over the wall' approach (Trott, 2002); there comes a point where the technologists have spent as much time, money and effort as can be afforded on the development, and it is then thrown over the wall to the sales and marketing people in order to recoup some of the investment. This approach can lead to technically innovative products that lack market appeal or are inconsistent with customers' needs.

In order to connect thinking between development and sales and marketing, the product lifecycle concept can be extended to represent the investment of time and money required to bring new products to market (Figure 2.3).

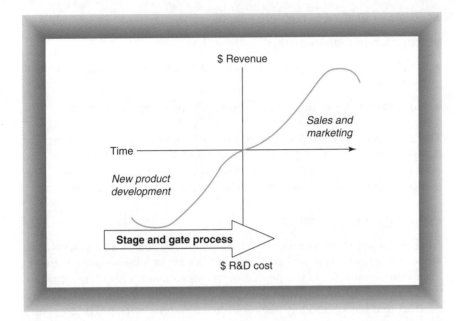

Figure 2.3
The development
and product lifecycle

Whilst there are many different models and formats for product development, one of the most widely used is the stage and gate process (Cooper, 1993). In principle the development process is divided into a series of steps, the stages, which represent discreet development activities. At the end of each stage the project is subject to scrutiny against a set of gate criteria. The project only proceeds if the criteria are met. Typically this is a team-based activity, with members of the team being drawn from across the functional areas of the organization. This means that there is a sharing of ideas and also ideology; often the first activity is an initial estimate of the market potential for the product, rather than technical development, before further resources are committed. The stage and gate process has wide application; some of the best exponents are pharmaceutical companies, for example. They deal with highly complex products requiring organizational-wide input, timescales are extended, and the costs of development are very high. Equally, the penalties for failure in bringing to market a product that is ineffective (or worse) are substantial.

When products eventually arrive in the marketplace, they represent a significant investment which then has to be repaid from sales revenue, as well as compensating for failed R&D projects and providing further revenues to invest in the next stage of development. This in a marketplace which is becoming ever more crowded and competitive, and in which product lifecycles are often truncated by new competitor products! The product lifecycle for a mobile phone is now less than a year, and a PC selling through retail outlets can have a lifecycle of as little as six weeks. Companies can no longer afford an unbounded 'blue skies' approach to development. The process approach to product development offers the following advantages:

- integration of functional and specialist skills
- early elimination of unpromising products and projects

- resources focused to high-potential programmes

- reduction in time-to-market

- investment in development is contained and managed against potential for return

- early market input improves opportunity for commercial success.

The stage-and-gate process is often used by companies for all forms of development activity, and not just for technology-led innovation projects. As it is a process, this management tool is applicable to most forms of pre-market activity, all of which need to be managed for optimum results.

Defining a new product

At first glance, the definition of a new product appears straightforward. However, various types of new product forms can be identified; this is important, as it reflects the degree of risk associated with their introduction. A new product, as far as the market is concerned, could simply be a product that has previously been sold to a different market. The company has wide experience with the product, and the incremental risk is marginal. Compare this to the new-to-the-world product that requires considerable market development work in order to generate awareness and educate the market as to the product's capabilities, and it can be seen that this is risk of a different magnitude. The degree of risk associated with new products can generally be related to the following:

- The extent to which they are *new to the market* – an incremental extension to the product range of an established supplier represents minimal risk and will probably be well understood by the market. As the supplier introduces new products or enters significantly different markets, then risk may increase. The Mars corporation grouped its various categories of food products under the umbrella name of Masterfoods. However, after a number of years the company is reorganizing and dropping the Masterfoods name in a number of its overseas markets, recognizing that it has not gained market acceptance.

- The *degree of technological innovation* – if the innovation represents the substitution of one technology for another, then there is minimal disturbance to the market. Varifocal spectacle lenses represent a different technology to conventional bifocals, but there is little challenge to acceptance of the product. A stepwise change in the nature of the technology can represent a much higher degree of risk. The introduction of CT and MRI scanners was a groundbreaking advance in the area of medical diagnostics.

These conflicts and dilemmas are summarized in Figure 2.4.

This suggests that incremental adjustments to the range represent a modest task in development terms and are likely to meet with a high degree of acceptance in the marketplace. However, the level of risk and, similarly,

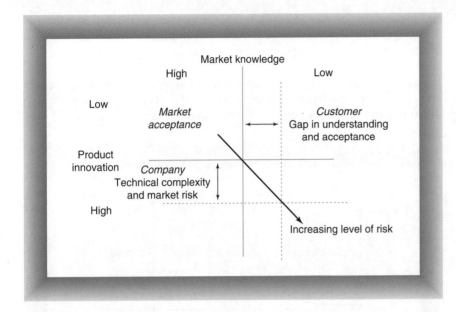

Figure 2.4
Balancing market and product focus

the potential for profit is low. Developing along either of the axes of the matrix represents increasing levels of technological innovation or market research and sensing in order to open the window of market acceptance. To undertake both of these tasks simultaneously within tight time and budget constraints requires considerable skill and expertise in the management of the new product development process.

Hence innovation is a potentially rewarding but high-risk process, and current products in the marketplace represent a substantial asset to the organization. Managing those products and continually reviewing them to ensure an appropriate fit to the market may be considered as renovation resulting in incremental changes to the product. A good example of this is provided by the ubiquitous confectionery product Kit-Kat®. The well-known four-finger wafer bar is available around the world, with variations in size, packaging, etc., to suit the needs of local markets. The product range is constantly reviewed and new products and innovations sought. The introduction of the single large bar in chunky format represented a significant change in the product range, whilst pack sizes and flavour variants (for example, mint or white chocolate and lime) are more incremental in their approach.

Product and market management

Having successfully introduced a new product, the classic role of marketing, and in particular the product manager, is to manage the product range over the lifecycle in order to optimize profitability. As Figure 2.5 suggests, by the time the product reaches the market it can have already incurred a substantial development cost. Some of the most expensive products to bring to market are patented pharmaceuticals that take 6 or 7 years to develop and may have only 15 or 20 years of patent protection, and incur a cost of up to $1 billion. This emphasizes the need for successful lifecycle management in order that development costs are recovered and investment in future products is maintained.

Figure 2.5 suggests a generic approach to managing the marketing mix and is built around the concept of the product lifecycle. This diagram also illustrates the experience curve, which will be discussed shortly.

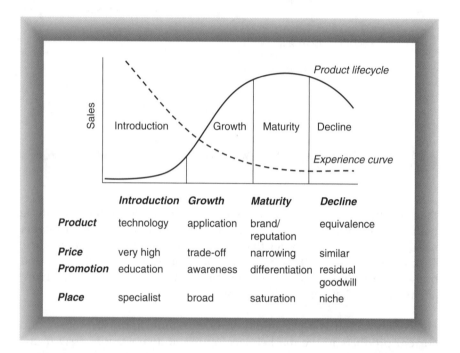

Figure 2.5
The product lifecycle and experience curve

	Introduction	**Growth**	**Maturity**	**Decline**
Product	technology	application	brand/ reputation	equivalence
Price	very high	trade-off	narrowing	similar
Promotion	education	awareness	differentiation	residual goodwill
Place	specialist	broad	saturation	niche

- *Product* – at the early stages of the product lifecycle, the features that are incorporated in new products can be particularly attractive to certain but limited parts of the market. Some customers will buy 'toys' in order to experiment with the features. However, it is not until the technology finds a worthwhile application, turning product features into user benefits, that the product is useful to customers. At this stage, the market experiences rapid user uptake. A good example is that of early personal computers. The Sinclair ZX80 and the subsequent ZX81 sold in large quantities despite the inherent poor quality of the product – only 1 K of memory, a very difficult to use keyboard, no software, and the fact that it had to be plugged into a television to be used. The Sinclair is now but a memory, if that may be said of a computer, having failed to become established as a mainstream brand. Currently, in-car satellite navigation is experiencing very rapid growth, GPS technology having found a very useful application. Eventually it will consolidate as the market rationalizes and the number of players reduce to a handful. The ability to build and retain market share has important implications for profitability, and establishing market/brand leadership is critical to success. Eventually the market becomes commoditized, as differences between products are largely determined by price.

● *Price* – when products are first introduced to the market there is a natural tendency for managers to think very carefully about price. The
intention is usually to optimize or even maximize price against volume
in order to gain a rapid, early return on the investment in product
development. As volume builds, there is a trend for costs to reduce.
Bruce Henderson, a founder of the Boston Consulting Group, described
this as the 'experience curve'. Working in a diverse range of industries,
he found that as cumulative output (that is to say, the total number of
products manufactured) increased, the cost per unit declined. This
could be ascribed to economies of scale, and learning effects such as
process development. Pilkington, one of the largest manufacturers of
glass in the world, developed the float glass process, which enabled the
costs of production to be reduced by 40 percent. This helped to turn
Pilkington from a regional, UK-based player into a globally dominant
company. An interesting question to ask is, does the market make the
price, or the price make the market? In other words, does the price
decline as volume builds, or does a reduction in price drive an increase
in volume? Japanese companies have used this principle to good effect
by developing a deep understanding of long-term costs, and setting
price in order to drive volume. Hence in the growth phase managers
need to consider carefully the trade-off between growth in margin and
volume. During this rapid phase of growth, market share (and hence volume) is an important determinant of long-term profitability. Managers
will inevitably need to manage the requirement for short-term profitability against long-term objectives (Figure 2.6). Eventually, as the market
matures and declines, prices become very similar and the premium
associated with brands narrows significantly.

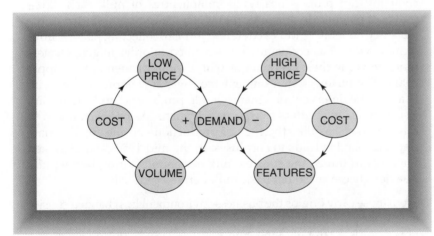

Figure 2.6
The price/volume
trade-off

● *Promotion* – the introduction of new products, particularly new-to-the-
world products, means that the market must be educated in their use.
Strong technical support helps potential customers to understand how
a product can be of benefit to them. In the IT sector, demonstration or
reference sites are used to inform customers; pharmaceutical companies will often sponsor medical research and technical conferences in
order to seed understanding of their products; food companies will

organize sampling and displays in supermarkets. As the market grows and expands, maintaining differentiation and awareness helps to secure long-term market share. Eventually, investment in promotion will be transferred to other, more promising new products.

- *Place* – consistent with the often technical basis of new products, specialist distributors with appropriate skills will be required to support and distribute the products. These are often quite limited, expanding to develop and fulfill demand. As the product becomes more ubiquitous, then saturation of distribution channels optimizes the opportunities for sales. Eventually, as the market declines – perhaps into a replacement market – niche distributors will stock the product. As an example, voice recognition software products are ubiquitously available from many high-street and online outlets. However, similar technologies that are adapted for use by the physically disabled and specialist markets for medical and legal applications are distributed through specialist outlets that can offer the appropriate support for effective use of the product.

Amul – the taste of India

Amul is India's largest dairy products company, with over half the market, leading other national companies such as Mother Dairy, and multinational food product companies such as Nestlé India and Hindustan Lever Ltd. Amul demonstrates how careful and consistent product stewardship combined with a deep and intimate understanding of the market leads to consistent growth and success. The company can process nearly 10 million litres of milk each day – orders of magnitude different from when the company started as the Gujarat Cooperative Milk Federation in 1946, collecting just 250 litres of milk a day. The cooperative was formed in order to give farmers more power in their negotiations with the middlemen of the supply chain. The business environment then was uncompromising, with heavy state intervention, many small producers, and significant issues in dealing with core aspects of hygiene. As has been found in other markets, as the efficiency of production and the supply chain improves so this leads to surpluses. In the mid-1950s, Amul looked for ways to utilize the surplus milk by manufacturing butter, milk powder, cheese and other basic milk-derived products.

From those early origins the business environment has changed considerably; the population has grown exponentially, and with industrialization there is a strongly emerging middle class. With double-income households becoming more common, this has led to higher disposable incomes and a rising demand for convenience-type foods. Alongside well-established ethnic products such as curd, ghee and paneer, demand is increasing for yoghurts and other milk-based convenience products. Multinational competitors have been quick to identify this trend, and have financial resources, expertise and established brands in this sector that enable them to move quickly to powerful effect.

Recognizing the needs of the marketplace, Amul has positioned itself as a producer of high-quality but reasonably priced products. More than that, it is integrated into the fabric of Indian society, from its roots in representing small farmers and the struggle of the poor and impoverished in difficult circumstances. Amul maintains and enhances its integration into society, reflecting and commenting upon social trends. Its long-running advertising campaign featuring a cartoon character of a small girl, known as The Moppet, features on billboards and in advertisements, commenting in a humorous but nonetheless insightful way on current events. The advertising is not afraid to challenge the interests of big business and politicians, reflecting the views of many ordinary citizens, and each week the next advertisement is eagerly awaited.

From its core products of milk and primary processed milk products, Amul has continued to expand its product range to include a wide variety of cheeses and milk-based drinks of various types, as well as ice cream, chocolate and health products, together with an expanded range of ethnic foods. Building on its expertise in producing mozzarella cheese, the company has also developed a range of pizza products. Amul has expanded into new markets, with export businesses to the USA (an agreement was recently signed with Wal-Mart) and the Middle East, with plans to go further afield in the future. A recent innovation has been the establishment of food kiosks, known as Amul Parlours, situated in high traffic locations such as railway stations, and also in-company with companies such as Wipro and Infosys. The kiosks are heavily Amul-branded, and sell only the company's products; they provide a wide range of snack and drink options. In 2006, the company diversified by opening its own television channel featuring Bollywood films and advertisements for Amul products.

Amul is strongly positioned in its domestic market, but has a low to mid-market positioning in terms of price. Multinational competitors have strong expertise with convenience and further processed foods. In the pizza sector, it will be interesting to see how Amul, an Indian company making an Italian product, competes against well-established, branded product specialists who are also entering the market. However, Amul also has the opportunity to export; with Indian communities established in many overseas countries providing a bridgehead for market entry, its expertise in ethnic foods is also to its advantage. The recent diversification into television is an exciting but potentially high-risk opportunity.

(Source: published sources, www.amul.com)

Product and lifecycle management

Marketers have a range of tools available for product and market analysis to assist in managing products over their lifecycle. The tools that will be discussed in this section include:

- the diffusion of innovation curve
- the product lifecycle
- the experience curve
- the Boston Consulting Group matrix
- the market attractiveness (McKinsey) matrix
- the Ansoff matrix.

Before discussing each of these tools, it is worth considering the relationships that exist between them. This is expressed diagrammatically in Figure 2.7, which shows the links between these various tools. The diffusion of innovation curve suggests that customers come into the market at different times. Cumulatively, adding together all sales, their participation adds up to the product lifecycle. As Figure 2.6 demonstrated, there is a relationship between price and volume. Hence, as volume increases so the experience curve effect becomes evident. The Boston matrix combines growth in market share, analogous to the experience curve, with market growth rate. However, the Boston matrix has only one variable on each axis, whilst the market attractiveness matrix combines a number of different factors. These tools are largely for analysis rather than for defining strategy, although it is common to associate generic strategies with each box of the matrix. The Ansoff matrix is a more appropriate tool for deciding strategy, summarizing the strategic alternatives. The lineage and suggested relationships between each of the tools is suggested in Figure 2.7. Each of these tools is discussed here.

The diffusion of innovation curve

Originally derived from sociology, the diffusion of innovation curve (Figure 2.8) suggests that customers have different propensities for the rate at which they enter the market and accept new products. The innovators represent a relatively small part of the market that has a strong inclination to purchase new innovations which at the time of first being marketed may be relatively underdeveloped for wider market applications. The early adopters are the next step into a wider market, and are prepared to pay a higher price in order to obtain a new product. The early and late majority represent the bulk of the market, managed by the trade-off between volume and price. The laggards are the last into the market, and are predominantly buying on price. There are a number of important points to bear in mind when considering this tool:

- *Product launch.* When introducing new products, the primary targets should be the innovators and early adopters. If they can be targeted, then this allows greater focus of marketing effort.

- *Technology versus products.* As the earlier example of the Sinclair computer demonstrated, feature-based, technologically driven products

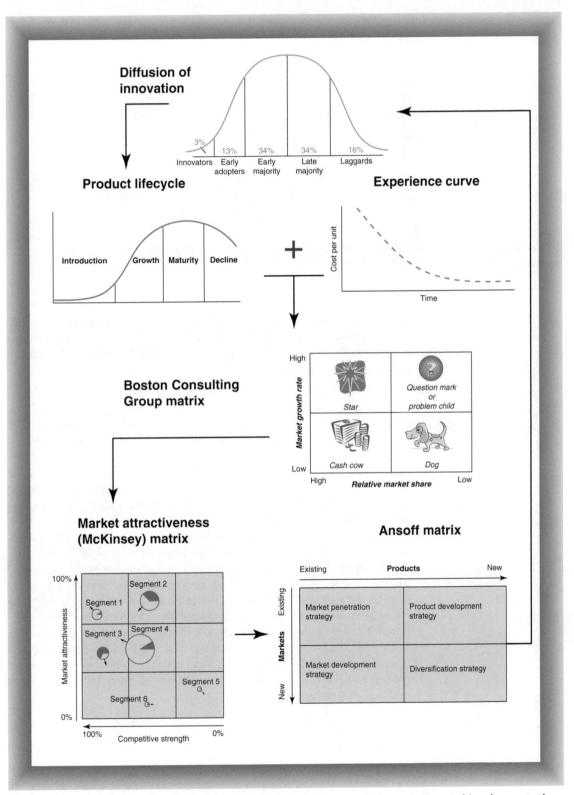

Figure 2.7 The relationships between marketing tools – analysis, strategy and implementation

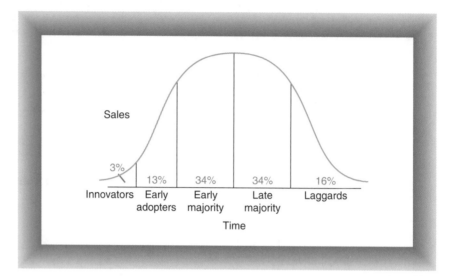

Sales

3%

13% 34% 34% 16%

Innovators Early   Early   Late   Laggards
            adopters majority majority

Time

Figure 2.8
Diffusion of
innovation

appeal to innovators and early adopters. However, to enter the main-stream market the emphasis needs to be on solving problems for customers. In the early post-launch period, market learning and feedback is essential in order to understand the circumstances of use.

● *Crossing the chasm.* This is a phrase made popular by Geoffrey Moore (1991), a renowned consultant in the area of technology marketing. The phrase refers to the gap that actually exists between early adopters and the early majority. Market uptake is not necessarily a smooth and continuous process. Innovators and early adopters will buy products because they are new, but the rest of the market purchases them because they are useful. However, the great majority of the market have solved their problem by other means, and 'crossing the chasm' implies that potential customers have to be convinced that they should change their habits, and stop using current products in order to use the latest ones. Take, for example, Linux versus Windows. Windows is the globally dominant operating system, and integrates with much of the functional Microsoft software that is used on personal computers. Whilst Linux may be technologically more sophisticated and is in principle free, due to the open source nature of the software, in order to adopt it many millions of users have to be convinced that the change is worthwhile. Ultimately, many might say 'what the hell, it's only an operating system, why should I be bothered?' Linux occupies some specialist market niches, but has yet to enter the mainstream of personal computing – and perhaps never will.

Product lifecycle

Very few products actually behave as shown in Figure 2.9 in the market-place; the product lifecycle is a conceptual tool that has been borrowed from the biological sciences. An analogy is made with living things, in that

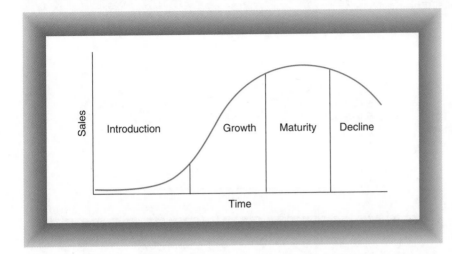

Figure 2.9
The product lifecycle

they come into existence, grow, mature and eventually die. This comparison gives the marketer a framework within which judgments can be made about the use of marketing resources. It is apparent that, particularly with the speed of technological change, products pass through the lifecycle more quickly than previously. They may well fail to progress to the later stages of the lifecycle, being superseded by competitor products. When using the product lifecycle, various points should be borne in mind:

- *Unit of analysis*. Careful thought should be given as to the subject of the analysis. It is quite common for marketers to confuse products and brands, for example. Brands may enjoy a life of decades or more, whilst various different types of products enjoying the benefit of the brand come and go. When comparing with competitors, take care to differentiate between products, product class and categories. The lifecycle can be applied at a number of levels of analysis – products, firms, industries, etc.

- *Prediction*. The product lifecycle is not a predictive tool, and does not suggest future sales. Estimates may well be made on the basis of the performance of similar and competitor products. Product lifecycles do not cause sales, but rather judgments about marketing actions using the product lifecycle as one of the inputs to those decisions are critical.

- *Single product*. The tool is mostly used in association with a single product or class of products. Most companies have more than one product and operate in markets in which there are many competitors. The tool is less helpful when considering a strategy for a range of products.

- *Integration*. The product lifecycle considers only sales revenue or volume on the vertical axis. It does not necessarily help in understanding the costs of product development and those associated with maintaining the product on the range.

The experience curve

The experience curve (Figure 2.10) was an interesting phenomenon that was uncovered in the 1960s when manufacturing industry was the subject

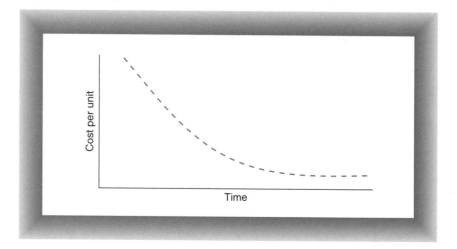

Figure 2.10
The experience
curve

of intense financial scrutiny. As a rule of thumb, it was found that, across a wide range of industries (aircraft production, electronic components, chicken meat), for every cumulative doubling of output – that is to say, when the total number of products that had ever been produced doubled and then doubled again and so on – there was the opportunity to reduce the cost of production by 30 or even 40 percent. This was found to be due to learning effects and the avoidance of mistakes, process improvements, and the adoption of best practice. However, when considering this concept there are a number of issues that should be taken into account:

- *Predictability*. As with the product lifecycle, the experience curve is not a predictive tool. The cost reductions implied have to be earned; they are not a reward for the increased output.

- *Calculation of costs*. The visibility of costs may differ depending on the perspective of the organization. In the short term some costs are fixed, but in the long term all costs are variable. The accounting practices of Japanese companies tend to take a much longer-term view of costs, whereas in Western organizations accounting tends to be more historically based. As a consequence, Japanese companies have been renowned for selling at relatively low prices in order to drive volume up and reduce costs. By contrast, Western companies take a more short-term view of costs, which can therefore appear higher and inhibit the opportunity to compete on price.

The Boston Consulting Group matrix

Sometimes referred to as the BCG, Boston or growth/share matrix, this tool (Figure 2.11) combines the concept of the product lifecycle, as indicated on the market growth rate access, with the experience curve, captured in the horizontal axis. Relative market share is regarded as an important indicator of competitive strength. As previously discussed, due to the experience curve effect a relatively high market share should give competitive advantage. The experience curve effect was promulgated by

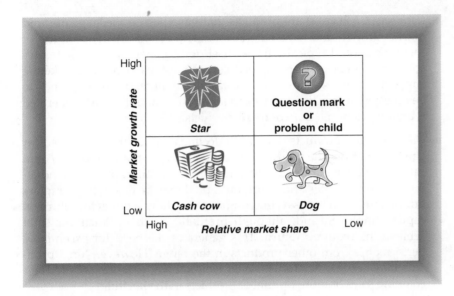

Figure 2.11
Boston Consulting Group matrix

Bruce Henderson, a consultant who later went on to found the Boston Consulting Group. From this it can be understood how the matrix came into being. It was originally developed as a financial management tool in order to help explain how cash was both generated and consumed in an organization. It is a portfolio management tool – that is to say, a number or range of products can be analysed by its use. The various boxes on the matrix help in understanding some of the issues involved in managing products and various stages of the lifecycle:

- *Question mark/problem child*. This is so named because, as is widely understood, most new products fail. This is the optimum point for products to enter the matrix. Here, market share is low but the potential is high. These are products of high promise, but with a number of challenges before they become established on the product range. High costs of development have been incurred at this stage, but little has been recovered from the marketplace. This represents the period of maximum cash exposure. Products of this nature are often assessed in terms of their potential by considering NPV. The net present value is calculated by forecasting the future income stream from the product, and applying a discount factor in order that different products can be compared in terms of the present-day value of their future potential. This technique is widely used, particularly for products with high development costs.

- *Star*. Stars are products which are moving ahead strongly in the marketplace and, although generating significant revenue, require substantial market support in order to maintain the pace of progress. These types of products both generate and consume cash, and are therefore cash neutral. Products in this category should be measured in terms of volume and revenue generation and growth against the market in terms of market share.

- *Cash cow*. Cash cows are products that have passed the stage of rapid market growth and have entered maturity. At this stage, products of this type should typically have offset development and market entry costs and will be consuming relatively modest resources for marketing support. Products of this type are cash generators, producing funds to be invested in question marks and stars. The amount of cash generated is an important measure of these products.

- *Dog*. Dogs are products that are in decline and may be considered for elimination from the product range. Too many of these products could cause the rate of earnings to be diluted. Whilst still capable of generating a return on sales, the return on capital may be below the company hurdle rate – that is to say, the company may have a target for return on capital employed and, although profitable, such products may not achieve the required return. This generates the need for exceptional performance from other products in the range. However, 'dog' products may serve other functions as well-known 'gatekeeper' products enabling sales of more profitable products in the portfolio.

As is apparent from the discussion so far, different types of products should be measured and managed in different ways and, in order to manage cash resources, a balanced portfolio of products is desirable. An important role for marketing is to ensure that the development pipeline is balanced with the requirements of new products, availability of finance and the needs of the market. When using the Boston matrix, a number of points should be considered:

- *Relative market share*. The matrix is largely used as an aid to thinking; it is unusual to see a matrix that has been correctly composed in detail. This is usually for practical reasons, as constructing the horizontal scale can prove difficult. Market share is proportional to that of the market leader, and in order to display the matrix meaningfully this axis is usually constructed using a logarithmic scale. This can often prove challenging.

- *Market growth rate*. Simply obtaining the data on market growth rate can be difficult. Deciding the upper and lower limits to anchor the scale can significantly change the interpretation placed on the matrix. The inappropriate positioning of the horizontal dividing line can alter the positioning of products above or below the centre line. A common trick is to set the market growth rate at the company growth rate, 'proving' what we already know – what great marketers we are!

- *Question the data*. Due to the difficulties in constructing the matrix, the data may convey an inappropriate perception of the product range; alternatively data can be actively manipulated to present the desired perspective. When reviewing a matrix of this type, the data should be questioned in order to establish the integrity and rigour of the analysis.

- *Scale items*. It should be borne in mind that the matrix uses only two criteria for the axes. Of course, there are multiple variables that can influence the success or failure of products, and other important criteria are ignored. In particular, it should be remembered that the concept of the experience curve and the competitive advantage given by a high market share is largely associated with manufacturing rather than service-based businesses, where economies of scale are much more evident.

The market attractiveness (McKinsey) matrix

The Boston matrix proved to be commercially very successful, and indeed is still in widespread use. This led to something of a battle between consulting firms to develop analytical tools. McKinsey, in cooperation with General Electric in the USA and Shell in Europe, developed a matrix which comprises a three-by-three, nine-box format, compared to the conventional two-by-two format (Figure 2.12). In addition, the scales for each of the axes were multifactorial, taking into account a number of factors that contributed to market attractiveness on the vertical axis and business strengths on the horizontal axis. The scores for each of the axes are calculated in the following way:

1. Decide the criteria for each axis – usually four or five; too many criteria lead to unnecessary complication and loss of focus.

2. Allocate weighting to the criteria – allocate a percentage to each criterion, denoting its level of importance.

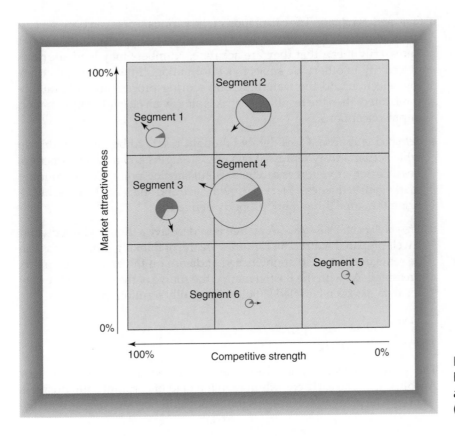

Figure 2.12
Market
attractiveness
(McKinsey) matrix

3. Decide the comparative scores – allocate scores to each criterion, usually on a marks out of ten basis; the tool is most effective when comparators are included, for example competitor products.

4. Calculate the weighted scores for each criterion – the score multiplied by the weight gives a weighted score, e.g. weight 30% × score 6 = weighted score 1.8.

5. Add the weighted scores for each criterion – this will give an overall score.

6. Plot on the matrix – place the factor concerned on the matrix according to the scores calculated for both of the axes.

7. Absolute and relative performance – include any additional information by plotting a circle at the intersection point to indicate volume or value and relative performance by market share.

As Figure 2.12 suggests, circles can be placed on the matrix with the size of the circle representing either the value or the volume of the market concerned. As an added sophistication, a pie slice can be placed in each of the circles to denote the market share of the company concerned. The principles embodied in this matrix are applied in many different variations and permutations. When reviewing such matrices, be careful to consider the following:

- *Apparent objectivity.* The calculation of the various scores can be to several decimal places. This means that the numbers are precise, but does not necessarily mean that they are accurate. Numbers may lend spurious objectivity to otherwise subjective information. If the process of criterion selection and the weighting and scoring process are not suitably moderated, then the resulting matrix is simply an elegant representation of preconceptions.

- *Selection of criteria.* Considerable thought needs to be given to decide which criteria truly represent business strengths and market attractiveness. Porter's five forces can be a useful starting point for determining market attractiveness. Market growth, size and share could all be measuring the same thing if not properly defined.

- *Presentation over substance.* A picture is said to save a thousand words, and a well-prepared matrix can capture a wealth of thinking. Conclusions can be seductively sold to an interested audience on the basis of the matrix presented. As with the Boston matrix, the source of the data and the way the data has been handled should be carefully scrutinized.

The Ansoff matrix

The Ansoff matrix (Figure 2.13) was developed in the 1960s by Igor Ansoff, one of the early contributors in the field of corporate and business strategy. The primary role for this tool is not situation analysis, as with the

Using matrix tools

The American Chemical Corporation distributed a wide range of chemical intermediate products through a network of European distributors. The process was becoming increasingly unwieldy, with variable distributor performance, poor quality management information and gradual loss of control, as Country Managers negotiated individual and one-off deals with their customers. The Vice President for Europe decided to assess the situation, and invited a firm of consultants to analyse the distribution practices and report their recommendations. The consultants selected five major European markets – the UK, France, Germany, Spain and Italy – as the basis of the study. Best practice established in these markets would then be applied throughout the rest of Europe.

The consultants developed a matrix tool which had two axes; supply chain value add (SCVA) and product value add (PVA). This was based on the principle of the market attractiveness (McKinsey) matrix. Distributors who scored highly on the SCVA axis provided high levels of service and realized good prices in the market. The PVA axis differentiated between commodity products which required a hard sell, at one end of the scale, and products that were in high demand and virtually sold themselves at the other end of the scale. The consultants developed a set of criteria together with weightings for each of the axes, and then worked with managers in each of the selected markets to apply and moderate the scoring process to ensure consistency between different markets. Each distributor was plotted on the matrix, and from this it could be seen that there was a significant minority who fell into the 'box shifter' sector of the matrix, with low SCVA and PVA, whilst others worked hard to add value across the range of products. This information was used to rationalize the product range and distribution channels, and to redefine the basis of the agreement between the company and its immediate customers.

previous tools discussed, but rather to take the understanding generated by the audit process forward into objective setting and strategy development. In principle, the matrix outlines the four primary options for the company. The output of the audit process is then iterated against the Ansoff matrix in order to develop clear objectives, robust strategies, and optimal targets and outcomes. The matrix can be used to consider alternative strategies in a process of gap analysis.

Many managers find themselves presented with the requirements to deliver volume and profitability; the Ansoff matrix provides a framework in which they can estimate anticipated outcomes and then work to close the gap against corporate requirements. Whilst it may not be possible to meet those requirements, the process develops a series of arguments and

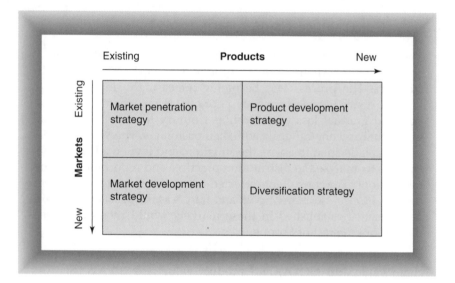

Figure 2.13
The Ansoff matrix

insights that allow a review process to take place against the background of the data.

It is important to remember that the core business – existing markets/existing products – represents the area of greatest knowledge and lowest risk for the organization. Diversification into new products/new markets is a move away from the area of core expertise, and therefore represents a high level of risk. The risks incurred need to be balanced against the profit that can be realized. Product development and market development opportunities enable the company to build on established strengths, and therefore represent lower levels of risk. When using the matrix, the following should be borne in mind:

- *Definitions.* The matrix presents only four boxes, but in reality there is no sharp definition between existing and new products, for example. As has been previously discussed, in considering product development there are many permutations regarding what might be seen as a new product.

- *Risk.* Risk is not necessarily incremental when moving from the core market to other areas of the matrix. A small shift in strategy could represent a substantially higher risk for the company.

- *Judgement.* The matrix is an aid to decision-making, and not a substitute for it. Simply because textbooks suggest a strategy based on one box or another, this does not imply that it is appropriate. As was said at one time, how unfortunate it would be if management thinking were to be reduced to a series of two-by-two matrices!

For more insight concerning these analytical tools, refer to www.market-modelling.co.uk and the matrix software tool. This also has a download-able, trial version of the software. The help menus and website itself contain much useful background information. The use of illustrations from this website is gratefully acknowledged.

References

Bowman, C. (1998). *Strategy in Practice*. Harlow: FT Prentice Hall.

Bowman, C. and Faulkner, D. (1994). Measuring product advantages using competitive benchmarking and customer perceptions. *Long Range Planning*, **27(1)**, 119–132.

Christensen, C.M., Cook, S. and Hall, T. (2005). Marketing malpractice: the cause and the cure. *Harvard Business Review*, **83(12)**, 74–83.

Cooper, R. (1993). *Winning at New Products*. Addison, Reading, MA: Wesley Publishing.

Kay, J. (2003). *The Truth About Markets: Their Genius, Their Limits, Their Follies*. London: Allen Lane.

Kim, W.C. and Mauborgne, R. (2002). Charting your company's future. *Harvard Business Review*, **Jun**, 77–83.

Kim, W.C. and Mauborgne, R. (1999). Creating new market space: a systematic approach to value innovation can help companies break free from the competitive pack. *Harvard Business Review*, **Jan/Feb**, 83–93.

Moore, G. (1991). *Crossing The Chasm*. New York: HarperBusiness.

Palmer, R.A. and Millier, P. (2004). Segmentation: identification, intuition and implementation. *Industrial Marketing Management*, **33(8)**, 779–785.

Trott, P. (2002). *Innovation Management and New Product Development*. Harlow: FT Prentice Hall.

3 Management and culture

Introduction

Working in organizations means more than just the functional tasks of actually doing the job; it involves engaging with colleagues who you report to and who report to you, and with many others within the organization. This chapter is concerned with how to understand this aspect of organizations, and how to manage the interface with the company and the people who work for the company. This area could be broadly referred to as corporate culture or, perhaps more colloquially, the politics of the organization and its more negative and sinister bedfellow, political correctness. These are intangible issues that are difficult to understand. You can't measure or touch them, but their influence is pervasive. The consequences for your career, and indeed your personal happiness and well-being, of failing to understand them can be at least as serious as inappropriate marketing decisions. This chapter considers these issues at the personal and organizational dimension, and introduces a range of tools to help in developing a framework of understanding and challenging your own thinking.

The personal dimension – what about you?

Are there certain companies or organizations that you would like to work for? Similarly, are there others that you would definitely not wish to be employed by? Perhaps you have experienced what it is like to be a member of a winning team, on the sports field or in the workplace. Many of us value our family and friends not only for the practical support they give us, but also for the faith that they show in our abilities. An understanding of the broad issue of culture and how we can understand our own view of the world and match that to our business lives is an important if not vital contributor to not just job satisfaction but also our overall well-being, as well as the avoidance of stress caused by the inner conflict we suffer due to lack of congruence.

Our family and our upbringing shape our early view of the world, but as we develop we can more actively take decisions about things that are important to us and which are consistent with our views and opinions. These underpinning beliefs, values and attitudes are central to our character, and contribute to our ethical and moral position. All of these contribute to the culture which surrounds us.

Attitudes – inherent drivers of our response to circumstances and people manifested by behaviour.

Values – the criteria by which we decide how things should be or ought to be, driven by our understanding of honesty, integrity and fairness.

Beliefs – strongly held assumptions about ourselves, others and the environment in which we live; things that we believe to be true.

Culture – a shared system of beliefs, values, behaviours and customs used by members of a society.

As we enter the world of work and develop our careers, these intangible but nonetheless substantial aspects of ourselves are important to our well-being. If there are companies that you would not like to work for, can you think why this is? Perhaps your view of the world would make you uncomfortable working for organizations that sell cigarettes, manufacture arms, conduct laboratory tests on animals or produce highly processed foods targeted at children. Perhaps you have strong religious beliefs that are important to you, or maybe you are a cash-strapped, debt-ridden student who simply wants to earn the maximum amount in the shortest possible time.

There are no rights or wrongs in this discussion; we all interpret the world in different ways and are entitled to our views and opinions. These contribute to our ethical position, our understanding of what we consider to be good or bad, and hence our moral conduct or behaviour is supported by this. When our views contradict those of the company or organization that employs us, this can lead to considerable personal stress. There are ways to deal with stress in the workplace, and in many ways stress can be a positive, but how much better to avoid the situation arising by carefully considering our own attitudes, values and beliefs and testing these against a potential employer or organization before joining it.

This chapter presents some interesting ideas regarding how we can think about culture in the context of an organization. As you walk around in an office, there are many clues and insights that can be gained. How do people greet and interact with each other? What is it that is posted on the walls and notice boards – the latest pictures of a successful sports team, or another memo from the finance director complaining about excessive usage of elastic bands?

In the upmarket Chancery district of the City of Auckland in New Zealand is a bronze statue of Lord Bernard Freyburg, a war hero and former Governor General. Carved into the stonework behind his statue are the words 'To Thine Own Self Be True' – a Shakespearian quotation.

Of course, this assumes that your attitudes, values and beliefs are clear and consciously articulated.

You and the organization

It is infrequently that we change organizations or have the opportunity to stand back and objectively consider the match between our culture and that of the company; more often than not we have to manage the situation as we find it, and of course organizations change and adapt over time. This could be as a consequence of external factors such as competitive moves or changes in legislation, or internal factors – and in particular changes in the senior management and leadership team. Leaders, especially, have a big responsibility for establishing and managing the corporate culture which is in turn evidenced by the way that people think, act and behave. Jack Welch, the former chief executive of General Electric and widely regarded as one of the best managers of the twentieth century, commented in his biography that GE actively sought certain types of management behaviour. The requirement for performance was a given, but Welch also wanted managers who could share best practice across the organization, and in particular he did not want managers who he described as 'kissing asses upwards and kicking like horses downwards'. Leaders, by their actions, establish what is acceptable and unacceptable within an organization. The checklist in Table 3.1 suggests some of the clues that point to the type of culture that exists within an organization.

Table 3.1 Corporate culture checklist

	Positive	Negative
Communication	Regular and open communication	Top-down only
Visibility	Senior management approachable and open	Closed-door mentality
Rewards	Rewards for appropriate behaviours, celebrate successes	Failure penalized, achieve results at all costs
When things go wrong	Open discussion to identify reasons why, seek to improve process	Blame allocation and scapegoating, punish the guilty and innocent
When things go right	Recognition of the contribution of all involved	Rewards to the few
Interpersonal relationships	Open and informal, information sharing, feedback given	Formation of cliques, rumour and speculation
Problem-solving	All invited to contribute	Tablets of stone mentality
Policies and procedures	Staff empowered to act individually when appropriate	Followed rigorously irrespective of consequences
Organization	Clear processes and good communication across functional boundaries	Strong silo mentality
Attitude	Let's do what we can	Let's do what we need to
Staff turnover	Very low	High, unable to retain good staff
Personal development	Seen as an integral to organizational success	An expense, why invest in staff who may leave?

Inevitably, cultures will change and develop over time as the success of the organization waxes and wanes and managers come and go. We have already discussed the importance of understanding your own personal attitudes and values and how these contribute to your behaviour. The types of behaviour that contribute to not only corporate success but also personal satisfaction include the following:

- *Personal mission statement.* Have you decided what you want to do with your life and how you will judge whether you are successful or not? Two brothers set up their own business; whether they used the term mission statement is debatable, but they set themselves a very clear ambition – to have fun and never borrow from the bank. We can all understand that.

- *Move on.* Things go wrong; admit mistakes and forgive those of others. Let go of the baggage.

- *Learn.* Review situations and circumstances, and remember mistakes are an investment in learning. Take advantage of opportunities for personal development.

- *Teach.* Share your skill and expertise with others, and encourage them to learn and develop. It is sometimes surprising how capable people are when given the opportunity to demonstrate their expertise.

- *Future focus.* Be clear as to the short-, medium- and longer-term objectives and actions required. Refer to Chapter 5 for ideas on how to achieve this.

- *Solutions focus.* Working towards a solution avoids personalizing problems and being drawn into an 'us versus them' frame of mind. Comment on ideas, not the people who articulate them.

- *Respect.* Treat others as you yourself would like to be treated, and make yourself approachable.

Corporate culture and market orientation

As marketers, we would all like to think that our organization is committed to the concept of marketing such that it is inherent in the way that it allocates resources and manages its business. In other words, it is market oriented. Several formal definitions of market orientation exist, but we might think of it as gathering, analysing and using information about customers to make business decisions. A wide range of terms are used which might encompass this – customer led, customer focused, market driven, etc. This is an underlying attitude that, whilst intangible, can almost be sensed in a company. We can all think of organizations that embody the spirit of marketing and might make exciting and interesting places to work. This marketing orientation may be made tangible in terms of the mission statement and explicit statement of strategies, but it is surprising how few organizations actually have such statements or even use them as guidelines for their business.

Some earlier work by Millier and Palmer (2000) identified the dilemma that this can sometimes cause managers, particularly if they are embarking on their career or taking a new job. Millier and Palmer offer a framework which is helpful in diagnosing the situation and in making this more understandable; this is shown in Figure 3.1, which is discussed below.

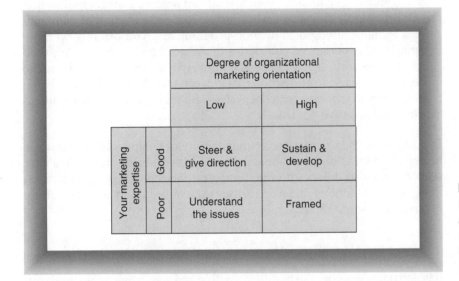

Figure 3.1
Matching personal and organisational marketing expertise (after Miller and Palmer, 2000)

- *Understand the issues*. Typically, organizations represented in this box will be focused on production and sales. From a personal point of view, you may well find that there is no such thing as a job description, and the marketing tasks that are expected of you are vague and lacking in any clear strategic direction. Typically, the marketing tasks in organizations such as this will be tactical sales support activities – producing literature, organizing trade shows and so on. Customer information will be disorganized and limited, and products may be technically excellent but often inappropriately sold.

- *Steer and give direction*. This could be the opportunity you have been looking for. These types of organizations are typically companies that have grown through technical excellence, but there is recognition by the senior management team that to grow further they must change the way they do business. Technical excellence will no longer win the order, and the competition is catching up. Often such companies will have large but disorganized product ranges, and the opportunity is to use an insightful understanding of the market and customer base to rationalize the product range and focus effort. Generating some early success, however modest, acts as an incentive for further investment and commitment in marketing.

- *Sustain and develop*. Organizations in this box are market orientated, and you will be working with a group of like-minded people where the role of marketing is appreciated and understood at senior level in the organization. Typically, a job role in this type of organization will involve rationalizing and improving effectiveness at a tactical level but also dealing with some 'big picture' issues which will enable the business to be driven forward and you personally to demonstrate your prowess. A role such as product or marketing manager in a business of this type would be a valuable addition to the CV.

● *Framed*. As a relatively inexperienced marketer, you will be coming into an organization which has well formalized processes and activities that will provide a rich learning experience. It is quite likely that there will be a formal training or induction program, and you can rely on more senior and experienced colleagues to mentor and coach you. Your job role will be very clearly defined, but this will also provide limits to the degree of discretion and action that you can take. You are likely to benefit most from working with the system and taking every opportunity to learn and improve your skills.

In addition to the orientation, an inevitability of business life is what has become known as organizational politics. This will be discussed in a later section, and also draws into the discussion the topic of political correctness. The next section will go on to discuss how we understand the culture at an organizational level.

The organizational dimension – managing culture

It is debatable whether the highly intangible and somewhat ephemeral concept of culture can actually be managed in an organization. An alternative argument would be that cultures simply are – they grow and develop over time in an evolutionary and self-reinforcing manner. Harold Geneen was the one-time leader of ITT, at that time a huge American conglomerate. He was a man with an all-encompassing knowledge of the business, driven and supported by a rigorous understanding of the finances. Each of his managers reported to him on a couple of sheets of paper containing the appropriate numbers and a commentary on them. Geneen would call a manager into his office from time to time to question him on his report. What he was looking for was 'a firm grasp of the unshakeable facts' by the manager concerned. One could speculate that this was an uncomfortable experience, particularly if Geneen had a firmer grasp than the unfortunate manager – and this was almost certainly the case. It can easily be seen how this approach and behaviour would strongly influence the culture of the organization. Johnson and Scholes (2002) have developed the cultural web as a tool for analysing and understanding culture (Figure 3.2).

The cultural web is the most popular tool that is used in this context. It is both simple and powerful; it captures the essence of the intangibles of what makes up a culture, yet presents it in a simple and easily understood format. This is an excellent example of how a management tool helps to reduce complexity to the point where we can understand it, without losing the subtlety of the detail. We can all understand the relevance of these seven items – try telling the salesforce that the type of company car they drive is not a reflection of their status. The chairman of one particular company insists on a strict dress code. Visitors, including customers, are offered a tie in reception should they arrive and not be aware of this requirement!

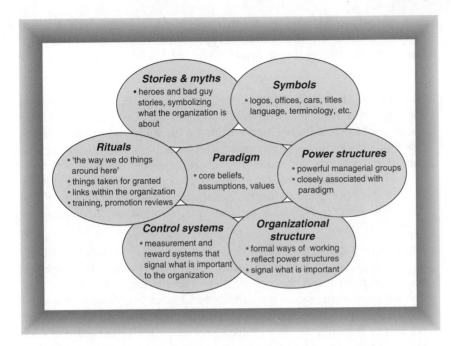

Figure 3.2
The cultural web

The type of culture that we operate in is the context within which our management actions take place. If you say to one of your staff 'I'm sure you can do better next time', that might be regarded as either threatening or encouraging, depending on the culture. The cultural web aids in understanding and categorizing some of these intangible aspects of culture, and then helps us to ask interesting questions – such as what culture do we think is desirable, and how is this to be achieved? Very often it will highlight the gap between what is said to happen and what actually happens, and even within organizations we can detect subsets of culture – the sales team might have a different perspective from production, for example.

An effective way to use this tool is with the management team; by focusing on the topic headings this can remove the temptation to personalize the discussion, and because this is somewhat abstracted it can be a very revealing process. In working through the cultural web the management team can highlight the relevant issues, use the tool to define a future ideal position, and then discuss the actions necessary to achieve this. Hence the process is:

1. *Summarize the current culture* – open, team-based discussion.

2. *Draw conclusions* – identify the key issues to be addressed.

3. *Define the desired culture* – use the headings in the cultural web.

4. *Decide and implement actions and next steps* – to make the necessary transition.

The degree of change that is required is sometimes referred to as 'rewebbing' or, in a more extreme case, 'dewebbing'. The latter implies a stepwise change within the organization.

Charles Handy (1985) presents another insight into culture which is useful in helping us to understand different types of cultures, but is not as helpful as a management tool in defining future actions. Handy identifies four types of culture:

1. *Role culture*. This is typical of hierarchies in which the job and place in the organization is very clearly defined. Personal power is derived from the type of job and its position within the hierarchy; as a consequence, this tends to encourage introversion and bureaucracy. Cultures like this can often develop a 'silo mentality' where cross-functional communication is poor; these types of cultures tend to be inflexible and slow to change. This is typical of larger organizations and those in which routine processing is typical – for example, continuous manufacturing operations.

2. *Power culture*. Rather than being described as a hierarchy, this type of culture can be better described as a web. A few people within the organization have power, and their connections radiate out in a web-like way. These types of organizations are flexible and quick to change, as a few but highly significant people have power, but this does tend to encourage congruent thinking as the powerbrokers agree with the boss and each other. These types of organizations can also become very political as members associate themselves with the powerbrokers. Family businesses and strongly charismatic leaders can encourage this type of culture.

3. *Task culture*. As the name implies, this type of organization is focused to task completion and problem-solving, with success being judged on outcomes. This structure tends to be flexible and dynamic, depending on the task in hand, drawing on the skills and capabilities of individuals who are respected for their knowledge rather than hierarchical seniority. Organization here can best be described as a matrix, with individuals often reporting to several different managers. Many consulting organizations will operate in this way.

4. *Person culture*. This is not very typical of most organizations, but here individuals become stars within the organization and have substantial power due to their specialist knowledge and expertise. Sometimes subsets of large organizations, perhaps specialist departments, can also adopt this type of culture. Charles Handy memorably described trying to manage this type of organization as 'trying to herd a group of tom cats'. Whilst these experts are brought together by the common interest of the organization, they nonetheless exert a high level of individual discretion; typically, this organization would include professional partnerships such as solicitors, advertising agencies, doctors, etc.

Handy's view of culture introduces an important element to the discussion. By linking culture with the structure of an organization, this poses the interesting question that if the structure is changed, does this mean that the culture is changed as a consequence? Generally speaking, the answer is no. Culture is composed of attitudes, values and beliefs, and in many instances changing organization structure is inappropriate as a tool to manage culture.

Anthony Giddens (1984) also discusses structure, not in the organizational sense that most of us understand it but in the social sense. What he means by this is that the society that we inhabit – in effect, the organization that we work for – has a set of rules and procedures in place, and resources available to it. Inevitably resources are constrained, and this sets limits or boundaries on what it is possible to do. What this suggests (Figure 3.3) is that in order to bring about change, simply changing the organization will not necessarily have the desired effect. In fact, the 'law of unintended consequences' could well kick in here as staff become concerned regarding their personal future and well-being, and lose sight of the customer and company objectives. After all, restructuring is the great euphemism for cost-cutting, which could mean your or my job!

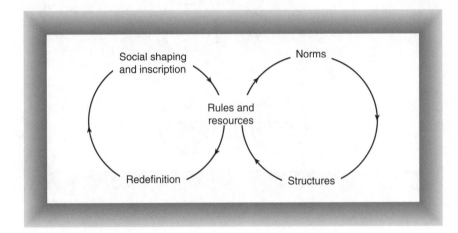

Figure 3.3
Social inscription and prescription (after Giddens, 1984)

Gidden's work identifies the central role of rules and resources, as noted in Figure 3.3. On first joining a company, you quickly learn the 'way things are done around here' – how the budgeting process works, how you get your expenses paid, where you go for lunch and so on. All of these are norms of the business and hence are part of the social structure. These procedures and processes are prescribed – that is, *they are* the way things are done here. As Handy's work suggests, the organizational structure overlays the social structure, and this puts boundaries on the degree of discretion and the opportunity for participation that is available. To bring about change we need to question some of these activities, which can become almost ritualistic in the way that they are conducted – the annual senior managers' conference, the budget presentation, the promotion process, etc. These are all things that we can go into and almost predict the outcome in some (if not many) cases. What we also know is that there are ways round rules and procedures, and things that we can do to get the job done despite the rules rather than because of them. In this way activities become inscribed rather than prescribed, and thus the culture subtly changes. Perhaps the organization has an 'Emperor's new clothes' moment and sweeps away all the old structures and procedures to bring about more decisive change.

So if we are to bring about change in organizations, we need to think not just of the hard and tangible things, such as organizational structure, but also of some of the more intangible things based around the way that people think, act and behave. The McKinsey 7S model is a useful tool that helps us to understand this (Figure 3.4).

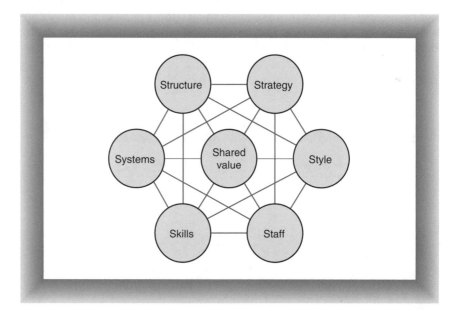

Figure 3.4
The McKinsey 7S model

The model is composed of three 'hard' Ss – strategy, structure and systems – together with the four 'soft' Ss of shared values, style, skills and staff. As one of the hard Ss, structural change has already been discussed. Many companies have excellent ideas about strategy; the real problem is implementing it, as a different strategy means change. In terms of systems, most CRM systems have failed to deliver the expected benefits. So focusing to the hard Ss without sufficient consideration of other factors may well not achieve the desired outcome. A well-known study (Orlikowski, 2000) used Giddens' ideas to try and understand change in the context of IT systems – as we have seen, CRM systems in the context of marketing are particularly problematic. This work found the change could be considered in three main ways:

1. *Reinforcing*, where technology is used to reinforce current procedures – for example, automating otherwise manual procedures such as data entry or order taking.

2. *Enhancing*, where technology is used to extend current business practice – so we could combine customer purchasing data with external market data to arrive at an understanding of market segmentation, enabling us to approach the market in a different way.

3. *Transforming*, where technology enables a complete change in the way that we do business – a good example would be how the low-cost airlines

have completely changed the nature of air travel together with the routes to market by which passengers purchase their tickets.

In these examples, and relating this to Figure 3.2, the reinforcing activity takes place within the right-hand circle whilst transformation focuses to the left-hand of the diagram. This suggests for managers that:

- managing culture is an intrinsic part of management
- changing the hard Ss may not bring about the desired outcome, and in fact could inhibit change
- questioning current practice and procedure encourages enhancing and transformation attitudes, but may be unacceptable in certain types of cultures
- failure to consider change is in itself a danger, as competitors make progress around you.

Disney

Walt Disney created a world of fun and fantasy through his cartoon characters and the development of theme parks. Steeped in the concept of service, visitors step into a fantasy world where belief in reality is suspended, to be entertained and charmed by the Disney Magic. The American theme parks, initially in California and then Florida, have grown into a series of theme and entertainment centres, and have spawned competitors and other attractions to entertain tourists. In 1983 Disneyland opened in Japan – virtually a copy of the original model, with only minor modifications to acknowledge the local marketplace. This icon of American popular culture was a big success in Japan. In 1992 the corporation expanded into Europe, with the development of EuroDisney just outside Paris. The northerly climate, notably damp and cool in the winter, was somewhat less attractive than the alternative location in Spain, but the decision was facilitated by the promise of financial incentives and developments to the transport system. However, this transplant of American culture into one of the intellectual centres of Europe underperformed significantly from its opening in April 1992.

There had been some tailoring to link into European culture, and a more international menu had been adopted in the food outlets. However, the American habit of 'grazing' – eating little and often whilst walking around – jarred with the French habit of sitting down to a substantial lunch accompanied by a glass or two of wine. Alcohol was not available on the Disney site. There were accusations of cultural imperialism, and staff were required to be bilingual although French was ostensibly the first language. The strict Disney dress code fell foul of French labour laws, and staffing and staff retention have

proved persistently problematic. Disney failed not only to understand eating habits, but also that Europeans were unlikely to spend
the whole of their holiday period at a theme park, preferring to dip
in and out for just a day or two to experience the rides and other
attractions. By comparison, Florida offers rather less diversity to
the holidaymaker than does Paris. All of this led to the theme park
in Paris being described as 'American imperialism – plastics at
its worst'. Critic Jean Cau went as far as to describe it as 'a horror
made of cardboard, plastic and appalling colours, a construction of
hardened chewing gum and idiotic folklore taken straight out of
comic books written for obese Americans'. The situation was made
worse by the high price policy adopted by the company, which was
thought to reflect through in low spending on merchandise and other
items in the park, and was not helped by the effects of the recession
in the early part of the 1990s. Rebranded as Disneyland Paris, there
are few who would claim that it has achieved the expectations placed
upon it.

(Source: Published sources)

Consumer products such as digital cameras, mobile phones and MP3
players now seem to be ubiquitous around the world. With globalization,
enabled by the low cost and rapid spread of technology, particularly since
the introduction of the Internet, it would be easy to assume that markets
are converging at the same time as consumers aggregate around a North
American/Western European-centric view. But we should be wary of this
assumption, as various examples illustrate the dangers of transplanting a
business model successful in one culture into another.

EuroDisney is a well-known and vivid example of cultural mismatch on
an international scale. As globalization becomes more of a reality for many
companies, this introduces the question of how companies can understand culture in different societies and environments. The most widely
used framework for understanding national and organizational cultures was
developed by Dutch sociologist Geert Hofstede (www.geerthofstede.nl).
Hofstede identifies five dimensions by which national and organizational
culture can be described:

1. *Power distance.* This refers to the level of inequality in individual power
   and wealth in the society. A low score indicates a high level of equality.
   Arab countries score high, Scandinavian countries low.

2. *Individualism.* This recognizes the degree to which individual or collective achievement is acknowledged. It also reflects the extent to which
   interpersonal relationships are built. An alternative to individualism is
   collectivism, whereby extensive relationships and mutual responsibility
   is acknowledged. The USA scores highest on this dimension.

3. *Masculinity.* This dimensional reflects the extent to which gender differentiation is expressed. When this is expressed to a high extent, achievement,

control and power are evident, which contrasts with low levels of discrimination and recognition of females in society.

4. *Uncertainty avoidance*. This considers the extent to which societies can tolerate ambiguity. Where there is a low tolerance, society will have institutional structures, rules and laws to exercise a high level of control. Where there is less concern and low uncertainty avoidance, a wide range of opinions can prevail. Mediterranean cultures have high scores in this dimension.

5. *Long-term orientation*. The fifth dimension was added to the original four following a study in China, and is derived from Confucian dynamism. It reflects the degree to which a society is future-orientated rather than having a historical or short-term perspective. Asian countries typically score highly on this, with a long-term perspective; European countries score much lower.

Organizational politics

'I don't indulge in organizational politics, I just get on with my job' is an occasionally stated but perhaps naive view of what it is like to work in organizations. If the interests of the organization and those of you and your colleagues do not coincide, then the rationalization process by which these interests, overlain with individual power, are resolved is a political activity. So organizational politics is about the way that we all work together within an organization, and whilst the 'rules' may not be overtly stated, this is the system by which the organization and individuals within it survive and hopefully thrive. Those who contribute to organizational success will no doubt have an expectation of personal reward, whilst others who may or may not have contributed to success nonetheless seek reward.

Here we have an interesting contradiction arising, where at the organizational level we work together to achieve success, however, whilst cooperating it is quite possible that at an individual level we are also competing. It is this lack of alignment that gives rise to organizational politics. One of the main ways this can be resolved in an organization is through the exercise of power – hence obtaining more power is an end in itself, and the more power a person obtains the more political that person is, and perhaps needs to be.

The International jetsetter

Horst Schneider is a Bavarian, from the southern part of Germany, employed by an American multinational pharmaceutical company. A degree in chemical engineering, a quick and alert mind and a good, near-fluent command of English proved an excellent basis for career progress with the company that he joined straight from university. He spent some time working in America at the head office in

New Jersey, home to many pharmaceutical companies. During his three-year assignment there he developed a friendship with an American colleague with a German background. His parents were first-generation settlers in America, arriving after World War II. Born and educated in America he was in every sense American, although the family still spoke German at home. Not surprisingly, Horst was a regular visitor there.

Some years later, both men had progressed in their careers. Horst was now General Manager for the German-speaking countries of Europe, and his American friend had recently been promoted to the prestigious position of International Vice President. Horst now reported to him in this role. The VP was a regular visitor to Europe, and meetings of European managers were usually held at a comfortable lakeside resort near Munich. In turn, Horst was a regular visitor to the US and other divisions of the company around the world. Horst found that some of his European colleagues were a little wary of him and his close relationship to the VP – something that was enhanced by their tendency to speak in German when together rather than using the company language of English.

A common problem in the pharmaceutical industry is that of parallel importing – the tendency for products to move from one country to another encouraged by differences in pricing and influenced by currency fluctuations. Pharmaceutical products are low volume/high value, and are therefore particularly prone to circulate in this way, assisted by a network of arbitrageurs who make a comfortable living by actively seeking and exploiting market opportunities. Horst was aware that product was entering his trading region and adversely affecting his topline sales performance. The regional profit-and-loss account was suffering, and Horst was beginning to feel uncomfortable at the detailed level of attention being paid by head office – and in particular by his friend and boss, the VP. By checking batch numbers and tracking deliveries, Horst strongly suspected that some of his European colleagues were 'product dumping' in order to meet their sales targets, probably by offering additional discounts by means of the numerous promotional and other budgets that were available to them.

As one of the company's most senior managers, Horst was entitled to first-class air travel. His next visit to the US was to discuss the shortfall in sales and declining profitability, and this was unlikely to be a comfortable discussion. In order to save money and demonstrate his commitment, Horst decided to travel economy rather than first class to the meeting. The discussions with his old friend the VP proved even more uncomfortable than anticipated. Horst's suggestion that performance was being impacted by product coming from other sales regions was not accepted; apparently other European managers were insistent that this was not the case and had provided evidence to support this. Not only that; Horst was told that he should not travel economy but stick to the company policy – if he were to travel economy then all the managers reporting to him would have their travel privileges adversely affected, and this was unfair on them. Despite his long friendship with the VP, he came away with demanding sales targets. Horst began to realize that he had been cleverly outmanoeuvered by other managers in the company who had been able to bring their influence to bear in a number of ways, and that his long friendship with the VP was outweighed by his friend's need to be seen to meet the expectations placed upon him.

As we can see from the Horst example – a real one that is presented anonymously – political behaviour can be used to achieve organizational objectives within the 'rules' that prevail, whilst individuals seek to achieve their own particular objectives. Political behaviour of this type can be understood by looking at Figure 3.5.

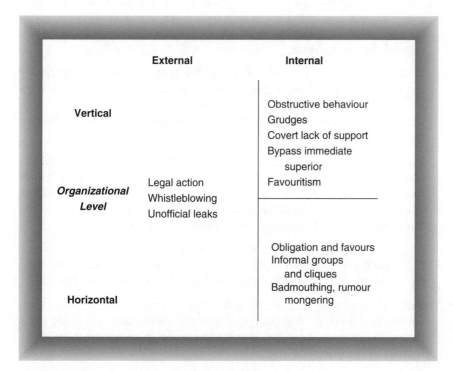

Figure 3.5
Types of political behaviour (after Farrell and Peterson, 1982)

A further aspect to consider is the degree to which the game of politics is played with a sense of equity. Whilst to some extent playing politics can be a positive and even enjoyable experience, there is a further and more unpleasant dimension in that coercive or personally threatening tactics may be used. Unfair behaviour, within the rules of the political game, treads a narrow line between denigration and harassment or more naked threats and aggression. Of course, this is behaviour that is practiced by others with lower standards of ethical behaviour than ourselves; we, of course, only indulge in practices which are fair and reasonable with respect to both the company and ourselves – well, at least as far as we see it.

Politics exist wherever people meet together, and, as every marketer knows, people do not necessarily act rationally and logically. Well, of course I do – it is the rest of you I have a problem with! Inevitably, rationality is overlaid with self-interest and self-actualization. For career success, it is not enough to accept that organizational politics exist; we have actively to exercise our political acumen.

Organizational politics – how to survive and thrive: a checklist

1. *People are people* – and not just organizational animals. Take time to remember somebody's birthday, congratulate them on the birth of a child or commiserate at the loss of a loved one. Simple but sincere gestures establish trust.

2. *Listen* – the grapevine is not necessarily an evil rumour-mongering machine, but one of the ways in which communication occurs within the organization. Listen carefully, and evaluate the quality and consistency of the information.

3. *What are the rules?* – How do people in the organization conventionally engage with each other? Is there an open, sharing culture, perhaps with meals being shared and social events organized, or is the culture more individual? Consider friendships and relationships, and how influence might be enacted.

4. *Criteria for success* – all organizations have a history; take time to talk to long-serving colleagues and find out what has worked and what hasn't worked. Think about how senior people have reached their positions, what they have had to do to get there, and how this is reflected in the attitudes that people express about them.

5. *Alignment* – consider how your ambitions fit with those of the organization; to achieve success it will inevitably be easier for you to change than *vice versa*, but this should be consistent with your values and beliefs.

6. *Build relationships* – link in to the information and powerbrokers; they are not confined to your function or department, so try to build links across the organization. Be prepared to trade information in order to remain fully up-to-date.

7. *To thine own self be true* – you have to be able to sleep at night and look at yourself in the mirror in the morning. Make sure that by your actions and behaviours you like what you see.

Political correctness

In discussing organizational politics, it is appropriate to mention political correctness – which is apparently related, but actually very different.

Whilst organizational politics is an essential part of everyday business life, political correctness has a rather different perspective. Certainly the concept is relevant to managers to a greater or lesser extent, but it is one that in many cases is seen to be largely negative. Some of the more academic literature discusses its corrupting nature and the consequences that it has for individual thought and action.

Political correctness attempts to impose language and descriptions which are deemed by the majority to cause minimal or no offence to others. This is particularly the case in sensitive areas such as race, religion, sexual orientation, and other aspects of personal thought and identity that may contrast with the received view of society. Mild examples are the use of the term 'flight attendant' rather than 'air stewardess', or 'Ms' for 'Mrs' or 'Miss', with the gender and status implications that these have. Hence the judgment about what is acceptable or otherwise is decided by society or, as one commentator put it, 'dictated by the mob', in contrast to the legal framework of the laws of public taste and decency and the judgments of libel and slander that can be made by courts.

There is a theory that proposes that the way that we use language reflects our understanding of the world and our consequent behaviour. Whilst not everybody will accept this, and leaving aside the extensive philosophical discussions that have taken place on this subject, those who are familiar with George Orwell's book *Nineteen Eighty-Four* will understand the essence of this. Rather than encouraging open debate, Big Brother attempted to control free speech, and hence the ability to think in unapproved ways, by inventing an English-like language, Newspeak, stripped of supposedly inappropriate words in order to limit nuances and subtlety of thinking. Of course, we are all amused by Scott Adams' *Dilbert* cartoon series that highlights the idiocies of business life, but somewhere between the works of George Orwell and Scott Adams lies an unpleasant reality.

As managers, we should recognize that our words have value and meaning, and they should be carefully selected and used. Are we prepared to accept the constraints imposed by political correctness, the shifting sands of sometimes ill-considered opinion, or do we say what we mean by expressing our own opinions and ideas, having weighed this against prevailing views? Perhaps the critical issue here is to think about the words that we use and the meanings that we imply, particularly when committing in writing and on the record, and this also means that we need to think through our own views and opinions and that we are prepared to defend them. The following list gives guidance regarding how to recognize and work with political correctness:

1. *Words and deeds.* Do the words that people speak and write match what they say and do? Consider whether this is due to bland and unthinking acceptance of political correctness or something else.

2. *Say what you mean, mean what you say.* Words have enormous power and significance. You might say 'restructuring'; I might interpret this as further staff reductions; you might have meant promotion!

3. *Ready, aim, fire* – and not the other way around. It is all too easy to speak in the heat of the moment without thinking through and presenting a cohesive argument. How many of us have reflected that perhaps we shouldn't have sent that email after all?

4. *Insult with intent.* If you do want to attack somebody, then do it knowingly rather than inadvertently. There is a vicarious pleasure in seeing a well-aimed barb firmly striking the centre of the target. Such insults will almost inevitably have consequences, sometimes far-reaching.

5. *Question and challenge.* Do not allow words to be used in order to conform to an ill-defined notion of political correctness if this is not consistent with the aim of the communication and your own views and opinions.

I will finish this section now, as I have to phone my bank – what's that – *'your call is valuable to us'*? Of course it is!

References

Adams, S. (1996). *The Dilbert Principle*. London: Boxtree Ltd.

Farrell, D. and Peterson, J.C. (1982). Patterns of political behavior in organizations. *Academy of Management Review*, **7**, 403–412.

Giddens, A. (1984). *The Constitution of Society. Outline of the Theory of Structuration*. Cambridge: Polity Press.

Handy, C.B. (1985). *Understanding Organizations*. Harmondsworth: Penguin Books.

Johnson, G. and Scholes, K. (2002). *Exploring Corporate Strategy, Text & Cases*, 6th edn, London: Prentice Hall.

Millier, P. and Palmer, R.A. (2000). *Nuts, Bolts and Magnetrons – A Practical Guide to Industrial Marketing*. Chichester: John Wiley & Sons.

Orlikowski, W.U. (2002). Knowing in practice: enacting a collective capability in distributed organizing. *Organization Science*, **13(3)**, 249–273.

Orwell, G. (1949). *Nineteen-Eighty-Four*. London: Secker & Warburg.

4 Organizations and the business environment

Introduction

As discussed in Chapter 3, there are many managers who will quake in their well-polished shoes at the mention of the word 'restructuring'. It seems that most senior managers when newly appointed to their roles will carry out a review of operations, resulting shortly thereafter in the restructuring of job roles and responsibilities. At the same time, the term 'restructuring' has become a clichéd euphemism for cost reduction, with the easiest and quickest costs to reduce being those associated with people. Not surprisingly, any suggestion of restructuring tends to generate an internal focus to what is happening in the organization, at the expense of customers. This results in 'heads facing inwards and ass to the customer', as Jack Welch, former and highly respected boss of GE, inelegantly but aptly put it.

This chapter seeks to understand some of the issues associated with understanding how and why organizations are structured, how work is organized, and how this is influenced and interacts with the external business environment. Johnson and Scholes (2002) describe the conjunction between structure, processes and relationships/boundaries as configuration. Here we will examine some aspects of configuration by discussing structure, some aspects of process and project management, and then considering the role of the business environment.

Organization

Taking a cue from the work of sociologist Thomas Burns, the development of industry, which is of course closely allied to society, can be thought of in three distinct phases:

1. *Pre-industrial*. This was the era of subsistence agriculture, where individuals produced their own food for their own consumption. In pre-industrial societies, labour may well have been exchanged as rent for land within a servant/master relationship. Goods and services were produced largely by individuals, and large organizations were few and far between, represented primarily by the church and the army – both of which had rules and hierarchies, and hence there was little need for what we today call 'management'. However, the legacy of the militaristic style of command and control can still be felt today.

2. *Industrial.* The UK was the first country to experience the process of industrialization. This was made possible by the 'enclosures' of the eighteenth and early nineteenth centuries, which dramatically shifted agriculture from a subsistence style of strip farming to a more efficient and effective form of agriculture as land became enclosed in larger fields, producing surpluses to feed city dwellers. At the same time this released labour from the land, which migrated to the emerging towns and cities. The factory system evolved to undertake simple, relatively high-volume, repetitive processes, complemented by skilled subcontractors who perhaps specialized in very specific tasks. For example, pins could be produced in large volume by drawing wire in a factory, but the making of the components of scissors was a more specialized and skilled activity. The nineteenth century was a period of great industrial development, with the UK leading the world and showcasing its prowess at the Great Exhibition of 1851. During this period factories were relatively small, as they were largely owned and managed by individuals who invested their own capital in commercial ventures. The introduction of the concept of limited liability, whereby companies could be formed, shares issued and downside risk managed, enabled further growth in the size of businesses. This in turn led to the emergence of a middle class of managers – foremen and supervisors, who organized the work and filled the gap between the owners of the businesses and their senior managers, and the labourers, who undertook the work. Improvements in technology, transport and communications enabled companies to develop on a national and eventually international scale.

3. *Post-industrial.* With globalization has come the migration of production to low-cost countries, with the so-called BRIC countries (Brazil, Russia, India, China) seen as the current and future workshops of the world. Post-industrial society in developed countries is now shaped around service and knowledge-based industries with technology enhancing and enabling economic growth. In the 1960s the then Prime Minister of the UK, Harold Wilson, made a speech in which he lauded the 'white heat of technology', suggesting that technology would solve society's problems. As we have moved into the post-industrial era there has been an increasing realization that technology brings with it disadvantages, such as the problems of environmental pollution and consumption of scarce resources. Social unrest, typified by the student riots in France in the late 1960s, and economic recession caused by the oil crises of the 1970s, can be seen as turning points in the transition from the industrial age. In the post-industrial era, the conventional hierarchical, command and control structure of the large manufacturing organization is replaced with fewer staff organized into cross-functional and cross-boundary teams, with layers of management removed, and responsibility and authority delegated downwards. This increases flexibility and the ability to act and respond to rapid changes in the business environment, and acknowledges the value of highly skilled knowledge workers empowered to act and decide.

Table 4.1 summarizes some of the difference between industrial and post-industrial perspectives.

Table 4.1 Comparison of industrial and post-industrial perspectives

	Industrial	*Post-industrial*
Organizational structure	Hierarchy Command and control, top-down management	Horizontal, team-based Empowered
Business environment	Local and national firms High demand for goods and products	Multinational and global environment Supply exceeds demand
Production approach	High volume Standard products Mass production	Lean, agile and 'le-agile' manufacturing to meet niche market needs and lower costs Process-driven service provision
Markets	Product-driven Low disposable income Local demand with barriers to trade nationally and internationally	Service and experience-led Highly discriminating consumers Global markets with high transparency of information
Society and culture	High social need – health, education, welfare Strongly conforming to social norms	High quality of life and life expectancy Paradox, fashion and ambiguity Celebration of diversity

That society and business has changed from the time of industrialization is self-evident. This has had significant implications for the way in which companies respond to these pressures. We will now examine some of the thinking that has unfolded during these times and which has led to our present-day understanding of how organizations are managed.

Scientific management

Henry Ford is the manufacturer who perhaps best epitomizes the industrial era. Coming from a farming background, his inventiveness and insatiable curiosity eventually led to him becoming the richest man of his time in America. The route to his success was the model-T car; 15 million were produced in a period of 19 years. What enabled this achievement was his invention of the production line – a thought put in his mind by seeing butchers in the meat packing district of Chicago reducing meat carcasses piece by piece as they passed by them suspended from overhead gantries. The production line was, in its day, the ultimate in standardization and increasing efficiency. Each component was fitted to the car as it moved past the operator. By increasing volume, cutting cost and increasing efficiency, Ford was able to more than halve the time taken to assemble a car, consequently reducing the end price to consumers, and at the same time he was eventually able to pay his workers more than double the daily wage rate. Whilst working on a production line was both boring and tedious, with very high labour turnover, it was at least remunerative. Ford increased his dominance of the market to hold a 60 percent share. Despite the fact that the price of the car had dropped from $825 when launched to only $290 in the mid-1920s, Chevrolet, under the leadership of Alfred Sloan, produced cars that appealed to buyers who appreciated the greater variety and sophistication of their products. Henry Ford not only manufactured cars, but is also responsible for a good stock of quotations as well. Perhaps the most famous of these is 'any colour you like as long as it is black'. Alfred Sloan made cars in any colour *other than* black, and rapidly eroded Ford's market share.

(Source: Published sources)

The industrial era and scientific management

In the early part of the twentieth century, Frederick Taylor developed the concept of scientific management. He was able to explain how high levels of efficiency, specialization of labour, deskilling of tasks and incentivizing output contributed to efficiency and profitability. This approach was also interpreted as a counter to the craft-based and specialist skills that workers held, and by which they could command higher wages. By removing the discretionary elements of work and controlling and supervising the workforce, profitability could be improved.

Taylor's approach could be summarized in his principles of management; based on work study, matching appropriate people to the tasks in hand in order increasingly to specialize their activities, providing financial incentives for increasing efficiency and ensuring that managers focus on the tasks in hand.

This highly rational view of organization and structure was based around managers who designed and oversaw the activities of others, and the workforce, which was simply a tool within the production process. Another insight from Henry Ford, allegedly, was that when he hired a man he got the pair of hands that he wanted, but also a brain. An understanding and sympathy for people and their potential to contribute to the success of the organization was marginalized in the scientific management philosophy, contributing to a gap in understanding between management and workers. Other aspects of society at this time contributed to this phenomenon.

From a European perspective, Henry Fayol, a French engineer, complemented Taylor's original ideas of scientific management, espousing such
principles as:

- *specialization of labour* – enabling increasing levels of efficiency
- *authority and discipline* – with clearly established power relationships
- *centralization, control and chain of command* – a clear line of command
  running from the top of the organization, where managers make decisions that are implemented by the rest of the organization
- *care of employees* – employees should be treated fairly and clearly understand their role in the organization, and turnover of staff should be
  minimized.

Science AND people?

Elton Mayo was an Australian-born social scientist whose ideas were
formed by his early experiences of labour unrest, which led him to
take an interest in the relationship between people and their work. In
the mid-1920s, a series of experiments were undertaken in what
became known as the Hawthorne studies. These were conducted in
the Hawthorne plant of a manufacturing company in Chicago. In
order to examine factors affecting productivity, workers in the plant
were put in a separate room and the level of lighting was varied
whilst the output was measured. The theory was that as the level of
illumination increased, so this would make it easier to undertake the
task in hand and output would increase. What was found was that
output increased even when the level of the lighting was lowered –
quite contrary to the theory. After analysing the data Mayo termed
this the 'Hawthorne effect', proposing that people at work are concerned with more than efficiency and output. His arguments ran
counter to the view of scientific management, and argued for collaboration and involvement of people in the workplace in order to
develop positive commitment to the organization's goals. His work
opened up a new area for research, and changed the perspective on
how organizations should be managed.

The increased questioning of the scientific management school of thought
was further fuelled by the global depression of the late 1920s and early
1930s. The early insights provided by the Hawthorne experiments opened
the discussion on alternative ways of managing, based not around rationality but rather on values and systems.

However, scientific management is not dead; anyone who has tried to
argue with an official about to issue a parking ticket will understand this!

Call centres are sometimes seen as the latter-day equivalent of the production line, with boring, repetitive tasks measured and managed by large displays showing calls waiting, average call time, etc., and monitored by supervisors and team leaders who listen in to calls and offer constructive criticism. Even in India, home of many outsourced call-centre operations due to the generally high standards of education and the English-speaking capability, call centres are experiencing high levels of sickness and absenteeism. Workers complain of pressure caused by the target-driven culture and poor career and development prospects (National Association of Software and Service Companies (Nasscom) – an Indian trade association; see www.nasscom.org). A more general term to describe the modern-day application of routinized, systematic and efficiency-driven management is 'McDonaldization' (Ritzer, 1993) – *'you want fries with that?'*.

The post-industrial era, values and systems

In a hierarchical organization driven by the concepts of scientific management, it is easy to understand how strict adherence to the rules can become an end in themselves – hence all the organizational requirements may be fulfilled and yet the ultimate objective is not achieved. Merton (1968) refers to 'trained incapacity' – the inability to be flexible in the light of changing circumstances. Some years ago Peters and Waterman (1982) published their book *In Search of Excellence*. They argued against bureaucracy, and discussed some of the softer issues of culture and vision within an organization that led not just to conformance to rules, but also to commitment to and achievement of objectives. This implies more than using people as tools to achieve the objectives, but rather recognizing their ability to achieve extraordinary ends by dint of their commitment. Hatch (1997) talks about organizations as 'living systems'; we can dissect a frog in a biology class at school or university and identify each of the individual parts, but they have to work in synchrony as part of the system in order to produce a croak.

Davidson (2002) contributed to this thinking in his book *The Committed Enterprise*, in which he identified the reasons why organizations are changing. These are paraphrased here:

- *Customer power*. Customers have wider choice and are more discriminating. They are increasingly sophisticated; satisfaction and loyalty are no longer guarantees of success. As their strategic value increases, customers cost more to acquire and become more difficult to retain.

- *Employee choice*. Talented staff are as hard to find as ever. The old concept of lifetime employment by employers has changed to one of lifetime employability, the responsibility of the employee. Employers can no longer expect loyalty in addition to commitment, as employees seek opportunities for personal growth and development with organizations consistent with their views and aspirations, in addition to remuneration.

- *Sophisticated financial markets*. Shareholders and city analysts seek more than short-term financial performance, increasingly taken as a given; they also seek further insight into strategy and the means by which future cash and profit generation will be delivered.

- *External stakeholders*. Companies increasingly recognize that they have a responsibility to more than shareholders, as CSR (corporate social responsibility) becomes much higher profile.

Such factors have produced new ways of working and organizing work. Whilst there is no single term, such as 'hierarchy' or 'bureaucracy', that sums up the post-industrial era, these types of organizations are often described using terms like:

- *delayered* – with few management levels in order to speed up communication and decision-making
- *horizontal* – communication takes place *across* an organization unencumbered by the vertical, functional organization and lines of reporting that hinder immediacy
- *processes* – customer-facing processes cut across the functional structure and act to combine the inputs of various functions resulting in customer relevant outcomes
- *empowered* – where decision-making rests with skilled and knowledgeable individuals prepared to accept and discharge responsibility
- *IT-enabled* – with suitable software tools underpinning the organization, speeding up decision-making and communication; in the extreme this can result in 'the virtual organization'
- *outsourcing, alliances, partnerships* – there are differences between these three terms, but let us not get particular at this stage about definitions. The principle is that the organization extends beyond the boundaries of the firm, to utilize and draw upon the capabilities of others to form a unit of competition. This is sometimes referred to as a 'network', and it is said that increasingly it is not firms that compete against each other, but networks.

The discussion so far has helped in understanding why organizations are structured the way that they are, and now moves on to consider the various types of structural organizations and the management implications that arise from these.

Structure

All organizations have some form of structure, which can range from highly formal and regulated to one which is negotiated between the participants concerned. Some formal structure is necessary for the following reasons:

- *Organization and allocation of work and resources*. Many organizations have some form of functional specialization, and hence this provides a framework within which tasks can be allocated and the appropriate resources identified, often through a planning process. In this way, individual responsibilities can be identified through a 'planning cascade' or other processes and procedures.

Competitive networks

There are three major airline alliances in operation – Star Alliance, Sky Team and One World.

Star Alliance	Sky Team	One World
Air Canada	Aeroflot	British Airways
Air New Zealand	Aero Mexico	American Airlines
ANA	Air France KLM	Qantas
Asiana Airlines	Alitalia	Aer Lingus
Austrian	Continental Airlines	Iberia
BMI	CSA Czech Airlines	Finnair
LOT Polish Airlines	Delta	Lan
Lufthansa	Korean Air	Cathay Pacific
SAS Scandinavian Airlines	NWA	
Singapore Airlines		
South African Airways		
Spanair		
Swiss		
TAP Portugal		
Thai		
United		
US Airways		
Varig		
Adria		
Blue 1		
Croatia Airlines		

As can be seen, each alliance is an interesting mix of major international carriers together with lesser-known airlines. By working together, each airline benefits. The larger airlines have the opportunity to extend their reach and allow their major international routes to feed into local destinations. This enables them to offer enhanced service and capture more revenue, but with minimal additional expense; smaller airlines have the opportunity to gain incremental business from those passengers wishing to connect with international flights. However, once the alliance has been initiated the members will all be looking to benefit their own business further whilst excluding competitors. As alliances form and develop, the opportunities for airlines not involved in the network progressively diminish. Unless an airline controls or can give access to a strategic destination, it has little to offer other alliance members. The chronic lack of profitability in the airline industry means that membership of an alliance is a powerful factor in competition and survival.

- *Job role.* This is a clear definition of the tasks concerned, often expressed in terms of processes or operations required, or standards of performance to be achieved. This also links to a definition of the capabilities required and appropriate reward and appraisal systems.

- *Decision-making responsibilities and information flow.* Information is an essential input to decision-making, as managers have to assess risk and make choices and judgments between alternative courses of action. Different types of information will be required, depending on the level and scope of the decisions to be made. There is often a link between the significance of the decision and the hierarchical authority of the decision-maker.

- *Relationships.* These can be defined at a number of levels. At an organizational level, organizations actively build and develop relationships with other organizations as part of a managed network. At an individual level, relationships may be formally defined as part of the job role, but can also be constrained by the organizational structure.

- *Culture, attitudes, values and behaviour.* The structure of the organization will also strongly influence its culture (see the McKinsey seven S model, in Chapter 3). These issues are discussed elsewhere, but it is easy to understand that the culture of an organization will vary depending on the nature of the task involved. The military officer determining whether or not to fire a missile will operate in a very different context to the professional partners in a law firm.

Configuration describes not just the structure of an organization, but also the processes, relationships and boundaries which make it operational. Processes will be discussed shortly, but structure can be considered in two main forms: hierarchical and matrix.

Hierarchical

This can be divided into the following:

- *Functional.* Here, the organizational tree is denoted by function. This is typical of smaller businesses, and allows a sensible balance between managers and operational staff, with subdivisions of specialization as appropriate. For example, the sales function could be further subdivided into internal sales, field sales and key account management. Such organizations tend to lack flexibility due to a 'one size fits all' approach; the needs of one trading region may be significantly different from another.

- *Product/market.* With diversification into different markets, perhaps with the same or different products, it may be appropriate to focus resources more specifically. This may well be the case as an organization grows and develops; this can often be accompanied by a discussion as to the degree to which the organization is decentralized, whereby central service functions such as HR, accounting, and research and development are distributed to the product/market businesses.

- *Divisional.* Product/market operations may in turn become stand-alone profit centres or strategic business units with agreed divisions of responsibility between the centre and the division. The basis of the division can be a source of much discussion – division by product, market or geography is commonly seen.

Matrix

The matrix management approach emerged from the complexities of managing large government-run aerospace projects. A matrix operates several types of structures in tandem with the objective of integrating specialist knowledge areas around common objectives in a grid-like structure. Those who work in a matrix will often have two bosses, which, combined with the politics of organizations, can often create ambiguities for the managers concerned. Hence the culture and attitude of those concerned in contributing to the overall objectives is an important factor. This has led to the matrix approach being described not so much as a structure but rather as a state of mind, and one that has proved problematic in practice. Sy and D'Annunzio (2005) have proposed five factors that compromise the operation of a matrix structure:

1. *Misaligned goals* – with (at least) two bosses there is always the opportunity for competition or conflict between objectives together with problems of communication and coordination.

2. *Unclear roles and responsibilities* – this is often seen as confusion regarding what is required and who should be referred to for guidance, resulting in tension and ambiguity.

3. *Ambiguous authority* – when there is only one boss it is explicitly clear who is in charge; lack of experience in working in matrix organizations can affect both manager and subordinate, leading to lack of clarity and delay in decision-making.

4. *Matrix guardian* – it is difficult to measure individual performance, therefore managing rewards may conflict with the way in which a matrix operates; this can be particularly difficult if the overall objective is achieved and the matrix structure itself is seen to be problematic.

5. *Functional focused employees* – a matrix structure contains within it the potential for tension, particularly if employees are attitudinally focused to their functional area of expertise, which could well have been instrumental in their career progress. This can result in a lack of trust, poor communication and reluctance to commit resources.

Matrix management

Dutch electrical giant Philips was an early adopter of the matrix style of organization, with both national companies and product divisions. There were persistent problems of accountability, with conflict between the two organizational units. For a while the national units prevailed, but a formal reorganization of responsibility gave power back to the product divisions in the early 1990s. Philips has now recognized that the company needs to work more on helping managers to change their attitudes, and that these changes will be brought about without the need for radical reorganization. As Gerard

Ruizendall, head of corporate strategy, says: whenever the company creates a new organization it creates a new problem. Now, the company says that most of the change required will be achieved by working with managers to change their attitudes.

(Source: Economist.com)

International and multinational firms

As industries and firms grow and develop nationally and internationally, issues of structure and organization become more complex. As firms develop global presence, a number of factors assume higher priority:

- *Worldwide value chains* – a further level of complexity is added when operating internationally; in particular, time can be a critical issue when the supply chain is diverse, and when dealing with food products storage conditions are also important. Zespri™ is a New Zealand brand of kiwi fruit that can be delivered halfway across the world within a 24-hour time window, guaranteeing that the fruit is in perfect condition for the supermarket shelf.

- *International firms, local markets* – there is potential for conflict when international firms enter into local markets where different standards, business practices, cultural conditions and other factors apply. A manufacturer of animal feed won a contract to supply food to racing camels in Saudi Arabia; a shortage of packaging materials at the plant led to sacks emblazoned with the logo for pig feed being inadvertently used, causing great offence in a strongly Muslim country.

- *Greater influence of NGOs* – non-governmental organizations, consumer pressure groups and other influences are capable of scrutinizing every element of a firm's operation. What may be considered acceptable practice in one market may be inappropriate in another. Does child labour exploit underprivileged and vulnerable people, or provide employment and income for those who would otherwise have no means of support?

- *Government intervention* – if trading or economic conditions change, then governments may act unilaterally in what they perceive to be their own best interest. Companies that have invested in overseas markets may find their activities constrained, their assets taken or markets denied to them. Countries affected by bird flu in 2006 found that exports of poultry products were quickly curtailed.

International or multinational companies face the challenge of managing global products and brands, and their international presence, but within local markets and diverse channels of distribution – perhaps with limited local knowledge. In such circumstances, the options for management and control can be summarized as in Figure 4.1.

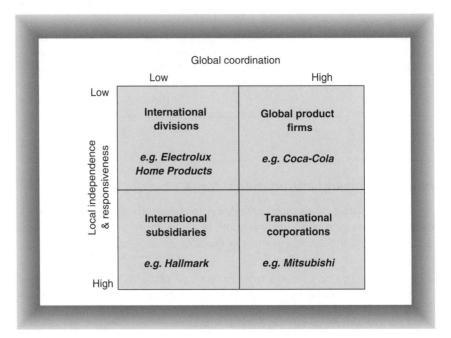

Figure 4.1
International
organization
structure

- *International divisions* – this structure enables the core business of the firm to develop strategy appropriate to the markets in which it operates, but with good vertical coordination between divisions.

- *International subsidiaries* – these are often internationally coordinated by means of financial and top-level planning; otherwise, managers enjoy a high degree of autonomy for operational matters and implementation.

- *Global product companies* – these have a one size fits all approach, with a high degree of central coordination; planning is often undertaken on a global basis.

- *Transnational corporations* – these often comprise many different business units as part of a network of interdependent operations providing local response and presence. The combined sales of three of the top six trading companies in Japan are equal to the combined gross domestic product of South America; transnational corporations are powerful economic and political forces, exercising significant influence over government policies.

Figure 4.1 helps to explain the boundaries and types of relationships that exist at corporate level. Changes in the external business environment can influence the nature of the relationship. With multinational corporations there is a tendency for adverse business performance to increase the tendency for centralization, for example.

Organizational dynamics

Peters and Waterman's book *In Search of Excellence* (1982), mentioned earlier, generated considerable discussion at the time of publication and also subsequently – not least because some 10 years or so after publication many of the apparently excellent companies had fallen from grace or even gone bankrupt. This demonstrates that management is not static but dynamic. Organizations are required to adapt, reflect and respond to change, but this is not necessarily reflected in many of the static and descriptive models commonly used. Greiner's model of organizational growth (Figure 4.2) provides a framework against which managers can derive not necessarily a prescriptive understanding of what they ought to be doing, but rather a framework within which they can assess and understand their own circumstances as a basis for decision-making.

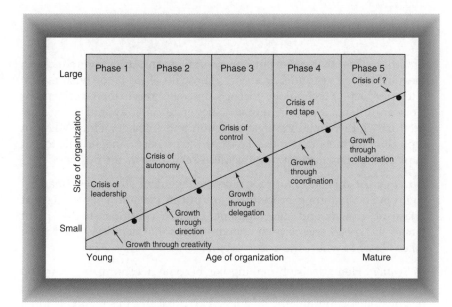

Figure 4.2
Greiner's growth model (Greiner, 1972)

Greiner's model identifies a number of dimensions which are important in the development of the organization:

- *Size of the firm.* With an increase in size comes complexity and potentially more levels of management and greater bureaucracy. Coordination becomes more difficult and communication slows.

- *Evolution.* This describes regular and steady growth with a relatively stable planning environment. In such circumstances, problems and their solutions are relatively self-evident.

- *Revolution.* This is a discontinuous phase with rapid change in the external environment; typically, we think of these changes as economic or technological. This requires a radical review of strategy, and survival of the firm may depend upon this. The publishers of the *Encyclopaedia Britannica* suffered a near-fatal shock to their book business when technology enabled Microsoft to publish an encyclopedia on a CD complete with colour, sound, vision and search facilities with text links to related subjects. In some cases these CDs were given away free, bundled with an inclusive package.

- *Age of the firm*. As time passes, history, tradition and the legacy of the past builds, unquestioned assumptions develop, and strategic vision can be narrowed.

- *Industry growth*. The rate at which an industry develops will also determine the speed with which various opportunities and threats emerge to challenge the organization. The mobile telephone sector has moved rapidly from market growth to saturation, and now faces the challenges of converging technologies which may or may not centre on a telephone handset-like apparatus. Vodafone has attracted criticism for failing to anticipate such change, and its share price suffered in 2005/2006.

Greiner's model identifies five stages of growth:

1. *Creativity*. This is where an entrepreneurial organization finds a niche in the market for its product or service. Those involved in the business are often product- or technology-focused, and solutions to managerial problems are often viewed in terms of better technology and more new products, rather than strategic direction and management. SMEs can typically become stuck at this level, as the owner/manager fails to put in place the management resource necessary to grow the business.

2. *Direction*. At this stage, appropriate management structures, financial controls and planning procedures are put in place to enable the next phase of growth and development. Growth continues to the point where the speed and pace of change means that decisions need to be taken closer to where the action occurs.

3. *Delegation*. Here, decision-making has become decentralized, with top management setting the performance criteria and operational managers responsible for running the business. Paradoxically, this relatively loose level of control gives wide freedom of action to managers, particularly if they deliver against objectives, which can lead to independent action contrary to the overall direction of the organization.

4. *Coordination*. Rather than trying to increase the level of control and regulation, perhaps a better solution is to look for more effective ways of coordinating activities. This might be by separating front-office and back-office activities, providing centralized resource to front-line activities, changing reward structures in order to influence behaviour; these are just some of the techniques that could be used.

5. *Collaboration*. As the organization continues to grow, so the coordination mechanisms become more difficult to manage and less effective; there is an inevitable tendency for rules and guidelines to take over, leading to a bureaucratic nightmare of red tape. Further evolution of the organization takes place not through greater 'vertical' management, but by 'horizontal' techniques such as team-building, matrix structures and process orientation.

This framework does not provide a prescription of solutions, but helps managers to understand the influences upon organizations and the possible routes to a solution. As ever, there is always another solution – as the example of W. L. Gore and Associates demonstrates.

W. L. Gore and Associates

Privately-owned W. L. Gore and Associates, maker of the ubiquitous Gore-Tex™ product, has 45 plants around the world and employs 6000 staff, always referred to as associates. The relatively small number of people employed at each plant promotes an entrepreneurial environment, and associates are encouraged to commit time and energy to innovation and new ideas. Underpinning the organization is a sense of ownership and equal participation based on four guiding principles – fairness to each other, the freedom to encourage, the ability to make commitments, and consultation with other associates. There is no hierarchy and no job titles, and work is team-based, with everybody expected to contribute to the success of the project and work effectively alongside other associates. There is also no salary structure; pay rises are *ad hoc* and are based on a poll conducted amongst fellow team members.

(Source: *Personnel Today*)

Where next?

Whilst the Greiner model suggests that matrix management and more people-centred styles of management represent the collaborative phase in his model, he speculated that further stages of development would be based on networks – managing beyond the organization. We started by discussing industrial and post-industrial styles of management; as we move beyond this into what is known as postmodernism, a strong anti-bureaucracy, anti-hierarchy trend starts to emerge. Fairtlough (2005) says that 'in a strictly hierarchical organization, the only learning that takes place is the learning of the individual at the top. Everyone else obeys orders'. Building on the example of W. L. Gore, the power of teams is apparent. Fairtlough also argues for more autonomy, counterbalanced by accountability.

Lars Kolind is the business brain behind the turnaround of a hearing-aid manufacturer, Oticon, which is now a global leader in its market sector. He articulates five principles underpinning his reform of the company:

1. Defining a meaning beyond profits.

2. Creating a partnership with staff, suppliers and customers.

3. Building a collaborative organization.

4. Leading through vision and values.

5. Implementing through change processes.

For more insight into what he terms his 'war against bureaucracy', visit his website at www.thesecondcycle.com. It will make you think.

Operations

As discussed earlier, Johnson and Scholes (2002) use the term 'configuration' to describe how the structure, processes and relationships/boundaries of the organization enable it to operate. Planning, as discussed in Chapters 11 and 12, is the means whereby resources are allocated to enable those operations to take place. This section will discuss primarily processes and projects, but accepts that the distinction between them is sometimes narrow. A distinction that can be made between them is that processes are ongoing and repetitive activities with clearly defined and allocated resources and which can be managed for increasing effectiveness and efficiency. Projects differ in that they are finite and non-repetitive, and are used in order to achieve predetermined outcomes.

In practice the line between the two can be somewhat blurred, as projects may be precursors of processes and processes themselves may be composed of discrete projects – as, for example, with new product development activities. In this case, new product development processes can be very clearly defined, but as each development activity or project progresses through the process, a go/no-go decision is eventually arrived at.

In principle, both products and services can be managed in this way; what is important is the way that value is added at each stage of the process, as the purpose of operations is to take inputs and turn them into value-added outputs. This is clearly a topic of considerable interest to marketers, and this section will focus on this topic. Michael Porter's concept of the value chain (Figure 4.3) suggests how different value-creating activities of

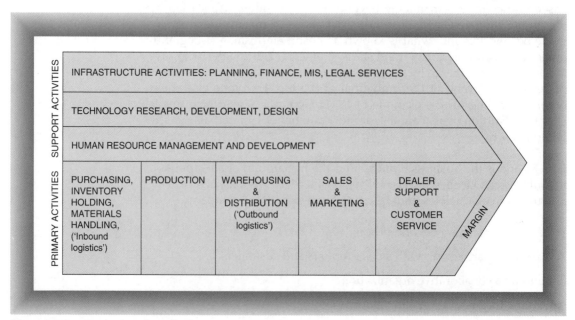

Figure 4.3   Porter's value chain

the organization link together, underpinned by supporting activities such as HR and accounting (Porter, 1985).

This value-based perspective of processes is conceptually elegant but rather more difficult to use as a management tool (see Chapter 12 for further discussion on this point). It helps us to understand how different activities link together across functional boundaries in order to achieve customer satisfaction, but it is more difficult to understand how this can give practical guidance to managers. As Figure 4.4 suggests, the components that are managed from input to output are both tangible (such as raw materials) and intangible (such as brand asset and commitment).

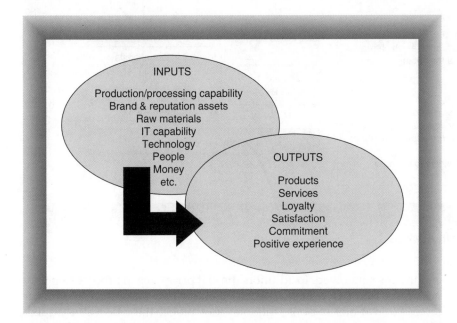

Figure 4.4
Inputs and outputs

By decomposing the activities involved into a series of steps, it is possible to gain sensible insight into how value is created within a process. This is done by calculating the costs of products and services as they enter each element of the process, adding the costs of processing then deducting these from the price realized at the end of the process. The value created is calculated by subtracting the costs incurred from the price realized. However, if costs exceed the price, then value has been destroyed. The price realized, together with frictional costs such as storage, transport and insurance, then constitute the entry cost into the next stage of the process. Figure 4.5 gives an outline of this activity. This helps in understanding where cost is incurred and value is created and destroyed. In turn, this can lead to decisions as to how the value chain can be reconfigured to allow comparisons between different routes to the market.

This technique is not entirely straightforward, as there are significant problems in identifying the processing activities of each stage of the chain

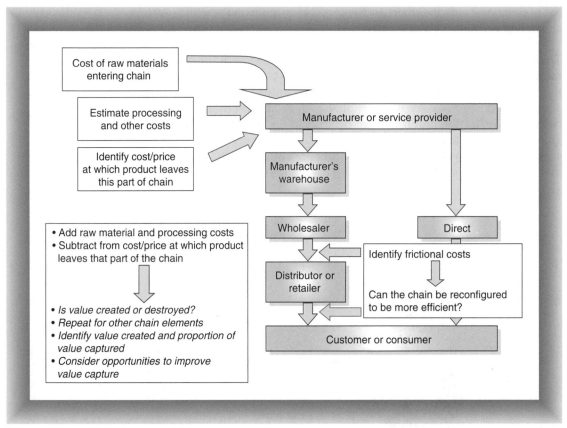

Figure 4.5 Value chain analysis

and the costs involved. In addition, the exit price of each process step may not be determined by the market, in that there may be an internal transfer price. For various reasons, this may not reflect the true value added. However, the final or end-user price does give a definitive view of how the customer values the product, but even this does not give insight into the intangibles of loyalty, commitment and the all important intention to repurchase. Numerous complications are involved, but this technique does allow for sensible estimates to be arrived at, and can give extraordinary insight.

In one case where this technique was used, with a large American manufacturer of packaging materials, it was found that the brand owners and their immediate customers, the retailers, captured 75 percent of the value created within the value chain. The packaging manufacturer and their immediate customer, who manufactured finished packaging materials for the brand owners to fill, realized only 6 percent of the value created. This realization encouraged the parties to work together to lever their 6 percent of value capture upwards, rather than arguing in a highly competitive and aggressive manner about how the meagre value captured was to be divided. The price negotiations between these two companies could have been described as epic; the insight given by an understanding of value creation and capture proved a turning point in their otherwise difficult relationship.

The purpose of a process or project is to create value at each stage of the process, and techniques are available which give at least some insight into this process. Slack *et al.* (2004) discusses five objectives that help in refining and improving processes (Table 4.2).

Internal perspective	Process objective	External perspective
Rapid throughput	Speed	Ready availability
High efficiency	Cost	Good value for money
Reliable, durable process	Dependability	Confidence and reputation
Organizational agility	Flexibility	Meet all needs
Right first time	Quality	Reliable, fit for purpose

Table 4.2
Process objectives and perspectives

As can be readily inferred from the points noted in Table 4.2, there are some difficult trade-offs and contradictions that arise. For example, the need to be flexible to meet a wide range of needs on behalf of the customer means that the firm has to decide to what extent it will manufacture customized products or deliver bespoke services. High levels of availability can incur exceptionally high costs, and these and many other trade-offs require judgment on behalf of managers. Some of the relevant decision criteria are as follows:

- *Value orientation.* High value or low cost? Does the firm add value by augmenting the product or service, or adopt a lower price/lower cost position with respect to the market? Differentiation must be durable and defensible. There is a need to assess the competitive threat and the degree to which change is required.

- *Process flexibility.* Is it easy to adapt, or rigid and inflexible? Processes can be built around high capability to deliver variety in product and service, or can be more focused to consistency, implying high volume and lower value. The balance between the two tends to be a zero-sum game.

- *Management and people.* Is it creative and flexible, or routine and task focused? There is little point in taking people where they do not wish or are not capable of going. As the example from Philips demonstrates, there is a need to manage culture in order to manage change.

- *Capability.* Diverse or narrow skill base? The degree to which the business is focused will suggest the extent to which change is feasible.

Business environment

As the night-time photograph in Figure 4.6 suggests, not just Europe but the world seems to be becoming a smaller place. We are increasingly recognizing that our organization is part of a larger whole, and that we must understand and react to the dynamics of the business environment.

Figure 4.6
Europe by night

This is an important aspect of the concept of configuration referred to by Johnson and Scholes (2002); the environment is one of the boundaries to the organization. Whilst tools and techniques for environmental analysis are discussed elsewhere, this final section will briefly discuss two concepts at the extremes of the configuration of the organization. The first is one that will enable us to develop deeper insight and broader vision regarding the possible influences of the business environment, and the second is a technique that enables organizations to respond to its most immediate consequences. The first topic to be discussed is scenario planning, and the second is crisis management.

Scenario planning

Typically, planning takes place with major underpinning and a sometimes unconsidered assumption – that the world of tomorrow is consistent with and much the same as the world of today. Such assumptions can be unfortunate, as the travel company that made a major acquisition on 10 September 2001, in order to develop a global network to support its target market, found out immediately after the terrorist attacks on America on 11 September that year, after which the travel sector entered a sustained period of decline. Figure 4.7 demonstrates the relationship between the possibility or likelihood of events happening, and their significance to our business. Planning, contingency planning and risk analysis all take place under the same assumptions of environmental continuity, and represent permutations of forecasting. Scenario planning takes us into the area of understanding the implications for the business of something that is very unlikely to happen, but which holds fundamental implications.

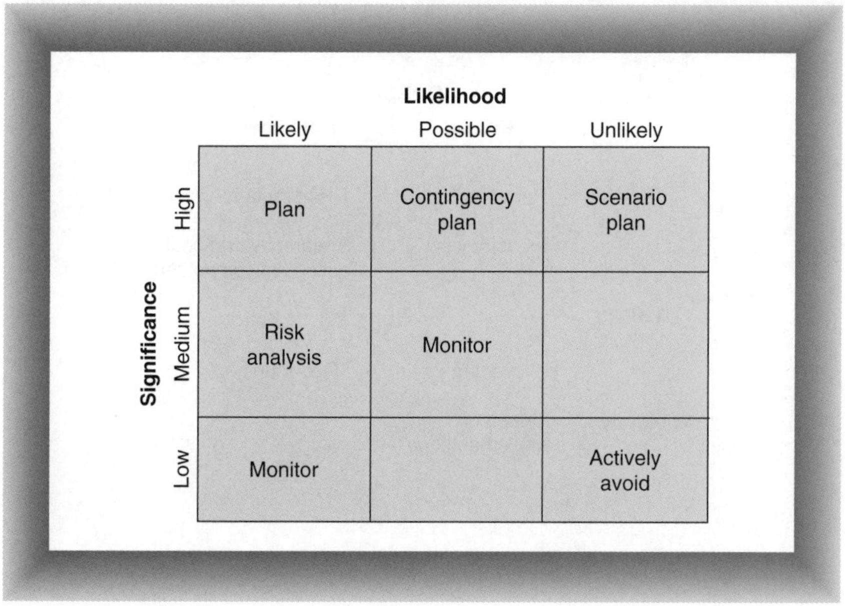

	Likelihood		
	Likely	**Possible**	**Unlikely**
High	Plan	Contingency plan	Scenario plan
Medium	Risk analysis	Monitor	
Low	Monitor		Actively avoid

(Significance on vertical axis; Likelihood on horizontal axis)

Figure 4.7
Planning and environmental certainty

Some quotations from Donald Rumsfeld, US Defence Secretary in the George W. Bush administration:

I would not say that the future is necessarily less predictable than the past. I think the past was not predictable when it started.

... as we know, there are known knowns; there are things we know we know. We also know there are known unknowns; that is to say we know there are some things we do not know. But there are also unknown unknowns – the ones we don't know we don't know.

As Donald Rumsfeld has attempted to suggest in his unique way, we cannot necessarily rely on the future resembling the past, and it is factors of which we are unaware and perhaps cannot even conceive that can comprise substantial threats. Scenario planning is one of the techniques that help us to recognize and step away from the constraints to our thinking, and identify new opportunities. Figure 4.8 overleaf attempts to recast the Rumsfeld quotation.

We will look at each of the boxes on this matrix in turn:

● *Known to us/known to others* – industries are sometimes surprisingly small, with key decision-makers perhaps having attended the same university, worked together in the same company, and at some stage possibly having been part of a trade association or professional body. In these circumstances inherent beliefs and assumptions about the industry develop, which can result in 'competitive convergence' as managers, albeit unconsciously, think and act in concert. Those interesting

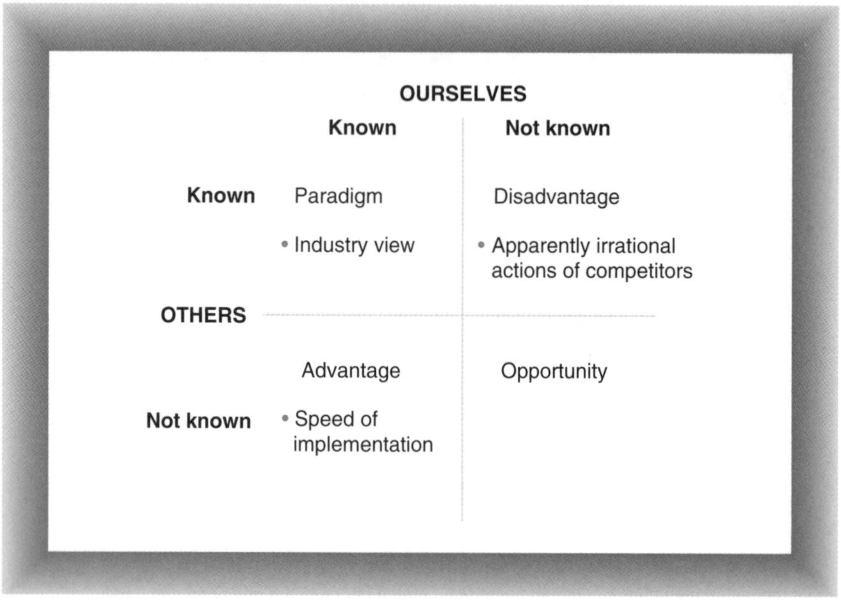

Figure 4.8
Scenario planning –
opening the
window

words 'well, of course, it is different here', heard by the consultant visiting a company, suggest that the industry paradigm is well-established, and indeed in some cases is being defended.

- *Known to us/unknown to others* – if our organization can generate unique insight and understanding, then this knowledge can be turned to competitive advantage – particularly if our actions and the reasons underlying them are unclear to the rest of the industry. Where competitive moves are more transparent, this leads to competitive imitation and a wide selection of 'me-too' products.

- *Known to others/unknown to us* – as managers in an organization with a reasonable degree of self-belief, it is all too easy to dismiss the competitive moves of others if they do not readily fit our own frame of industry reference. Such blind arrogance can sometimes be swiftly followed by a period of retrenchment as the advantage generated by competitors becomes more apparent. In the highly competitive UK retail market, the Tesco Clubcard was introduced in the mid-1990s and was dismissed as a gimmick by the then market leader, Sainsbury's. The unexpected success of its competitor led Sainsbury's to an about-turn, and they introduced their own loyalty card. Some 10 years later, Tesco now has a 15%+ market share advantage over Sainsbury's, which has slumped into third place behind Asda. The success of Tesco is largely attributed to its loyalty card and the insight into customer buying behaviour that this gave them.

- *Unknown to us/unknown to others* – here, in the 'opportunity' box, lie some of Donald Rumsfeld's 'unknown unknowns'. Scenario planning is a technique that enables managers to explore these different worlds and understand the implications for their business.

Conventional planning techniques often work on the basis of forecasting, but in times of high uncertainty these can prove less effective. The development of scenario planning techniques is largely attributed to Shell, which, in the 1970s, was trying to deal with the instability and uncertainties of the oil industry at that time. In principle, the technique aims to elicit the primary drivers of change and then to understand their various combinations in terms of a range of outcomes or scenarios, from unfavourable to favourable. Careful development of both the driving factors and scenarios will help managers to identify the implications for their business. The technique generates flexibility and awareness of the factors driving change, and encourages managers to consider the implications while at the same time dealing with the complexity of issues posed. In times of dynamic and unpredictable change the technique is gaining in popularity in order to help managers remain alert to the implications of environmental change. The technique is not concerned with predicting or forecasting the future, but with exploring the implications that it may hold and thinking through the consequences.

Numerous websites provide further detailed information on the process of scenario planning, and give examples of such scenario plans. See, for example, the global business network (www.gbn.org), www.chforum.org, and www.themanager.org. Many public bodies publish their scenarios on the Internet, and these too make interesting reading.

Crisis management

In a fast-moving and dynamic business environment, with cheap and powerful means of communication and with high levels of consumer awareness and involvement, there is both higher potential for adverse events to occur and a greater need to manage them. Crisis management is an example of contingency planning, where factors of high significance are considered against their possibility to damage the interests of the organization (Figure 4.7). Of course managers continually assess and offset risk in the course of their day-to-day decision-making, but what differentiates a crisis is the speed with which it may strike and the potential for damage to a reputation or business interests.

Crisis management

One of the most famous examples of crisis management concerns Johnson & Johnson and the headache/painkiller product sold under the brand name of Tylenol. In the early 1980s, the product was market leader and contributed nearly 20 percent of the company's revenue. A small number of packs were tampered with and contaminated with cyanide, resulting in the deaths of seven people. The company immediately withdrew all products from their retail outlets and advised health-care professionals and others as soon as possible of the problem. Jim Burke, the chief executive officer of Johnson & Johnson, was highly visible, and expressed commitment, concern and empathy for those involved and affected. In the longer term, the product was produced in a different format and packaged in tamperproof, sealed packages. It was reintroduced with a major advertising campaign, together with money-off coupons to compensate users for having to empty their bathroom cabinet, and sales quickly rose to around the same level previously enjoyed. The company was seen to have acted responsibly during the crisis, although the culprits were never identified.

By contrast, the problems associated with Firestone tyres fitted to Ford Explorer sports utility vehicles in the US is acknowledged as having been a fiasco in public relations terms. By October 2000, 119 people had reportedly died in accidents involving a Ford vehicle fitted with Firestone tyres. When the tyres failed, the tread tended to peel off and the vehicle then overturned. In addition to the deaths (and there were thought to be many more than those recorded), there were many thousands of injuries. In August of 2000, Ford and Firestone agreed to a product recall. The companies issued a statement, but declined to answer any further questions. The relationship between Ford and Firestone declined, with each blaming the other. Ford noted the high defect rates associated with the Firestone products, and compared this to the absence of problems experienced with tyres supplied by a competitor, Goodyear. Firestone refused to admit that there was any problem with the product, although it was strongly associated with one of their production plants in the USA. Firestone argued that incorrect recommendations for tyre inflation pressures were implicated, together with problems specific to the Ford Explorer. It later emerged that Ford may have been forewarned of the problem due to similar experiences in rather more distant markets such as Venezuela and Saudi Arabia. The two companies continued to blame each other, with the end result of damage to share prices, profits and very substantial legal payouts. This case has been described as 'the largest vehicular product liability crisis in the history of this country'.

(Sources: personal.psu.ed, iml.jou.ufl.edu, *Business Week*, firestone-tire-recall.com, regesterlarkin.com, atla.org)

The way that a crisis develops can be explained, using the lifecycle analogy, with four distinct phases (Gonzalez-Herrero and Pratt, 1996):

1. *Issues management* – at this stage, there is a search for early indications of a crisis emerging by monitoring consumer groups, lead users, etc.

2. *Planning prevention* – by this stage it is apparent that there is a problem, which can be curtailed by swift and decisive action. By working with the media this action can be presented as evidence of involvement and concern. A figurehead spokesman, typically the chief executive or other very senior manager, should present the case clearly and sympathetically. At this stage, a process should be in place to deal with inquiries and actively to provide information to fill the rumour gap.

3. *Crisis stage* – by failing to act pre-emptively, rather than leading events the organization ends up responding to them. Intel failed to respond sufficiently quickly to problems associated with their latest iteration of the Pentium processor, but eventually had to replace all the faulty Pentium chips at a cost estimated at around US$400 million.

4. *Aftermath* – by this stage, events have unfolded; the main task here is to finalize issues associated with the crisis, learn from the experience, and put in place procedures to enable more effective management in the future.

Management action can be planned around each of these phases, based on the principles of openness and honesty, acting responsibly even if blame is not established, expressing concern and empathy, and putting in place a communications management program to deal with the short- and long-term issues that will be generated. Preparation, perhaps having a suitably prepared website and trained and briefed managers, combined with decisive action will help to neutralize the sting of a crisis. It is also inevitable that there will be some short-term costs involved. With a crisis, the only real option may be whether to pay now or later. The Tylenol example suggests that swift, decisive and early action enables the company to recover and move on far more effectively.

Scenario planning and crisis management dovetail neatly together as ways in which the interface of the organization with the external business environment that is most acute can be managed and defused.

In a vivid management development exercise associated with a food product, the managers involved worked through a scenario enacted over a period of 48 hours. The scenario involved the use of real journalists questioning the managers concerned at a press conference, with reports being 'broadcast' on television and radio, and articles appearing in specially prepared newspaper articles the following morning. Facts, figures, rumours, telephone calls, emails and fax messages poured into the organization, and managers developed a very real sense of the issues involved for them, their organization and their products.

References

Davidson, H. (2002). *The Committed Enterprise; Making Vision and Values Work*. Oxford: Butterworth-Heinemann.

Fairtlough, G. (2005). *The Three Ways of Getting Things Done: Hierarchy, Heterarchy & Responsible Autonomy in Organizations*. Axminster: Triarchy Press.

Gonzalez-Herrero, A. and Pratt, C.B. (1996). An integrated symmetrical model for crisis-communications management. *Journal of Public Relations Research*, **8(2)**, 79–105.

Greiner, L.E. (1972). Evolution and revolution as organizations grow. *Harvard Business Review*, **21(4)**, 1022–1054.

Hatch, M.J. (1997). *Organizational Theory: Modern, Symbolic and Post Modern Perspectives*. Oxford: Oxford University Press.

Johnson, G. and Scholes, K. (2002). *Exploring Corporate Strategy*. Harlow: FT Prentice Hall.

Merton, R. (1968). *Social Theory and Social Structure*. New York: Free Press.

Peters, T. and Waterman, D. (1982). *In Search of Excellence*. New York: Harper & Row.

Porter, M. (1985). *Competitive Advantage: Creating and Sustaining Superior Performance*. New York: The Free Press.

Ritzer, G. (1993). *The McDonaldization of Society*. London: Sage.

Slack, N., Chambers, S. and Johnston, R. (2004). *Operations Management*. Harlow: FT Prentice Hall.

Sy, T. and D'Annunzio, L.S. (2005). Challenges and strategies of matrix organizations: top-level and mid-level managers' perspectives. *Human Resource Planning*, **28(1)**, 39–48.

Part II People

5 Management skills

Introduction

An organization is only as successful as the skills it has acquired and developed, and the way in which it utilizes those skills. We will briefly remind ourselves of some of those essential skills and then concentrate on marketing management. We will cover leadership and team skills in Chapter 6.

What follows are brief descriptions of the technical, functional and marketing management skills required by organizations.

Technical and functional skills

Every job requires skills of some sort, from a simple skill learned on the job from a more experienced colleague (for example, processing an order) to highly technical skills acquired after years of learning, training and experience (for example, a surgeon operating on a brain).

As we have seen, when organizations become larger their structures reflect the need for more functional specialization; people are required to develop skills that enable them to become experts. However, this expertise often results in narrowly defined roles and skills, which is necessary in some industries but causes problems in many organizations. Such problems include:

- poor use of organization resources, people only skilled in one limited area
- demotivated employees, lack of interest or opportunities for job rotation or progression
- lack of workforce flexibility at peak times or times of change.

The answer lies in multiskilling – ensuring people can undertake more than one task. This has obvious advantages, such as a climate of learning and adapting, and effective coverage of skills.

The danger is that in broadening skills development we fail to deepen skills – that is, we are able to cover a diverse range of skills but are not particularly good at any of them; we fail to develop expertise. If multiskilling has become part of the work climate, the challenge for managers is to find a balance between breadth and depth – multiskilling, and developing expertise.

The manager's role becomes one of orchestrating a diverse range of skills across teams in pursuit of organization goals. Managers can only do this if they know:

- what skills are required – technical, functional/professional
- where they can be found – externally and internally
- when they should be utilized
- how they can be harnessed and deployed
- how they can be developed and maintained.

Industry technical skills and trends

Many industries require skills that transfer from industry to industry – for example, general finance and engineering skills. However, many industries require skills specific to that industry, obvious examples being the medical and legal professions. Other examples include:

- the chemical industry (for example chemists)
- the IT industry (for example software developers)
- financial services (for example actuaries).

It is important for organizations (usually HR) to keep track of what skills are available now, and the trend for the future. Some industries in some countries are finding themselves facing a serious skills shortage. Organizations susceptible to such shortages are risking future success, even survival, if they do not have a plan to overcome these problems, and it is management's responsibility to acquire and retain these skills.

Skills shortages

OECD economies have experienced the longest continuous period of economic growth for decades. As a result, labour and skills shortages are widespread. Across Europe organizations are experiencing common problems with skills shortages in education – particularly sciences, engineering and the service sector. In France construction is a problem, and in Austria there are shortages connected with ICT. Germany predicts 75 000 unfilled vacancies in ICT. Of the hard-to-fill vacancies, 50 percent are in low and unskilled categories, including agriculture, fisheries, hotels and restaurants. Retail and consumer services are also suffering from shortages.

This situation is aggravated by demographic trends in Europe, with an aging workforce, and predictions are that these problems will exacerbate skills shortages as early as 2015.

(Source: OECD)

Business functional skills and professional institutions

Organizations also require functional skills. Functional (professional) skills can be acquired by studying for and qualifying as a member of, for example, one of the following:

- Chartered Institute of Marketing (CIM), for marketers
- Chartered Institute of Personnel and Development (CIPD), for HR practitioners
- Chartered Institute of Management Accountants (CIMA), for accountants
- Institute of Incorporated Engineers (IIE), for production managers.

These are just some examples of professional qualifications that provide the functional skills required by organizations.

The above may seem obvious examples, but some organizations struggle because of either a lack of professionally qualified people with the skills for functional roles or an imbalance caused by (for example) engineers or accountants taking on other functional jobs which they are not qualified for or experienced to do. There is now an expectation that people do not just hold a degree but also have a professional qualification that equips them with the functional know-how to do the job.

Such institutions provide for both the academic rigour of understanding a functional role and also the application – how concepts are applied. This provision begins early, with many qualifications starting at a basic certificate (tactical) level and leading to a postgraduate diploma (strategic) level. For example, functional skills development within the Chartered Institute of Marketing (CIM) includes:

- marketing research
- marketing communications
- marketing planning
- marketing management.

These skills are broad headings, each of which can be broken down into component parts (see Figure 5.1).

Managers are responsible for ensuring that they know what skills are required to do a job and for acquiring or developing these skills.

Management skills

As well as the functional or technical skills of a marketing management job, what other skills are required of a manager? Skills could include:

- planning, organizing and coordinating
- analytical and evaluation

- problem-solving and decision-making
- creativity and innovation
- communications
- motivation.

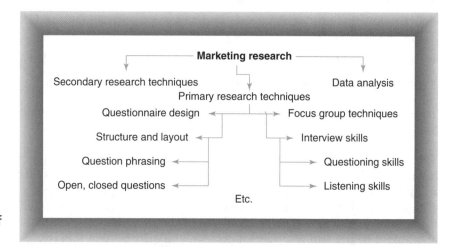

Figure 5.1
Component parts of skills development

We will be reviewing the above skills and more in the following chapters. Different levels can demand different skills, or the same skills but a different emphasis. For example, problem-solving at a tactical level could be speeding up a purchase procedure or improving an aspect of the production line. This might take hours, days or possibly a few weeks to solve, and involve relatively few people, probably at one level and within one department. Problem-solving at a strategic level could be changing the structure and culture of an organization. This would take years, and involve the whole organization at all levels and across the organization.

A reminder of a typical organization context is provided in Figure 5.2.

In a management context, managers are responsible for utilizing the resources available and managing people and tasks. This requires planning and controlling activities.

The management activities identified by Fayol (1949) in his studies were planning, organizing, commanding, coordinating and controlling. His findings are as relevant today, although commanding or directing is less popular in some cultures. Figure 5.3 shows a more up-to-date interpretation, placing motivation as central to a manager's role. Motivation is deliberately set centre stage for two reasons:

1. Planning, organizing, coordinating and controlling can be very demanding, and therefore it is easy for managers to focus on these aspects. They also have a task bias, which is often easier to deal with than motivating people.

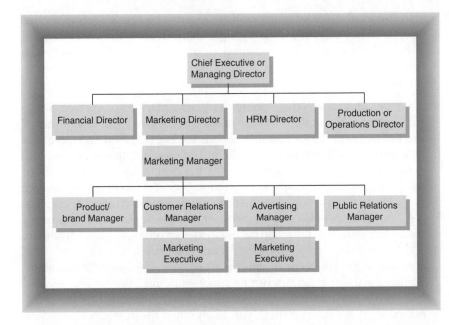

Figure 5.2
Organization
context

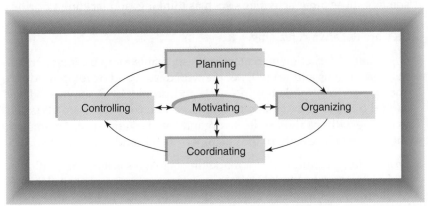

Figure 5.3
Management
functions and
motivation as
central to
management's role
(©2002 Juanita
Cockton)

2. If we do not focus on motivation, we are in danger of some or many of the workforce being disengaged and indifferent to organization goals. It is not something that can be left until last or dealt with as an afterthought; it should be central to everything managers do.

Organizations either manage these functions clearly and formally with established processes and procedures guiding activities, or they are not formalized and the execution may not be so obvious. Factors affecting formalization include the size and bureaucracy of the organization, the type of industry, and the product or service produced. However, research shows that managers are more inclined to spend their time 'doing' than 'managing'. So in practice, what and how should marketing managers be managing?

Management functions interpreted for marketing

● *Motivating.* Marketing managers need to identify marketing employee needs and motives, and design the work and environment to motivate staff to contribute. Marketing staff are responsible for delivering service and customer satisfaction. If they are demotivated, the customer will suffer. Motivation will be covered in more detail in Chapter 8. The remaining management activities should be designed and executed to motivate.

- *Planning*. This means developing marketing plans to deliver customer satisfaction. This requires the use of the tools, models and techniques of marketing planning to establish where the organization is, where it is going and how it is going to get there, and ensuring that it arrives. The marketing manager is responsible for the design and development of marketing strategy and marketing action plans (marketing mix), as well as for internal marketing plans that communicate to and motivate employees. Marketing people can plan out their day, week, etc., but the nature of their jobs means that things do not always go according to plan. Customers and key stakeholders in particular cannot be expected to wait until it is convenient for you to deal with their problem. This might mean abandoning the plan to sort a customer problem immediately. A way around this is to allow time for 'the unexpected' each week, and if the unexpected does not happen (highly unlikely) then the time can be used for some of those other activities – such as thinking, and tackling Priorities 2 and/or 3. Marketing people must plan for being responsive so that they are not always reacting.

- *Organizing*. Marketing managers are responsible for marketing personnel (individuals and teams), people who design and develop products and/or services, marketing research and promotional activities. They should build effective marketing teams and ensure tasks are allocated to people with the right skills. In organizing marketing tasks, managers should never lose sight of the customers' needs and expectations.

- *Coordinating*. A critical role for marketing managers is the coordination of the marketing mix. Marketing managers are not in control of all elements of the mix, and in many organizations they actually have little influence. The marketing mix delivers value to the customer, so marketing managers must have input into design and development and ultimately take responsibility for delivery. Marketing management coordination requires an organization-wide approach, incorporating the customers' touch points or 'moments of truth' and identifying whether or not the customers' experiences are positive or negative. Marketing must collaborate with other functions to ensure the customers' experience is positive.

- *Controlling*. Marketing managers establish realistic and achievable (but challenging) targets. They set standards of performance, and equip people with the skills and resources to achieve these standards. They must ensure customer satisfaction targets are included in measurement. Measuring effectiveness of all elements of the marketing mix (sales volumes, enquiry conversion rates, media reach, awareness, channel profitability, price performance and customer service) will be part of the control process. Marketing measurement goes beyond quantitative measures on costs, volumes, revenues and profits. Marketing managers establish mechanisms for measuring people's performance in the context of the customer experience. How satisfied and loyal customers are, the number of repeat purchases, referrals, etc., are all part of establishing whether or not the organization is successful.

- *Managing communications*. As well as external communications with customers and/or stakeholders, marketing managers need to take greater responsibility for managing internal communications. As the customer interface they are responsible for ensuring that employees know who the customers are and what they want. Communications play a key role in keeping customers at the centre of the organization.

- *Managing time*. Customers and/or stakeholders are the first priority. Everyone in the business is there to serve the customer, but this is particularly the case for marketing people. Marketing people are often interrupted by customers, and these interruptions should be handled differently to other interruptions. If a customer has a problem, it is a legitimate interruption and must be dealt with immediately. As a manager, the way you manage your time significantly affects your staff – so make sure it has a positive impact. For many managers it may be obvious that customers come first, particularly in business-to-business markets where face-to-face contact is typical. However, as a consumer who has experienced a problem and poor service, how often have you been allowed to speak to a manager to resolve the problem when things go wrong?

- *Managing delegation*. Planning and organizing events and marketing programmes is very much a feature of marketing jobs. This is an excellent opportunity for practicing planning and for taking on responsibility. Delegating the planning and organization of an exhibition, coordinating an advertising campaign, etc., are all opportunities to develop and motivate marketing people, and for the marketing manager to work more efficiently and effectively.

- *Managing environment*. As key information gatherers and communicators with stakeholders (customers in particular), marketing people need the equipment and technology that allows them to do this job efficiently and effectively. Marketing people have visitors to offices/factories, etc., from customers, suppliers and distributors – to mention a few. It is important therefore that there is space for visitors that is well designed, spacious and welcoming. Physical evidence is an important aspect of the marketing mix, and should not be overlooked.

- *Managing information*. Everyone in the business has to manage information of one sort or another. Marketing people in particular have to manage lots of information – more than most. For this reason, it is vital that information gathering is selective and time is allocated to converting data gathered into marketing intelligence. If the marketing department wants the information to be used, it must allow time to prepare and present the information in a way that is informative, persuasive and digestible.

- *Managing thinking*. Marketing managers are responsible for the customers and for ensuring the business is competitive. This requires using conceptual skills, and creativity and innovation. Generating new ideas and new approaches to executing tasks requires time to think, to brain-storm, etc. The marketing manager both contributes to this process and facilitates contribution from others.

Improving management often means breaking old habits, and that can be difficult. It requires doing things a different way – maybe doing different things. It can be tempting, unintentionally, to slip back into old ways, but the rewards for improving management are too great to ignore:

- excelling in your job, possibly being an example to others, *and* not being stressed

- having more time for people that matter – family, friends, work colleagues, subordinates

- having time for personal growth and development

- having time for hobbies and adventures, whatever they are.

Henry Mintzberg provided a different definition of what managers do, which is particularly pertinent for marketing managers. This is adapted in Figure 5.4.

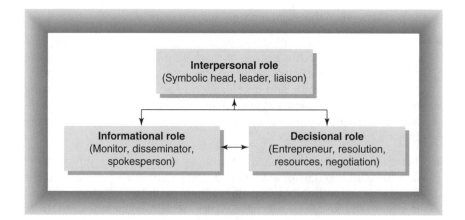

Figure 5.4
Managers' roles (adapted from Henry Mintzberg, 1973)

In practice, what does this mean for marketing managers?

- *Interpersonal role.* Leading by example is important in marketing management. Managers must demonstrate their commitment to the customer, and time and effort spent actively building relationships with customers and other stakeholders. They are the interface between the customer and the organization.

- *Informational role.* Marketing managers in particular are key to ensuring that data is converted into marketing intelligence that informs business decisions and planning. They should also use their communication skills to inform, educate and persuade employees of business intentions, activities and events. Knowledge management is an essential role in managing people.

- *Decisional role*. A marketing manager's decisions are focused on the customer and what the business needs to do to keep customers happy and loyal. Decisions will include information requirements, how the marketing mix should be designed, and how competitive strategies will be designed.

Marketing functional and technical skills

Trying to decipher job titles in marketing could be the subject of an entire book, so it will not be attempted here. Job titles change and new titles emerge – for example, corporate social responsibility director, chief marketing officer – and these new roles are being interpreted in many and varied ways. Old titles can change as a result. A lack of standardization has contributed to many job titles becoming confusing and unhelpful, providing little idea of what the person really does, and organizations vary in their interpretation of job titles because of industry context. Also, the smaller the company the less likely it is that there will be many people with marketing titles. In small and in larger companies, marketing activities can be outsourced, reducing the need for marketing personnel.

In some organizations, sales and marketing are separate with a sales director, sales manager, etc. In other organizations, sales reports to the marketing director; a third option is a sales and marketing director, with the marketing manager and sales manager reporting. In small to medium-sized companies there would be fewer levels of management – a flatter structure with fewer marketing people. There may be two to three marketing executives reporting to a marketing manager. Outsourcing marketing activities to (for example) advertising agencies and marketing research agencies would enable a smaller business to have access to marketing expertise and resources.

We will focus on broader management skills and look briefly at:

- skills required by marketing managers
- responsibilities at strategic, operations and tactical levels.

As well as planning, organizing, coordinating, controlling and motivating, marketers have three key functions at the centre of everything they do; these are information, innovation and communications. Marketers:

- provide marketing intelligence that identifies stakeholder value needs and informs decisions on strategic direction, competitive position and how to differentiate the organization's offer
- through innovation, identify new value opportunities from the marketing intelligence
- communicate internally and externally at a strategic level to broad stake/shareholder targets to build organization reputation, and to customers to promote offers.

How these are interpreted at different levels will depend on the industry and organization, but an example is provided in Figure 5.5.

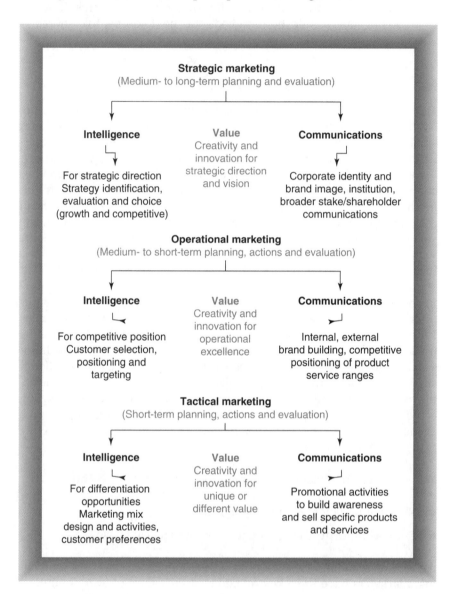

Figure 5.5
Levels of marketing skills

The above themes have been discussed in Chapters 1–4, and will be explored in more detail throughout the following chapters. Creativity and innovation are central to what an organization does, and as managers move into more strategic roles, as well as functional skills, managers and leaders will increasingly utilize their conceptual skills (see Figure 5.6).

Marketing managers need to be aware of the transition they are making from predominately using technical skills to predominately using social and human skills, and increasingly using conceptual skills. Conceptual skills are important in creativity (this is discussed in Chapter 7).

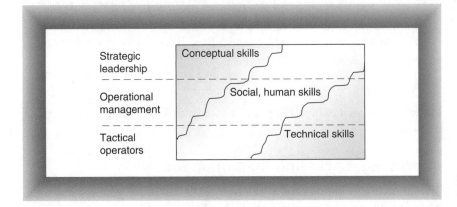

Figure 5.6
Conceptual skills

Research example: the management challenge

Research from various sources has revealed that the demands of the modern workplace are putting managers' ability to utilize their skills to manage effectively under increasing risk. Our fast-moving business environment and organization responses with regular, sometimes continuous, change has resulted in many managers finding themselves in a constant state of the unfamiliar. Changing structures, cultures, staff turnover and the changing nature of skills needed by managers means they are constantly juggling the demands of senior managers to achieve a vision, and the demands of employees, to make sense of their work.

Managers have responded by doing what they think is right and expedient, empowering people. There is, however, a subtle difference between empowering people and under-managing. Empowering people takes time, effort and considerable management skill. The skills a manager needs include:

- planning, organizing, coordinating and controlling
- communications, interpersonal and motivation skills
- delegation
- problem-solving and decision-making
- analysis and evaluation.

To develop these skills requires time for training, and to utilize these skills properly to empower employees also requires time. The perpetual dilemma in fast-changing environments is lack of time. Managers need a more active role in the day-to-day managing of people. This should not be confused with over-supervising, but rather with increasing interactions so all involved can communicate and share needs, concerns and ideas regarding solving problems. The shared goal of these interactions is improving overall performance.

Hands-off management is only valid when the necessary groundwork has preceded managers taking a step back from hands-on

> management. Empowering employees requires investment in time to delegate and develop employees so they have the competence and confidence to take responsibility.
>
> (Sources: Various web and print)

We will now review how we might develop skills required by marketing managers.

Improving marketing management

The following guidelines for developing skills can be for you as a manager, and also for developing your staff. Whether you are responsible for the design of learning and development or not, you are responsible for influencing the design, and for briefing whoever is in charge, regarding your requirements for yourself and for your staff. This is not something that can be delegated to a third party. HR and/or training providers will be responsible for designing learning to meet your requirements, but only you can determine what these are. Through a consultative process, you can agree learning and development initiatives that are of benefit to all involved.

Training courses are an obvious answer to developing skills, but they are not the only answer, and any development solutions should be a carefully planned and blended mix of events. Development and improvement starts with assessment of needs and ends with measuring the outcomes (see Figure 5.7):

- skills assessment, gap analysis and establishing learning needs
- skills development and improving use of resources
- transfer of learning into the workplace
- measuring performance and improvements.

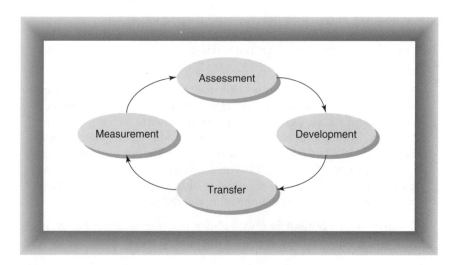

Figure 5.7
Development and improvement cycle (©2002 Juanita Cockton)

In Chapters 6–12 we will cover skills that we feel merit special attention for marketing management.

Skills assessment

Chapter 12 covers measuring performance in detail, and at the end of this chapter there is brief guidance on performance measurement which is also relevant here because it both starts and ends the development cycle, so please refer to that section. However, assessment has an added dimension in that its purpose is also to establish learning and development needs.

Our skills assessment should aim to establish current competence, required competence, and any gap that may exist between the two. We want to be able to assess our strengths and weaknesses, and prioritize these in terms of essential strengths and undesirable weaknesses. It is not appropriate to try to sort everything out at once, so prioritizing is useful.

If you work for a larger organization, your HR department will have clearly established levels of competence. In recent years there has been a concerted effort by various institutions, including government, to define competence and move towards a common understanding of what this is. Management and marketing competences have been through a fairly rigorous review, management more so than marketing, and the resulting competence frameworks are useful but are not necessarily aligned with each other.

There are still a number of versions that exist, and be wary of those that are woolly and ambiguous in description. In trying to establish a common standard and uniform approach there is a tendency on occasions to try to fit everything across functions and levels into one mould, which is often not representative of what really goes on in organizations. However, developing a universal framework of competences is helpful to managers, and you can take what is available and modify it to suit your particular requirements.

If you are not fortunate enough to have a competency framework from an HR function or some other source, there are the marketing standards developed by the MSSSB (Marketing and Sales Standards Setting Body). We have provided an example of competences, focusing on marketing and aligning against general management (see Table 5.1). It is by no means an exhaustive list, and under each of these headings would be a subset of specific competences. Some competences you would expect to see at every level – for example, interpersonal skills.

We have not attempted to cover the specifics of other functions, but have provided general management descriptions. The competences could also be broken down and aligned by each function.

Skills assessment can be achieved by or through:

- performance appraisals with managers, where skills needs will be identified

Table 5.1 Management and marketing competence

Senior management competence Defining vision and strategic direction Defining change to achieve organization goals Allocating resources across organization to attain goals Measuring organization performance	*Senior marketing competence* Influencing vision and strategic direction Defining change initiatives from customer perspective Allocating resources across marketing function Measuring marketing function performance
Middle management competence Interpreting corporate strategy, designing work to achieve goals Managing change Allocating resources to management activities Measuring management activity performance	*Middle marketing competence* Interpreting corporate strategy, designing marketing strategy Managing and influencing customer-focused change Allocating resources to marketing activities Measuring marketing activity performance
Junior management competence Implementing strategy Implementing change Using and managing budgets Measuring individual performance	*Junior marketing competence* Designing, implementing marketing mix Implementing customer-focused change Using and managing marketing budgets Measuring individual marketing performance
Administrative competence Executing and improving activities and work flows Feedback on activities and work flows to management Team and interpersonal and skills Ideas and problem-solving	*Administrative marketing competence* Executing and improving customer experiences Feedback on customer experiences to management Team, interpersonal and customer skills Ideas and problem-solving for customers

- diagnostic tests, from (for example) simple questionnaires and Likert scales to more sophisticated techniques such as psychometric tests

- feedback from colleagues and peers.

Management skills, particularly the softer skills, can be difficult to assess. The more objectivity that can be brought to the process the better, but avoid it becoming over elaborate or complex. Weighting and rating of strengths and weaknesses might be appropriate, or a reasoned assessment based on high, medium and low grades. If this assessment is reached in consultation with others who are qualified to make such judgments, it will be valid.

Learning and improvement objectives

Once you know what you want to improve, the next step is to set clear objectives. Objectives must be set, or you cannot measure improvements. Primary and secondary objectives can be quantified. For example:

1. Increasing personal time for managing (as opposed to doing) by 10 percent through delegation of tasks to suitable subordinates within the next three months

2. Use the 10 percent increase in time . . . to ensure 95 percent of targets reached with timescales . . . for individual development of staff.

Skills development

Now we have established objectives, the next step is to identify opportunities for development and improvement. Training courses and studying for qualifications are two options that might be appropriate, but we will not be covering those methods here.

Another option is to look for work-based opportunities to help aid understanding and develop and improve skills, or for opportunities outside the workplace – for example, serving on the committee of a local professional body or charity. The following are broad headings where you can look for examples and then select an assignment or project:

- *people* – for example, improving motivation, team behaviour, productivity, communications

- *process* – for example, improving tools, techniques and frameworks for carrying out tasks

- *task* – for example, planning and organizing using planning tools, techniques and frameworks.

Some projects can cover a number of skills development objectives – for example, a marketing information system programme or a customer relationship management programme would have an impact at all levels. You as the manager, your staff and others in the organization can form a project team to do this and ensure that learning and skills improvement objectives and plans are also part of the project.

The opportunities to learn and improve are many, and we should not underestimate the value of learning from others with whom we work. Our learning can vary from being very simple and costing nothing to being expensive and via a highly structured programme. Learning typically is a blend of approaches. As you move into management, if your organization does not structure your learning for you, particularly management development, you will need to take responsibility for this yourself. Even if your organization does have a productive HR and/or learning department, you still need to take responsibility for your learning. In this case, you want to influence the learning and development provided.

On-the-job learning

As a manager, you will have experienced many examples of management practice and behaviour. Subconsciously, you will have observed and analysed this behaviour and made judgements on whether or not the examples were good or bad. If you have not been making these observations and judgments, it will be helpful to start deliberately learning from these experiences. You can observe:

- *how managers behave* (reflecting attitudes, values and the impact on others)
- *how managers manage* (plan, organize, coordinate and control events).

You can then interpret these observations and formulate your own management style. Particularly useful, when moving into management, is either a coach (someone who provides instruction) or a mentor (someone who listens and advises on your performance) who can provide valuable support in the early stages.

For your staff, you may be the coach or mentor helping them to improve their technical and interpersonal skills.

Blended solutions

Other learning events include:

- *online learning* – good for knowledge-building and testing, and information sharing
- *training courses* – good for networking and softer skills development
- *private study* – using academic text books and case studies, and even broadening knowledge by increasing the breadth of regular reading (for example newspapers, journals, industry reports, etc.)
- *conferences and seminars* – industry-based and for your particular profession
- *secondments* – opportunities to spend time either in your own organization but in another function or division, or with a different organization
- *management development programs* – which will be a combination of the above but in a deliberate structured programme for developing executive talent for promotion.

Transfer of learning

Training courses and workshops, online learning and many other forms of off-the-job learning can be very beneficial to individuals and the organization. However, a step that too often gets missed out in skills development and improvement planning is that of transferring the learning. Time, money and effort is put into learning something new, and then the enthusiastic learner returns to the workplace to find no provision has been made to support or facilitate the transfer of learning into work practices.

If we are to realize the benefits of learning and achieve desired improvements, we need to actively manage the transfer of learning.

It is important during implementation to have someone (or possibly more than one person) that can give support and guidance. A mentor who can provide input when appropriate and monitor progress can be a valuable asset.

Learning, or training, needs to be thought of slightly differently. We should not think of training interventions as discrete packages of learning with stop-and-start points, as depicted in Figure 5.8.

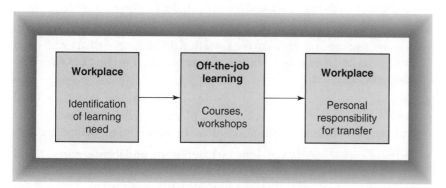

Figure 5.8
Discrete learning and *ad hoc* transfer (©2002 Juanita Cockton)

Off-the-job learning should be as seamless as on-the-job learning in terms of an integrated learning environment and transfer process. The way training needs are identified and evaluated, the beginning and end points, will be an indicator of how integrated or not this learning process is. Therefore, learning and its transfer might look like Figure 5.9.

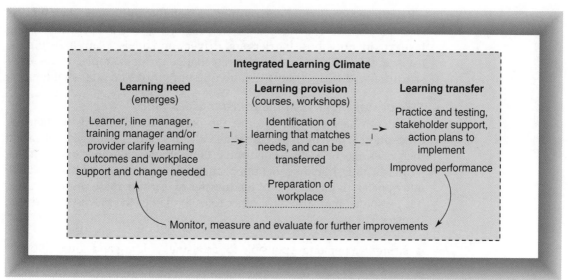

Figure 5.9   Integrated learning climate (©2002 Juanita Cockton)

It is the lack of integration that causes problems for the transfer of learning. The identification of learning needs must be linked to outcomes, and utilizing the learning and evaluating its effectiveness should be part of one process with all stakeholders involved.

Workplace factors that influence learning and its transfer

Our place of work will have a number of influences on our ability to transfer learning. These include the following:

- *department structure* – hierarchy, leadership and management, delegation, nature of tasks, direct or indirect customer contact, direct or indirect input into the product and/or service the customer receives.
- *rules, regulations, policy and procedure* – rules, etc., that govern work practices are usually laid down in organization documents such as terms and conditions and manuals. Conduct and standards of performance are also often documented.
- *processes, systems* – the formal processes and systems that have been established to carry out work, formal planning processes, information gathering, models and techniques used in planning, reporting lines.
- *design of work* – goes beyond the task definition and job description and covers how the job is integrated and linked to other jobs, the routines and patterns that are formally and informally established.
- *measurement* – what is measured and how.
- *time* – attitudes to and use of time.
- *working conditions* – the physical working conditions and environment.
- *relationships* – the way in which people work together and relate to each other, teamwork ethic, equalitarian or authoritarian relationships, support and harmony.

All of these factors can have positive or negative influences; they will act as either barriers or drivers in the transfer of learning. Part of the learning task is to identify those barriers and drivers, and devise plans to secure the transfer of learning. This might mean change to, for example, processes or structure, and will certainly require the support of some stakeholders.

Role of stakeholders in the transfer of learning

Employees have specific roles in the organization, defined by their job description. They may be operators, administrators, managers, etc., and their roles may be easily recognizable. How employees impact on the transfer of learning should be identified, and their support gained to help facilitate transfer. In the context of the transfer of learning these roles still exist, but personnel may also have other roles to play in the process of learning transfer. For example:

- *mentor* – a person responsible for advising, guiding and counselling
- *coach* – a person responsible for supporting learning through demonstrating, answering questions, explaining, etc.

- *liaison representative* – someone who keeps those outside the learning process informed of what is going on and acts as a point of contact between those outside and those within the process

- *independent observer* – someone who might be assigned a role of observing or overseeing the process and encouraging a broader perspective on the issues involved

- *control group* – studies have shown that if you give people enough attention, they will perform better without learning. We would not recommend this as a strategy, but one aspect of learning transfer that will be difficult to evaluate is, what improvements would have occurred without the learning? It may be that circumstances have provided an opportunity for improvement not originally thought of. A control group can be helpful in some circumstances. For example, if the learning is to be tested in one area and then rolled out to the rest of the organization, other areas not involved in the learning can be monitored for improvements during its transfer. It is another way of checking the validity of learning and effective use of resources. It need not be a burden or troublesome 'extra' workload. If the organization already has in place performance evaluation processes, the only 'extra' would be to establish a start and finish point that might be different to the normal period of assessment.

We will pick up the theme of transfer of learning again in Chapter 8.

Learning from experiences

For a manager, keeping a learning log can be very useful and should become a habit. It forces you to reflect and contemplate on what you have learned from formal and also from informal events and activities. The danger is that you rush on to the next challenge without thought about what has been learned, and therefore how you or others can benefit. It is a useful skill to develop in itself, and has the advantage of encouraging you to think constructively about what you have learned. It can also improve your ability to articulate and synthesize experiences.

Learning logs force us to adopt a more structured approach to the experience of learning, reducing the usually haphazard nature of learning experiences in everyday life. The intention is to log significant learning experiences, reaching brief conclusions. This is followed by a commitment to action – the next stage of learning – and when this will take place. Keeping a learning log should not be time consuming or require great effort other than thinking. Such logs need to be brief, or we can quickly get disheartened and not bother. A learning log should cover:

- key significant learning experiences

- conclusions

- commitment to courses of action

- the time when the action will happen.

Honesty is vital if the learning is to be meaningful. You should try to log your learning experience as soon as possible, while it is still fresh in your mind, but allow enough time for reflection (Figure 5.10). Do not be over ambitious, with actions that will be difficult to implement. Keep them manageable.

Example Learning log **Date:** 20.01.200..

Significant learning experience: During a briefing session with a member of my staff today he kept interrupting and asking questions about what he was to do. He clearly was not listening to me as the briefing was about what he was to do. We both ended up getting frustrated and he went off saying he would do the best he could.

Conclusion: At the time I was angry that he was not listening and probably showed it. On reflection it may be that he was not listening because he had some concerns/fears about his ability to do what was being asked of him. I should have spent a bit more time listening and less time talking. I should have used probing questions to ascertain his concerns and addressed these before rushing ahead with the brief.

Actions: I need to go over the brief again but this time before I do I will encourage him to talk to me about the brief and any views he has about potential problems etc. I will think through some questions to ask him before we meet.

Deadline: Tomorrow first thing

**Figure 5.10
Example learning log**

Finally, we need to measure the outcomes – have the objectives been achieved?

Measuring performance and improvements

Measuring performance will be covered in more detail in Chapter 12, so we will only cover a few points here regarding measuring the performance of people.

Outcomes versus inputs

Establishing the right measures of performance does not appear to be as easy as it should be. There are many examples of poor measures, including the following:

- *Ombudsman for financial services*. The target was improving the turn-around of complaints handling. There was a financial bonus for speed, and the outcome was questionable decisions (fairness, justice), rise in complaints about the process, calls for change, and negative publicity.

- *Cleanliness of hospitals*. The target was the cheapest tender, which has involved using unqualified and untrained people; the outcome has been a dramatic rise in incidents of the superbug MRSA.

- *Councils' decision to charge for rubbish taken to tip*. The target was a revenue stream, but the outcome was a dramatic rise in fly-tipping estimated to be costing £100 per minute (89 000 incidents per month across the UK) for councils to clear away.

- *Direct enquires telephone number 118118*. The target was the speed of answering a query; the outcome was that callers were given any number, with accuracy being unimportant, lost customers, and negative press coverage.

Problems arise in setting measures for two reasons:

1. Measures are selected because they are quick and easy to do – for example, quantity, speed.

2. Measures focus on inputs rather than outcomes.

The second point in particular is a chronic problem in organizations. In all of the above examples, if managers had asked themselves two questions:

1. What result do we want here, what are the desired *outcomes*?

2. What are the possible interpretations and consequences of the measures we have established?

– then they would have been more likely to achieve the right outcome and minimize or even eliminate the negative consequences of establishing poor measures – bad publicity being just one of these consequences. It requires going beyond the immediate financial gain and identifying other consequences, including long-term financial loss.

Objectives and targets

Measurement starts with objectives and targets, and this is why it is so important to set quantified objectives rather than woolly statements that cannot be interpreted or measured – such as:

Improve your communication and interpersonal skills over the next year.

OK, we have a timescale, but how do you interpret the rest? What communications skills – all of them? This is far too broad and vague, and is open to interpretation in many different ways. A person could put time and effort into improving listening skills when the problem was actually giving instructions and briefings. What is the desired outcome – for example, it might be that a person's verbal communication style is perceived by other team members as being abrasive and often causing offence. This is an uncomfortable area for a manager to deal with, and it is too easy to slip into an emotional response that will not focus on the desired outcome. In such circumstances, it is useful to get the individual to identify his or her own problem:

Identify your personal positive and negative verbal communications style with the team in different situations and describe the nature and impact of negative communications style on team members (provide evidence). Devise a plan with your manager to improve any specific interpersonal skills identified as needing improvement.

As a manager, you can support this by encouraging the observation of others who are good or bad at communications and reflecting on the impact on team members of positive and negative communications. This can then be followed through with practice.

Objectives must be challenging but also realistic, or they can demotivate staff. A manager can also lose credibility in the eyes of employees if objectives and targets are perceived as being unrealistic, the assumption being that the manager does not know what he or she is doing or what is going on.

A typical example of an improvement target is:

Improve customer retention and value of the top 10 customers.

Personal interpretation might include 'improve (specified) interpersonal skills'. This would need to take into account both external and internal factors. External factors might include market conditions (industry and economic), levels of competition and competitive actions, and consumer behaviour and demand. Internal factors would include resources available (e.g. budgets, office support) and supporting promotional activities.

Measuring performance – what can we measure?

The most common measures are quantitative, and broadly include:

- *quantity* – targets achieved (volumes, revenues, productivity, etc.)
- *time* – reduced time taken, increased speed, timeliness
- *cost* – reduced cost, increased value for cost.

Some measures require quantitative and qualitative measures, for example:

- *errors and mistakes* – reductions (for example complaints), improvements, accuracy, precision.

Quantitative measures are essential but must be balanced with qualitative measures, both external:

- customer/stakeholder satisfaction, perceptions
- loyalty and referrals

and internal:

- ideas, innovation and creativity
- knowledge
- morale and confidence.

Qualitative measures are of course more difficult to measure, and can take longer. However, they can provide greater insight into, for example, customer needs and employee motives.

Measuring performance – how can we measure?

Assessment can be undertaken in a number of ways. The first is by observation – for example, you can observe your staff (or be observed yourself):

- interviewing
- giving presentations
- undertaking exercises
- debriefing and providing feedback
- giving input and contributing to a discussion, at a meeting
- resolving conflicts
- giving instructions.

Some things are either difficult or impossible to observe, and require evidence in the form of assignment documentation – for example:

- planning a program of activities (evidence in the plan and a report describing the planning process)
- managing a particular initiative, such as change (evidence in a report describing how you managed the change)
- implementation of a new system (evidence in a report describing how you managed the process)
- negotiating between two parties to resolve a conflict (evidence in a report on how you managed the preparation and conducting of negotiations).

Parts of negotiations can be observed, but in such often emotionally charged situations it is inadvisable to have an 'observer', as this may be seen as threatening and antagonistic.

Criteria

To be truly effective in evaluating performance, there should be criteria against which you are measured. Criteria must have some sort of weighting and rating. For example, assessment criteria and weighting for improving time management might be as shown in Table 5.2.

An alternative way of allocating marks to performance might be, for example:

A	Exceptional	(9–10 marks)
B	Good	(7–8 marks)
C	Adequate	(5–6 marks)
D	Inadequate	(3–4 marks)
E	Poor	(0–2 marks)

Insights into customer perceptions of customer service can be obtained through questionnaires or interviews using Osgood's semantic differential

Table 5.2
Assessment criteria and weighting

Prioritizing tasks Identifying tasks to prioritize Organizing tasks by priority Executing tasks	5	4	3	2	1
Delegating Identifying and selecting staff for delegating Preparing staff for delegation Briefing	5	4	3	2	1

The scores are as follows:

5 Comprehensive understanding and excellent knowledge demonstrated through full explanation of the theory and skilled use of the tools and frameworks

4 Good understanding and knowledge demonstrated through good explanation of the theory and use of the tools and frameworks

3 Adequate understanding and knowledge demonstrated through adequate explanation of theory and some use of tools and frameworks; lacks explanation and application

2 Inadequate understanding of knowledge, little demonstration or explanation or use of the tools and frameworks

1 Poor understanding, no evidence of learning

scale (Osgood *et al.*, 1957) or the Likert summated scale. Figure 5.11 is an example of a semantic differential scale.

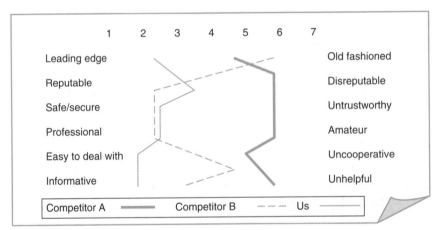

Figure 5.11
Example of a semantic differential scale

Measuring performance requires a balance of quantitative and qualitative measures, must be focused on outcomes rather than inputs, must be relevant, and must be agreed with individuals. Finally, remember the objective. Was it achieved? That is the ultimate test of how well you are doing.

Summary

If we want collective organization performance to excel and to differentiate the organization from competitors, we need to have excellent skills of the right quality and in the right quantity. This requires recruiting people with the skills that meet organizational needs, and investing in training and development to ensure continued personal growth.

We only benefit from training and development if we prepare the workplace to receive new learning, and plan to transfer the learning.

Hands-on management is fine as long as someone is managing. Managers are responsible for planning, organizing, coordinating, controlling and motivating people and tasks, and need these skills to use resources efficiently and effectively. Marketing managers have the added responsibility of using these skills to ensure value creation and delivery is centred on selected customers.

References

Fayol, H. (1949). *General and Industrial Management*. London: Pitman.

Mintzberg, H. (1973). *The Nature of Managerial Work*. New York: Harper & Row; reprinted 1980, Upper Saddle River, NJ: Prentice Hall.

Osgood, C.E., Suci, G.J. and Tannenbaum, P.H. (1957). *The Measurement of Meaning*. Champaign, IL: University of Illinois Press.

6 Leadership

Introduction

Effective leadership is something that can be learned. Leaders may have innate characteristics that make them good leaders, but effectiveness comes from the experience of good leadership. Education and training can also significantly improve leadership qualities.

Many people, influenced by their cultural background, assume that leaders are 'born, not made'. This assumption creates a number of problems. First, leaders with characteristics that indicate an ability to lead are uncommon. Secondly, recognizing who these leaders are from the crowd is not easy. Thirdly, these assumptions are subjective.

One of the most interesting insights into leadership is a book called *Great Military Blunders* by Regan (2000). This book examines some of the great battles fought in the last millennium in terms of leadership. It looks at the reasons behind why certain decisions were made and actions taken. In such circumstances it is not unnatural to assume that decisions and actions are the result of a logical, objective evaluation of all the options, based on sound information and in the best interests of one's men and country. However, it was revealed that leaders can be prone to making decisions and taking actions for reasons of personal political ambitions, personal failings, lack of confidence and an inability to see the bigger picture. The consequences, under these conditions, were catastrophic.

We all have personal ambitions and strengths and weaknesses, but with leadership comes responsibilities, and we should have a goal of being an example of good practice.

Regan's book reveals that leaders are not necessarily born, and it is particularly interesting because of the parallels that can be drawn with business.

There are salutary lessons for leaders in business. Mistakes, some financially expensive and damaging in terms of the human cost, have been and still are made in business, and the reasons behind the mistakes would not hold up well to scrutiny. For example, Enron and Worldcom became infamous in 2001 and 2002, respectively, when leadership fraud was exposed. Enron was the biggest bankruptcy in US history, and 4000 jobs were lost. The accounting firm Arthur Anderson was brought down in the scandal, and the CEO of Enron was sentenced to 185 years in prison. The Worldcom fraud amounted to $3.8bn, and its CEO was sentenced to 25 years in prison.

There are many reasons why leaders fail in organizations, including the inability to think strategically or to adapt to different management styles, insensitivity to others, betrayal of trust, arrogance or over-ambition. While this knowledge of why leaders can fail is not new, there are some interesting clues in this list that many managers still ignore. The importance of trust, for example, is often disregarded. If staff cannot trust their leader, there may be little reason left to make any sort of effort for the business – in other words, staff will do what they have to when they have to, and nothing more.

Inability to adapt the management style is another interesting reason for failing. In today's rapidly changing markets with the need to be able to manage across borders, leaders, as never before, must be able to adapt their style as the circumstances dictate. This is not to suggest that leaders or managers can or should *change* their style, but rather that they need to be able to bend and flex enough to reflect the needs of the situation faced. Managers will inevitable have their own particular style that essentially will not change; it is part of who they are. This personal style can continually improve with learning and experiences, and can adapt when necessary.

Being a good leader is not easy, and can be one of the most difficult jobs. The leader is the one in the spotlight trying to reconcile many, often conflicting, interests. It can be a lonely job.

There is no template or formula for good leadership. Different circumstances, situations, eras, etc., all require different approaches to solving problems and building successes. While leaders can benefit from past experiences – their own and other people's – they still have to lead the business and people through the current situation with the current skills and with some understanding of how future events might evolve.

Effective leadership

Much research has been done on leadership, and characteristics have been identified to try to establish some sense of what good leadership is. One of the most well-known writers on leadership is John Adair (1989). Looking at the most frequent traits of leaders, they are:

- adaptable
- assertive
- cooperative
- fair
- decisive
- energetic
- self-confident

- tolerant of stress
- willing to assume responsibility
- humble.

These traits are balanced with the most frequent skills of successful leaders. Looking at these skills, leaders are:

- clever
- conceptually skilled
- creative
- diplomatic and tactful
- fluent in speaking
- organized (administrative ability)
- persuasive
- socially skilled.

The reality is that not all leaders can have all these traits and skills; however, if we look at leaders we admire, we will undoubtedly find that they possess many of them. The idea that one set of characteristics defines a good leader assumes that the circumstances leaders find themselves in will always be the same, requiring the same responses. We know this is not true, particularly in these days of rapid change.

The way we use these skills will determine whether or not we are effective leaders. John Adair believes that leaders must be focused on three key functions, as illustrated in Figure 6.1:

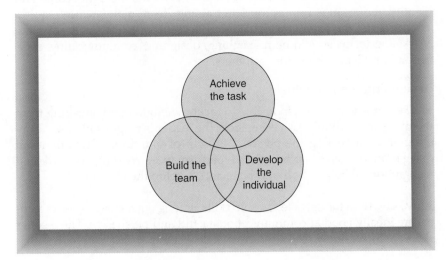

Figure 6.1
Action-centred leadership

1. *Task.* A leader must ensure that people are briefed properly. This involves setting clear objectives, explaining why the task is being done, describing what has to be done, demonstrating how it is to be done, and establishing

when it has to be done. Leaders must ensure that they achieve that task efficiently and effectively.

2. *Team-building and maintenance.* This is how the task is to be completed. Most organizations require a number of people to achieve the task, and to do this both efficiently and effectively the people within the organization need to work as teams, playing to each others' strengths – the whole is greater than the parts.

3. *Developing the individual.* Team work is important, but teams are made up of individuals, each of whom has specific and often different strengths to bring to the team. Individuals also have weaknesses, and these need to be either minimized or improved.

A bias towards one aspect of performance – for example, achieving the task – results in neglect of other essential parts of performance. From time to time leaders may need to focus their efforts on one particular aspect in response to a particular need, but overall they should balance the demands of the task, individuals and the team.

In a marketing context, what does this mean?

Defining the task

The reason for the organization existing, the purpose of the business, is to deliver something of value to people. A marketing leader is responsible for ensuring that the marketing task determines what that value is and then organizes work to deliver that value. Customers buy benefits, and benefits are the result of combined tasks that make up the marketing mix.

Building and maintaining the team

Marketing leaders should ensure that marketing teams are focused on customers. Building the team requires the leader to recruit the right people, and identify and arrange for appropriate training. Team maintenance requires ensuring that the team is well balanced in terms of skills and team roles. Marketing teams should be researching, designing, communicating, serving and problem-solving for customers.

Developing the individual

Marketing leaders are responsible for acknowledging and engaging team members individually. Once engaged, the leader is responsible for motivating and supporting the personal growth of individuals. Rotation and delegation of tasks, appraisals of performance, training, reward and recognition all help to both motivate and develop the individual.

As we saw from the list of leadership skills, among other characteristics leaders are ideally good at communication, tactful and persuasive. These softer skills are increasingly seen as essential to leadership.

Emotional intelligence

The concept of emotional intelligence (Goleman, 1998) as a quality essential for good leadership is now part of our business vocabulary. It is not that we did not have this quality before, but rather that in some societies – particularly Western industrialized societies – we actively avoided, denied or frowned upon the notion of 'emotional' anything in the workplace. In fact, there are some deep-rooted beliefs that emotions are a sign of weakness in many working environments.

Emotional intelligence is not about 'being emotional', even intelligently; it is about how we manage emotions – our own and others. In Chapter 5 we outlined many competencies required by employees and managers, and many of these can be described as cognitive skills – for example, technical skills for the job, or analytical skills. Other skills require a combination of thoughts and feelings with functional skills – for example, problem-solving or interpersonal skills – and these are described as emotional competences. These skills can be much more powerful in leadership roles, and are learned from a much broader mix of experiences.

Personal emotional competence includes:

- *self-awareness* – emotions, knowing strengths and weaknesses
- *self-regulation* – self-control, integrity, conscientiousness, adaptability, innovation
- *motivation* – achievement-driven, commitment, initiative, optimism.

Social emotional competence includes:

- *empathy* – awareness of others feelings, needs and concerns, such as being perceptive to others' feelings, developing others, having a service orientation, leveraging diversity, political awareness
- *social skills* – adeptness at inducing desirable responses in others, for example influence, communications, conflict management, leadership, change catalyst, building bonds, collaboration and cooperation, team capabilities.

Looking at social skills, for example:

1. *Influence* – build rapport, convince. People with this competence typically:
   - are skilled at winning people over
   - fine-tune presentations to appeal to listeners
   - use complex strategies like indirect influence to build consensus and support
   - orchestrate dramatic events to make a point effectively.
2. *Communication* – mood and meaning, keeping cool. People with this competence typically:
   - are effective in give and take, registering emotional cues in attuning their messages

- deal with difficult issues straightforwardly

- listen well, seek mutual understanding, welcome sharing information fully

- foster open communications and stay receptive to bad news as well as good.

3. *Conflict management* – reading the signs, negotiating channels, resolving conflict creatively. People with this competence typically:

- handle difficult people and tense situations with diplomacy and tact

- spot potential conflict, bring disagreements into the open and help de-escalate

- encourage debate and open discussion

- orchestrate win–win solutions.

4. *Leadership* – give energy, ripple effect, know when to be tough, virtual leader. People with this competence typically:

- articulate and arouse enthusiasm for a shared vision and mission

- step forward to lead as needed, regardless of position

- guide the performance of others while holding them accountable

- lead by example.

5. *Change catalyst* – transformational leader, emotional craft. People with this competence typically:

- recognize the need for change and remove barriers

- challenge the *status quo* to acknowledge the need for change

- champion change and enlist others in its pursuit

- model change expected of others.

We learn these skills informally as we grow up and during our working lives; they are part of being human. These skills can be poor if learned from a bad example, or excellent if we have benefited from good examples. We can also engage in deliberate learning to develop and improve these skills.

What is obvious is that these skills are central in determining whether or not we are good leaders and marketing managers. They also play a central role in the style of leadership and management, and in organizational culture.

Leadership and management styles

Leadership styles vary depending on the circumstances and organizational culture. There is no single right way when it comes to leadership style, but there can be some wrong ways. The nature of the task plays a significant part in determining style. For example, a military leader in the middle of a battle is not going to sit down with the entire team and discuss the issues, explore possible alternative actions, and attempt to arrive at a consensus on how to proceed. The decision-making must be informed, but it must also be swift and authoritative – men and women going into battle have to believe that their leader knows what he or she is doing.

It is the same in business. Employees must be able to trust leaders to make the right decisions and agree the right courses of action when leading employees into the battle for customers in the marketplace. There are times when management style can be consultative and a consensus desirable, and times when a rapid decision has to be made without consultation.

Leadership and management styles have been researched for decades, providing insight into senior management behaviour that affects organizational culture and employee morale. One of the best known studies is illustrated in Figure 6.2.

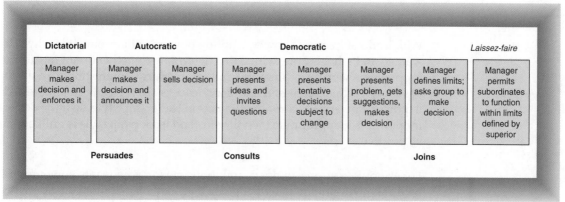

Figure 6.2   Management styles continuum (adapted from Tannenbaum and Schmidt, 1973)

A dictatorial style is rarely appropriate and can have a negative effect on employees, including an unwillingness to take responsibility or initiative. A *laissez-faire* style can have drawbacks if people are not competent or there is no leadership.

Case study
Leadership in the spotlight

As if leadership is not difficult enough, for some this challenging job is further complicated by the attention of the media. As England football manager, Sven Goran Eriksson was no stranger to media attention, and every move and decision he made was scrutinized publicly. This was not helped by all the invented decisions, actions and interventions he could be accused of. So what makes a spotlight leader tick?

In the first instance, he appears not to allow the spotlight to influence his leadership. Sven Goran Eriksson's management style is democratic, and good communication skills are seen as essential. He is a good listener and negotiator, and he works at achieving consensus when there are differing points of view. This requires paying attention to individuals, persuading and convincing people of a particular course of action, and building respect and trust. While he is accepting of failure and mistakes, he has a strong positive outlook that is used to focus on success. He is quick to praise and slow to criticize, and never pretends or expects to know it all, being happy to defer to experts.

His style of leadership is calm and reassuring in spite of the pressure of media attention. Most difficult of all, he calls the shots, not the media, and that requires strong leadership and self-belief.

(Sources: Various web and print)

Power and leadership

With leadership comes power. Wanting power is not wrong; it is why it is wanted and what is done with it that determines whether or not the desire for power is worthy, or immoral and/or unethical. Interestingly, research has revealed that successful and good leaders are typically not interested in power. Power has a strong influence on leadership style, so if the desire for power is inappropriate then the effect on leadership style is unlikely to be positive.

For example, a strong-minded, ambitious person who wants power for its own sake will pursue personal goals that may or may not coincide with organization goals. This may include taking credit for other peoples' successes, or aggressively pursuing targets that may lead to short-term gain but are either damaging or in conflict with other targets, or damaging to long-term goals. As well as being aggressive, the personal style may possibly be bullying. As the ambitious individual becomes more successful and such behaviour is seen to be rewarded, this style becomes a pattern of behaviour that others either withdraw from, becoming isolated, or try to emulate as a defence mechanism. The resulting style is unlikely to utilize softer skills or emotional intelligence.

Sources of power

Power by virtue of position alone reveals a certain weakness in leadership qualities. Having power simply because a person has reached a certain position, such as marketing manager, is not enough. Knowledge, experience and technical skills may all be valid reasons why a person is promoted to marketing manager, but once there the role changes to one of leading rather than doing, and leading requires the different skills described earlier. It will be these different skills that determine whether or not the marketing manager is a good leader. If these skills are absent or are not used, the only source of power left is position. Without evidence of actual leadership skills, power can very quickly diminish.

Dominance, an old favourite source of perceived power, is never valid. It shows a significant weakness, and in fact the weakness is an inability to lead. Dominance often requires a coercive or bullying style of leadership, so by its very nature is not leading but rather harassing people into doing what the leader wants.

Some managers go for popularity as a source of power – 'If I am liked, people will do what I want'. It is a rather shortsighted view, as leaders often have to make unpopular decisions. In such a situation, managers could find themselves struggling with the need to remain popular and thus make the wrong decision, or lose their power (based on popularity) by making the right decision.

We often hear about charismatic leaders, and there are undoubtedly people who are charismatic. They have charm and a presence that makes them well-liked. However, times change, as do attitudes and perceptions. Charisma can change too. It may have the potential to be give power while it lasts, but it also has the potential to fail. Charisma alone is not a valid source of power.

Why do people admire and follow leaders? The two greatest sources of power for leaders are respect and trust. Part of the respect comes from the leader's knowledge, experience and skills – what they do. Trust comes from the way in which leaders treat people, with honesty and integrity, and from the decisions they make – the right ones, most of the time. So leaders are good because of what they do, why they do things, and how.

Power and politics

In Part 1 of this book, we discussed power in organizations. We cannot talk about leadership without reviewing the influence of power and politics. Most of us might like to think we behave rationally and make rational decisions based on the facts and information available. Anyone who has worked in organizations for any length of time will know, of course, that this is not always the case.

Power and politics have a significant influence on decisions. While formal processes for decision-making may exist, informal politics will be shaping decisions and actions. This complex milieu means that decision-making is not confined to specific people undertaking a specific task; it can involve many people from around the organization. This pool of participants may not all have the same perspective on the decisions being made – different people can have entirely different interpretations of decisions and desired outcomes.

Different interpretations, perceptions and goals result in the decision-making process sometimes becoming unnecessarily complex. It can bring people into conflict with each other, and result in behaviours that are not always transparent.

Conflicts can often be the reason people engage in political behaviour in organizations. When people have to compete for resources and influence decisions, they are likely to use whatever skills they have to secure their desired outcomes. This leads to political manoeuvres, persuading, convincing, etc., to get what they want. This can be positive, ensuring that money is spent on the right people or technology, but it can also be negative, used to improve power and influence for its own sake rather than for the good of the organization or others. The problem with negative politicing is that this, in turn, can lead to conflicts.

Power can be cultivated through politics by networking with those who have influence, and manipulating situations so people become dependent – for example, by being the only person that understands a particular process or technology, or by working in areas of high uncertainty.

We need to be aware of and realistic about political behaviour. Sometimes it can be positive and justified, but more often it is not. Sometimes we can challenge the outcomes of what appear to be flawed decisions, and sometimes we cannot. It can be very frustrating if decisions are being made that we know will waste resources and not achieve the desired outcomes, but sometimes we have to live with them.

Ways in which we as managers can influence positive behaviour will be discussed under managing change, motivation, and communications.

Context – so what leadership style is appropriate?

Industries and the type of products and services provided do affect leadership style. In industries where dangerous products are manufactured (for example, chemical industries) or where life-and-death decisions are made (such as the armed forces), some decisions have to be made quickly and with little or no time to consult.

In other industries (for example, social services) consultation is vital – a decision cannot be made until all the parties involved have contributed what they know and agreed a desired outcome.

It is also a reality that a mix of leadership styles can be appropriate in the same industries and organizations. The circumstances can determine the appropriate style. For example, during times of calm, involving staff in decision-making and development of plans is an opportunity to both develop and motivate staff. However, if the same organization suddenly finds itself under attack from external changes, a competitor or an advance in technology, the need to be decisive and move fast reduces the opportunities to involve staff in decision-making and developing plans to any great degree. The staff role then becomes one of implementing. There are drawbacks to lack of staff involvement as a regular way of working, though, and we will discuss this later.

Other occasions when it might not be possible to try to get employee agreement include:

- when the leader is unable to make known all the information necessary for decision-making
- when the problem is clear and the solution can be formulated logically
- when employees do not share the organization's goals.

Occasions when it is inappropriate for leaders to fail to consult employees include:

- when the leader does not have the relevant information which will affect the quality of the outcome
- when the nature of the problem is unclear and needs discussion and clarification
- when lack of employee consultation will result in lack of acceptance.

As discussed in Part 1 of this book, organization structure and culture also affect leadership style.

Leaders, like the rest of us, have strengths and weaknesses, and they need to consider these objectively when taking on the role of leader. It will affect decisions about how they manage. A good leader will also think about what the desired outcomes are, and therefore what the most appropriate style of leadership is in order to achieve the desired outcomes.

We need leadership – someone who has the bigger picture and is ultimately prepared to take responsibility, make decisions, unite people, coordinate and orchestrate. It is not appropriate for leaders to relinquish responsibility, or lack of leadership can degenerate into chaos, with people and tasks becoming progressively less efficient and effective.

Increasingly, there is a trend (where appropriate) for a more consultative or democratic style of leadership. This has the advantages of involving staff, so motivating them and gaining their commitment, and also of ensuring the leader is well informed and understands the implications of decisions made from the perspective of those who implement them.

Values, attitudes and integrity

Leadership and management styles, power and politics are all outcomes of the values, beliefs and attitudes held by leaders and managers. Values, beliefs and attitudes are coming under scrutiny as never before as corporate social responsibility is forcing its way into boardrooms and onto corporate agendas.

Those who have reassured themselves that corporate social responsibility is a passing phase and a choice are in for a nasty shock. It is here, and here to stay. Briefly, drivers include:

- corporate governance
- consumer pressure groups that are activating globally
- Non-Government Organizations (NGOs) increasing power and influence globally
- depletion of natural resources and protectionist measures by governments
- increasing government legislation on waste and emissions
- an increasing number of organizations genuinely prepared to commit to CSR, shaming those that do not
- growing evidence of the commercial credibility of CSR
- growing value of the ethical investor market and growing expectation by traditional shareholders of ethical behaviour.

While there is no escaping the inevitability of CSR, there is a reality and dilemma for organizations and consumers. How 'green' is it possible to be today? So much depends on us all acting together, and we are a long way from that. It is not just acting together in our local community and in our organization, but across countries. To be truly socially and environmentally responsible requires that we act differently in everything we do, and that takes time. However, we can make a start, and early realistic goals might be to improve our corporate social responsibility credentials incrementally.

Carroll (1991) defined corporate social responsibility as a pyramid of essential building blocks of values and behaviour (Figure 6.3). Managers have an

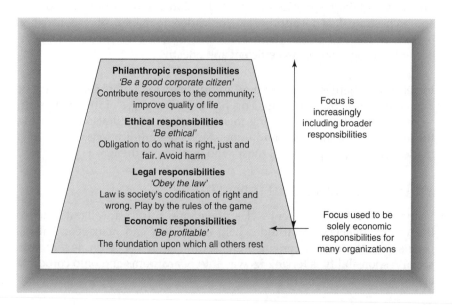

Figure 6.3
Pyramid of CSR
(Carroll, 1991)

economic responsibility to ensure that the organization is financially sound, and unless they get this right, pursuing desired social responsibility is futile. The next building blocks are the legal responsibilities organizations have to comply with, and legislation on environmental and human rights issues are increasingly demanding and are also not optional. Many (but not all) ethical and philanthropic obligations are optional, and whether or not these are pursued depends on the leadership style and values held by those leaders.

At the heart of CSR is a genuine intention to do the right thing, to be responsible and act with integrity. This behaviour comes from leadership, and is most effective when leaders are committed. The word 'genuine' is used because some organizations have jumped on the bandwagon with a cause-related marketing activity that is nothing more than a PR stunt.

The difference between an organization that is strategically committed to corporate social responsibility, as opposed to using (for example) cause-related marketing as a PR stunt, can be found in the CSR objectives that change the way the whole business behaves and operates. To be truly committed to corporate social responsibility, the orientation is strategic and total. As we have already acknowledged, achieving a truly social, ethical and environmental orientation is going to be difficult, and some organizations may never achieve a complete transformation; however, they can become greener.

Many organizations are now on a journey aimed at being greener. All will start at different points and have different challenges and approaches, and some may only achieve part of the journey. Organizations make compromises – some for practical operational reasons and some for financial reasons. The bottom line is often used as an excuse to avoid the commitment to invest in CSR. However, even this long favoured last line of defence is being challenged as more organizations prove that the goal of become greener encourages efficiency and innovation, resulting in financial gain.

A strategic and committed approach to CSR is also reinforced by the way performance is measured. Measures have been available for some time that put CSR at the core of business behaviour.

The 'triple bottom line' (Figure 6.4) can provide a framework for CSR performance analysis. Performance is measured against the triple bottom line,

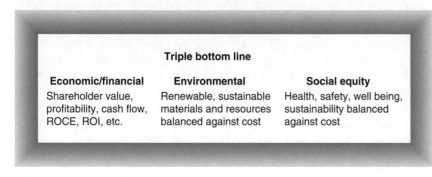

Figure 6.4
Triple bottom line

which is the simultaneous pursuit of economic/financial prosperity, environmental quality, and social equity – not just a single financial bottom line.

The Coalition for Environmentally Responsible Economies (CERES) 1989 also developed a range of measures, as did the Business Impact Taskforce (2000) – for example:

- workforce indicators (absenteeism, grievances, health and safety record)
- marketplace indicators (customer complaints, advertising complaints, anti-competitive behaviour, late-payment bills, customer satisfaction and retention, provision for special needs)
- environment indicators (energy consumption, water usage, waste produced and disposal, environmental offences, emissions such as ozone, recyclable waste)
- community indicators (cash value support of community, company/ staff time in community, positive/negative media comment)
- human rights indicators (compliance with international human rights standards, wage and employment agreements).

For the professional manager who worries that integrity is being compromised by misuse of power and destructive political behaviour, these values and measures have the advantage of forcing a more ethical dimension into organization practice and individual behaviour. Therefore, a CSR agenda can be a powerful vehicle for dealing with these concerns and conflicts.

Case study
A familiar brand with a well-kept secret

WH Smith (WHS), the stationery store, sits on the high street of most UK towns and many shopping malls. It has been out there since the eighteenth century and has evolved over time, and while it is rare to find a WHS customer devoted to the brand, we all expect it to remain on our high streets. Some might say its evolution has been questionable and has not gone nearly far enough, with some surprising diversifications in the 1980s and 1990s, WHS seemed to lose its way.

However, the twenty-first century sees WHS more focused. Improvements in its brand-building activities have yet to be realized, but WHS has a secret that could have potential for its brand.

When thinking about WHS – assuming you ever give it a thought – you would not immediately think of its green credentials and choose the brand because of its commitment to the environment. If thinking about the environment, you would not necessarily immediately recall the WHS brand. However, for some years WHS has been among the leaders in pursuing a corporate social responsibility agenda and, whether intentionally or not, this is driving strategic change not only through their own business but also through the businesses of their partners and supply chains. Each year WHS sets new targets for eliminating waste, recycling, fair trade, improved health and safety and working conditions for employees, sustainable forest sourcing, literacy projects, etc.

WHS's commitment to corporate social responsibility has seen significant results that have benefited the environment and communities, and, for shareholders, has led to a business operation that is improving in efficiency and effectiveness.

Perhaps the brand is the next challenge?

(Sources: Various web and print)

Leadership decisions – strategic direction

Any decisions should be the result of a consultative approach that involves and encourages contributions from all parts of the organization. However, at some point decisions have to be made, and by those most qualified to do so. Decisions are hierarchical and interdependent. Functional decisions and strategies emerge from strategic decisions and strategies. In reality, it does not always work like this. Managers and staff struggling with a lack of direction usually take the initiative and develop operational and tactical plans in the absence of strategic direction. They must do something and better to deliver goods and services to customers, rather than do nothing, even if this is not set in the framework of a clear and distinct vision and corporate strategy.

This is not ideal, but nor is it uncommon. Senior managers are responsible for communicating their expectations to those responsible for implementing strategy.

Developing a view of the future

Before the senior management team starts making decisions, members should be clear about where they are going. Our future is not entirely within our control; market conditions and trends sweep us along. If a course is set without consideration of market currents, managers are likely to find themselves swimming against the current, putting considerable effort (and resources) into getting nowhere.

Developing a view of the future is a strategic process of anticipating likely changes, opportunities and threats. There are seven key factors driving future change:

1. Customer needs.

2. Channels.

3. Technology.

4. Regulation.

5. Finance.

6. Competition.

7. Innovation.

It is not the intention in developing a view of the future to predict exact quantities or behaviour, but rather to anticipate likely trends regarding how markets will evolve. The purpose of this activity is to develop an understanding of possible future market conditions, thereby allowing the management team to consider future direction and vision in light of this understanding.

It is the responsibility of the senior management team to develop a view of the future, and it is the responsibility of marketing to inform this view. This requires marketing to manage the process of coordinating knowledge and views from across the organization.

Trying to assess how markets might evolve can be a risky business, and taking risks is discouraged by many organizations. However, as custodians of marketing intelligence, marketers should be informing and leading their organizations and can reduce risk by employing intelligence.

Making sense of the future

First look at the past. What changes have taken place, and to what extent were these predicted? Where has the most change occurred, and to what effect? Evaluate the effectiveness of past predictions and look for reliable sources of information. Who were the visionaries? Establish the past chain reaction that led to change.

It is important during this exercise to ensure that you are clear about the facts of change – the real causes. It is also important to ensure that any anticipation of future changes, guided by past changes, takes account of the different market circumstances. The world in the future will not be the same as the world in the past. The future chain reaction will be different – for example, there is the changing nature of distribution channels, there are better informed consumers, and there is the increasing influence and power of pressure groups.

Anticipating future developments requires scenario planning and a lot of imagination and creativity. Developing a view of the future that will help the organization to understand its markets will not be achieved with cautious, risk-avoiding individuals. A 'blame culture' is also not conducive to engendering creativity and free thinking. Teams should be created that are visionary, creative and not averse to going off on a tangent to explore ideas. However, there is the need for leadership that can manage and coordinate the team to ensure the objective is achieved.

Steps include:

1. *Evolution* – identifying possible trends and patterns of behaviour that will lead to future conditions.

2. *Relevance* – describing the organization's possible roles in possible future conditions.

3. *Interpretation* – evaluating what the organization's future role in future conditions means in terms of value, people and operations.

4. *Clarification* – defining the vision and confirming the mission for the organization.

We discuss teams later in this chapter, and in Chapter 7.

When the senior management team has established a sense of the future and clarified strategic direction, leaders can then make decisions about how to achieve the vision and deliver the mission.

Leadership and management decisions

The structure and process of decision-making depends on the nature and size of the organization. Multinational enterprises have strategic business units (SBUs) across the world, and the holding company manages a portfolio of SBUs. The ultimate goal of the holding company is to answer the question, how will we make money? In these circumstances, the holding company decisions may include investment in diversification, vertical integration, acquisitions, new ventures, allocation of resources between business units, and divestments.

How integrated the individual SBU goals and plans are depends on whether the organization has a global strategy or whether SBUs offer very different products in very different markets and operate independently.

For strategic business units or organizations that are not multinational, strategic decisions start with the question, what business are we in? The purpose of the organization is clarified through a mission statement. The next decision is, how do we make money – or, for non-profit organizations, how will we achieve our goal of . . .? For example, how do we raise funds to eradicate homelessness? Only now can leaders and managers start broadly deciding which products fit into which markets. Marketing should have a significant role in influencing these decisions, but as it affects the entire organization it must be made by the senior management team responsible for allocating resources and setting objectives across the organization.

Marketing managers will also be very influential in deciding how the organization should compete and/or position. These decisions include how to differentiate, market positioning, and competitive strategies. Competitive positioning affects the entire organization, so should be a collaborative decision. It is a strategic decision because it affects not just what is done but also the way in which it is done.

Non-profit organizations still need to be clear about what the purpose of the organization is, but rather than 'competing' they might be deciding how they 'position' – that is, distinguish themselves from other providers. Charities do, in fact, compete. There are over 600 cancer charities in the UK alone, all competing for donations and funding. The public sector is increasingly compared by region, and even with the public sector in other countries. To compare favourably and be seen to be spending public money wisely, they have to be seen to be efficient and effective.

Figure 6.5 shows the relationship between strategic, operational and tactical planning, and cross-functional planning.

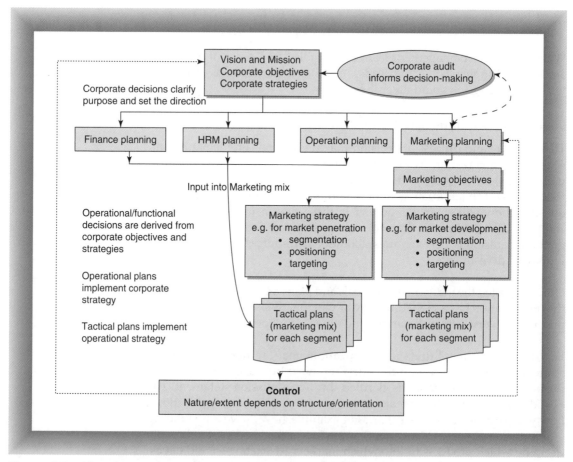

Figure 6.5 Planning route map: vertical planning systems and decisions (©1997 Juanita Cockton)

Strategic decisions and strategies also include, for example, changing the structure of an organization or its culture. It involves everyone, and will require resources allocated across the organization.

Corporate strategies are the selection of growth strategies and formulation of competitive strategies. At the next level down, we see how the organization strategy breaks down into functional unit decisions and strategies.

Functional and operational decisions and strategies

Functional decisions include setting objectives and the allocation of resources within a particular function to achieve the objectives. They also determine how strategies will be achieved – the detailed action plans of who will do what and when.

Functional strategies include:

- *human resource management* – for example, recruitment and training of staff to ensure that labour and skills are available
- *operations* – for example, procurement plans, production schedules to produce products and services
- *finance* – for example, work in progress and cash flow plans
- *marketing* – for example, segmentation, positioning, targeting.

Functional plans are designed to achieve the desired goal and implement organization strategy. For marketing, these are the plans that differentiate the organization from other providers. They reflect the desired competitive position. Marketing strategy segments markets and positions the organization's offer, and tactical marketing mix plans deliver value to each segment being targeted.

Leadership role – horizontal management

When the chief executive and senior management team have established the vision, mission and strategic direction, functional/unit managers can design plans to implement organization strategies. Part of the role of senior management is overseeing functional strategy design and implementation. However, the main role of the senior management team is to manage horizontally and coordinate goals and policies *across* distinct but interrelated functional and divisional units and/or departments. The senior management team activity is to employ horizontal planning designed to achieve synergies and maximize advantage, competitive or otherwise, for the whole organization. Horizontal planning links different vertical plans.

Disadvantages of not having horizontal planning include the following:

- *inconsistency*, caused because business units evolve independently and different approaches can lead to weak performance in some areas (for example, customer service)
- *an indistinct and weak position*, caused by different approaches to communications, brand building and competitive activities
- *expertise being diluted*, due to lack of transfer (or processes to transfer) across the organization
- *conflict*, caused by conflicting objectives, business units competing with each other which is counterproductive, costly and can lead to failure.

As with vertical planning, horizontal management needs a recognized process for managing across the organization (see Figure 6.6).

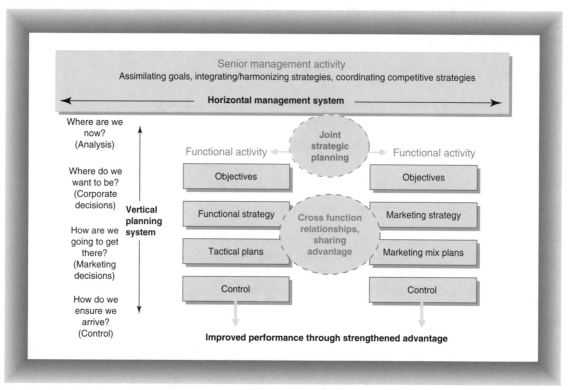

Figure 6.6   Horizontal management (©1997 Juanita Cockton)

Horizontal management allows practices that build a common understanding and accord, and encourage a unifying theme. Leaders manage conflicts (sharing authority, coordination), provide examples of strong values, and acknowledge how everybody contributes to overall success.

Horizontal management may require change to existing operations and practice:

- *Horizontal culture and identity*. Even in a small organization, culture can vary across it. If the organization operates in different markets, this can be complicated by national cultures. Allow some flexibility, but encourage acceptance of a corporate culture that will facilitate horizontal management.

- *Horizontal relationships*. This involves actively encouraging relationships across the organization and beyond. Some relationships will be more influential or important than others, and relationships should be categorized according to their impact on the organization and on value creation. Identify reciprocal relationships where sources of advantage can be shared – for example, personnel rotation among departments (or SBUs) or with other partners (for example suppliers and distributors) promoting from within.

- *Horizontal structure.* The organization should be designed to reduce perceived and actual barriers between departments and functions. Form joint functional planning teams at an operational level, and facilitate the sharing of information, expertise and ideas.

- *Horizontal processes and systems.* Uniform vertical planning processes should be introduced where possible, to make horizontal management achievable. Horizontal procedures should encourage inclusive practices and communications flow across the organization. Horizontal incentives should recognize and reward cooperation. Use technology to reduce any negative impact of geographic separation or distance.

As we established at the start of this chapter, a leader's job is not an easy one, and while leaders are managing vertically and horizontally, the one thing they must never lose sight of is the customer or stakeholder – the reason the organization exists.

Leaders cannot delegate this responsibility to others; they can share it with others, but leaders are as responsible for customers as is the employee serving the customer face-to-face.

Case study
Customer-focused leadership

Entrepreneurs are passionate about their business. It starts as their idea, grows and develops through careful nurturing, and succeeds because of a passion for a particular idea. One entrepreneur's idea becomes another generation's family business. A difficulty for entrepreneurs is when the business grows, requiring a more structured and formal approach. Part of this difficulty is being prepared to hand over responsibility for customers to others.

John Timpson, of Timpson's shoe repair and key-cutting business, has no such problem. He is quite clear about where responsibility for customers lies, and therefore how the business operates. He believes that the staff repairing shoes and cutting keys are the most important employees, and all other employees – including management – are there to serve those front-line employees. The concept of managers 'serving' customer-facing employees puts customers right at the centre of the business. Front-line staff are expected to see customers as their priority, and if they are committed to this objective, power comes with responsibility.

Timpson's approach has the benefit of keeping it simple and effective. If the company wants staff serving customers to deliver a level of service that keeps them coming back and recommending Timpson to others, then everyone else in the business is responsible for making sure front-line staff can do their jobs well.

Timpson's approach to looking after staff includes holiday homes, training schemes, having birthdays off, a hardship fund, and newsletters.

> Employees are part of the Timpson family business and are encouraged to enter the business at the bottom and work their way up, following a structured career path. A little under half of new employees are introduced by those already employed.
>
> When leaders are focused on customers, it establishes a prevailing culture of customer focus.
>
> (Sources: Various web and print)

As well as customers, leaders are responsible for change – and how change is managed will depend on management attitudes to change and their knowledge, experience and skill in managing change.

Managing change

Why change?

Change is now a fact of life; if an organization wants to survive, it has to change. Change can be threatening and uncomfortable, and is often unpopular. However, the problems of change are less to do with the change itself and more to do with the *way change is managed*. The intention here is first to accept the reality – change will happen and is sometimes painful – and secondly to improve the way change is managed.

Some change has been concerned with efficiency drives. Increasingly, change is now also concerned with effectiveness – particular the goal of marketing orientation or customer focus. Some change appears vague about what the desired outcome is, which could be the result of poor communications or, more worryingly, because the management team does not have a desired outcome. It is sometimes mistakenly believed that change for its own sake is good. It is not. Change is expensive, time-consuming and potentially damaging to the mental health of the organization. If managers do not know why they want to change, or just have a vague idea that 'it would improve things around here', they need to identify what it would improve and why.

Managers must be able to explain and justify change, or it loses credibility before it starts. The objective may be to get rid of incompetent people, but poor management of change usually loses the competent people. The objective may be to improve performance, but again, without clear thinking about what performance and how it can be improved, managers can spend a lot of time achieving very little.

A valid reason for change is to achieve a marketing orientation. The goal is to ensure that management and employee focus is on the needs and wants of selected target markets. This requires improving structure, processes and systems to meet those needs – for example, a marketing intelligence system as part of the decision-making process, and marketing programmes tailored to meet the needs of specific targets. A marketing orientation also requires a focus on the people recruited and the way people are trained and managed. It is important not to lose sight of this during change. A preoccupation with internal issues and activities designed to change and improve performance can often result in forgetting the customer, and in particular the customer experience. Any change must be designed to protect existing good practice and/or improve the customer experience. A customer might be forgiven for thinking that most change in organizations today is designed to do the exact opposite.

There are various reasons why change is required in an organization, including:

- innovation
- new technology
- changing marketing conditions and trends
- competition
- government legislation
- changes in organization structure and/or operations
- mergers and acquisitions.

So what's the problem with managing change?

There are many examples (too many!) of change that has been managed poorly. The results can be devastating to employees, and damaging to the organization. People resist change when it is not understood and appears threatening. If they are not involved in the change in any way, it will inevitably be threatening and cannot be understood.

If you are not convinced, here are one or two brief examples of managing change:

- Rumours across the organization suggested imminent redundancies. To address this problem, senior management called the entire workforce onto one site (on a Thursday) to reassure and confirm that there would be no more redundancies – an expensive and time-consuming exercise. The following Monday, senior management started the next round of redundancies.

- Those being made redundant had their names called out over the public announcement system. The entire workforce sat in silence and waited to hear whether their name was to be called. Management wondered why they were so miserable.

- Over two years, thousands of workers (some long-serving and valued members of the workforce) were made redundant because of falling profits. Some 200 management consultants were on site during this period, advising on strategy to improve profits. Not only did they not improve profits; the consultants also cost the company £15 *million*.

These examples show a blatant disregard for humanity that is unacceptable. We can do better.

There are many reasons why change is poorly managed. Change affects people in different ways, and has different perspectives. Change usually takes place at all levels of the organization, but affects different levels in different ways.

- *Senior management level.* Senior managers are usually the initiators of change. They are responsible for identifying strategic direction and the necessary changes to achieve that direction. Problems arise when all they can 'see' is the bigger picture (not a problem in itself), but if they do not involve those who implement the project it is doomed from the start.

- *Middle management level.* These people are responsible for managing the change; they often have the toughest time because they have to meet the demands and expectations of senior management as well as the concerns and fears of employees.

- *Operations level.* These are the people who implement the change. Quite simply, they know what will work and what will not work. If these people are not involved, not only do you risk implementing something that has failed to take account of current business operations, but you also risk antagonizing the workforce and will encounter resistance.

If it were as simple as understanding the levels and therefore how people might be affected, managing change could be easy. However, it is not this simple. We discussed earlier the effects of power and politics, and another dimension to change is that existing power bases are often threatened – and this can result in destructive political behaviour, defending a power base at all costs.

Senior management can have a credible vision of where the organization should be going, and recognize that change is needed to achieve the vision. What happens next is where the success or otherwise of change will be determined.

For some senior managers there is a DIY mentality to change-management initiatives. It may be for the best intentions, and the assumption is that managers are competent and should not be supervised. In DIY change management, the vision is followed by nothing more than an instruction to managers to 'make the necessary changes'. However, it is a disconnected approach at a time when integration will be fundamental to success, and creates a number of problems:

1. Expectations have not been communicated with the instruction; there is no explanation of what is required or justification for the change.

2. Interpretation creates conflict due to the lack of explanation and justification; people will interpret requirements in different ways.

3. Engagement will be limited and self-motivated; those who can see opportunities will support change, but even these people will come into conflict at some stage, as everyone is not pulling in the same direction with the same purpose.

In DIY change it is down to managers to interpret the instruction, and without guidance, preparation or a process, each manager will interpret differently depending on his or her own experiences and training. The result of different interpretations is a chaotic mix of approaches to managing change.

Some will decide to ignore the instruction, and believe the best approach is 'business as usual'. This can become obstructive to change and actively builds barriers, reinforcing the *status quo*. It is an effective weapon for resistors of change, the argument being that 'at least we are doing something productive, and management have not made it clear what they want'.

Others who feel threatened and incompetent to deal with change can become aggressive and demanding, and believe 'forcing it through' is the answer. They will not be sharing information or involving people in a productive process of change, as they have no understanding of why change is being implemented or how to do it. There may be open resistance or (more likely in these conditions) a quiet withdrawal.

Some willing enthusiasts may interpret change management as an opportunity to experiment. Experimentation is important, but without a process for change the experimentation becomes 'let's have fun', and is likely to be random, ill-advised and inappropriate, with no useful outcomes. Learning from haphazard experimentation will not be formalized. This approach rarely moves on from experimenting, and usually stops when enthusiasts get bored.

Even those using best-practice concepts to achieve the goal will have limited success because of the disorganized efforts of the rest of management. The real damage in these circumstances is that a professional approach by able managers is condemned as failure because of its limited success, and therefore others can reassure themselves that good concepts do not work.

There are many more ways in which change is managed and mismanaged, and you will have had different experiences. We can all learn from good and bad experiences and use them to improve the way change is managed.

Managing successful change

Our starting point must be to understand possible reactions to change and how change affects people. Change affects people in different ways, including:

- a lack of sense of direction
- changing relationships and loss of friendships
- growing insecurity
- self-doubt and feelings of incompetence in newly defined roles
- a loss of territory.

Employees typically go through phases during the change process. These phases are shown in Figure 6.7:

- *shock* – difficulty taking things in
- *denial* – refusing to acknowledge what is happening
- *hopelessness* – employees may passively withdraw or actively resist
- *experimentation* – exploring, redefining and finding a role, beginning to come to terms with change
- *acceptance* – beginning to make sense of change, confidence growing
- *commitment* – settling down to new tasks and a new role.

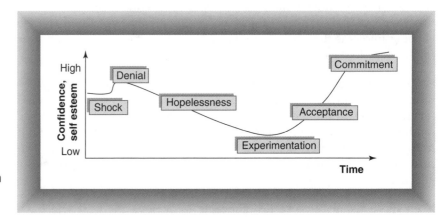

Figure 6.7
Change transition curve (adapted from Sheard and Kakabadse, 2002)

Understanding employees' reactions

People are likely to go through these phases, or something similar, even if change is managed well. The difference is that if change is managed properly, either they will go through these phases quickly and resistance will be minimal, or they may even miss some of the more negative phases. If change is not properly managed, people will not only go through these phases; they may never begin to accept the new order, and quiet resistance becomes a way of life.

To understand better how people may react, internal markets must be segmented. During periods of change, segmentation will not be based on levels of the organization or departments and functions. People are more likely to segment according to their attitude to change. For example:

- *Neutrals* do not feel strongly about the change one way or the other; they have yet to be convinced it is a good or bad thing, or are possibly indifferent – which can create a different problem to solve.
- *Resistors* feel threatened and will resist change. They are not convinced of the benefits (assuming these have been communicated), and want things to remain the same.

- *Drivers* are enthusiastic about the change, and believe it is right for the organization and is the way forward. From these people you will find your 'change champions' – the people who will help to drive the change through.

The targets or segments will be represented across the organization, and from the top of the organization to the bottom. In every change event there will be winners (they have more power, or territory, or status, etc.) and losers (they may lose what winners gain plus the issues raised above).

Change, by its nature, means taking a step into the unknown, and inevitably brings uncertainty, but a plan for change can reduce the risk of potential chaos and failure. It encourages us to identify potential problems and explore solutions to those problems. It also provides opportunities to communicate expectations, and a framework for involving people (see Figure 6.8).

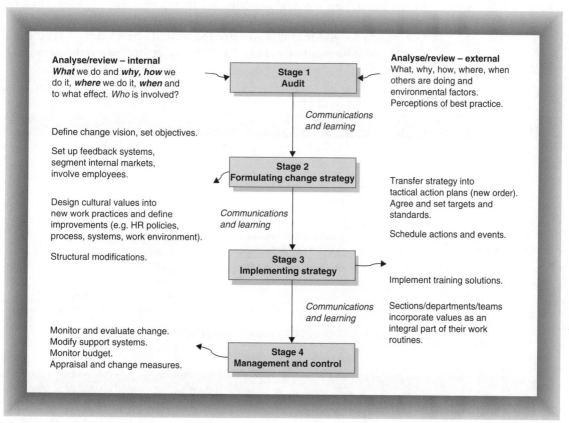

Figure 6.8   Managing change stages – route map (©1997 Juanita Cockton)

Any change plan should incorporate and deal with the transition phases people may experience (see Figure 6.9). Experience and professionalism help to define future outcomes, and the actions needed to achieve the outcomes. However, change is unpredictable, so any change plan must be flexible and iterative. Managers and staff must be prepared to learn and adapt where needed if actions and outcomes are not evolving as intended. If it means going back to the drawing board and starting again, it is better to do this than to carry on regardless with a plan that is not going to achieve the desired outcomes.

However, sometimes reality forces us to accept something that is less than ideal but is the best that can be achieved in the circumstances. It can sometimes be better to accept a less-ideal solution that is workable rather than pursuing elusive perfection. Change is about learning; we can learn from other people's experience, but we learn most from the change we manage ourselves.

Managers need to be alert to individual transitions. A plan to manage the change phases cannot assume that everyone is moving at the same speed, and this can obscure the progress through the planning stages.

When describing leadership styles we mentioned that in some circumstances it is not always possible to involve employees in decision-making, but acknowledged that this was not the ideal. During change, employee involvement is essential and can mean the difference between success and failure.

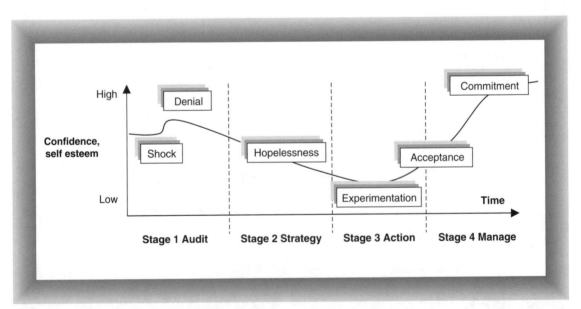

Figure 6.9 Managing the change transitions

During the *audit stage*, people who are in shock or denial, or even embrace change, need to be able to make sense of why change is happening and what change means. At this stage, by involving people in an audit they can come to terms with why change is needed. They come face-to-face with organization problems, external pressures and future challenges. This may not result in acceptance, but it should result in understanding. Also, because people have been involved in the audit they begin to feel part of the process.

Before concluding this first stage, identify budget and other resource needs, including training. As we move into the next stage, the change vision is re-evaluated and clarified, and objectives are set.

In spite of a better understanding, the *strategy formulation stage* inevitably reveals how things will change and what this means for people personally. As we have said, winners are unlikely to resist or to experience hopelessness. They may, however, experience uncertainty before the new order takes shape. Others may well feel a sense of hopelessness even if they are not losers. The uncertainty and an increasing awareness that old familiar routines and social circles are changing brings with it doubt about the future.

Segment internal markets according to needs and concerns, how people will react to change and are affected by it. With this understanding of segments you can set up support designed to deal with reactions and concerns, and feedback systems that ensure you are keeping a finger on the pulse of the organization. Monitor morale and activate support as required.

The more people are involved in shaping the new order and have control over development, the less threatened they feel. Because they have input into change, they begin to become familiar with the new order before it is implemented. Encourage and facilitate creativity and innovation to ensure that solutions and improvements offer advantage. Allow experimentation and testing of ideas. Involving employees in strategy formulation also has the advantage of ensuring that whatever is implemented is workable.

By the time people get to the *action stage*, their familiarity with the new order and ownership means they are now willing to accept change and increasingly committed to making it work. Training precedes adopting new work practices, and it is important to allow time for adjustment. Business will *not* be as usual – the goal is that it will be different – and that requires time for people to adapt. During implementation, it is important to continue to allow experimentation and testing of solutions. Test runs can both eliminate problems and build employee confidence, providing there are formal learning mechanisms for evaluating progress.

The final stage of *managing and controlling* the implementation should be a move to a less unsettled and more productive stage if the first three stages have gone well. By now, people are committed to new practices and new work routines that are becoming increasingly familiar. This stage is more about making sure that the change is embedded and people do not slip back into old habits. Support systems may need to be modified as the requirements for support will diminish and change. Support will be less about dealing with fears and concerns, and more about making sure that people have access to any development needs – for example, coaching and accessing information.

Support is also provided through appraisals, which should reflect change issues. The change itself must be evaluated and measured in terms of both the change process (how well we managed change) and the outcomes (the desired improvements).

Communication at all stages

Communications play an important and central role in change management. Good and timely communications can go a long way to minimizing the negative impact and speeding the process through the transition phases, and even eliminate the more negative aspects where possible.

Managing the phases – dealing with reactions and emotions

- *The announcement.* There should be no shocks – at least, not overwhelming ones. If communications are properly planned, it reduces the element of surprise – desirable in these circumstances. The senior management should signal commitment, and explain and justify why change is needed. Communications are designed to allay uncertainty and fear, and to educate and inform regarding the need for change, create dissatisfaction with the current set-up and a desire for the new. The learning at this stage is to assess employee morale and views on change to determine the communications task going forward.

- *Denial.* Again, communications have a vital role in reducing perceptions of threat, by informing, explaining and reassuring. Communications are designed to reduce confusion and the risk of detachment, and to interpret new values and/or purpose as meaningful *and* personal to all. Two-way communications are now essential, and learning about employee reactions, concerns and ideas continues.

- *Depression.* This may be unavoidable for some people. You are dealing with emotions and feelings, and sensitivity and tact is vital. Personal communications are essential, and acknowledging and expressing feelings and emotions should be established as acceptable. Openness, transparency and honesty are important, even if it means confronting the less agreeable aspects of change. Trying to make people feel better by making promises that cannot be kept, or by putting a gloss on less favourable aspects of change, does not fool people and can make matters worse.

- *Acceptance.* Communications are designed to build confidence and reduce self-doubt and hesitation. Reinforce benefits and improvements, promote and translate success opportunities into something individuals understand from their own perspective. Provide forums for discussion and the exploration of issues and ideas from which every one can learn. It helps get things out in the open, and reassures as people learn that others have similar reactions and concerns.

- *Experimentation.* Allow exploration and focus on priorities, training and support. Use communications to share and exchange information, experiences and learning, and reinforce a culture value of mistakes being acceptable and blaming for failures unacceptable. Begin to focus people on shorter-term goals to move them from experimenting with ideas and possible solutions to consolidation change.

- *Commitment*. People need a sense of achievement, and communications can promote successes achieved and reward achievements through recognition. Establish longer-term goals and move people from a pre-occupation with the current to a view of the future. Be prepared to share the change management failures as well as successes; learn from them and encourage all to contribute ideas on how change in the future can be managed better.

And the customer?

Change management means we are preoccupied with internal issues and events. Marketing people have the added responsibility of making sure that customers and stakeholders are also managed through change. Hopefully, in most cases external stakeholders will be unaware of changes, except perhaps of improving performance. What they must not experience are the problems, upheaval and potentially demoralized employees that can come with change. Marketing needs a plan, particularly communication that manages relationships during change, and this may require openness about what is taking place and/or a mechanism for customers and stake-holders to feed back their experiences and concerns.

Change management in the hands of experienced and skilled managers can be a far less traumatic, and even a positive, experience. There is no doubt that most change involves some negative experiences, and in these circum-stances managers can do much to try to minimize the impact. Leaders can delegate responsibility for managing change to managers and staff, but they cannot be absent from the process. Their role is to ensure that the change is on track for achieving the desired vision, and to coordinate change horizontally. Leaders should defer to managers on issues of making change work operationally, and managers should defer to staff who implement. This, of course, requires people to trust each other.

Project teams will play an important part in achieving change. How teams are formed and managed for change, or for various marketing activities, will determine successful team performance.

Managing teams

As increasingly rapid and complex change in the business environment affects organizations, working together in teams becomes a necessity. Work can be more demanding and complex, and a range of experience, skills and ability is required.

Teams do not happen automatically just because people have been brought together. Creating an effective team is deliberate, and building and main-taining an effective team takes considerable management effort.

If you are going to manage a team, it is important to understand the type of team you are managing and the relationship with other teams.

Senior management teams lead the organization, set corporate goals and object-ives, develop corporate strategy which involves all aspects of organization, and manage horizontally supporting managers in executing their jobs.

Middle management teams set detailed operational objectives and design operational strategy, allocate resources and tasks, disseminate information, and manage vertically and cooperate with horizontally supporting staff in delivering value to stakeholders.

Junior and administrative teams are responsible for getting the job done; they transfer inputs into outputs, and deliver value to customers or stakeholders directly or indirectly.

Depending on the organization, there may also be technical teams who set technical, production or service standards.

Benefits of teams are that they:

- provide support and help to members
- coordinate activities of individuals
- generate commitment
- meet the basic human need to belong
- provide learning opportunities
- enhance communications
- provide a satisfying, stimulating, enjoyable working environment.

Barriers to effective teams include:

- lack of agreement regarding objectives, direction, commitment
- the wrong balance, with essential skills lacking
- a lack of contribution by team members
- the leader being isolated from the team
- poor communications – a lack of honesty and openness
- evident and counterproductive competition and conflict
- hidden agendas – personal objectives such as trying to impress the boss, scoring points, etc.

The purpose of managing people and teams is to ensure that we have satisfied profitability customers and satisfied stakeholders. If we do not want a team that habitually fails, we need to design one that will succeed. Typical reasons why teams fail include lack of mental ability, having no clear team role, lack of skills, and being the wrong size.

Successful teams are the result of careful design, structure and maintenance (see Figure 6.10). The reasons a team succeeds include appropriate leadership, a spread of mental abilities and personal attributes, and distribution in responsibilities of members to match different capabilities. Teams need to share common objectives and work together to achieve them.

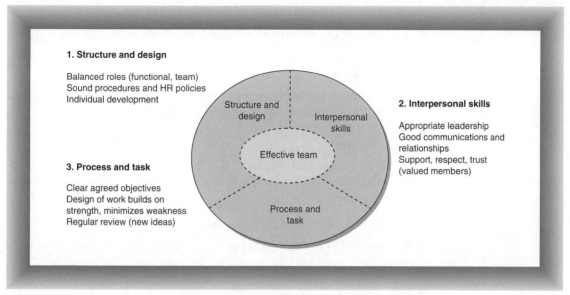

1. Structure and design

Balanced roles (functional, team)
Sound procedures and HR policies
Individual development

2. Interpersonal skills

Appropriate leadership
Good communications and
relationships
Support, respect, trust
(valued members)

3. Process and task

Clear agreed objectives
Design of work builds on
strength, minimizes weakness
Regular review (new ideas)

Structure and design   Interpersonal skills   Effective team   Process and task

Figure 6.10   Foundation of effective teams (©2004 Juanita Cockton)

Some teams form and the individuals remain part of the same team while they remain with the organization – for example, working for a particular functional department. Some teams form to tackle a specific task, and when this task is completed they break up and re-form (with different team members) to tackle a different task.

Before teams form, some thought is needed regarding their design. There should be a selection process, as with any job, to ensure that the right people are recruited. Recruitment is usually from within, although sometimes a new team member or team needs to be recruited from outside the organization.

Structure and design

Team audit

Forming a team starts with an assessment of the task (rather like a job analysis) followed by an assessment of the knowledge, experience and functional skills required (rather like a person specification).

The next stage is to recruit people for the team, and this requires a personal skills audit. Sources of information include company records, particularly personnel files and appraisals. Any original selection tests that were done may also provide useful information on what sort of team skills the individual has. However, people change, develop and grow, so make sure the information is up-to-date and relevant.

Obtaining further information about people through team role questionnaires, psychometric tests and observation can help to ensure the right balance of people is recruited into our team.

Once we have completed the audit, we can then ensure that our team is structured to provide the best results. Technical competence is essential, and easier to identify and achieve.

Team structural design should include the following:

- a functional role based on technical knowledge and skills
- a team role based on behaviour, the way in which one team member interacts with others in facilitating progress
- balance across the team in both functional and team roles, and mental ability (ideal blend depends on goals/tasks).

Functional roles

We need to ensure that our team has the experience and technical skills required. We have discussed marketing functional roles, but as a reminder they are listed here:

- new product development manager
- business development manager
- marketing research manager
- advertising and promotions manager
- sales manager
- regional sales manager
- category manager
- customer relationship manager.

At executive and administrative levels there are similar sorts of job titles; they are the next levels down from manager, concerned with doing rather than managing. In large organizations, functions can be broken down even further – for example, there may be a consumer research manager and a business-to-business research manager. Teams may be made up as management teams and executive teams, etc., and also members from these teams can make up other teams across organization levels.

In small organizations one or two people are responsible for all these jobs, and the tasks will be simple and uncomplicated.

Examples of marketing teams include:

1. A sales team. This can consist of one or a mix of the following:
   - field sales people
   - sales engineers
   - sales technicians
   - office sales staff
   - export salesforce.
2. A marketing research team. This can consist of one or a mix of the following:
   - market analysts
   - market researchers
   - interviewers.

3. A product management team. This can consist of one or a mix of the following:

- research and development engineers
- design engineers
- packaging and design specialists.

Team roles

In building our team, it is not just functional and technical skills we need; we also need skills that reflect particular behaviour suited to different purposes. Some of those skills were identified when we discussed leadership and emotional intelligence.

Studies on teams carried out by Belbin (1981) resulted in the identification of a number of team roles that had specific attributes. Table 6.1 summarizes these team roles.

Table 6.1 Belbin team roles

Role type	Typical traits	Value to team	Limitations
Implementer (organizer) (IMP)	Conservative, dutiful, predictable	Organizing skills, practical, hard-working, self-disciplined	Lacks flexibility, unresponsive to unproven ideas
Co-ordinator (CO)	Calm, self-confident, controlled Responsive to contributions, focused on objectives, open-minded	Unassertive	
Shaper (SH)	Highly strung, dynamic, outgoing	Drive, challenges (inertia, ineffectiveness, complacency)	Easily provoked, irritated, impatient
Plant (PL)	Individualistic, serious-minded, intellect, unorthodox	Genius, imagination, intellect, knowledge	Up in the clouds, inclined to disregard practical details or protocol
Resource investigator (RI)	Extrovert, enthusiastic, curious, communicative	Networking, exploring new ideas, responsive to challenges	Can lose interest quickly
Monitor evaluator (ME)	Sober, unemotional, prudent	Judgement, discretion, hard-headed	Lacks inspiration or ability to motivate others
Team worker (TW)	Sociable, mild, sensitive	Responsive to people and situations, promotes team spirit	Indecisive in crisis
Completer finisher (CF)	Diligent, orderly, conscientious, anxious	Capacity for follow-through, perfectionist	Reluctance to let go, absorbed in minutiae
Specialist (SP)	Single-minded, insular	Technical expertise, skills	Lack of interest in others

Case study

Team diversity

Teams come in all shapes and sizes, and with very different purposes. Some teams are analytical in nature – for example, marketing research teams – and some are highly creative. Some are formed for the long term, and team members never change until or unless they leave the organization, while others change after the completion of every task.

Production companies provide an example of teams that change membership regularly.

Film production

Hollywood has seen a shift from permanent production teams to short-term project teams following changes from large bureaucratic production studios to small production companies. The project production teams have become very skilled at moving from forming to performing very quickly, as they pull together all the people need to produce a film. Belbin's team-role techniques have been particularly useful in helping teams to improve their performance under demanding conditions and tight deadlines. This has helped team members better to understand their role in the team, how they contribute, and the process they are going through.

Project production teams experience problems not typical of many other teams, having a large number of highly creative talented perfectionists. Emotions often run high, and these people need managing sensitively and with tact.

Theatre production

Theatre productions are different in that there are members of the team that remain the same. A theatre may have the same floor manager, stage designers, lighting engineers and even directors and producers for different productions. They may even have the same actors, year in year out, or these may change for every production.

The Royal Shakespeare Company (RSC) is well known for its performances, and the expectations of audiences are high. The RSC was concerned about how well all participants in the production of a play felt they were part of a team. This concern extended to actors who would have periods with the company alternating with periods touring with the company, or even performing at other theatres across the country.

Actors in particular, often following demanding schedules, felt isolated. Following a survey, the management team made some changes to the way people were managed and improved communications with all members of the production team, whether they were permanent or part-time members. Regularly sharing information about the RSC and team members helped to provide a sense of inclusion and being part of the RSC team. Making efforts to encourage personal development and change or adapt work practices to improve working conditions all led to staff feeling part of a team.

(Sources: Various web and print)

An evaluation of your particular team role can establish your primary team role, your strongest team skills, and your secondary team role. Some people have equal strength in two roles, or a balance across as many as four. As with any evaluation, the results are only a guide; however, they are useful for assessing team strengths and weaknesses, and why teams might be good at some things and not at others. It is not suggested that every team has to have nine members, one for each role, especially as few of us will score very highly in one role and not at all in another. Typically, we will use more than one team skill – particularly if a team role is missing.

Belbin identified that different tasks required different team formations. This is particularly useful for marketing managers. If we want to generate innovative ideas for a new product, we will not get very far if we have a team of monitor evaluators. Conversely, if we want to streamline order processing, we are unlikely to achieve our objective with a team of plants. Belbin's team roles do not provide the only example of how teams can be defined, but this system is one of the most well known.

Teams utilize their range of skills better if team members are encouraged to recognize the value of each others' strengths and compensate for each others' weaknesses.

Team size

Team size depends on the work to be done, but usually, the larger the team the greater the problems. Large teams of, say, 10 to 16 members may work if each member has a clearly defined office or role.

Larger teams typically experience problems caused by lack of:

- communication
- involvement
- coordination
- control.

Smaller teams also have their problems, including:

- lack of ability (technical and team role skills)
- they often become leaderless
- they can be unstable in moments of crisis (there are not enough people to share the load)
- absence making meetings redundant
- relationships being too personal, so emotions are involved more.

Under favourable conditions, a good size for a team is around five to six members. This can provide for a broad enough range of skills, allocate specific tasks and roles, and provide the opportunity to participate in group discussions.

Other writers on teams have used different terminology, but describe essentially the same stages. Mike Woodstock (1989) uses the following terminology:

- Stage 1 – the undeveloped team
- Stage 2 – the experimenting team
- Stage 3 – the consolidating team
- Stage 4 – the mature team.

Having established our team, we now need to manage the stages of team development.

Interpersonal skills and team development

Now we have a team, we can get on with the task. Or can we? It is an added benefit if team members are compatible and can get on, but this is not necessarily going to happen, for a variety of reasons. Personalities that cannot get on, different communication styles and different outlooks can all result in team dynamics that are less than harmonious. There is also the added impact of what happens to teams as they develop.

Research conducted by Tuckman (1965) suggests that teams go through four stages in team development, and explains what typically happens during these stages (see Figure 6.11).

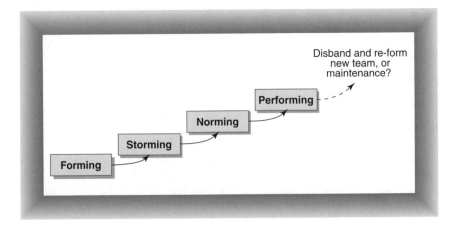

Figure 6.11
Stages in team development (adapted from Tuckman, 1965)

We will first discuss briefly what happens at each stage, and then go on to discuss in more detail key issues and how each stage can be managed.

1. *Forming.* This stage is characterized by uncertainty and the unknown; new team members wonder where they are going. They are mentally summing each other up, deciding who they like, admire or respect, and who they might have trouble getting on with. They are making decisions about whether the situation requires them to withdraw physically

and/or psychologically if they feel threatened. The doubts and insecurities result in confusion.

2. *Storming*. At this stage, people begin to assert themselves, express their opinions and views. The likelihood is there will be a polarization of views as expressions of individuality emerge. This is the most likely stage for conflict, as members test each other to determine who will make appropriate partners when and if psychological games start. If people are intent on 'playing games', the group will experience a lot of storming and have difficulty moving on to the next stage.

3. *Norming*. By this stage, team members are recognizing each others' strengths and weaknesses and roles are becoming clearer. Members are ready to sort out relationships with the leader and each other. It is now possible to establish some harmony, and cohesiveness begins to develop. Standards start to evolve.

4. *Performing*. Members can now relax and settle down to the task – the reason the team was formed. Team members now focus on the job and their personal contribution. Each team member recognizes and acknowledges the strengths of others, and is no longer intimidated by his or her own personal weaknesses. Members are now communicating effectively, are prepared to listen to each other and are willing to share views and opinions.

As you can see, knowing the likely stages teams go through can be very useful, but only if we give some thought to how we are going to manage these stages.

Managing teams – so what do we do?

Ideally, there should be a stage after auditing and recruiting and before forming.

Briefing and pre-forming

We want to reduce the time spent in each of the first two stages and move on to being a productive and effective team as quickly as possible. Our objective is to persuade team members of the value each brings to the team. Details of the team can be sent to new team members, highlighting the strengths each brings to the team and the technical skills they have. We should use this opportunity to clarify functional roles. The briefing should be positive in tone and style.

Managing the forming stage

Now you have to manage the forming stage. This stage needs to be short and focused.

A social aspect to this stage is useful, but it must be realistic. For example, suggestions such as going away for a weekend break together are not always realistic, quite apart from people not wanting to spend a weekend with others they do not yet know. The reality is that very few organizations would do this, and even fewer could afford to. Socializing can range from something as simple as having an informal lunch together in the canteen, to something more formal, such as a dinner. Whatever the social event, in most circumstances the less formal it is, the better. Think about the people involved, the purpose of the team, and plan something appropriate. Do not lose sight of the objective; this is about people having the opportunity to get to know each other. They cannot do that with their heads stuck down a pothole feeling sick with claustrophobia.

Activities during this forming stage should also be relevant to the reason for the team's formation and task. Team members could introduce themselves or each other; it could be light hearted. They could do a brief presentation on the team's proposed work.

Managing the storming stage
This is another stage that is best kept short, but this will very much depend on your skills as a manager and the personalities involved.

While we do not want people 'storming' for long, it is important to bring conflicts out into the open and deal with them. Use this opportunity to demonstrate that the team norm of open communications is expected.

Focus on positive aspects of what each individual brings to the team, and convert threats into opportunities. If and when appropriate, use humour to reduce tension.

Managing the norming stage
During this stage, we want to encourage team members to start using their skills, so tasks should encourage them to use problem-solving skills, decision-making skills, creativity and innovation, etc. Brainstorming activities will be particularly useful at this stage. Present team members with a marketing problem and encourage them to solve it creatively. Do not allow them to slip back into storming; ensure that they recognize the value of each other's contributions.

Managing the performing stage
Good communications skills are important for you as a manager and for your staff, and they are certainly helpful for managing team interpersonal skills.

For the manager, good personal communications are essential to effective management of people, whether we are briefing, debriefing, instructing, appraising and giving feedback or even just having a casual conversation. As marketing managers, we have to be examples of effective communications practice. For the team, part of customer service and the customers' experience is communications, and if customer service is one of the few ways left in which an organization can differentiate itself, managers and staff have to have good communication skills. These can be learned – and what a difference this can make to the customer, in the workplace and in our personal lives.

It is not the intention to cover good interpersonal communications skills in detail in this book, but the following is a brief reminder of the factors that improve personal communications with individuals and teams, which can lead to improved communications with external customers and stakeholders.

Team communication skills: listening

Sometimes people deliberately avoid listening, but mostly it is unintentional. There are two types of listening – real and simulated – and a lot of simulated listening is disguised as the real thing.

Reasons for not listening include:

- thinking you have something better to say yourself
- already having the answer to what you know is the problem
- the speaker giving you no motivation or reason to listen
- previous experience means you know that the message will be too complicated or simple.

Take care when trying to interpret signals – for example, sometimes people gaze or doodle because they are concentrating and listening.

Blocks to listening

Many of us use blocks to listening, both intentionally and unintentionally. The following are some of the examples of listening blocks:

- *Advising* – continually jumping in with well-meaning advice to solve problems. Advising requires a continuous search for information to be able to provide the next piece of advice. Searching makes it difficult to listen.
- *Being right* – some people cannot accept a different view and will not listen. They will alter facts to support their case, and if all else fails may become aggressive.
- *Judging* – prejudging people enables the listener to label people as, for example, stupid, and therefore negates the necessity to listen to what they have to say.

This can be typical behaviour in teams, and blocks prevent people from listening. We all use different blocks at different times and for different reasons.

In situations with customers, internal or external, our lack of listening can sometimes be the result of something that has nothing to do with the customer. An argument with a colleague can result in a preoccupation with this recent event, and can result in failing to listen to customers.

Developing active listening skills

Some of the best customer feedback we get is informal and face-to-face; therefore, developing good listening skills is essential. Being a good listener requires effort and skill, and more than just sitting quietly. As listeners, we also have responsibilities in the communication process. We need to participate fully to ensure effective communications. This requires us to take part in an exchange; we ask questions for clarity and we comment. This exchange results in a more comprehensive understanding of messages.

Techniques for improving your listening skills include:

- *Paraphrasing* – use your own words to summarize; for example, 'So the result was . . .'. Paraphrasing demonstrates that you are listening, and avoids misunderstandings.

- *Clarifying* – check out what is being said by questioning, ascertaining facts, etc., this keeps you focused.

- *Feedback* – an opportunity to express your views and reactions in a positive way. That does not mean you have to agree with everything that has been said.

- *Openness* – show that you can listen and take part in a conversation that expresses views different to your own.

- *Empathy* – you cannot always understand the feelings, emotions or experiences of others, but empathy requires that you do not make judgements or offer advice.

- *Awareness* – be alert to all the messages you are receiving. Are they consistent, or are you receiving mixed messages?

Good listening skills are also essential in problem-solving and in creativity and innovation.

Team communication skills: non-verbal signals (body language)

We communicate the intended and the unintended, and some people are better at hiding the unintended than others. As well as verbal messages we use non-verbal communications – for example, disbelief in something someone is saying may be clear in our facial expressions, and distrust may exhibit itself in the way we stand or even how closely we stand to someone.

The most believable aspects of messages break down as shown in Figure 6.12.

As well as thinking about what we are saying, we should be aware of our non-verbal habits. However, do take care. Too much attention to non-verbal messages can be our undoing. A few years ago it was very fashionable in organizations to understand non-verbal signals, and much time and effort was put into training people to understand the subtlety of body language. It was taken to extremes by some, and resulted in the wrong messages being picked up – for example, if a person scratched her nose simply because she had an itch, this was wrongly interpreted as doubt.

Salespeople were often the victims of the body language 'fashion' – for example, being told that once people had uncrossed their legs and arms

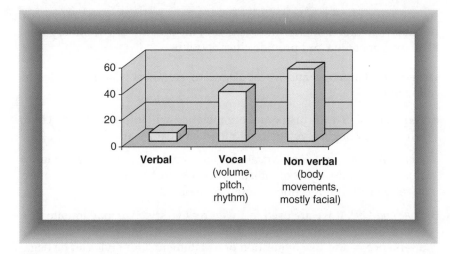

Figure 6.12
Breakdown of
messages

they were ready to deal (amongst other non-verbal signals). Unfortunately, this was not always the case. Experienced and expert salespeople are usually way ahead of the latest theories on the psychology of body language, as they are intuitively dealing with it every day.

Never underestimate our natural and unconscious ability to interpret non-verbal messages. We have being doing it since we were children; we just want to do it better. We should also be aware of cultural differences, as different cultures exhibit different non-verbal messages.

Team communication skills: verbal communications

We get what we want through communicating with others. If asked, most of us confidently believe that we are reasonable and straightforward when communicating. Surely, then, there should be no misunderstandings? Few of us believe we are not making sense when we communicate. This self-image, the way we see ourselves, may be different from the way other people see us.

It is our responsibility as communicators to ensure that we use the appropriate language, tone, etc., so that our messages are received and understood.

We use verbal messages for a number of purposes:

● to convey information

● to establish and maintain relationships

● to influence others

● to question and clarify.

We use a range of verbal techniques (intentional and unintentional) to convey our messages. Our accent, the volume at which we speak, our tone, the structure of sentences, the frequency with which we repeat ourselves, our ability to link thoughts and ideas, and the breadth of vocabulary used all convey meaning and provide clues about us.

Aspects of language and vocabulary are significant, and include the following:

1. *Plain English*. The industry and organization will influence the extent to which plain English versus convoluted language is used.

2. *Jargon and slang*. Business vocabulary is acceptable; it is the language of a particular industry or organization. Some jargon is legitimate business vocabulary, but if it is not it should be avoided.

3. *Style and tone*. If we are used to an aggressive style we may imitate this, not realizing how it comes across to others. Tone and rhythm can make a sentence sound like a question or a statement. Our style can be negative or positive, and be reflected in our behaviour:

   ● aggressive – forcing a particular belief, opinion or point of view without consideration of others

   ● non-assertive – allowing yourself to be swayed, even bullied by others to comply

   ● assertive – standing by your opinions and views, holding firm on a particular position *but* being willing to hear and consider other views/perspectives.

The organization's style of language and vocabulary will typically be reflected in communications with customers and other stakeholders.

Process and task

Finally, how do we make sure tasks are performed effectively? If we have taken care over the structure and design of our team, and practice effective interpersonal skills, managing the task should be the easiest part. Managing the task requires a simple process:

1. Set objectives – our starting point is to establish clear objectives for the team.

2. Plan – plan who does what, where, when and how.

3. Standards – communicate expected standards, such as quality and quantity.

4. Control – control budgets, timescales, and how performance and success will be measured.

You may want to add methods of communicating, learning and knowledge management, and other issues that are specific to your job, organization and industry.

Objectives communicate your expectations of what exactly is required. There is the overall team objective for the activity or assignment that must be completed within a particular timescale. There will also be personal targets for each team member and the expected contribution by them to the team objective.

Planning requires a uniform approach unless there is a valid reason otherwise. It makes it easier to exchange information and ideas, and to monitor and compare performance. A planning process provides a framework for developing plans – the start and finish points – and identifies the stages involved.

Standards and levels of expectation must be communicated. This avoids the risk of misinterpretation, confusion or conflict over quality of performance. For marketing teams, standards often involve levels of service to customers or other stakeholders, so consistency of standards of performance is essential. This is where the greatest potential for conflict might arise, among team members who may have different views of standards – some too low and some too high. Standards are set from the customers' perspective – what they expect and are willing to pay for.

Control has three key functions:

1. Identifying and monitoring the budget.

2. Developing and monitoring the schedule of activities.

3. Monitoring and measuring task and team performance.

Ideally, the team should share responsibility for control with other team members and their manager, rather than it being imposed by management. Reviewing team performance and relationships should be part of performance measurement, and the team should be encouraged to identify team improvement goals going forward.

International teams

Team-building can become more complex when moving across borders, particularly if the culture is not understood. The same rules for building effective teams can apply, but extra consideration should be given to the following:

- *National cultural influences.* National cultures were discussed in Chapter 3, and Hofstede's dimensions inevitably affect team behaviour and relationships. An understanding of the culture will help to determine whether team-working is a strong cultural norm, or whether extra communications and training will be needed to encourage team-working and harmonize team relationships.

- *Motivation.* Work varies across cultures, and therefore managers need to identify cultural influences on motivation and adapt motivation practices as appropriate. For example, in Hofstede's low individuality dimension, team-work is a cultural norm and moving people between teams to increase personal growth and development will not necessarily be a motivator and could even demotivate.

- *Functional and team roles.* In some cultures different functions are valued equally, but in others a different emphasis may be placed on the value of technical expertise. We also cannot assume that team roles, for example Belbin's, work in quite the same way. If valuing someone's contribution is based on hierarchy, other attributes may be seen as subordinate.

There is also the challenge of making sure that overseas teams feel a valued part of the parent company. One such company that has put in place a deliberate strategy to ensure that effective teams are created in overseas markets, and that these teams feel as though they belong to the organization, is B&Q.

Case study
Managing in international markets

China has for some time been the gold-rush destination of organizations wanting to expand their overseas presence. The opportunities in this big emerging market (BEM) are unquestioned, but the demands of managing an operation in China are not always properly thought through.

In reality there will inevitably be a lot of learning on the job, but there are things managers can do to minimize problems.

B&Q has been in China since 1999, and by 2003 they had eight stores, growing to 58 by 2005. B&Q's approach to setting up operations was planned to maximize performance and acceptance in the market and minimize problems. The company did this by:

- using roving mentors. B&Q kept expatriate involvement to a minimum, with a very clear brief: transfer knowledge and skills to local employees, and then move on.

- networking and career progression. Expats were in regular contact with HQ, supporting the sharing and exchanging of information, and career plans were in place for the returning expats.

- recruiting and retaining employees. This required adapting processes to reflect local expectations and behaviour, and educating local employees of the expectations when applying for jobs. To attract the best, B&Q provides personal development opportunities.

- employee exchanges. Chinese employees visited the UK to learn more about the organization. This had the added advantage of learning about B&Q's culture and practices, providing a better understanding of why things are done in a particular way.

(Sources: Various web and print)

Summary

Effective leadership can be learned. There are innate characteristics and traits that can mean an individual has leadership potential, but many skills can be developed to improve leadership. Marketing leaders in particular are responsible for coordinating value creation across the organization to maximize advantage.

Marketers must influence change to protect customer or stakeholder value, and be able to manage change to produce positive outcomes for the organization and its stakeholders. A process for change ensures that credible outcomes are identified, and explanations and justification are communicated. Communications are essential throughout the process of change, for educating, informing and persuading people of the benefits of change and for recognizing individual and team contributions and success. Learning is part of change, and being prepared to modify and adapt as we learn is part of the change process.

Effective teams are the outcome of a deliberate design and plan to create and maintain teams. Managers or team leaders are responsible for team performance, and their skill in identifying team members and creating a team environment that utilizes strengths, harmonizes relationships and focuses on outcomes produces high-performing teams.

The next challenge for leaders and managers is how to solve problems, and this is the subject of Chapter 7.

References

Adair, J. (1983). *Effective Leadership*. London: Pan.
Belbin, M. (1981). *Management Teams, Why They Succeed or Fail*. Oxford: Heinemann.
Carroll, A. (1991). *Toward the Moral Management of Organizational Stakeholders*. Oxford: Elsevier.
Goleman, D. (1998). *Working with Emotional Intelligence*. London: Bloomsbury.
Regan, G. (2000). *Great Military Blunders*. Osceola, WI: Motorbooks International.
Sheard, A.G. and Kakabadse, A.P. (2002). From loose groups to effective teams, the nine key factors of the team landscape, *Journal of Management Development*, **2**, 131–151.
Tannenbaum, R. and Schmidt, W.H. (1973). How to choose a leadership pattern. *Harvard Business Review*, **May/June**, 162–175, 178–180.
Tuckman, B.W. (1965). Development sequence in small groups. *Psychological Bulletin*.
Woodstock, M. (1989). *Team Development Manual*. Aldershot: Gower.

7 Problem-solving, creativity and decision-making

Introduction

We solve problems and make decisions every day; sometimes they are solved easily and quickly (for example, small routine problems), and sometimes solving them takes time, resources and considerable effort. The outcome of problem-solving, creativity and decision-making should be a solution or improvement of some sort. Ideally, this process is also an opportunity to learn.

Problem-solving requires both a methodical approach to ensure problems are solved efficiently, and creativity to ensure they are solved effectively. Problem-solving and creativity lead to decision-making – evaluating alternative solutions and deciding which solution best solves the problem. These three distinct activities require distinct and different skills and processes, but should be linked together. A problem is not solved unless a decision is made, and problem-solving and decision-making must be creative if they are to provide potential sources of competitive advantage and differentiation.

A systematic problem-solving, creativity and decision-making process is illustrated in Figure 7.1.

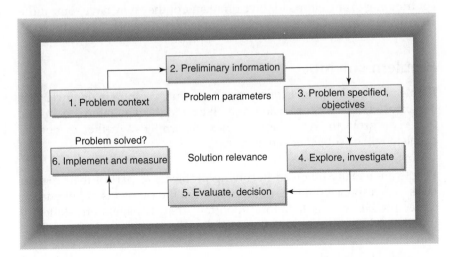

Figure 7.1
Creative problem-solving and decision-making (©2004 Juanita Cockton)

The benefits of a systematic and methodical approach to problem-solving include:

- encouraging information gathering, and ensuring that problem-solving is informed

- encouraging discussion and agreement on problem definition before the problem-solving begins

- encouraging creativity, and exploring and generating alternatives that might provide sources of advantage

- the use of objective techniques to evaluate alternatives.

A systematic process encourages a more productive and objective approach to solving problems. It is the point of reference by which we can establish progress and check the validity of our problem-solving activity; have we considered everything we should, and are the alternative solutions realistic?

The factors to take into consideration when solving problems and making decisions are:

- the person/people who have the problem

- constraints (internal and external, such as resources, government restrictions)

- controllable variables (quantitative and qualitative, for example production capacity)

- uncontrollable variables (PEST factors, competition)

- possible outcomes.

People in particular must be considered. They may be supporting and contributing to any efforts to solve problems, or they may have some influence over resources, or impact on the implementation of any solutions.

Problem-solving

Problems arise for all sorts of reasons. Customers complain, inefficiencies are exposed, mistakes are made, and all lead to the inevitable conclusion: there is a problem. What happens next determines whether or not the problem will be solved effectively.

People are usually involved in solving problems as part of their regular tasks and responsibilities, and for marketers the problems are often customer problems. It is therefore important that managers are skilled at problem-solving and ensure they develop the problem-solving skills of their staff.

Problem-solving dilemmas

In our busy lives, we too often feel we do not have time to solve problems. It is a fallacy to think that a problem ignored will go away: it will bite you sooner or later. Time is not saved by not solving a problem; instead the time is used poorly and inefficiently, often resulting in more time being wasted – i.e. constant fire-fighting.

While the purpose of some organizations is actually fire-fighting (metaphorically speaking) and crisis management, for most it is not. It is not suggested that organizations will never experience fire-fighting; this is not realistic. Even the best organizations can be faced with the unexpected, the unanticipated, and find themselves fire-fighting. What does not have to be a reality is fire-fighting as an organization norm. This leads to increasing inefficiency and ineffectiveness. It also leads to stress, demoralized staff and lost customers.

There can be the problem of not seeing a problem, or not seeing the right problem. People can be so wrapped up in the minutiae and volume of their daily internal activities that they may not see or understand problems from the customers' or even each others' perspective.

There are arguments for adopting a systematic approach to problem-solving – mainly improved objectivity. There are also arguments for adopting a creative approach to problem-solving to improve the organization's ability to innovate and thereby differentiate.

Problems can be the result of:

- planning systems
- processes (operating systems)
- people
- control
- communications.

A lack of a systematic process for problem-solving can result in other problems, particularly those caused by human behaviour. Marketers typically love diversity in their work, so solving a problem initially is exciting and holds the attention; however, it may not hold their attention long enough to actually solve it. Our discussion on team-building can help show how to avoid this problem.

People get distracted, other urgent priorities push out the urgency of solving the problem – which is often seen as an extra workload, and so gets pushed down the priorities list. A lack of good problem-solving skills and process also creates problems – for example, lack of observation, and lack of investigating or communicating. The problem in these circumstances never gets solved, reinforcing the view that 'the problem can't be solved, so let's not waste time'.

Step 1: Describe the problem in context

It is important to establish what the problem *really* is. The danger is that people do not identify the problem, and only see its symptoms.

Everyone's view of what the problem is may not necessarily be the same. Someone from outside the department or organization may see the problem differently from someone on the inside. A boss may see the problem differently from a subordinate. If the problem reflects badly on someone, a friend may be inclined to minimize the problem.

The problem context is the workplace and/or market, and comprises both internal and external factors. Internal factors include:

- departments and the physical working environment
- the people involved, directly and indirectly
- operating systems and processes
- materials and locations.

External factors include:

- economic/market conditions
- competitive behaviour
- channels, partners' influence
- customer/stakeholder behaviour.

Another valuable outcome of describing the problem in context is that we now know what skills and people are required to solve the problem. The final action of Step 1 is forming the problem-solving team, which was covered in Chapter 6.

Step 2: Collect preliminary information

This step is a fact-finding mission. Sort out facts from opinions, excuses, etc. Through establishing the what, where, when, how, who and why, a picture should begin to emerge of potential causes of the problem. Information can be gathered from:

- records, reports, appraisals, etc.
- surveys, customer/stakeholder feedback, etc.

During this stage, talking the problem through with people involved can sometimes be enough to resolve the problem. If this is not the case, continue to Step 3.

Step 3: Problem specified; set objectives, timescale and budget

Is the problem as originally described, or different? Enough information should now be gathered to describe the problem in detail and with clarity. Symptoms will have been separated from causes. With this clarity, it is now possible to set objectives and establish the desired outcomes.

If the objective is to identify a new product or service opportunity, or to increase demand or reduce time to do something, it is usually easy to define. For example:

> Develop a new product to meet an identified need (specified according to research on customers) within 6 months.

> Find a way to reduce the paperwork by 20 percent and time by 30 percent for order processing within 2 months.

However, if the objective is solving a complex problem or change, it can sometimes be difficult to define until after analysis – in which case state an aim or goal. For example:

> Improve the way services are delivered to customers to improve satisfaction and loyalty within 12 months.

Defining and quantifying the aim can act as a constraint early on in the process, so is not always appropriate. It should be possible to define and quantify as you move through the process. For example, we could add detail to the above objective:

> Improve employee knowledge of service products to 100 percent within 4 months.

> Improve employee interpersonal skills by 20 percent, from 70 percent to 90 percent, within 6 months.

Any problems expanding beyond your own personal authority will require approval from those who it affects and those who are involved. The formality of this approval will depend on your particularly circumstances.

Some problem-solving benefits from setting organization boundaries, usually when the problem directly or indirectly affects a number of areas of the organization and can become indeterminate. Apart from the issue of authority, there are time and other resource constraints, and we need to contain the problem-solving activity. This may require identifying essential and immediate issues from non-essential or non-immediate issues, and prioritizing what must be dealt with over issues that can either be dealt with at a later date or delegated as peripheral activities. It may require separating responsibility for those aspects of the problem that are not directly within your control, and informing those who are responsible that these aspects will not be part of your problem-solving. If the problem is infiltrating different areas, it may be necessary for a number of function- or activity-specific problem-solving teams to be set up, with a senior manager coordinating the different team projects.

A realistic timescale will be part of the objective-setting activity, balancing how urgent the problem is against the time needed to solve it. One way of persuading people that it is worth investing time is to understand the consequences of not providing the time. Rather than asking the question 'Have I got the time to solve this problem?', ask 'What are the consequences of not solving this problem?' A document providing examples can act as a reminder of consequences and explain that if the problem is not solved or is not solved properly it will lead to other problems (specify) and more time needed to do the job (specify), and probably cost more (specify). These factors can be quantified, which usually gets people's attention. Other factors such as demoralized and stressed staff, dissatisfied and lost customers might be more difficult, although not impossible, to quantify.

Timescales are essential for two reasons:

1. To ensure that people are working to a deadline. Problem-solving can become a way of life if there is no deadline. Critical issues are not addressed, and there is a lack of responsiveness to changing external conditions.

2. To ensure that the problem is solved before it either creates more problems or results in some catastrophe because it was not solved soon enough – for example, solving a production-line problem before the launch of a new product.

Finally, agree a budget. At Step 3 there is a much better understanding of what the problem is and therefore what is required to solve it. This also helps in explaining and justifying the need for resources. As already mentioned, people tend to focus on what it will cost to solve the problem rather than what it will cost if the problem is not solved. Both must be considered. Organizations always have constraints on resources, and resources for problem-solving will compete with other priorities.

Step 4: Exploration, investigation and creativity

At Step 4 we move into solving the problem, and there are tools and techniques that need to be identified for the task. These include marketing research, simulation tests or experimentation techniques.

People need to have the authority to challenge the *status quo* and the freedom to explore the less obvious or relevant. This freedom is essential to creativity. If we define our exploration and investigation by what we know and are familiar with, it constrains creativity and thinking differently.

Creative problem-solving

Creative problem-solving has two opposing requirements; the need for method and order, and the need to break free from method and order. The manager must know when it is time to be outrageous, to deviate, challenge and explore, etc., and when it is time to be rational, methodical, objective and practical. During the early stage of our analysis, Steps 1–3, there will be some formal and semi-formal process and techniques to help clarify the current situation. The process becomes informal during Step 4, and in the later stages it reverts to being formal and requires structure, a process and procedures.

The goal of creativity and innovation is people creating things people want and need, and solving problems and finding solutions. Creativity and innovation require a certain attitude and way of thinking, as well as natural and learned skills and competences.

Creativity dilemmas include:

- *attitudes* – values and beliefs held by individuals (personality) and organizations (culture)
- *behaviour* – rigid adherence to habits, stereotyping, emotions (fear, anxiety)
- *skills* – lack of education, training and experiences
- *communications* – inappropriate style, process and media
- *environment* – poor structures, equipment, facilities
- *systems* – lack of process or techniques.

Problem-solving usually requires creativity if it is to lead to innovation and provide any source of advantage. Creativity is about going one (or more) step further, asking 'what if?' and pushing the boundaries. This informal, unstructured and flexible stage is the time to think the unthinkable and challenge current practices. Informality is required during idea generation, and people need to be unrestrained by whether or not something will work or is a good idea, and left to explore, experiment and break free of parameters.

Therefore, creativity requires a cultural norm of openness and no blame, and opportunities to experiment and try out new ideas. Over-supervision and control act as barriers to creativity. Brainstorming and thinking laterally, 'outside the box', tends not to be part of everyday life for most people, and requires the manager to create the right environment.

Stimulating information

Information comes from the analysis, the information that sets the context, informs and guides our thinking, and allows us to check progress against our objectives and plan. We also need information to stimulate thinking. Sometimes it is factual, specific and related information, but for creativity it can also be completely unrelated, non-specific, and fiction or fantasy. For example, a good sci-fi book can stimulate very different thinking, as can fairytales, jokes and bizarre behaviour atypical (or typical) of the human race.

Some people may struggle with fiction or fantasy, and be uncomfortable about moving away from tried and trusted information. This is exactly what you want, but manage this process with sensitivity. Make sure that people are not feeling threatened or so uncomfortable that they withdraw. Sometimes it may mean slowing down while people adjust to unfamiliar territory, but the rewards in new ideas could be worth it.

Creative space

Managers are getting better at setting the scene for creativity. In the past, and still today, there is the bizarre notion that creativity can be put on the 'to do list' and people will immediately slip into creativity mode and produce the most amazing ideas. In reality this is unlikely to happen, and most managers need to create an environment that will enable people to think differently, or at all. Creativity needs space:

- *physical space* – somewhere to play, literally; a room or area that is relaxing and has an atmosphere conducive to creativity. This may be different for different people, and will most likely be different from other physical space in the organization. Thought given to providing appropriate surroundings makes a difference

- *mental space* – this is time and permission to think, play and experiment. Being silly is not encouraged in the workplace, and for some very good reasons – health and safety among them. However, ideas come from allowing the mind to wander, and sometimes having fun leads to ideas

- *time* – allow time for creativity. Trying to fit it around everyday work routines is rarely going to achieve a leap of imagination or a result, and it suggests that you are not taking creativity and innovation seriously.

It is not suggested that everyday work routines are sterile of ideas; they are not. People have ideas at the most unexpected moments and at any time. Discussions in routine meetings, sitting in front of the computer or a mundane conversation during a coffee break are moments when an idea can suddenly materialize. However, other immediate pressures are always vying for attention, so creative space can provide for creative ideas.

Case study
Creative solutions

Encouraging creativity in an organization often requires creative solutions – being brave enough to do things differently. Some organizations have recognized this, and with impressive results.

The leadership of Cemex, a Mexican cement manufacturer, decided to take an active role in encouraging employees to be creative. The Vice President personally invites employees to submit ideas around a particular theme. This has the advantage of focusing people on specific areas without becoming too narrow and restraining creativity.

The invitation precedes 'innovation days', of which Cemex has nine a year. These invitations have led to up to 250 ideas being generated, some of which can be implemented with immediate results. This creative process has the advantages of:

- demonstrating senior management commitment
- being able to demonstrate successful results
- engaging employees.

An important factor in Cemex's approach is allowing time for innovation and demonstrating its value by dedicating a number of days to it.
(Sources: Various web and print)

Challenging the status quo

Creativity sometimes requires understanding the context in more subtle ways – the environment and its influences, interconnecting relationships and behaviours.

Analysis should provide a picture of how the situation is understood from different points of view. If something different is to emerge – something new, better, or just a solution – then the next task is to challenge. Without challenge, there is no stimulus for creativity. Challenging often requires thinking differently.

Thinking

Vertical thinking is traditional logical thinking, where you move from one informed state to the next and build the mental picture piece by piece. A characteristic of vertical thinking is continuity. The intention is to select and make the 'right' choices. It therefore searches for proof, and identifies links, connections and relationships to establish an understanding of what is being studied. It is analytical by nature.

A characteristic of lateral thinking is discontinuity. Its purpose is to generate and stimulate movement from one state to another, one concept to another, but not necessarily in an orderly and methodical way. The nature of lateral thinking is exploratory; can new forms be identified and, by restructuring, can a different interpretation emerge? Lateral thinking deliberately provokes and challenges assumptions and the *status quo*.

Lateral thinking enables us to be imaginative and creative; it frees thought from parameters that can act as constraints on thinking about problem-solving, and idea and solution generation.

It is the combination of these different ways of thinking that is most powerful. If we adopt one way of thinking and exclude others, we are in danger of rigidly following protocols without ever allowing a new thought or idea to emerge, and therefore being left behind. Alternatively, if we are only creative and never convert ideas into workable solutions through an efficient and effective process, we fail to solve problems.

Idea cultivation and creative techniques

Sometimes one obvious answer quickly becomes apparent, and it is tempting to go with the obvious – the justification being time saved. However, exploring more than one option encourages creativity that either allows a better solution to emerge or improves on the obvious solution. Remember, solving problems should always been seen as an opportunity to improve something or create some advantage.

Examples of techniques that can be used in the creative process include the following:

1. *Categorizing*. This is the process of identifying, linking and grouping various elements with similar characteristics. Categorizing allows us to classify elements into something that is familiar and recognizable by all people involved. This classification provides added meaning to the grouped elements. It may require us to define a category that has some new meaning in a new context. The process of categorizing by those involved helps us to come to some agreement and mutual understanding of what the category is.

2. *Mapping*. This allows us to make sense of the relationships and connections between concepts. There are three main types of maps:

   ● *perceptual maps*, which can be developed from statistical techniques to map various elements (which can be complex or simple depending on methods used). For example, a questionnaire to customers identifying what they value about a particular brand and prioritizing these values might result in a perceptual map as in Figure 7.2

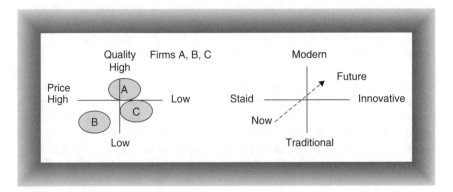

Figure 7.2
Perceptual maps

   ● *mind maps* (Figure 7.3), which are most useful for identifying key elements and their relationships. They encourage grouping of elements, and establish links and connections between elements

   ● *cognitive (cause) maps*, which result from a process of analysis and the inferences that can be made from that analysis, through trial and error and by searching for information or by asking for help. One or all of these activities can be used to arrive at a conclusion or some outcome. We learn as we go through a variety of methods, and the outcome will

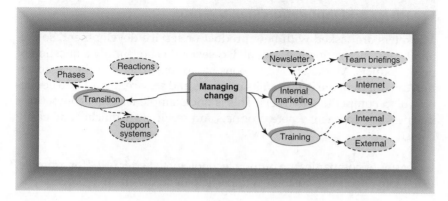

Figure 7.3
Mind map

be a better understanding of the system, problem or environment we are studying. We build a mental picture of the combined elements, our view of the world, problem or situation. There can be a difference between reality and perception – for example, the reality of how long it takes to get somewhere or do something can be different from our perception of how long it takes. Our cognitive map does not necessarily match the reality, but is nonetheless real to us.

3. *Visualizing and guided imagery* – visualizing a problem or thoughts and ideas encourages us to bring some structure to what we are doing. It can also help to bring some meaning. If we can convert our problems, thoughts and ideas into pictures, maps and models, etc., it can expand our means of expressing what we mean and communicating it to others. Those involved can then modify, refine and adapt the picture contributing their own thoughts and ideas. The process moves from the individual to the group. It can also provide descriptors to help others conjure up the same images to communicate our meaning – for example, 'if you were to use an animal to describe your organization, what animal would that be?' (tiger, pussy cat, elephant, mouse, etc.). We can also encourage people to draw images; their interpretation of an object, problem, situation, etc., and the drawing can be symbolic or illustrative. It can be very useful in getting people to think outside the realm of the known, the organization and its environment, and into the unknown, using your imagination to think up unlikely scenarios. This can change and/or enhance thinking.

4. *Focus groups* are usually research interviews with a group of participants who discuss the topic under the direction of a moderator. The role of this moderator is to facilitate the discussion between the participants, to make sure all are involved and that the discussion remains focused on the topic. It can reveal underlying beliefs, values and attitudes regarding different situations, objects and events.

5. *Role play* can be useful in imitating typical organizational behaviour. People given a particular task and situation to role play may unwittingly display the behaviours and symptoms of their real environment. In doing so, they are presented with the opportunity to acknowledge and explore the behaviour exhibited, and to search for meanings and solutions.

Creativity and innovation in marketing

Marketers are tasked with new product or service development, so creativity and innovation is essential. However, it is not simply a question of new products. Marketers are responsible for ensuring that the organization can differentiate itself and its products and services in order to be successful in competitive markets. This is not a simple task in a competitive business environment where products and services are quickly and easily copied.

Increasingly, companies are putting technology to better use – for example, using it to encourage customers to participate in the creative process.

Inviting customers into the creative process

BMW designed an online toolkit that facilitated the involvement of their customers in the innovation process. Customers were delighted to be invited to engage in the creative process, and some visited engineers for direct input into new product and service ideas. This creative process has the advantage of engaging customers and acquiring successful ideas at little cost.

(Sources: Various web and print)

Differentiating the organization is often only possible at the customer service level, and yet this seems to be an increasingly weak area. For example, voice-activated answering systems, from the *customers'* perspective, are poorly designed, hopelessly ineffectual, frustrating, and have nothing whatsoever to do with customer service but everything to do with internal convenience and cost reduction.

Marketers have the rather sensitive and difficult responsibility of ensuring that any internal cost efficiencies not only do not have a negative impact on customers, but also should be seen as an opportunity to identify what value might be added from the customers' perspective. Now there's a revolutionary idea!

When we have identified alternative solutions to problems, it is time to make decisions. The process of problem-solving may have led to a single, obvious and irrefutable answer. However, in most cases we arrive at alternative courses of action and we have to decide between them.

Step 5: Evaluation and decision-making

Decision-making

We now move into a formal and structured stage if ideas are to be translated into problems solved, innovation and improvements. Good ideas need to work, so they must be evaluated for their feasibility and workability.

Generating alternative solutions to problems requires making choices on which course of action to take: we have to make a decision. One of the anxieties for managers making decisions is the fear of making the wrong decision. Decisions can be made using systematic processes that can reduce risk in decision-making. A critical factor in decision-making is intelligence; all decisions, where possible, should be informed, and this requires quality intelligence.

Factors involved in decision-making include:

- *Intelligence* – has all intelligence been provided to help make the decision?
- *Alternatives* – have all possible options been explored?
- *Evaluation* – have feasibility, suitability and acceptability to the organization been considered – the physical, human and financial implications?

If decision-making incorporates the above, working through the consequences of certain actions, managers can be reassured that they have been as objective as possible. It does not mean that their decision-making is infallible, but it does reduce risk and increase the chances of success.

What must be avoided is prevarication and delaying decisions until *all* intelligence has been gathered, *all* alternatives have been explored, etc. Decisions in business today have to be swift, and delaying decisions can be more damaging than waiting for the perfect time or answer.

Organizations make many decisions daily – hundreds or thousands for large organizations – but should not lose sight of what, essentially, decisions are about. Decisions and courses of actions are always susceptible to the unknown; we do the best we can with what we have. We can rarely identify perfect solutions or get it right all of the time; it is not realistic.

Decision-making in organizations

Organizations make long-term strategic, medium-term operational and short-term tactical decisions. Decisions are typically made vertically (Figure 7.4), and small decisions can be integral parts of larger decisions. Decisions will typically be broad in perspective at strategic levels, and at the operational and tactical levels become increasingly narrow and specific.

Effective decision-making will not just be a top-down process; it should also encourage bottom-up decision-making. People doing the job, meeting the customers, solving front-line problems have knowledge that will be valuable to the decision-making process. Top-down decisions will inform employees of strategic intentions. Bottom-up decisions will inform management of the detail of courses of action to achieve the strategic goals and incorporate customer and market intelligence.

Horizontal decisions, particularly those that can be part of other decisions, have broad implications for the organization – for example, if marketing

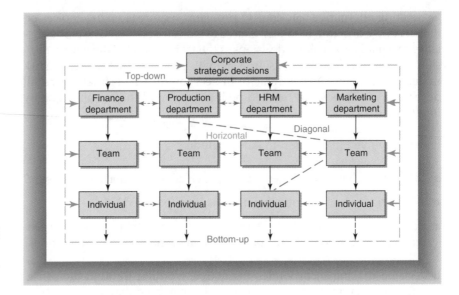

Figure 7.4
Vertical, horizontal and diagonal top-down and bottom-up decisions

decides to develop and launch a new range of products or a service. As a result of this decision, HR may need to recruit more people or train existing personnel, finance will need to make decisions on budgets, and operations will need to make decisions regarding the operational implications.

There are also diagonal decision-making processes, usually informal and used to overcome bottlenecks or obstacles to getting things done.

Will it work?

Experimentation and testing of ideas will have checked out the workability of an idea, and whether or not it provides the solution or solves the problem. When making decisions between alternatives a number of factors may need to be evaluated, including functional, technical and human criteria, and these can occur at a number of levels:

● *Strategic fit* – will it fit with corporate goals, image, reputation, position, impact on organization's culture, image, current product range, social and environmental responsibilities?

● *Operational fit* – will operations need to change or be modified, will it improve operations, utilization of resources, internal and external constraints, extent of risk and magnitude of reward, ability to adapt and change?

● *Tactical fit* – will processes and procedures need to change, will changes, modifications and solutions be required, and what will their impact be versus the benefits offered?

The impact of most problems or creative ideas does not tend to be so widespread, but sometimes is. Sometimes the impact is not obvious but can have serious repercussions. A common example is operations changing the way in which a product is made or a service is delivered in order to be more efficient, and this having a negative impact on the customer or stakeholder.

Decision-making dilemmas

Remember our discussion on power and politics? These factors also affect decision-making, and we must be realistic about the impact. For example, marketing research is often commissioned to help the organization to make the right decisions and is then ignored when it does not confirm what managers want to hear. Sometimes the marketing research design is contaminated to ensure that it confirms decisions already made.

These are the realities of working in organizations. However, the consequences usually catch up with people sooner or later. Our decision-making should provide us with a rigorous and methodical process that enables us to arrive at the best decision in the circumstances.

Decision-making is not always a rational process for various reasons – for example:

- lack of, poor or untimely information

- the time taken to make decisions, and the stages and people involved (too many or too few of both); the greater the time taken, the more frustrated people become and thus the more likely to 'do their own thing'

- lack of decision-making skills, where people have not been provided with any guidance or training on decision-making techniques or processes

- the complexity of the issue involved – if it is particularly difficult then people may try to simplify the decision-making process, resulting in a flawed decision

- the personalities involved – there may be people who do not or cannot get on and will argue with each other for the sake of it; there may be a particularly powerful or dominating person involved who will ensure that the decisions made are what *they* want, without proper reference to the broader knowledge available

- a blame culture – decision-making in a blame culture tends to result in people not wanting to make a decision, diluting a decision, or going for the safest option – which might not be the best

- hidden agendas involving the power and influence of people who are part of the decision-making process, and some outside the process; these people may have goals or aims not necessarily connected with the decisions, but their hidden agendas affect the decision-making such as decisions that could affect their promotion aspirations.

As we have identified, there can be a certain amount of fear associated with decision-making – particularly if there is a blame culture or people are constantly fire-fighting. Other reasons, including the following, also contribute to the fear of making decisions:

● rewards may be adversely affected by the wrong decision

● the wrong decisions could damage promotion prospects

● social, esteem or status factors may be damaged by flawed decisions.

Sometimes it is simply not possible to know what the 'right' decision is, as a number of alternatives might look attractive. It can be reassuring for people to go through a process of eliminating decisions they know to be wrong or less attractive from the evaluation that has taken place. Left with a range of attractive options, the decision-making process could be gone through again, for example developing another set of criteria or re-working probable values, etc. If there are still difficult choices, it is important that the decision made is supported by all those involved, even if there is an element of doubt.

Decisions are associated with risk. The risks include money, reputation, stakeholder relationships, customer numbers, and demand. The greater the risk, the more difficult the decision, but if we have gone through a process of trying to identify likely scenarios and have good-quality information, robust criteria can be used to evaluate the likelihood of the risk happening and the impact on the organization. In a risk matrix (Figure 7.5) the likelihood and impact of risk are ranked from high to low. The decision-makers need to agree the ranking, and then agree how likely it is that the risk will happen and the impact it will have. The lower the likelihood and impact, the more attractive the option or solution is.

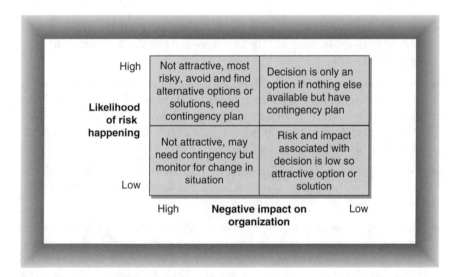

Figure 7.5
Risk matrix

Other useful multifactor matrices have been popular for evaluating decisions for decades, evolving from the Boston Consulting Group matrix (BCG) to the GE matrix referred to in Chapter 2.

Organizational culture and the attitudes of people will play an important role in ensuring that there is a supportive environment for decisions. If it turns out to be the wrong decision, responsibility must be accepted by all those responsible, and the occasion treated as an opportunity to learn.

Decision-making process for problem-solving

The decision-making process for problem-solving includes the following:

- *making a decision in outline* – bringing the decision into focus, identifying what broadly needs to be decided and who is involved

- *revisiting the desired outcomes* – determining what it is we want to achieve and why, which requires agreement, honesty and openness

- *validation* – testing responses to decisions and gaining feedback

- *evaluation* – using tools and techniques to help us reach a decision objectively, developing criteria to ensure that we consider every aspect, angle and consequence; this requires objectivity and a methodical process.

Sometimes solving problems challenges the *status quo*, the accepted way of doing things. This may well be what we want. However, we must make the effort to present the solutions in a non-threatening way, starting with what is familiar and known and gradually revealing the new and unknown. Potential solutions therefore need to be explained and justified to win over those who doubt or will be inclined to resist new ideas and ways of doing things.

Decision trees (Ross, 1970) (Figure 7.6) can help to structure the decision process. A decision tree requires the decision-makers to examine all possible outcomes, desirable and undesirable, and helps to communicate the decision-making process to others, adding credibility to decisions reached. This process allows decision-makers to discuss all the alternatives.

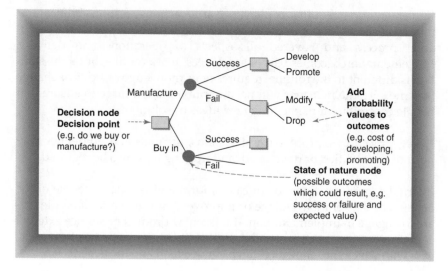

Figure 7.6
Decision tree

The probability values allow decision-makers to assess the costs involved in various courses of action, and the possible returns. This requires quality intelligence, and while it may not always be possible to provide accurate figures, reasonably reliable information can help to reduce risk and increase the chances of making the right decision.

Marketing decisions

Marketing decisions are always influenced by customers or stakeholders, directly or indirectly. For example, obvious decisions might include:

- product or service innovation and improvement
- customer service innovation and improvement
- information gathering and processing
- marketing communications design and development
- employee motivation and development.

Less obvious decisions that may require the marketer convincing people they should be involved include:

- operational change and improvements (that might affect customers)
- internal communications design and development
- the physical environment (where customers into contact with environment)
- performance measurement across other functions (where indirect performance affects customers).

Step 6: Implement and measure

Implementation

Implementation requires a plan to clarify actions, responsibilities and timescale. Feasibility of implementation will have been part of the evaluation process and covered all aspects of operations and delivery. Implementation becomes part of employees' work routine, but if the solution is different to the routine, requires new knowledge or skills or change of some sort, the manager will need to put a plan in place to ensure that people commit to implementing new ideas or solutions.

Policy, procedures, processes and systems, manuals and guidelines may need to be modified or developed, and training may also be required.

Internal communications to educate, inform and persuade people of the benefits of the solution, change or improvement is essential if employees are to engage in implementation. If it is a new product or service external communications are also essential, and consideration must be given to the ease with which the innovation can be understood and the benefits it offers.

Measurement

Measurement has been discussed in Chapter 5, and is covered in more detail in Chapter 12. For the purposes of problem-solving and creativity, we may need to review current measures and modify or develop new measures to determine the effectiveness of the solutions and the problem-solving process.

Problem prevention

Here's a thought: how can we prevent problems? We always have problems; it is a natural part of life. However, some problems really are unnecessary, and managers have a responsibility for ensuring that we are not continually or regularly solving problems that should not have occurred in the first place. We also need to check that we are not suffering from a recurring problem that apparently refuses to be solved.

Prevention is better than cure. If problems can be prevented in the first place, this can save a lot of time and money. More importantly, if the problems involve customers, it can avoid us losing them.

Problem prevention requires:

- monitoring and measuring effectiveness
- anticipating problems, brainstorming the 'what ifs?', and future events and contingency plans
- good communications
- planning and control.

Contingency planning and the 'what ifs?' really do require a creative approach. Brainstorming the unlikely, unusual or even impossible is not particularly easy, but it should be part of the creative stage.

Creative problem-solving and decision-making teams – attitude, passion and teamwork

We have covered teams in Chapter 6, but will just say a few words here about creative problem-solving and decision-making teams.

In most cases, problem-solvers ideally should be the people doing the job rather than people assigned to solve other people's problems. This is not to say that you cannot have a trouble-shooting team, which is different. Trouble-shooting teams are highly trained experts at solving particular problems, and are essential in organizations where the problem can lead to devastating outcomes – such as an explosion on an oil rig.

It may be necessary to employ temporary workers (or staff from other areas) who can quickly be recruited to cover the more routine and simple tasks while employees solve the problem. Training in problem-solving techniques must be provided.

People have to take responsibility for solving their own problems. However, they have to have the authority and be equipped to do so. This requires certain skills and resources.

Problem-solving skills include being:

- analytical
- systematic, consistent
- questioning, probing, investigative
- imaginative
- resourceful.

Individuals can be very creative on their own, but some of the best ideas can result from people coming together to brainstorm ideas. A key driver of innovation is *attitude* – for example, people being interested in leading not following, wanting to be first and/or different. This attitude will extend to people particularly good at understanding the implications of implementing ideas and meticulous in thinking through the detail of what is required. Attitude will affect the type of innovation – revolutionary or incremental. Revolutionary innovation is usually the result of either a leap made by the organization, or occurs in response to dramatic advances externally, and can be more expensive, cause greater upheaval and be more difficult to manage. Incremental innovation builds on what is currently available – gradual modifications and improvements. It is usually less expensive and easier to manage than revolutionary innovation.

We need people who are creative, good at idea generation, never satisfied with the *status quo*; the awkward ones who are never content, always challenging, questioning and trying to change things. We need rebels and troublemakers, as long as what they are doing, more often than not, is in the end productive.

It is not enough for organizations to have people with good or brilliant ideas; we also have to turn these ideas into gainful solutions (whether profitable for profit-making organizations or productive for non-profit organizations). Some people are not predisposed to idea generation or leaps of imagination; their strengths lie in other areas. We need analysts, people who thrive when evaluating, and implementers, pragmatists who will make the ideas work. These people, with different knowledge and skills, will explore and evaluate fully the validity and implications of implementing solutions.

How these teams are formed means the difference between success and failure, and it is not simply a case of putting all the people with the right combination of skills in the same room. 'Creativity' requires different characteristics from 'Analysis' and 'Making it work'.

A mix of people with different strengths, skills, thinking and processes is the best possible combination. However, they need to communicate with each other so teams will form and re-form for different aspects of the creative and innovative process.

Key collaborators in the creativity and innovation process include the following:

- *Actual customers/stakeholders* – they are the ultimate consumers of whatever an organization produces, and they will decide whether or not their needs have been met. Using customers as co-creators in value has become easier with the Internet and the ability to network. They are a source of organization competence that should not be overlooked.

- *Employees* – these are the people who are responsible for developing, designing and delivering what customers want. They have unique insights into the process of getting products and services through the value-adding process to the customer.

- *Employers* – we should not exclude those who own and run the organization. In small to medium-sized businesses, these people often include the entrepreneur who originally developed an idea that was marketable; they tend to be creative and innovative.

- *Intermediaries* – if we are reliant on our channels to get to our customers, our distribution chain is critical to our success. Members of the chain may be the only contact with our customers, and therefore have knowledge that informs creative and innovative ideas.

- *Suppliers* – these are part of the value adding supply chain. Their knowledge of supplies and developments in the supply chain can enable them to provide useful insights and ideas from a different perspective.

- *Potential customers or non-users* – there may be a reason why these people do not buy or use the product or service, other than that they do not need it. It may be that the product or service in its current form does not solve their problem or meet their need. These people can provide unique insights into new and quite different ideas.

You might also use an innovation or idea company, such as IDEO or Idealab. Other people that can help with ideas, creativity and innovation include:

- *Academics* – people who research and think about our environment and business systems, provoke and challenge old ways of thinking and doing, and present ideas on new ways of thinking and doing.

- *Industry experts and analysts* – depending on the industry, these people could be the captains of industry who challenge traditional business practices and evangelize their ideas or experts in a particular technology or craft.

- *Authors, journalists* – these people, as well as coming up with their own ideas, will be well-read and, as part of their job, collectors of ideas and thoughts from a wide variety of sources. They can make connections between diverse ideas and thoughts, industries and organizations that can lead to creativity and innovation.

- *Anthropologists* – these people study societies and customs across the globe, and can make connections between different civilizations, behaviour and product/service use.

- *Inventors* – you may know some! Perhaps you know a neighbour or someone in the local community, or are able to access inventors through writings in journals, etc.

Problem-solving team communications

We have discussed interpersonal skills in managing teams, but as communications are both important and complex, it is worth acquainting ourselves with what can happen to communications in problem-solving teams.

Research was conducted based on groups of five engaged in a number of problem-solving tasks. They were permitted to communicate with each other by written notes only, and not everyone was always free to communicate with everyone else. Figure 7.7 shows the patterns that emerged and link our review of teams and problem-solving.

What can we learn from this? It is extremely helpful for thinking about how we design the problem-solving team, how we manage information, and the communications skills that will be needed. It will also affect the problem-solving process. If we have a very simple localized problem, we do not need an elaborate process for solving it. We can set fairly aggressive deadlines, expect a quick resolution and allocate appropriate resources.

If, however, our problem is complex and spans several parts of or the entire organization (and beyond if it involves the supply chain), a different approach is required. We require more flexibility in the design of the problem-solving team, it may require more than one team, timescales are more difficult to predict, and resource needs may change as the full extent of the problem emerges during the early stages of problem-solving.

It helps us to decide:

- the extent to which we centralize or decentralize control and allow freedom
- the type of leadership appropriate to solve the problem
- the interpersonal skills required
- the team design required and how we motivate
- information requirements.

Learning from problems and knowledge management

Finally, through this problem-solving and decision-making process, we can capture the learning and development – what we have learned and what improvements have resulted.

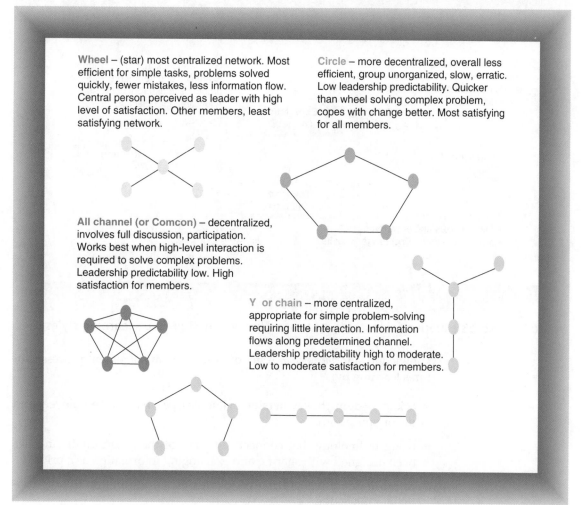

Wheel – (star) most centralized network. Most efficient for simple tasks, problems solved quickly, fewer mistakes, less information flow. Central person perceived as leader with high level of satisfaction. Other members, least satisfying network.

Circle – more decentralized, overall less efficient, group unorganized, slow, erratic. Low leadership predictability. Quicker than wheel solving complex problem, copes with change better. Most satisfying for all members.

All channel (or Comcon) – decentralized, involves full discussion, participation. Works best when high-level interaction is required to solve complex problems. Leadership predictability low. High satisfaction for members.

Y or chain – more centralized, appropriate for simple problem-solving requiring little interaction. Information flows along predetermined channel. Leadership predictability high to moderate. Low to moderate satisfaction for members.

Figure 7.7   Patterns of communications/networks (Bavelas, 1948, 1951; Leavitt, 1951, 1978)

It is difficult to go through the creative and innovative process without learning something, and there is no point in going through this process unless it leads to improvements of some sort. We gave an example of a learning log and how it can help the individual. At a team or department level, this could take the form of team meetings and briefings with some formal record of the learning – reports, or an intranet-based learning site.

Our problem-solving process should incorporate a process for encouraging learning – learning loops and designing mechanisms for ensuring that learning takes place and is distributed throughout the organization. For example, if we combine Kolb's learning cycle (Kolb, 1985) with Honey and Mumford's learning styles (Honey and Mumford, 1992), we can review how this would provide a framework for learning (Figure 7.8).

Learning and knowledge management should always be managed as one process, as some sharing of knowledge provides learning for those receiving

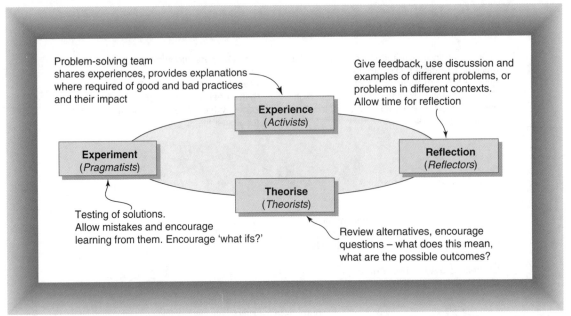

Figure 7.8 Kolb's experiential learning cycle and Honey and Mumford's learning styles

knowledge, and *vice versa*. A good knowledge management process captures learning by:

- acknowledging the ownership of knowledge (shared by employees and the organization)
- using technology that connects all parts of the organization and has been designed with sharing and exchanging information as a priority
- rewarding and recognizing people for their contribution to organizational knowledge.

Part 3 of the book will cover this information in more detail.

Finally, what improvements? The problem-solving process should result in some sort of improvement. This may be an improvement in people's behaviour and/or competences, process improvements, or an improvement in the way tasks are executed. For the marketing manager, ideally the improvement either leads to some sort of advantage or contributes to it.

Summary

Problems do not solve themselves, and a problem ignored can create more problems. An unsolved problem results in fire-fighting, wasting time, and the risk of becoming increasingly inefficient and ineffective. It can also result in people becoming stressed. If a customer's problem is not solved, we lose the customer.

Creativity requires time, space and freedom. It also needs the right mix of people, and a willingness to make mistakes and experiment.

A decision-making process can improve objectivity and reduce risk. It can also play a part in reducing negative politicking and destructive power struggles.

It is essential that the marketing manager does not lose sight of the customers' or stakeholders' perspective during the creative problem-solving and decision-making process.

The process is summarized as follows:

- *Step 1: Describe the problem in context.* Establish a common understanding of what the problem *really* is from different perspectives.

- *Step 2: Collect preliminary information.* Establish the facts and separate them from opinions; build a picture of potential causes of the problem. Talking the problem through with people can sometimes be enough to solve the problem.

- *Step 3: Describe problem precisely and set objectives.* Is the problem as originally described, or different? Set objectives, timescales and the budget.

- *Step 4: Explore, investigate and use creativity.* Establish which tools and techniques are required, such as software programs to model or simulate a process or activities. Allow people to be creative and challenge the *status quo*.

- *Step 5: Evaluation and decision-making.* From the alternative possible solutions generated, used objective techniques to evaluate solutions and make a decision regarding which solution is most appropriate.

- *Step 6: Implement and measure.* Make an action plan to implement the solution and targets, and establish standards to measure success.

If we want individuals and teams to be productive and willing to engage in creativity and innovation, and to solve problems, we need to be able to motivate. This is the subject of Chapter 8.

References

Bavelas, A. (1951). *Communication Patterns in Task Oriented Groups*, in H.N. Lassell and D.O. Lerner (eds), *The Policy Sciences*. Stanford, CA: Stanford University Press.

Bavelas, A. (1948). A mathematical model for group structures. *Applied Anthropology*, 7, 19–30.

Honey, P. and Mumford, A. (1992). *The Manual of Learning Styles*. Maidenhead: Peter Honey.

Kolb, D.A. (1985). *Experiential Learning: Experience as the Source of Learning and Development*. Upper Saddle River, NJ: Prentice Hall.

Leavitt, H.J. (1978). *Managerial Psychology*, 4th edn. Chicago, IL: University of Chicago Press.

Leavitt, H.J. (1951). Some effects of certain communication patterns on group performance. *Journal of Abnormal and Social Psychology*, 46, 30–50.

Ross, S.M. (1970). Applied Probability Models with Optimisation Applications. San Francisco, Holden Day.

8 Motivation

Introduction

We all understand the importance of motivating people, so why is this still something that is neglected by management? Motivation is another of those areas that people think they understand but all too often do not. Another view is that it is just too hard or time-consuming to motivate. Motivation at some levels is just meeting fairly basic needs. Managers should be able to do that. For example, something as simple as respect and recognition can motivate.

Good leaders know how to motivate people, and anything they do will reflect their careful consideration of the impact on people of their behaviour and the actions they take.

Why do people work?

Most people need to work to earn money to live, and it could be assumed that money is the primary motivator to work. If that were true, why do some people choose the jobs they do, why do some individuals work with enthusiasm and others appear disinterested? Reasons for working and the different value put on earnings (even if of the same financial worth) have different meanings for different people. For example, time rates, piecework, profit-sharing, individual and small or large group bonuses, and holidays all have differing effects and appeals.

Motives, incentives and disincentives – what are they?

It is worth clarifying the difference between motives, incentives and disincentives.

- *Motives* are needs and desires existing within us which act as driving forces causing us to search for satisfaction, contentment, a sense of well-being and happiness.

- *Incentives* are the external 'carrots' or satisfactions – some object or goal or circumstance outside the individual which he or she feels will satisfy a need.

- *Disincentives* are the external circumstances or behaviours that cause individuals to lose interest and/or withdraw.

Motives are inner drivers that are highly personal and varied. The outcome of pursuing a motive is the act of engaging in something that satisfies an inner need, and it is therefore motivating. We may need to feel valued at work, and therefore be allowed to contribute in some way and be recognized for our contribution. We may desire to achieve something worthwhile; for some people this may be to serve others in need, while for others it means being part of a team or the desire to be creative in some way. People have different motives, and they are not always obvious, easy to recognize or tangible.

Incentives are tangible and recognizable. Incentives are a means to an end; they are not in themselves motivating. In work, they include financial benefits such as salary or bonuses, job security through contractual or employment terms, physical working conditions and promotion. A person has a need for a home, for material possessions, and to be able to buy goods and services, and a salary satisfies those needs. It is not the salary that motivates, but what the salary can buy. Working conditions may satisfy the need to work in a prestigious, comfortable environment, or the desire to be outdoors.

Disincentives can be caused by situations and conditions (for example, poor prospects at work or a poor working environment) or by behaviour (for example, conflict and difficult working relationships, or lack of recognition of a job well done). These are disincentives because they prevent people from being where they want to be, doing what they want to do, or being recognized for what they do.

How do we know when we have a motivation problem? Symptoms include:

- working to rule
- absenteeism and poor timekeeping
- decreasing productivity
- aggressive and/or defensive behaviour
- complaints and obstruction
- staff turnover.

If we want to understand motivation, we need to start with understanding individuals.

Understanding the individual

Individuals have common needs which are met to varying degrees by taking part in work with others. The common task provides opportunities for developing a sense of achievement, gaining status and recognition, while the group allows our social needs to be met, along with a sense of belonging. Money is primarily a means of exchange that allows us to convert work in one specialized activity (such as selling a product) directly into the results of other kinds of activity (food, drink and shelter) that meet our physiological needs.

Causes of demotivation include:

- dissatisfaction with pay and benefits
- poor working conditions
- management by threat or criticism
- poor communications
- poor induction, training and job match
- unattainable targets and unclear standards.

Individual needs are especially important in relation to motivation. Motivating people was traditionally a combination of rewards and threats – the carrot and stick approach. More recent thought and research recognizes that individuals motivate themselves to a large extent by responding to inner needs.

Motivation is also affected by the national culture within which people live, referred to in Chapter 3.

We will not attempt to cover all the theories on motivation – and there are many. We will review some of those that are best-known and most enduring.

Motivation – management assumptions about people

Douglas McGregor (1957) pointed out that managers often operate under one of two sets of contrasting explicit or implicit assumptions about people. He used the descriptions Theory X and Theory Y.

McGregor made the point that what we believe about a person can help that person to behave in that way (the self-fulfilling prophecy). If you tell people that you believe they are lazy and worthless, for example, they will tend to live up to your estimate of them. If you have a high regard for them that is not strictly justified by the facts, they may well rise to meet your expectations.

Theory X assumes that people:

- are innately lazy and untrustworthy, they do not like work and will do as little as possible
- lack ambition, dislike responsibilities and prefer to be led

- are self-centred, indifferent to organization needs and resistant to change
- lack creativity.

Theory Y assumes that people:

- are naturally inclined and willing to work in the interests of personal growth
- are keen to realize their full potential and will seek responsibility
- are self-disciplined and controlled in pursuit of goals, and concerned about outcomes
- are creative and innovative, and this is often underused.

If we make these assumptions about people, we will treat them accordingly. Theory X assumptions may result in the organization structure being designed to ensure maximum supervision and control. Management style is more likely to be autocratic.

Theory Y assumptions may result in a flatter structure with less emphasis on supervision and control, and that allows some flexibility in interpretation of how tasks are done – which in turn encourages creativity. Management style is more likely to be democratic.

In Chapter 6 we reviewed Tannenbaum and Schmidt's management styles continuum, and if we link these styles to Theory X and Y assumptions it reveals the potential impact on motivation (Figure 8.1).

Within an organization there will be a variety of management styles in use, and therefore different levels of motivation and engagement of employees.

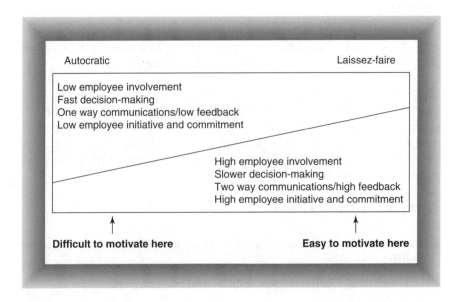

Figure 8.1
Management style
and impact on
motivation

Motivation theories

Maslow's hierarchy of needs theory

We pointed out that individuals have needs. Maslow's (1943) concept of hierarchy of needs (Figure 8.2) is useful for helping us understand this. He suggested that individual needs are arranged in an order of dominance, with the stronger at the bottom and weaker (but more distinctively human) at the top of the pyramid (Maslow, 1943, 1987).

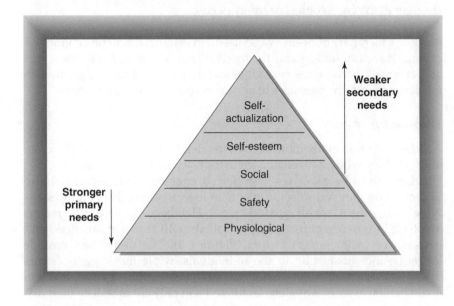

Figure 8.2
Maslow's hierarchy of needs (modern Western societies)

Starting at the top of the pyramid:

- *Self-actualization* needs include realizing one's own potential, continued self-development, creation in the broadest sense
- *Self-esteem* needs include egoism, self-confidence, independence, achievement, competence, knowledge, status, recognition, appreciation, deserved respect
- *Social* needs include the sense of belonging, acceptance of people, association, giving and receiving friendship
- *Safety* needs include lack of danger and deprivation, and a role as family provider
- *Physiological* needs include food, drink, sex, rest/sleep, shelter and protection from the elements.

Stronger needs have to be satisfied before a person can move on to satisfying the weaker needs. However, if we have moved up the hierarchy of needs and attained, for example, our esteem needs but one of our stronger needs is threatened, we then move back down the hierarchy to defend it. You do not worry about status if you are starving. Therefore, if you appear to threaten people's security by proposed changes you should expect defensive behaviour.

A satisfied need ceases to motivate. When one area of need is met, the individual becomes aware of another set of personal needs. These in turn now begin to motivate.

As with many concepts, the needs are culturally specific – for example, in China following the Cultural Revolution the social need to belong was far stronger than physiological or safety needs.

Maslow's hierarchy of needs is also useful in external marketing communications. If we can understand the motivational factors and influences that affect people's perceptions, behaviour and decisions, we can design marketing communications messages to appeal to specific needs and wants.

Two-factor theory

Another writer on motivation is Frederick Herzberg, an American Professor of Psychology who involved himself in industry far more than Maslow did. Herzberg and his associates interviewed engineers and accountants to find out why they found some events in their working lives highly satisfying and others highly dissatisfying. Herzberg divided the factors involved into two groups, which he called motivators (or satisfiers) and hygiene (or maintenance) factors (Figure 8.3). The motivators provide longer-lasting satisfaction to the individuals, while the hygiene factors cause dissatisfaction if they are missing or found wanting. However, if you give a person more of a hygiene factor you will only either reduce their dissatisfaction, or else give them a short-lived sense of satisfaction (see Herzberg, 1959).

If there is dissatisfaction with, for example, working conditions or job security, then no matter how much effort is put into motivating people

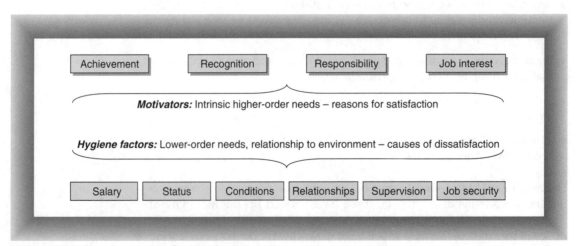

Figure 8.3   Herzberg two-factor theory

through interesting jobs or more responsibility, the chances are people will not be motivated.

McClelland's achievement, affiliation and power needs theory

In the early 1960s David McClelland identified three kinds of needs – for:

- achievement – to be responsible for satisfactory outcomes
- power – to control and influence
- affiliation – to belong and have relationships.

McClelland's studies (McClelland, 1988) indicate that the strongest need will affect and change a person's behaviour. Thus a person (and accepting that people's behaviour is affected by many things) with a strong affiliation need will spend time and effort on building relationships. This person will want feedback on his or her interpersonal skills and relationship status.

If the dominate need is achievement, a person is driven by the need to succeed. Such people spend timing thinking about how to improve the way they do things, and are only interested in feedback that is task-relevant. These people tend to be successful in business and are promoted rapidly. They receive substantial financial rewards. The promotion and financial rewards are only of interest as a measurement of their achievement. Salespeople are often motivated by achievement.

A strong power need will result in a person pursuing a job that allows him or her to influence decisions, mould and control events. If this power need is derived from a desire to improve the overall success of the business and people associated with it, it can have a positive effect. A power need can result from a need for freedom and having control over your own destiny. However, if the power need is driven by egotistical desires it is unhealthy and negative.

Expectancy theory

Victor Vroom's 1960s expectancy theory (Figure 8.4) assumes that people are motivated by different needs because they place different values

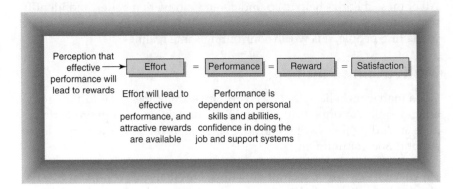

Figure 8.4
Vroom expectancy theory (adapted)

on rewards. The effort they put into something is based on their expectation of what they will get out of it, and each person has a different expectation (Vroom, 1964).

Key to successful motivation is employees being able to relate what they are getting to what they are doing. So, for example, if the management team has designed a sophisticated or complicated reward scheme for the sales team that is not easily understood, it will not motivate because the sales team will have difficulty connecting more effort or harder work with the rewards they will receive.

Vroom described the level of need as *valency*. High valency is indicative of a strong need for something, and low valency indicative of a weak need for something. The higher the valency, the more likely it is the person can be motivated by meeting this need. Low-valency needs are less likely to motivate. A high-valency need will only motivate if the person believes that the desired outcome is achievable.

Figure 8.5 shows how this might vary from one person to another.

Person A is motivated by money

Effort	Performance	Reward
Extra long hours over the next 6 months	Exceeding stated targets	Financial

Person B is motivated by power and recognition

Effort	Performance	Reward
Identifying new overseas markets	Detailed profiles, successful appointment of distributors	Promotion

Person C is motivated by personal development and achievement

Effort	Performance	Reward
Managing complex project over time	Improving efficiency of product design process	Public recognition

Figure 8.5
Varying valency

All of these theories help us to understand motivation better, and identify opportunities for improving motivation. Before we look at motivating marketing people, it is worth confronting some realities.

Motivation realities

Good managers believe that it is worth investing time and effort in motivating people. An organization where all are striving to improve performance, including the way people are managed, is rewarded with employee support and commitment.

However, it is worth just reminding ourselves that such conditions are not always the reality; other realities exist, and we need to be aware of these.

National cultural context

Our deeply held cultural beliefs, attitudes and values, particularly religious, will affect our internal motivation – for example, spiritualism versus materialism. The manager's national culture, as described in Chapter 3, may be the same as that of the employees, in which case there will be an innate understanding of national cultural motivation.

However, in international organizations managers can find themselves in a different culture, and in these circumstances it is essential that the manager makes some effort to understand the national cultural influences on motivation.

Organization context

This has been discussed, and of course it will be obvious to you that in some organizational cultures it will be difficult, even impossible, to motivate. In these circumstances, the manager needs to look realistically at what is possible.

It is possible for managers to improve motivation in their own team in a hostile organization environment. There is nothing to stop the manager from using effective communication skills and motivation techniques such as job enlargement, praise and recognition to motivate. However, in these circumstances it is essential to be honest with staff about other predominant organization behaviour and how it might impact on them. The manager can provide the necessary support, and can be in the position of a buffer. Don't lose heart if this happens to you; in such circumstances managers can find themselves leading by example and changing behavioural norms to something more positive and productive. Early signs of an emerging effective leader?

Individuals

Many managers are not equipped to motivate, and we have all had experiences where we know that if people were treated better and/or differently they would behave better and/or differently. Theories X and Y remind us how we can condition people to behave in a particular way. Some motivation theory suggests that every individual can be motivated. We are all different and therefore will be motivated differently; we just need to find out what will motivate. However, in some cases workplace motivation seems to be elusive, and anyone who has been in the workplace for any length of time will have come across people who are just not interested in work or in being there. The causes of their disinterest will be varied and perhaps complex, but after a period of exploration and effort to resolve the problem a manager needs to recognize when some problems cannot be solved. The individual might be in the wrong job or organization, and in these circumstances changing one or both is the only solution.

In our determination to be good and better managers, the danger is that we can spend a lot of time on these people. This then raises questions of how this impacts on individuals who are working hard, producing results and engaging positively in work. There comes a point when the manager needs to accept that an individual is not going to be motivated, and any more extra time spent on that individual will be wasted and lead to productive workers being neglected.

The problem is how to deal with these people, particularly with today's employment laws that (quite rightly) make it difficult to fire people without good cause and evidence to support it. Because the situation is often both difficult and emotional, and will be time-consuming, the tendency is to want to ignore it. If you have an HR function, in these circumstances its involvement is essential.

Dealing with a difficult-to-motivate individual

1. Communicate clearly your expectations of objectives, goals, required performance and interactions with others.

2. Provide opportunities for feedback, encouraging the individual to interpret his or her understanding of your expectations.

3. Deal with any discrepancies.

4. Provide reasonable opportunities to improve performance and interactions with others (for example training, coaching, appraisal, one-to-one feedback sessions), and encourage the individual to take responsibility for his or her behaviour.

5. Track performance with the involvement of the individual concerned, and encourage him or her to identify any problems, issues or gaps.

6. Encourage the individual to identify acceptable alternative solutions if he or she is unable to engage. Solutions might include a transfer to a more suitable job in another part of the organization, or helping to find a job for the individual outside the organization.

7. Record your decisions and actions to provide evidence that you have behaved reasonably, and done all you can to provide support and opportunities.

There are two more realities:

1. There are, fortunately, very few individuals who it is just impossible to motivate.

2. Take care not to mistake the quiet, reserved introvert for someone who is not motivated. It takes all sorts; people do not have to be happy and bouncy to be motivated, and the culture may result in predominant behaviour that not everyone responds to openly or in an obvious way.

Summary

Motivation requires cooperation. Managers have a responsibility to improve motivation of individuals and teams, to engage people and get optimal performance. However, employees also have a responsibility, particularly if managers are making the effort, to engage positively in work; it cannot be all one way.

In summary, we need to ensure that the hygiene factors are not going to cause dissatisfaction, that we understand what motivates the individual, and that the balance between challenging work and support from managers and the organization are designed to motivate. All of these theories have something to offer in helping us to think about how best we might motivate people.

Case study

Motivation and the role of communications

In many examples of organizations that have set an objective of improving staff motivation, the starting point has been a survey conducted with employees. What follows next reveals different approaches to improving motivation.

Civil Aviation Authority

After carrying out a survey, the Civil Aviation Authority sent managers on a course to improve understanding and the issues of implementing good motivation practices. Employees were sent on a course to explain the process, which was not just about informing them of what was going to happen but also had the advantage of beginning the process of engaging them. The Civil Aviation Authority believed that the success of motivation was dependent on the quality of communications, and encouraging staff to take more responsibility in the two-way interactions with managers – for example, staff gathering evidence of their performance for appraisals, rather than managers having sole responsibility for this.

Woolworths

Following a staff survey, Woolworths developed an index for measuring how motivated employees were and from which it was possible to assess how managers were performing. This feedback enabled managers to work with employees to better understand their needs and concerns, and together they developed performance improvement targets. Again communication was seen as central – first to gain feedback and then to discuss and agree ways forward that were acceptable to both managers and employees. Managers were able to communicate their expectations, and employees the practical implications and needs.

(Sources: Various web and print)

Motivating marketing people

The different management styles that lead to a variety of motivation climates within an organization can be problematic for marketing managers.

Where people are motivated, customer experiences are more likely to be positive – providing people are competent and trained. Where motivation is a problem, customers are likely to be encountering poor service and unsatisfactory experiences. As marketing managers do not have control over all aspects of customer experiences, the challenge is to influence and persuade management of the need for a consistent approach to motivation.

What can we learn from motivation theory, and how can we use it?

First, we need to understand individual needs; we cannot make assumptions about what these might be, or that everyone in our department or organization can be motivated in the same way. People have different emotional needs that influence behaviour, including self-respect and respect from others.

Secondly, we must realize that money, often used as a motivator, is unlikely to motivate, and if it does, it will not do so for very long.

Thirdly, we must understand that different people are motivated by different needs, and these needs can change over time and depending on the circumstances. Organizations change over time, as do their circumstances. This can affect people's needs – for example, the threat of redundancy will change the need for weaker secondary needs and result in people being concerned with their stronger primary needs.

We know that incentives might include:

● money

● better working conditions

● promotion.

The next step for the marketing manager is to identify motivators for marketing people. These might include:

● opportunities for personal growth

● opportunities for achievement

● the chance to learn new skills

● challenges

● a sense of usefulness.

Keep it personal

A good starting point for motivating people might be to practice what we preach, and understand our staff better rather than just know them. This is not necessarily going to be as simple as it seems. We could start with understanding what they do from their job description, which provides some insight into the nature and type of work. However, this is too much like being product-orientated rather than customer-orientated.

A good manager who has worked with a team for some time will have some idea of personality types among the team, and know their staff well enough to be able to describe at least some motives for doing things. However, if we want to be more objective and thorough, we might want to use some diagnostic tools to provide insights into motivation. Some of these you may already be familiar with and have access to, others not. Some are not specific to motivation but provide insights, for example personality profiles, and some are specific to motivation.

There have been a number of developments on identifying personality traits, leadership styles, learning preferences, etc., and for the workplace here are just a few well-known diagnostic tests:

- Myers–Briggs Type Indicator – showing characteristics frequently associated with particular personality types
- DISC Personal Profile System
- Saville & Holdsworth 17 motivational factors
- Work Motivation Inventory – Chartwell Bratt
- Situational leadership questionnaire
- Belbin team-role questionnaire
- Honey and Munford learning styles questionnaire.

Any one of these tests provides some insight into internal motivators and what is likely to disengage a person. We should also not overlook the value of just talking to people and asking them what they want out of work and life, and what they believe motivates them. What do they feel passionate or excited about?

Armed with this knowledge of possible internal drivers and motivational theories, we can now apply it. The challenge for the manager is getting internal motivators to fit with external motivation and reward. The following is an example, using expectancy theory.

Assume we have three people hoping to be promoted to marketing manager – a self-actualization need (Maslow). Each may have a different perception of how to achieve this promotion:

- The first person might believe that the way to achieve this promotion is by consistently exceeding targets, and so will put in extra hours and effort to deliver that goal in the expectation that the reward will be promotion.
- The second person might believe that the key to success is demonstrating interpersonal skills, so will put extra time and effort into building relationships, possibly using opportunities to solve people's problems or act as an arbitrator in a dispute.

- The third person might believe the only way to achieve promotion to marketing manager is to have a professional qualification so puts extra time and effort into attending evening classes and studying for the Chartered Institute of Marketing Diploma.

We have three different approaches and outcomes, all to achieve the same goal. The danger for the manager responsible for making this promotion is that the decision will be perceived differently by all three, and therefore potentially will be seen as unfair by two of the three. This can lead to dissatisfaction and demotivation. How do we ensure we are seen to be equitable and fair?

Establishing context, conditions and performance expectations

By understanding the possible internal motivators and external context, we can make some reasonable assumptions about employee expectations. By identifying employee expectations, we can ensure that in setting a goal (for example, a job promotion) we also establish our expectations (Figure 8.6). It is important that we are reasonable and fair, and that we are *perceived* as being reasonable and fair. Our communication skills are going to be essential in this process.

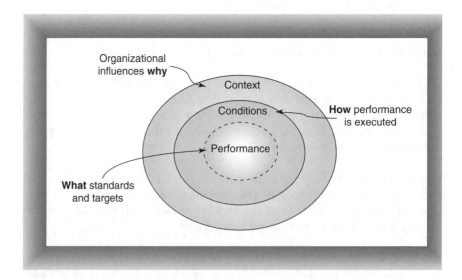

Figure 8.6
Context and conditions for motivation (©2004 Juanita Cockton)

Context is important because organizational culture influences why people behave in a particular way. If we take the example of a person working in a power culture (described in Chapter 3), then the perception may be that building relationships with key executives is the route to promotion. If the company has a role culture, then abiding by the rules, conforming and delivering exactly what is expected will eventually lead to promotion. If the manager's expectations are at odds with the cultural norms, this will create the potential for misinterpretation of what is required. Underlying the organizational culture is the national culture within which people live, which may also influence perceptions.

Conditions range from the normal work environment and work-task circumstances to special incidents that have particular requirements. Timescales are usually part of the conditions. Conditions are about how we expect something to be done. Normal work conditions will be important in demonstrating an individual's talent and potential, but special circumstances may require something extra. Again, our job promotion is a useful example. A manager can agree that one or a number of options could lead to promotion, but if more than one option is available then it must be clear that all options have the same potential to demonstrate talent and lead to promotion. Projects and assignments designed to stretch candidates to perform beyond their normal competence provide a challenge to test their ability and willingness.

Performance standards and targets are part of performance expectation, and these are usually communicated to individuals through job descriptions and appraisals that clearly state what is expected. In special circumstances, additional performance expectations might need to be communicated. In our job promotion example we might want the individual to demonstrate a number of specific skills, including:

- leadership skills – for example, developing strategy

- management skills – for example, reorganizing a process or task

- coaching skills – for example, through delegating a task.

Competences are often used to clarify expected performance. Competences provide a common language and can bring clarity to expected performance, but make sure they are not too prescriptive and do not stifle creativity and initiative. In any job, whether an employee is aiming for promotion or just trying to do the work better, the freedom for individuality can be a real asset and has the added advantage of motivating.

Figure 8.6 illustrates the context and conditions for motivation. By taking into consideration the context within which we are motivating, we can understand why individuals will behave in a particular way and the cultural influences that affect perceptions of what is required to achieve a particular goal. By establishing the conditions, all those involved are clear about how to achieve a particular goal. By clarifying performance, we communicate what is expected – which reduces variations in perceptions and interpretation of what success looks like.

Examples of inappropriate context, conditions and performance are as follows.

1. *Context*:

- a blame culture where, when things go wrong, effort is focused on finding people to blame rather than on learning

- leadership and management styles that are distant, impersonal and controlling do not create a climate in which people can be motivated; indecisive or incompetent managers tend to lack respect or trust and will find it difficult to motivate

- a process orientation – the focus on task and the attitude of processing people develops a 'factory' environment.

2. *Conditions*:

- knowledge and information that are not shared – information is power, and there may be an unwillingness to share information and knowledge

- equipment and facilities that are out of date or poorly maintained, or the lack of appropriate tools for the job, can result in people's efforts being consumed by sorting these problems instead of doing the job on which they will be measured; even the physical space within which people work can influence performance

- systems and processes that are inefficient, complex and bureaucratic or simply a lack of systems can lead to frustration, particularly if people are made to look incompetent because of the systems they are using.

3. *Performance*:

- unrealistic targets that are out of touch with either the organization or market situation can be very demoralizing

- woolly statements that cannot be measured make it difficult for people to understand what exactly is required of them

- little or no feedback on performance means people are working 'in the dark', and this uncertainty can result in them either taking things into their own hands and interpreting what is required in their own unique way, or doing the absolute minimum to avoid risking poor performance.

Marketing managers have a duty to promote a positive climate for motivation (Figure 8.7), especially as marketing people are usually at the forefront of customer contact and experiences. Motivated, committed and loyal employees are, not unsurprisingly, more likely to deliver superior service and create a positive experience for customers.

Managers sometimes fail to make the connection between how employees behave towards customers and how managers behave towards employees. It is often a mirror situation, and customers are savvy to this fact even if some managers are not. Customers increasingly do not complain to employees, because they are aware that the problem or poor service is not a reflection of the employees' performance but rather a reflection of management performance.

Managing individuals, teams and tasks

The design of work needs to take account of the challenge we can create and the support we give (Figure 8.8). If we challenge people without support,

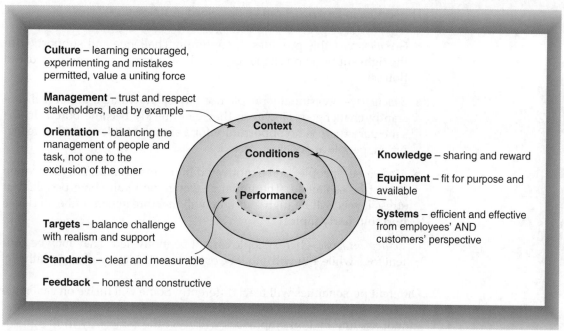

Figure 8.7 Promoting a positive climate for motivation (©2004 Juanita Cockton)

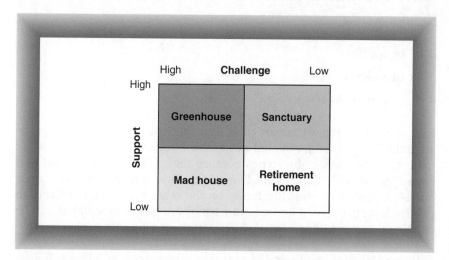

**Figure 8.8
Managing
motivation**

they can quickly feel threatened and demotivated. It is the management team's responsibility to ensure that employees have the right level of support to do their work.

Whatever challenges we pose for marketing personnel, appropriate support systems need to be in place. If we understand the level of challenge and support (from high to low) and possible mix of challenge and support, we can begin to understand under which circumstances we might be able to motivate and, conversely, it will be difficult to motivate.

The sectors in Figure 8.8 can be described as follows:

- *Greenhouse* – this provides the optimum challenge and support; with the right support and challenge, people should be easily motivated and flourish.

- *Sanctuary* – occasionally people need to feel nurtured and not feel constantly challenged. However, they can quickly become bored. In the sanctuary there is no opportunity for a sense of achievement or recognition; people are over-protected.

- *Mad house* – people can be motivated in the mad house, but motivation cannot be sustained. The initial challenge will suit some people, but stress levels will be high and they will feel threatened and experience burn-out fairly rapidly.

- *Retirement home* – here, people cannot be motivated. They may be content for a while, but will either be or become disinterested and apathetic.

Different personalities will react differently. Some will thrive on challenge and little support, while others will immediately switch off. The manager cannot assume that all employees will react the same way in the greenhouse, and can be managed in the same way. For example, the DISC personal profile system identifies four personality types:

1. Dominance (D).

2. Influence (I).

3. Steadiness (S).

4. Conscientiousness (C).

Each of the four types has particular characteristics. 'D' personality types are quite likely to be motivated in the 'mad house', surviving for longer than the other personality types because they are result-orientated and have a 'get on with it' mentality. Even 'D' types will eventually experience burn-out here. 'I' personality types, on the other hand, are not likely to survive long in the mad house because they are people-orientated, can be emotional and require praise – which is in short supply!

In the greenhouse quadrant different approaches are needed for different personalities, and the challenge for the marketing manager is to match the challenge and support with the individual's personality and motivators.

Marketers can identify opportunities for challenges and support, and assess their implications for motivating (Figure 8.9).

Examples of how we might challenge people include:

- *improvements* – for example, improving efficiency or effectiveness of some kind (reliability, speed, delegation, sales/awareness targets, team-working)

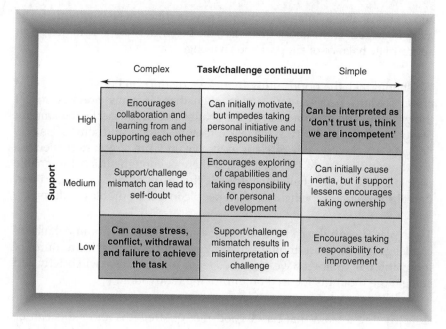

Figure 8.9
Managing challenge and support (©2000 Juanita Cockton)

- *problem-solving* – for example, a recurring or particularly difficult problem, perhaps constraining the time within which the problem has to be solved

- *creativity and innovation* – for example, new products or services that are unique or offer strong differentiation, new processes, ways of team-working

- *decision-making* – particularly where information is in short supply or there are a number of attractive options and it is therefore more difficult to make a decision.

Examples of how we can support people include:

- one-to-one interviews to allow feedback and resolve individual problems

- team briefing and debriefing sessions to inform, keep team members up-to-date, and allow open dissent and discussion to overcome problems and objections

- access to technology and processes that allow exchanging and sharing of information, ideas, concerns, etc.

- learning and development to support skills requirements.

Finding the right balance of support and challenge is dependent on the manager's knowledge of the people involved, and on preparation.

As we have already said, different people respond differently to both support and challenge, with some seeing support as for the 'weak and insecure' and others unable to imagine tackling a new or different task without it. The more managers know about their staff, the better they are able to design an appropriate balance of support and challenge.

We should take the opportunity to make a distinction between *stress* and *pressure*. Many people work better when there is some pressure to get things done. The pressure can be the challenge of a timescale, the amount of work or the complexity of the task. Pressure is good, and some of us cannot get started without it. Stress is excessive pressure. Pressure challenges, but the conditions are favourable and there is enough support to enable people to rise to the challenge. Stress is the result of lack of support and unrealistic demands being placed on people in unfavourable conditions.

Tasks play a central role in motivating and, with an optimum balance of challenge and support, thoughtful design of work can provide a source of motivation. In Chapter 6 we discussed team-work, and we will briefly add some more thoughts focused on improving motivation.

Constructing a team that has a good mix of strengths and skills can be motivating. Optimizing individual strengths – matching tasks to people's strengths – allows people to contribute something of value. Matching tasks to people's strengths means that we avoid tasks being performed by people without the necessary skills, and team-working provides the range of skills needed. It has the added benefit of focusing people on success rather than failure.

Optimizing personal growth involves developing people's expertise where they have strengths, but also, with the support of the team, diminishing weaknesses and developing new skills by learning from each other.

Our work tasks are a mix of day-to-day essential routines that keep the wheels in motion, and irregular events that require more thinking, creativity and skill. Marketing people are often motivated by diversity in tasks, are drawn to new challenges, dealing with crises and solving problems. There are usually plenty of problems of various sorts to solve, from small and simple to large and complex. Managers can use this to their advantage.

Large projects are a regular feature of many organizations today, to optimize the supply chain, re-engineer the business, etc. They can be daunting and too often lose their way, which can result in employee dissatisfaction and demotivation. Breaking down large projects into manageable mini-projects is the responsibility of managers. The opportunities provided by mini-projects and assignments are often overlooked. They provide a framework for improving or changing something specific within a relatively short timescale. They have the advantage of being manageable, so balance challenge and support, and of being achievable, so are more likely to motivate.

The experience of the most motivational managers reveals some common practices, including the following:

- ensuring that objectives and expectations are clearly communicated and are demanding
- providing varying levels and types of support appropriate to the situation
- actively resourcing and encouraging personal learning and development
- allowing the freedom to take initiative and act.

These managers command respect and trust, and inspire extraordinary loyalty from employees along with a commitment to doing the best job they can. What more can you ask?

Preparation is an essential part of setting challenges for staff, and the best form of preparation is learning.

Motivating through learning and development

Unfortunately for many, childhood experiences of learning are not happy and can put people off the idea. Fortunately this rarely lasts long into adulthood, and most people realize that learning is not only very interesting but can also be fun. Learning and development can be a great motivator, and very beneficial for the organization too.

We identified in Chapter 5 that sometimes the haphazard nature of learning and development means it can be a demotivator rather than motivating, particularly when learning is not successfully transferred into the workplace.

This is all too familiar for trainers. A delegate attends a course, enthusiastic and willing to participate – the perfect delegate. The lament, however, is 'but I won't be able to make a difference back in the workplace'. This is caused by two serious omissions:

1. No proper learning needs analysis to ensure that the delegate's learning is matched to his or her objectives and performance.
2. No attempt to prepare the workplace to transfer and implement the learning on the delegate's return – 'business as usual' reigns.

The missing ingredients are not only an obstacle to motivation but also a waste of time and money, with no strategy for exploiting the investment in learning. There are factors that need to be in place if learning is to motivate the individual and benefit the organization.

The manager, learner and selected colleagues should work together before the learning event to anticipate the likely change and support needed to transfer learning into work practices and improved performance. This could be the briefest of discussions where quick and simple decisions are made, or may require more time, planning and change. What must be avoided is no discussion or decision; this signals a lack of commitment and real intention to use the learning. After the learning event the precise nature of change and support can be identified, and a plan of action designed to transfer learning for all to benefit. Useful ways of preparing the workplace can be:

- *process review* – what processes are likely to be involved, and will they support or block learning and improvement?
- *task review* – what current tasks are performed, what are their value and outcomes, and how can learning improve task execution?

Preparing people includes:

- mini-presentations to colleagues on learning, and invitation for feedback
- team briefings
- seminars to encourage further ideas and developments.

As well as the waste of money and time, if learning is not transferred an organization cannot be a learning organization – which constrains its ability to be a creative and innovative organization. It is currently fashionable to be creative and innovative – the latest goal of many organizations – but how many have learning at the centre?

A lack of transfer of learning also demotivates learners. They may take some personal satisfaction from learning something, but this will be tempered by the frustration of not being able to do anything with it.

Figure 8.10 shows the cycle of learning and motivation.

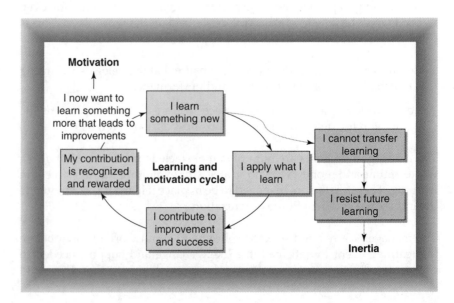

Figure 8.10
Learning and motivation cycle
(© 2002 Juanita Cockton)

Learning can switch people on, and poor management of the experience they want to bring back to the workplace can switch them back off again. In many cases these newly trained employees will start looking for a job in an organization that will allow them to use their learning.

There are no losers, only winners, in transferring learning into the work-place, and yet this still remains a major stumbling block for many organizations. It is getting better, but there is room for considerable improvement.

Motivation adaptation and evolution

Wouldn't it be wonderful if, having gone to the effort of establishing the organizational framework for motivation, understanding the individual internal motivators and developing a motivational climate, we could sit back, relax and reap the rewards of our efforts? But sadly no, we cannot.

People change, situations change, and managers have to be vigilant to the need to adapt and evolve motivation.

If we look at what is happening in the workplace today, we can easily see how motivation changes. At one time training and development was seen as a motivation. This is now expected, and to motivate today the nature and planning of learning and development, as discussed above, is essential. Some trends are being driven by legislation, but some of those driven by forward-thinking managers to keep good employees include:

- extended maternity leave (three years or more in some companies)
- paternity leave
- flexible working arrangements – not just adjusting arrival and leaving times by 30 minutes or so, but providing real flexibility, including opportunities to work from home
- job-sharing and secondments within the company and outside
- sabbaticals – an opportunity to take time out for travel or to pursue/ support a worthy cause
- corporate social responsibility – again, encouraging staff in supporting worthy causes but also to find innovations to enable the organization to be more socially responsible. This has proved highly successful in both motivating and improving profitability for some organizations.

Only two decades ago, the idea of three years' maternity leave was unthinkable for any but the most enlightened. However, this not only retains highly talented staff but also leads to motivated, very loyal and committed staff.

This is a good moment for another reality check. Small organizations or charities are not in a position to offer, amongst other things, years of maternity leave or sabbaticals. In fact, small organizations are being crippled by such employment and other legislation. However, they do have the advantage of being flexible, and can offer job enrichment and enlargement opportunities. If buying learning and development is too costly, try a creative approach. Who is particularly good at what? There are two motivation opportunities here:

1. The expert can develop coaching and possibly managing skills by training others.

2. Others can benefit from being coached by experts.

Feedback loops for both can help to refine and develop skills.

Summary

Motivation is not difficult for good managers, and they see it as an essential and natural part of the job. For some it is instinctive, for others it is not. For those that do not have a natural flair for motivation, what we have covered in this chapter shows us that, with a little thought about the people who work for us, the way we design jobs and the way we communicate, a lot can be achieved in motivating employees.

During our review of managing teams we discussed the fact that interpersonal skills and good communications are at the heart of effective motivation. If our communications style is respectful, encouraging, supportive and honest, we are more likely to motivate. If our communications style is aggressive and lacks integrity, and we like to name and shame, for most people it will demoralize. There are of course bound to be some masochists that enjoy being ridiculed, and others that love the chance for a good fight – but probably less than you think!

As we have already established, our communications style and the motivation of staff will affect the customer experience, so let's get it right. Getting it right does require understanding the particular circumstances within which you work. National culture, organizational culture, industry and profession all affect motivation needs and drivers. Salespeople have to be competitive to survive, so working in an environment that has been designed to be non-competitive and thus non-threatening may well disengage them. There is an interesting dichotomy at the moment in many Western cultures where we are trying to both 'damp down' emotions in the workplace (so scary for everyone) *and* allow people to be emotional – part of the political correctness we referred to earlier. Some cultures (and even industries) are more aggressive than others in the way they interact with each other, and constraining emotions will demotivate.

Communication is also at the heart of motivating customers, and in Chapter 9 we will be looking at how we can integrate communications to improve the overall performance of the organization.

References

DISC Personal Profile System (1972). Minneapolis, MN: Inscape Publishing Inc.

Herzberg, F. (1959). *Work and the Nature of Man*. London: Chapman and Hall.

Maslow A.H. (1987). *Motivation and Personality*, 3rd edn. New York: Harper and Row.

Maslow, A.H. (1943). A theory of human motivation. *Psychological Review*, **50**, 379–396.

McGregor, D. (1957). *The Human Side of Enterprise*, Penguin.

McClelland, D.C. (1988). *Human Motivation*. Cambridge: Cambridge University Press.

Vroom, V. (1964). *Work and Motivation*. Chichester: Wiley.

9 Communications and relationships

Introduction

We have identified that there are three key functions that marketing managers are responsible for: information, value creation and communications. Central to value creation is creativity and innovation. Value creation is also dependent on skills, leadership and management, team-working, managing change and motivation. In this chapter we will explore the connection between communications, relationships and managing people, and in Part 3 of this book we will discuss information in more detail.

Marketing managers have two distinct communications roles and responsibilities. The first is the functional role, that of marketing communications with external customers and other stakeholders. The second is *effective* communications with internal staff.

Amongst other goals, communications plays a significant role in motivating employees, and in improving customer service and building customer relationships. Therefore, marketing managers need to communicate effectively both internally and externally, and lead by example. Marketing managers have a pivotal role in linking internal employee communications with external stakeholder communications.

The purpose of marketing communications

Considerable resources (time, personal effort and money) are invested in developing products and services. If the organization has also invested in marketing research, it is not unreasonable to expect success and returns in selling these products and services to customers. However, the task of ensuring a profitable exchange requires communicating with customers.

Promotional activities have long played a significant role in communicating with existing and potential customers. As customers have become more sophisticated and better understood in terms of their aspirations and needs, so have communications become more sophisticated.

Effective marketing communications can:

- create a need
- create, build and maintain awareness, image and reputation

- educate

- inform

- provoke a response

- reinforce competitive advantage

- influence

- build a relationship

- increase profits.

It is not enough just to be creative at marketing communications. We communicate in many different ways with customers and other stakeholders, and they all need to be consistent or they create confusion and even damage the efforts of our marketing communications.

Barriers to effective communication

Obstacles to effective communications that cause messages to be misunderstood, or simply not received at all, include the following:

- *Variation in style or tone* – for example, marketing communications being informal and friendly and written communications such as a letter being officious and threatening.

- *Disconnection between word and deed* – saying what people want and expect to hear, but not following through with actions.

- *Distance* – even with today's technology, people communicate less if there is distance between them; the misuse of email has not helped this problem.

- *Stereotyping* – making assumptions (usually negative) about people because of, for example age, sex, religion or race. This is also true externally when organizations fail to segment their markets, or group together a heterogeneous mass – for example, 50–80-year-olds are often seen as a single segment.

- *Overload* – too much information and/or communication in various forms; a real problem in organizations today.

- *Not listening* – distractions or preoccupation with something else can result in messages not being heard at a personal level and, externally, no mechanisms or process for listening to customers.

You may have industry- or organization-specific examples of barriers to communications, as well as departmental, team and individual barriers. We tend unconsciously to try to work around these barriers. A useful starting point in improving communications is to identify the barriers, understand the impact they have, and try to eliminate or reduce them.

It becomes more complicated to try to understand the possible external barriers to communications that are stopping you reaching your customers or stakeholders. Apart from the 'noise' we are familiar with (for example all the other organizations communicating with external markets), there are less obvious barriers, such as the internal prejudices and filters stakeholders use. The proliferation of media in itself makes it increasingly problematic trying to ensure the right media have been identified and selected.

The purpose and role of integrated marketing communications

There are many very good books on Integrated Marketing Communications (IMC), and it is not the intention here to attempt to provide a comprehensive coverage of the subject. We will provide an overview of IMC and make the connection between marketing communications, customer relationships and the management of people.

Integrated marketing communications is precisely what it says – it integrates not just marketing communications, but all aspects of how an organization communicates with its stakeholders. Some marketing communications are instantly recognizable, such as advertising or merchandizing, and others are less obvious, such as tone of voice and body language.

Some organizations are good at making sure that any employee who comes into contact with stakeholders in any way is trained to communicate effectively, including verbal, non-verbal and written communications.

In other organizations, some aspects of communications are neglected or ignored all together – for example, verbal, non-verbal and written forms other than marketing communications. We have all had experiences of inconsistent messages. The marketing communications can be slick, sophisticated and have appeal, but then when we try to buy a product or service the customer experience can be abysmal. Product experts are wheeled out in retail outlets, but know less about the product than you do. A favourite must be getting a telling-off for asking something unreasonable such as 'where do you keep the widgets?', or that look when you have inconsiderately interrupted a far more important conversation the sales staff were having with each other.

Such experiences are not just confined to customer-facing staff. Chief executives' *faux pas* have given us some lighter moments in recent years, such as the CE who announced to his shareholders that their products were 'crap'. (Remember Gerald Ratner's speech to the Institute of Directors? An estimated £500 m was wiped off the value of the company; he was pushed out of the company 18 months later, and the company was renamed from Ratner to Signet Group.) Why was this CE surprised when it hit the front pages of the national newspapers? A sign that these problems are endemic and deep-rooted is the near-abusive way in which some managers respond when you complain about service. If a manager lies and uses this contact with you as an opportunity to 'put you in your place', the organization has a serious problem.

Suddenly, the brand is not looking so slick or sophisticated. In extreme cases, if a manager makes customers or stakeholders angry enough, their *raison d'être* becomes exposing the organization and taking legal action. This can drag on for years, and the media love it because it is newsworthy. There will be plenty of media exposure without having to make any effort at all with marketing communications, or spend thousands or hundreds or millions of pounds!

Strategic focus

There are several reasons why integrated marketing communications requires a strategic focus. These include:

- the expectation that you will measure the effectiveness of communication activities, for example Return on Investment (ROI)
- the growing importance and visibility of corporate status and reputation
- corporate governance and ethical behaviour.

The need to add value and differentiate the organization through effective positioning has forced organizations to recognize the strategic role of the brand and the importance of integrated marketing communications. This affects the whole organization, not just the marketing department. It requires an understanding of how the entire organization communicates with its public, and the impact those communications have. It requires a commitment to managing communications at all levels and across the organization to maximize favourable customer and stakeholder perceptions and protect the organization's reputation. Figure 9.1 shows the communications planning relationship with corporate and marketing planning.

An organization's image and reputation is achieved through a combination of the following, and therefore IMC broadly includes:

1. *Culture and behaviour*, personality, values, attitudes, behaviour towards each other – management, employees and other stakeholders – interpersonal skills (verbal and non-verbal), performance (competitiveness and, for example, reliability) and integrity (conducting business, for example social and environmental responsibilities, ethics).

2. *Promotional tools* and techniques, for example public relations and advertising, and written forms including all written material (annual accounts, manuals, letters and email, etc.).

3. *Personal selling*, for example field salesforce and internal sales people.

4. *Products/service* – the actual benefits received.

5. *Customer service* – the *personal* service to provide a product or service; the *processes* that customers use and that are used by staff to serve customers; and *physical evidence* – for example, the atmosphere created by the premises, the décor and surroundings, logos, colour.

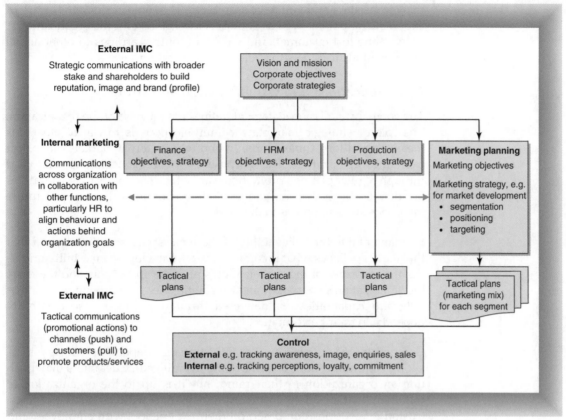

Figure 9.1 Integrated marketing communications planning relationships (©2000 Juanita Cockton)

As we have acknowledged, as managers progress up the organization they are increasingly expected to manage horizontally as well as vertically, and this is particularly true for marketing managers managing the organization's integrated marketing communications.

Marketing communications are most often interpreted as a series of promises made to customers and/or stakeholders about 'what the product or service can do for you'. The challenge for marketing managers is that any customer experience, including even a small amount of service, also communicates something. The customer experience is not always within the control of marketing and, even if it is, human beings are different, behave differently and interpret service differently. These intangible customer service experiences can be positive, negative or neutral, and without efforts to define and manage the service will most certainly be inconsistent.

Difference is not a problem, and can in fact make an experience personal and valued as opposed to impersonal and unwelcome. Inconsistency is a problem. Employees might all have their own way of delivering service, and if all experiences for customers are good then this is successful. If, however, some experiences are good, some are bad and others are neutral, it is inconsistent and you have a problem. The same customer is at risk of experiencing poor as well as good service. The risk for the organization is at least one lost customer, and word-of-mouth warnings to other actual and potential customers to avoid the organization.

Communications and vision, mission and strategy

The company's mission statement defines the purpose of the organization. The role of strategic marketing communications is to clarify what this means to and for people internally, and what external markets can expect from the organization. The purpose of the organization is reinforced through regular planned promotional activities. The company's aspirations are defined in the vision, and marketing communications signal future intentions and aspirations to the market.

Fundamental to the believability of these messages is credibility, and that the market believes what is communicated. Developing credibility underlies the messages of the organization's purpose and vision, and therefore the organization's know-how and capabilities are given prominence. Know-how and capabilities are delivered through employees, so credibility depends on their performance.

Competitive positioning and growth strategies depend on effective marketing communications to achieve the overall goal. Customers may position an organization in their mind, but it is up to the organization to influence that position positively and in line with its strategic goals. Customers will position based on their experiences with employees and processes, and so the organization must ensure that any messages that make claims about what customers can expect will be matched by their experiences. Obvious? Yes. So why are so many customers complaining about poor and very poor service?

Messages to customers are often by nature promises of what can be expected. To retain customer respect, and build loyalty and long-term relationships, promises must be kept (Figure 9.2). Promises lead to expectations, and if they are disappointed customers will simply walk away. Marketing managers have a duty to ensure that communications do not raise expectations or make claims that will not or cannot be met.

Communications, organization culture and management style

The culture of the organization, its personality, is expressed through the behaviour of all the people working for it. Organizational culture increasingly plays an important role in adding value to the organization brand. The organization's reputation is built through a mix of quality, reliability, innovation and behaviour, etc., which can all contribute positive attributes and have the potential to become core communication messages.

The issues we raised regarding leadership and management style, teamworking and motivation, and even problem-solving, are potential brand

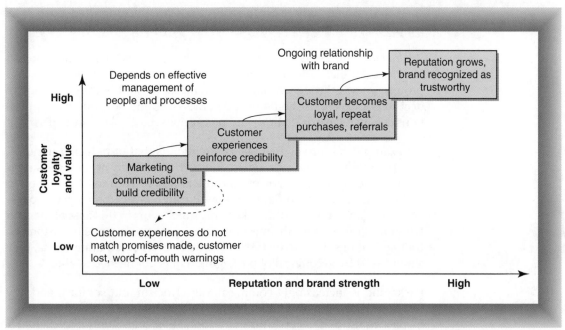

Figure 9.2   Integrated marketing communications (©2006 Juanita Cockton)

attributes. Trust and respect is passed on to customers through employee attitudes to service. Customers will feel either that they have been processed or that they have been served. The result of this communication with the customer is either an impersonal experience that results in the customer feeling uncomfortable, unhappy and/or unsatisfied, or a personal experience where the customer feels valued and expectations are at the very least met or exceeded.

Communications and integrity

The growing importance of corporate social responsibility (CSR) as part of corporate strategy requires a review of marketing communications for its honesty, integrity and intelligence.

Unfortunately, the early response of some communication programmes was to misuse CSR issues, seeing it as an opportunity to make claims about being 'environmentally friendly' that were at best naive and in some cases misleading. Many communications messages were suggestive of a commitment to CSR, but the words were not supported by actions. Meaningless claims of 'recycling' materials that are recycled anyway, or any other claim that is not supported by evidence of a real change to the way things are done, is dishonest and is viewed as such by consumers.

We can even get ourselves into trouble unintentionally. Our preoccupation with 'business as usual' means that quite rational decisions and actions can suddenly throw us into a crisis. Shell underestimated the strong feelings of customers when attempting to dump an oil rig in the sea. In countries such as Germany, where green issues are strongly supported, customers simply stopped buying products that had anything to do with Shell.

It is not enough to say that an organization is responsible in conducting its business. All that it does and how it does it must support the claims and promises made through various communications. Part of the evaluation of decisions and actions should include CSR issues and how our communications can manage expectations and perceptions, particularly in a crisis.

An example of an issue that needs attention is that of reducing unnecessary packaging. Having struggled and battled our way around the supermarket and shops and got our products home, we then have another battle – that of trying to fight our way through layer upon layer of packaging. Organizations could make some quick wins in this area alone, and we should think about the message excess packaging sends to customers. If organizations want to be taken seriously about eliminating waste, they should start by getting rid of packaging that is not needed at all.

Packaging is increasingly coming under criticism and scrutiny, and any forward-thinking marketing managers will be planning now for changes in packaging that meet future environmental legislation *and* customer expectations. One such example is the drinks industry.

Case study
Environmentally friendly consumption

There are incentives for companies to find creative solutions to reducing landfill waste. Savings in landfill tax make the effort worthwhile, and with consumer behaviour actively making choices based on an organization's environmental track record, the question is whether companies can afford not to find creative solutions.

After a faltering start, supermarkets are slowly responding by changing packaging to materials that break down into a harmless substance in home recycling bins. The move away from PVC plastics and towards more recyclable plastics is a positive step. Boots and Coca-Cola are among those experimenting with different and new materials to overcome the problem of destructive packaging.

Allied Glass, working with the Waste Resources Action Programme (Wrap – a state-sponsored organization aiming to create markets for recycled materials), is responding to the challenge of reducing the quantity of class used in its whisky bottles. In the trial alone it has succeeded in reducing the amount of glass used by 4788 tonnes, and there has been a positive response by various drink producers, including some supermarket own brands, signing up for the lightweight bottles. The benefits go beyond the amount of glass saved from landfill sites and include the bottles being lighter to transport and requiring less energy for production.

(Sources: Various web and print)

All these organizational issues are interwoven, and it is the responsibility of marketing to ensure that they are productively and successfully integrated. It is a tough call, because it is not just a question of taking responsibility for what marketing has authority over. Marketing must influence others, and this requires internal marketing that educates, informs and persuades people to communicate, in all forms, in a particular way. For external stakeholders, all these forms of experiences and communications become symbolized by the brand.

Brands and their role in building relationships

Managing brands at a tactical level was always easier; it did not require coordination across the organization or consideration of integrating organization behaviour to represent the desired meaning and values of the brand.

Once brands appeared on balance sheets as assets, managers began to realize their true potential. Ever since, brand management has become much more strategic. This requires investment, long-term commitment and innovation. Brands are central in establishing a competitive (or distinctive for non-profit organizations) position in the market.

Positioning takes place at two key levels. At the strategic organization level, decisions determine the unique position in the market that differentiates the organization from others. This has implications for marketing and marketing communication strategies. Any strategy must reflect the competitive position and be designed to create, build, maintain or improve this position as dictated by the positioning statement. Messages must reflect the actual and/or desired position.

Once a strategy is adopted, everything in the organization is organized to deliver products and services based on that position, and this will influence marketing decisions, the design of marketing strategies and the marketing mix.

The marketing mix is the next level that affects positioning decisions (Figure 9.3) – the specific benefits and values associated with products and services. These include both rational and emotional values attributed to brands.

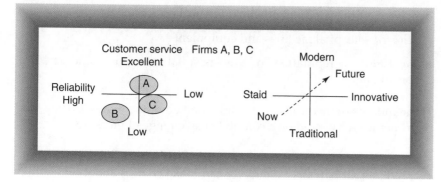

Figure 9.3
Positioning maps

Communication messages will reinforce positive benefits and values attributed to the offer, and the brand can play a significant role as a source of competitive advantage and a means of building customer loyalty.

A brand is more than just a physical product or service, and can help to build relationships with customers, shareholders and other stakeholders. This is particularly important in markets where the organization has no face-to-face contact with customers, such as fmcg. A brand is also more than just the component parts that make up a product or elements of service; it has additional values attributed to it by customers (Figure 9.4).

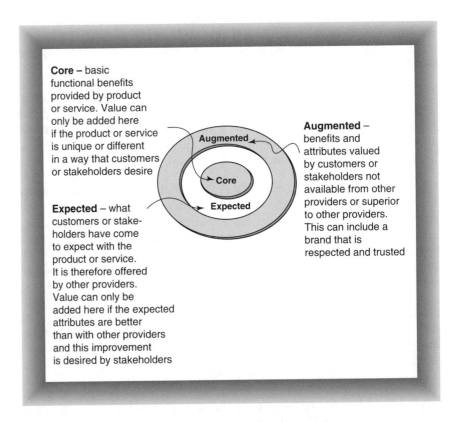

Core – basic functional benefits provided by product or service. Value can only be added here if the product or service is unique or different in a way that customers or stakeholders desire

Expected – what customers or stake-holders have come to expect with the product or service. It is therefore offered by other providers. Value can only be added here if the expected attributes are better than with other providers and this improvement is desired by stakeholders

Augmented – benefits and attributes valued by customers or stakeholders not available from other providers or superior to other providers. This can include a brand that is respected and trusted

Figure 9.4
Brand value and attributes (Collins, 1989)

If we take a hospital as an example, patients might expect the following:

- *core* – medical care from qualified medical professionals

- *expected* – hospital facilities and equipment

- *augmented* – reputation of the hospital, surgeons and medical consultants.

The standards of medical care, facilities and equipment are all rising, and performance is assessed on a comprehensive range of measures.

Some patients have always had the choice between state and private provision. Now all patients potentially can make choices about where they will be treated within the state sector – something that was inconceivable a few years ago. Expectations regarding the treatment you can get depend on which country you are in. However, the trend of rising expectations is set, and service is increasingly seen as part of treatment.

Hospitals are now brands, whether this is intentional or not, and performance is being compared with hospitals both across the country and in other countries.

A brand adds value to the product or service. Added value often has more potential to differentiate one offer from another than the core and expected functional benefits sought by customers. For the hospital, this might be investing in the latest technology and attracting the top medical practitioners in the industry to build a reputation for leading-edge care, possibly in a particular field. Other hospitals might focus investment on care in the community. Hospital decisions are complicated by political agendas and the local community, which also plays a part in determining what the hospital might focus on.

The communications effort, amongst other things, should be concerned with promoting positive associations with the brand that are meaningful and valued by customers. Sony is a good example of a brand that is perceived as trustworthy, gives high-quality performance and is reliable. This reduces the customer's need to take time deciding between brands. The Sony brand is trusted and reduces risk (Figure 9.5).

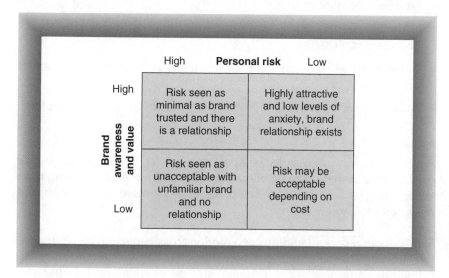

Figure 9.5
Brands and risk
(©2000 Juanita Cockton)

Consumers want to reduce risk when making purchases, particularly if the purchase is financially or emotionally expensive (reflects their self-image). When evaluating the different offers, they are looking for clues as to what can be expected from the offer. A brand is the organization's means of providing clues to what can be expected. What the brand stands for represents the values attributed to it by consumers.

Creating a brand

Name

Getting the name right has never been more important, particularly if international or global markets are to be pursued. Even in domestic markets, customers are better educated, more mobile and aware of foreign places, so are more likely to respond negatively to a name that can cause offence or just result in a giggle. Considerable research effort now goes into finding the right name (and they can still get it wrong).

The name is a signal imbued with values; a clue to what can be expected. It can play an important role in providing associations for customers that help to describe the brand more fully. The name can also act as a barrier to other entrants and competitors. If names come to mean the product or action – for example, we 'Hoover' a carpet rather than 'vacuum' a carpet – then customers go into outlets asking for a Hoover rather than a vacuum cleaner. Velcro and Formica are also names that have become synonymous with particular products. Establishing the name as a trademark can provide better protection than patents, which are often time-consuming, expensive and difficult to get.

Names should:

- reflect useful and if possible unique associations (for example friendly, reliable, fast)
- be able to be symbolized
- be memorable (being different and creative helps, providing it does not become complex)
- pronounceable (people will not remember names they cannot pronounce)
- avoid unfavourable associations (requires a search of the wider context).

Symbol

A symbol cannot necessarily be spoken; however, it has the advantage over a name in that it can be more universal and memorable. It can have faster impact than a name, and embrace so much more in terms of brand representation and meaning.

Symbols can represent and inspire emotions for people that result in positive attitudes to the brand. Cartoon characters can be fun and amusing (sometimes reflecting regional traits), and people relate to the character and therefore come to like the brand – take, for example, the Tetley Tea Folk and the Pillsbury Dough Boys.

Symbols should:

- portray something of the brand; there should be easy association with positive feelings evoked by the symbol

- be able to evolve over time to avoid becoming dated

- be protected from competitors externally and enthusiastic promotions campaigns internally; no promotions should be allowed to damage the symbol or what it represents.

Slogans

Names and symbols, particularly together, can do much to indicate what the brand represents, and are stronger if they evolve with the times rather than changing. However, there is a limit to what they can do, and more is needed to help customers with brand transitions. With strong competition in many markets, more is needed to ensure that the brand is easily recognized and quickly delivers the desired associations.

While names and symbols should be relatively constant, a slogan provides a much greater opportunity to reflect the brand's current and future aims. Slogans can be adapted to reinforce the current positioning strategy or support repositioning intentions.

Slogans should:

- provide additional associations to the name and symbol

- reinforce the name and symbol

- be specific, relevant, brief, and memorable.

The name, symbol and slogan should provide competitive advantage. If they do not, it's back to the drawing board.

Developing the brand with the product and service development

Traditionally, products and services are launched onto the market and advertising and selling are used to build sales. As time passes the product name becomes a 'brand', recognized and valued for what it offers. When a replacement product is launched under the now brand-name, it is the brand that builds sales.

New product/service development processes need to incorporate the meaning of the brand in all its markets right from the beginning; it must not be added as an afterthought. It is not enough to be concerned with the mechanics of the product or service; the values of the brand are also significant. The product or service must convey the full meaning of the brand, and both rational and emotional attributes must be designed in during the new offer development process.

Product/service brand development therefore needs to define brand quality while still on the drawing board.

Brand quality

Quality is relative to the customer's perception of quality, what it means to the customer. A lot of effort and resources can be invested in improving quality to be competitive, and yet still fail to maintain the existing customer base and/or attract new customers. This can happen when quality is defined by managers without reference to customers; this will not deliver the desired results. Customers' definition of quality is relative to their needs, uses and motives for buying. This criterion is often a mix of both tangible functional benefits, which can be objectively measured, and intangible emotional benefits, which are far more difficult to measure objectively. Even rational benefits are susceptible to subjective evaluation.

Quality is derived from a number of sources:

- *component quality* – the ingredients of the product

- *process quality* – the way in which the product or service is made or delivered

- *service quality* – how the product or service is delivered through personal service.

Perceptions of quality can be influenced by a number of factors, some of which are a result of deliberate strategies by the organization and some of which are not. Those perceptions that are not a deliberate strategy can be positive or negative – for example, good or bad press coverage, or accidents. Marketing communications is responsible for forming and maintaining positive perceptions.

Customer service and communications

Product/service and brand development must also include customer service development. This is essential if it is to differentiate the organization. The competence of people in making products and services will affect qualities such as reliability. Process and personal quality are delivered through customer service. Customer service is about how customers and stakeholders receive their product or service.

Processes create perceptions by being simple, fast, accessible, responsive and reliable – how simple and fast depends on the product or service. These perceptions can be positive or negative and become brand attributes. Sadly, poor processes can negate the impact of good personal service. However, sometimes good personal service can negate the impact of poor processes – but we should not leave this to chance.

Personal service also creates perceptions through competence and credibility, accessibility and responsiveness, integrity, courtesy, helpfulness and understanding, reliability and security. Again, customer experiences of personal service will become brand traits, and whether or not they are values depends on good or bad experiences.

Neglect either processes or personal service and we communicate very damaging messages to our market. Effective training and development ensure that we prepare employees to deliver high-quality service. Good leadership and management practices influence behaviour, maintain standards, and can minimize the risk of unintentionally communicating the wrong messages through service.

Processes are used as a tool in communicating – a means of developing and delivering communications – but they are not always thought of as a of communication message in themselves. They should be. Customers are increasingly affected by processes; online or telephone contact, cash machines and tills in retail outlets are all regular features of customer experiences. Slow and unreliable processes can be frustrating, and inaccessibility is increasingly seen as a major criticism by customers. Paradoxically, online and telephone contact, which should provide the greatest accessibility, is actually designed to do the exact opposite in many organizations. These experiences damage or prevent relationship-building with customers.

Perceptions of quality are also influenced by brand associations – another aspect of building a strong brand.

Brand association

Brand association comes from the connections people make between names, symbols and slogans. McDonald's is associated with the symbol of the golden arches; Cadbury's chocolates with the colour purple; Sainsbury's with the slogan '*Try something new*'. The value of the brand is represented in these associations, and provides meaning to the values attributed to the brand. Associations can contribute to the success of the brand by:

- speeding up evaluation through easy retrieval and processing of information
- provoking positive attitudes towards the brand
- broadening definitions of the brand's know-how and ability
- aiding and enlightening the interpretation of the name, symbol and slogan
- providing a context for positioning through the circles in which the brand moves.

Brand associations are not just derived from the name, symbol and slogan, but also from a number of other sources. Associations are also not confined to the activities of the organization, such as the marketing mix. Brand associations can also include:

- the industry to which the organization belongs (for example 'high tech')
- personalities used in promotions (for example celebrities or a figure of authority)

- a high-profile leader (seen, for example, as adventurous, anti-establishment or a pillar of the community).

All these associations say something about the brand to the customers. Brand-building is multifaceted, and the factors that affect brand-building are complicated further if trying to build a global brand.

The same rules for creating and building a brand apply to building global brands, but there are additional factors to consider. One of the problems of building a global brand is how the brand is interpreted. Can the brand be interpreted in the same way, with the same meanings and values, and will this be valid in all markets? Translation of the brand goes beyond the name and ability to pronounce it, and a major problem in some developing markets is the lack of legal protection.

Favourable conditions for global brands include:

- social or cultural change

- new sectors

- universal values.

Brand loyalty and customer relationships

Ultimately, our goal for the brand and marketing communications is to build loyalty and relationships with customers and stakeholders. There are degrees of loyalty, and it is helpful to understand these because they determine the marketing effort and activities necessary to achieve the goal (see Chapter 1, Figure 1.7).

Part of the marketing task is to identify who the loyal and potentially loyal customers are, their attitudes to the brand, and other buying-behaviour characteristics. Quite distinct and individual marketing activities will then need to be designed for each group of customers identified.

Marketing's goal is to improve customer loyalty so that customers become advocates of the brand – active supporters and promoters. This requires designing the marketing mix to meet specific needs, and communication programmes that talk personally to the customer groups. Communications that 'talk personally' to customers are focused on needs and motives; the organization knows what the customer needs and focuses messages on those needs.

More difficult to manage is the marketing mix, because in one way or another the whole organization is involved (including outlets such as distribution channels). To ensure the promises made through communication activities are kept, all activities must be coordinated, integrated and consistent. If they are not, customer loyalty is difficult to achieve or maintain, and a relationship cannot be established.

Developing integrated marketing communications strategy

All we have discussed so far in this chapter encapsulates how people build relationships with customers and stakeholders. We provide the following as a framework for developing an integrated marketing communications strategy, and the key issues that need to be considered.

If we want our integrated marketing communications to build customer loyalty and relationships, we need to be able to target specific groups of customers and design communications to appeal to those groups.

Target audience

Communications effectiveness is dependent on making choices about the customer groups to serve. During the development of the marketing strategy, segments will have been identified and selected as those most appropriate to target. A product (business strength/s) will be matched with markets (customer opportunities).

We should remember that we often communicate with a broader stakeholder target than just people we are selling to. Other stakeholders include shareholders, suppliers, distributors, financial institutions, regulatory bodies, the government and, of course, the media. Different communication strategies are needed for different purposes.

The process of segmentation ensures that we have a comprehensive understanding of the selected targets. This enables products and services to be designed to meet needs, and communication messages to be designed to attract attention and break through the 'noise'.

Before any communications campaigns are designed, we need to know:

- to whom are we speaking
- what motivates and influences them
- how buyers behave.

If we can understand the motivational factors and influences that affect people's perceptions, behaviour and decisions, we can design marketing communications messages to appeal to specific needs and wants. At a very superficial level, influences include:

- social class, age, sex, family
- reference groups, family lifecycle
- race and religion
- income and occupation.

There are more sophisticated segmentation techniques, for example:

- psychographic – by personality and lifestyle

- geodemographic – combining geographic and demographic information with patterns of purchase behaviour, including lifestyle (for example MOSAIC and ACORN).

Each method of segmentation has something to offer and provides some essential but limited information to help us communicate effectively with our target audiences.

Segmentation should be a source of competitive advantage, providing insights into what customers need and want – and that requires quality intelligence. The organization's own segmental analysis to gather information on customers is more likely to provide insights not available from other sources. Customer intelligence will be discussed in the following chapters.

The Decision Making Unit (DMU) is another way of segmenting and understanding better the people being targeted. It is typically used in organizational buying, and can also be used in consumer markets. The DMU consists of a number of people who affect the decision to buy, rather than just one person making the decision. DMUs typically consist of:

- *users* – people who actually use the product or service

- *influencers* – people who may have some technical expertise and can advise on the purchase, or people who have power and exert that power to influence decisions

- *buyers* – people who have the formal authority to purchase.

There may also be approvers, who sign off a purchase decision, and deciders, who have the ultimate say; all DMUs are different, and depend on the size and complexity of the organization. The value of the DMU is that marketers can identify the likely needs of different members of the DMU, and make sure messages promote solutions to their specific problems or benefits sought.

To construct effective communication programmes, the information from segments should provide insights into who you are talking to and why – the customer evaluation criteria:

- *rational needs* – functional benefits sought from products/services (tangible benefits such as quality, speed, reliability)

- *emotional needs* – expressive value, motives for buying products/services (intangible values such as status, aspirations).

The emotional values can often be the key to competitive advantage, so it is important to include them in the overall brand offer. Some motivational techniques discussed in Chapter 8 have been used effectively in marketing communications, particularly Maslow's hierarchy of needs. When we have this information, we can develop our marketing communications for specific targets.

Essentially, the role of communications is to persuade people either to continue or to change attitudes, which in turn reinforces or changes behaviour. Behaviour is influenced by what we know (or think we know) and believe (*cognition*). Attitudes are learned from, for example, experiences, opinions and observation, and are often expressed as feelings and evaluations (*affection*). Behaviour is influenced by our knowledge and attitudes, and results in actions or behavioural tendencies (*conation*).

The role of communications is to move people through these stages with a positive result (persuasion):

- *cognitive = thinking* – individual becomes aware of the brand, acquires information and forms beliefs

- *affective = feelings* and evaluations are formed about the brand

- *conative = behaviour* – intention to purchase (or not) a particular brand.

Marketing communications objectives

Communications objectives are derived from the marketing objectives, and can simply be setting an awareness objective – for example:

improve awareness from 30 percent to 65 percent of target audience by the year 20XX.

For business-to-business markets, you would expect an awareness objective to be much more ambitious – even 100 percent, depending on customer numbers and levels of competition.

A number of response hierarchy models (Figure 9.6) have been developed which attempt to understand the process of buyer behaviour, and therefore what we need to achieve with our communications.

Taking the AIDA model, for example, if we have already achieved *awareness* then the task is to generate *interest* and move potential buyers through the stages of *desire* and *action*. When the task is understood, it is usually easier to estimate the time it may take to achieve it.

These sequential models are not foolproof. One challenge is trying to establish what stage people are at, and, as we have already suggested, the more we know about our target market the better we can design our communications. People may not go through all the stages or in sequence; however, used as a guide, the models do provide a starting point for setting communications objectives.

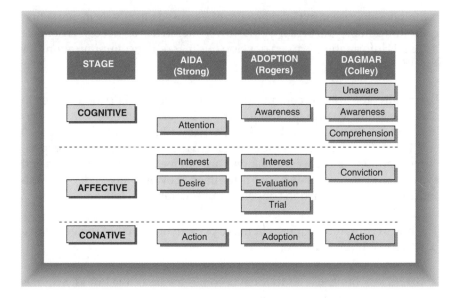

Figure 9.6
Response hierarchy models (Strong, 1925; Colley, 1961; Rogers, 1962)

Communications strategy

Communications strategy was originally essentially a combination of push and pull. Chris Fill (2002) added another important dimension to communications, and defined communications strategies as follows:

1. *Pull strategies*. Pull strategies are targeted at customers, consumers and end-users, and are designed to 'pull' the customers into outlets, etc. Key to this strategy is generating awareness, helping to form attitudes and motivate certain behaviour that ultimately results in demanding the availability of the brand.

2. *Push strategies*. To ensure that supply meets demand for the brand, push strategies are targeted at channels or networks that provide the brand. Key to this strategy is encouraging suppliers to hold stocks and allocate resources to actively selling the brand.

3. *Profile strategies*. Profile strategies are strategic and are targeted at all stakeholders of the organization, both external and internal. Key to this strategy is the creating, building and maintaining of the desired image of the organization, what it stands for and its reputation.

Push and pull strategies will be linked to and integrated with profile strategies. Profile strategies increasing focus on building the corporate brand.

Positioning and messages

Positioning and messages brings us back to the product or service, our brand values and our communications objectives. Our messages will be a mix of rational benefits that can be expected from the product or service, and emotional benefits that are represented by the brand – for example, security, innovation or stability.

Promotions mix selection

Promotional activities are the organization's key means of communicating with its public, customers, suppliers, distributors, financial institutions, etc.

During marketing research, the identification of target markets will have included assessment of the best ways of reaching the targets through appropriate channels with the appropriate promotional mix.

Key factors affecting promotional mix selection include:

● whether it is a business-to-business or consumer market

● whether it is mass-market, has numerous segments or is a niche market

● whether it is a product or service

● technology (in terms of both product/service and media channels).

The selection of promotional tools will also be determined by the objectives set and the people being targeted. For example, if we take the AIDA model we can see how advertising is good for creating and building awareness, but not necessarily good at getting action. Personal selling is highly effective at getting action, but poor at creating awareness (Figure 9.7).

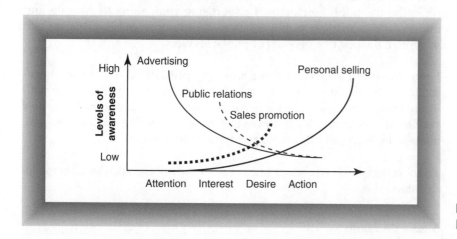

Figure 9.7
Levels of awareness

It is not as simple as the graph in Figure 9.7 suggests, and does depend on the industry and the products and services sold. Television advertising to mass markets can be highly effective at pulling people into retail outlets to purchase the product. The more aspirational the product or service, the more aspirational advertising can achieve in persuading people not just to buy but also to take action. However, the more technical or complex the problem, the more likely it is that personal selling is needed to achieve action.

Figure 9.8 shows the promotional mix available to the marketer. The promotional tools to the right-hand side are more likely to be used in

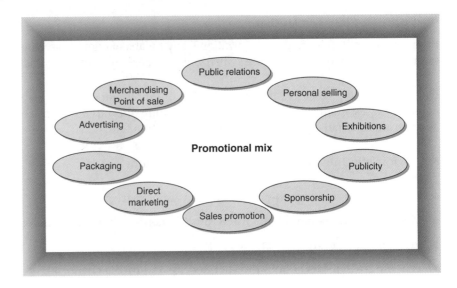

Figure 9.8
Promotional mix

business-to-business markets, and those to the left-hand side are more likely to be used in consumer markets. However, this is not a rule, and both markets use a range of promotional techniques. In the public sector it is unusual to see sales promotion being used, but not unheard of. More typically, the public sector uses advertising campaigns to educate and inform, and to manage public relations to minimize public criticism and maximize the positive benefits of public services.

Large charities have become much more sophisticated in the use of promotional tools, and use a wider range of techniques. Small charities with limited resources tend to be more creative and keep promotional activities very local – for example, fundraising days sponsored by local businesses, mail shots, even exhibitions, if appropriate, can be used.

The next decision is where our messages should appear, and these are media decisions.

Media decisions

There are two types of decisions facing the marketer:

1. *Inter-media* decisions concern which media to use (for example TV, press).

2. *Intra-media* decisions concern which medium to use within the category (for example *Daily Telegraph* or *Times*).

The media channel(s) selected should provide the best match in terms of access to the target audience the company is trying to reach. The objective is to reach as many of the target audience as possible and as cost-effectively as possible. The development of new channels is opening up opportunities for businesses that were previously not available.

Control

Budgets

Marketing and communications budgets are arrived at in a variety of ways, including:

- percentage of turnover or profit
- incremental budgeting (this fails to prioritize and encourages spending for the sake of it)
- competitive parity (this assumes that competitors know what they are doing).

Percentage of turnover or profit is the most common method, and does have the advantage of being realistic about what can be afforded. However, these and other methods fail to take account of the objective and what is realistically required to achieve it. The objective and task method does make such allowances, and allocates a budget that will support all tasks needed to achieve the objective. Smaller organizations may have to balance this with what is affordable.

Budget allocation across different promotional activities depends on the industry (business-to-business or consumer markets), objectives, target audience and messages. Expenditure is monitored throughout the period of the plan.

Scheduling

All plans have a planning horizon – a time within which the plan must be executed and objectives achieved. Activities are also often dependent on each other; one activity must be completed before another can commence, so scheduling activities to make the best use of time is necessary.

Gantt charts (Figure 9.9) and, for planning that involves hundreds of activities, critical path analysis are useful techniques for ensuring that activities have deadlines and are scheduled according to sequence.

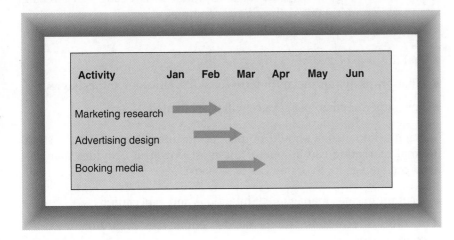

Figure 9.9
Simple Gantt chart

Measurement

Measuring promotional activities are advertising (queries generated and conversion rates, attitude change pre-, during and post-testing), PR (column inches) and sales promotion (sales volume and sustainability).

Measuring integrated marketing communications are:

- *strategic communications* – perceptions of position, brand strength and reputation, internal morale, loyalty and commitment
- *relationships* – longevity, value, repeat purchase, referrals
- *customer service* – people (attainment of targets, problem-solving, courtesy), processes (reliability, speed, simplicity), physical evidence (perception of, for example, atmosphere, décor, etc.)
- *marketing mix* (product, price, place) performance.

This integrated marketing communications strategy is designed with the intention of building relationships with customers, either directly or indirectly. If directly, the emphasis in promotional activities will be personal, face-to-face contact; if indirectly, the brand has to work much harder to build relationships with end-users that the organization does not come directly into contact with.

The plan must also take account of publicity not within the control of the business – for example, bad press, word of mouth, etc. Crisis management is part of communications planning, as is influencing the less obvious communications.

Internal marketing

Effective internal communications seem to be a problem for many organizations, even for those who make a concerted effort to do it better. The danger for internal communications is if it becomes a 'passing-on data process', which is not necessarily always communicating.

As we saw in Figure 9.1, IMC includes internal marketing and aligning internal communications with external communications. If an organization is promising customers superior customer service, employees need to know:

- that this is expected of them
- what precisely this means in terms of skills, attitudes and behaviour
- how superior customer service will be evaluated.

Managing knowledge should be part of an internal marketing system. Internal marketing can be one of the most powerful activities management can engage in, for a number of reasons:

- it communicates management intentions and expectations
- it informs, educates and persuades employees regarding intended courses of action

- it motivates

- it clarifies responsibilities.

Internal marketing is an activity that unites the workforce behind organizational goals. It involves the use of formal processes (such as the internal marketing plan and lines of communication), semi-formal processes (for example, team meetings) and informal processes (such as one-to-one conversations).

By communicating management intentions, including the justification for embarking on a particular plan, and revealing how all in the organization will contribute to the implementation of an intended strategy, management can reduce conflicts that might arise from the 'them and us' syndrome. The information distributed through internal marketing activities promotes better understanding of why the organization is following a particular direction. A better informed and motivated workforce can be a real source of competitive advantage.

In communicating with internal target audiences, organizations should be clear that they are usually informing, educating, persuading, etc. There should be a clear objective and purpose to the communications, rather than just moving data around the organization – which serves no real purpose other than increasing data overload. One of the most common examples of this is the 'everybody on the distribution list' syndrome.

Internal marketing can overcome various problems, particularly during mergers and acquisitions.

Case study

Communicating to unite

Mergers and acquisitions are a common feature of organizations today, and one of the problems that comes with a merger or acquisition is the 'them and us' syndrome. If mergers and acquisitions are not managed effectively, the original benefits of bringing two organizations together often fail to be realized.

One such challenge faced an advertising agency when it acquired a PR consultancy. During the run-up to the acquisition there was much speculation, rumour and gossip about what this meant for employees in both companies. The company had effectively managed external communications with customers and other stakeholders, but realized that planned internal communications had been omitted.

It set about developing an internal communications plan to establish a more open and transparent approach. The first stage was to inform all employees of the benefits and necessity of the two companies coming together, to remain competitive. The second stage was to invite employees to engage in identifying all the potential issues involved in bringing the two companies together.

Emails were used to update staff on developments. A specially designed website was set up, with employee biographies and contact details. It also had a frequently asked questions section, with answers and the opportunity to email personal questions. Job loss was a main preoccupation, and this allowed people to air their views on the way things had been done and concerns about how things were going to be done in the future. This feedback to management helped to identify some changes to management practices.

The speed and interactive nature of the website and emails meant that concerns could be dealt with quickly, even if they could not be resolved right away. This prevented destructive and inaccurate rumour and gossip taking over, and encouraged the uniting of the two companies.

(Sources: Various web and print)

Technology promised much for communications, internally and externally, and there is no doubt that it has delivered much. However, it cannot be the only way to communicate either internally or externally, and to be most effective the methods must be selected to suit the purpose of the communication and the target being communicated with. Too often, technology is used inappropriately – the commonly cited example is that of people using email when a telephone call would have sorted the problem in a quarter of the time.

Key factors affecting success

Senior management must be committed to the concept of internal marketing, and be prepared to commit resources to it. Employee cooperation in positive and effective communications is also important. Open communications, honesty and trust should be a cultural norm, and attention to developing communication skills part of everyone's development. Figure 9.10 offers a framework for internal marketing.

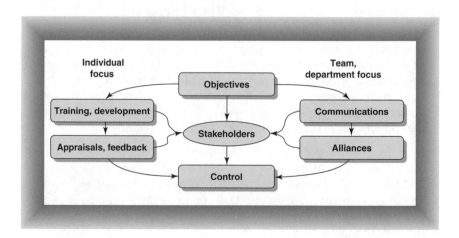

Figure 9.10
Internal marketing communications
(©2000 Juanita Cockton)

Objectives

Clarify what is to be achieved, the desired outcomes and by when. Sometimes it may be difficult to quantify objectives, in which case state internal marketing goals. These might include:

- unite the workforce behind organization goals, strategies and plans
- promote organizational change and marketing orientation
- encourage sharing and living the organization values
- establish commitment to total quality
- encourage commitment to customer service
- improve interdepartmental relationships
- improve knowledge and information sharing.

Timescales can always be included, and where possible try to quantify the goal.

The purpose of the internal marketing program determines the style and tone. During change, education and information are important. During difficult times, reassurance and transparency take priority.

Stakeholders

Identify internal stakeholders and their perceptions and expectations, what their needs, motives and concerns are (individuals and teams), and how the objectives will affect them. We discussed internal segments during managing change, and if the initiative is change they may be appropriate. If, however, the goal is to improve interdepartmental relationships, segments will be different – and not necessarily simply by department. Attitudes to interdepartmental relationships will be different, and these need to be established.

Communications

What messages are to be communicated? Do we need to educate, explain, inform, reassure, persuade, convince, etc.? Design communications to address the interests of different groups. Manage expectations – establish two-way communications and feedback mechanisms, regular, honest and timely communications.

Design a range of internal promotional activities. This can include newsletters, an intranet, team briefings, seminars, and personalized communications and messages. The more difficult the situation – for example, managing change – the more personal the communications should become. Make sure messages are specific and relevant. For example, newsletters can slip into becoming superfluous and irrelevant, just to fill space.

Timing and frequency of communications should avoid information overload, and should not be dictated by arbitrary decisions on a 'once-a-week' basis and the number of issues. If there is nothing to say, do not say something just because, for example, the newsletter is always produced once a month and is always eight pages long.

Alliances

Alliances involve personnel exchanges across different departments or divisions. Exchanges can be a very powerful way of improving the understanding of what other people in the organization do. They promote better relationships and should establish and encourage networking, can break down departmental barriers ('them and us' syndromes) and improve idea and information sharing. They also have the benefit of encouraging people to see things from a different point of view, so can improve problem-solving. These exchanges can be secondments or even visits of anything from an hour to several days, and can involve shadowing staff, presentations or briefings on what the department does, or a combination.

Training and development

Equip people with the knowledge and skills needed so they are competent to do whatever is expected of them – for example, improve customer service, improve communications, and improve creativity and innovation.

Appraisals and feedback

There are the usual appraisals and feedback mechanisms, but when a part of an internal marketing program these should reflect components of the objectives of the program. This might include specific two-way feedback on progress towards achieving the goal – for example, improving the quality of service or the way in which behaviour is reflecting new values.

Control

As with the external marketing communications plan, an internal marketing communications plan requires a budget, a schedule, and performance measurement.

The human resource management team is predominately responsible for communicating with all staff on issues concerning people policies and conditions. Marketing is often the driver of strategy and change, and therefore must take responsibility, in collaboration with others, for internal marketing, aligning people behind organizational goals and strategy, and in particular encouraging a behaviour norm that leads to quality customer service and experiences.

This internal dimension to marketing communications and coordinating communications across the organization is a relatively new challenge for marketing managers. In smaller organizations it is much easier to manage and coordinate the complex components of factors that impact on communications, but in larger organizations it can be extremely difficult.

This is not helped by structures that separate marketing activities – a typical example being the establishment of a customer relationship management department that does not report to marketing, which is bizarre and more common than you might think. Perhaps this explains so much in terms of the failure of many CRM initiatives.

Communications is central to building customer relationships, so to separate the two and treat them differently is designing in failure.

Summary

We build customer loyalty and relationships through integrated marketing communications that deliberately manage and influence:

- *organizational culture and behaviour* – leading to consistency in outward expressions of values and performance and in all written forms

- *product, price and place* – these are designed to meet needs and match customer perceptions of quality

- *customer service and personal selling* – these are designed from the customers' perspective. Processes are efficient for us, effective for customers and support employees in doing their job. People are training to service customers to a standard that will positively differentiate the organization from others

- *communication activities* – messages are tailored to specific targets, and we only make promises we can keep.

All these activities are required to be consistent in style and tone. Internal marketing is part of the means of achieving this consistency.

References

Colley, R. (1961). *Defining Advertising Goals for Measured Advertising Results.* New York: DAGMAR, New York Association of National Advertisers.

Collins, B. (1989). *Marketing for Engineers, Management for Engineers* (D. Samson, ed.), Melbourne: Longman Cheshire, 347–409.

Fill, C. (2002). *Marketing Communications Contexts, Strategies and Applications*, 3rd edn. Upper Saddle River, NJ: Prentice Hall.

Rogers, E.M. (1962). *Adoption, Diffusion of Innovations*. New York: Free Press.

Strong, E.K. (1925). *AIDA: The Psychology of Selling*. New York: McGraw-Hill.

Part III Resources

10 Time and technology

Introduction

Resource is a precious commodity when we implement a marketing strategy. There are a number of ways to consider the resource issue: manpower, knowledge, money and support technology, but, above all, time. We can consider manpower as a function of time; the classic triad of money, quality and time come into play here – given that the implementation has to be to a set quality (as demanded by the market), the balance of time and money remains.

In this chapter we need to consider the application of time and technology to the marketing implementation. We must consider these two resources in terms of:

1. Time to market.

2. Technology available in the market, thinking here about both:

    ● technology for product innovation and

    ● technology available as a support function in the company.

We need to consider these aspects because time-to-market is a function of our expected hold on the development of the market; and technology because it is a measure of either:

● the customer's perception of our status in the marketplace, or

● the automated support in the workplace.

A further series of questions arise about their nature:

1. Why is time important? Is it:

    ● timing that is important (for example a relative activity, such as 'first-to-market'), or

    ● time itself (for example an absolute activity, such as 'launch on 1 September')?

2. What is technology in this context? Are we asking about:

    ● *industrial technology* (for example the development of long-life egg powder for a cake mix, or special lightweight toughened plastics for soccer boots, or sub-Etherband digital radio, or 5 GB USB portable memory stores, or non-corrosive bleaching agents) which we intend to incorporate into our products for innovation or product enhancement; or

● *workplace technologies*, that is the application to marketing of practical scientific principles (for example database development for storing, retrieving and processing customer data; computer modelling for pricing)?

Technologies in the workplace (rather than technologies developed for customer products) could be considered as fulfilling four roles (Figure 10.1):

1. Improving the speed of an activity, for example computers.

2. Improving the precision of an activity, for example satellite navigation.

3. Overcoming limitations, for example rocket science, nano-technology.

4. Reducing costs, for example electronic publishing.

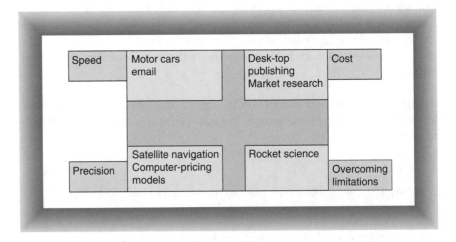

Figure 10.1
The four elements of technology

We could reduce these four elements to two:

1. *Overcoming limitations.* If getting to the moon means reducing the distance between the moon and me, then hot air balloons, whilst reducing that distance (and an advance on jumping up and down) will never allow man to reach the moon. Aircraft, while offering superior height to the balloon and reducing the distance between the moon and me still more, rely on a limiting technology (for example movement in a viscous fluid) and aero-engineering is still an insufficient technology to get Man to the moon, let alone beyond. The best optical astronomical telescope will never 'see' what radio telescopes can see.

2. *Improving speed.*

● Precision is a manifestation of speed and overcoming limitations; we could work at any level of granularity, given sufficient time, but at the limit of precision newer technologies are required to achieve the next level of granularity.

- Cost is a manifestation of time: were it possible to take as long as necessary to achieve the same outcome, the cost would be significantly higher.

In our case, then, in terms of *workplace technology* we should think of it as primarily something which can reduce the time taken to do something, and which can overcome limitations imposed by the laws of the environment. Workplace technology should be considered as a manifestation of time.

Time

Why is time important?

To meet the customers' expectations faster implies the faster delivery of 'best value' – which infers that we have to strategize faster, implement faster, and thereby meet the customers' expectations of best value faster than the competitor. In other words, we are not talking about absolute time, but about relative time. When you and your friend are being chased by a bear, you don't have to run faster than the bear – just faster than your friend.

Attitude change is also related to time. Changing perceptions is a fundamental part of marketing. We can historically look back at change and wonder why it didn't happen faster. Indeed, in the history of marketing there are several events where too fast a change resulted in failed product.

So how do we consider relative time over absolute time?

Stalk and Hout (2003) regard time as the next competitive advantage. His main thesis lies in the reduction of waiting time to gain absolute time advantage. As one wag put it, 'Marketing success is like going to a dance: be first there and best dressed.' However, reducing waiting time can also be employed in making more absolute time available, thereby giving flexibility in the use of relative time. We need to consider how relative time gives competitive advantage, while traditionally absolute time has been regarded as critical.

Time and industrial technologies

Historically, there has been a relationship between first-to-market and sustained market share. Clark and Wheelwright (1992) found a relationship for consumer electronics (see Figure 10.2).

This is not, however, a universal law. It assumes that the market is ready for the innovation displayed in the new product, or at least in assimilating it.

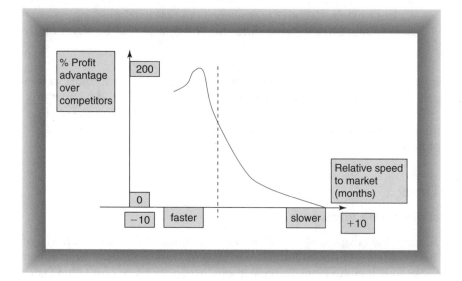

Figure 10.2
Relationship between first-to-market and sustained market share (Clark and Wheelwright 1992)

In the early 1980s, ICL developed an integrated desktop computer – the One Per Desk (OPD, also sold by BT as Tonto). This brought together a desktop computer and an integral telephone provided with a word processing package; a spreadsheet; a file database; and a telephone directory with autodial. It was bought and used by some very eminent personages – Prince Philip, the Duke of Edinburgh, being one. But OPD was a failure. It failed not only (as many commentators have argued) through commercial difficulties, but also because, at the time of its introduction to the market, desktop integration was so far in its infancy – particularly in the integration of the telephone directory and computer – that the market had not yet understood how to use it. Once the advantages of an integrated desktop computer with telephone were more widely understood through greater familiarity, the requirement was obvious; Microsoft Office was born, and OPD was relegated to the lists of failed products. It failed because it was too far in advance of the market understanding. It had absolute time advantage when relative time advantage was actually what was driving the market.

ICL had a similar lack of success with the integrated entertainment centre; the integration of television, radio, recorded music, home computer and the Internet. Only now, with the advent of digital television, is the same concept becoming readily accepted – some 10 years later.

(Carmichael, 1998)

Perhaps at this stage we ought to consider what we mean by innovation; in this context we are considering products which use new technologies to solve customer needs. In other words, we can consider innovation in the context of new products as shown in Figure 10.3.

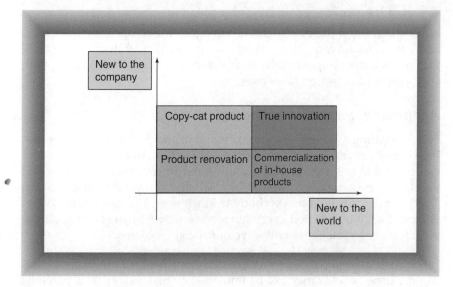

Figure 10.3
New product
taxonomy

Innovation usually implies both:

- an increased level of complexity through the use of advanced industrial technologies, and

- an increased risk, both to company and user – the market must be ready for that level of increased complexity and risk; in other words, the market needs to have been educated in the benefits of the use of the new industrial technology.

An interesting conundrum arises here, particularly in systems and products using new or advanced industrial technologies, and we can see a number of stages:

1. On the product's (and therefore the technology's) introduction to the market, the standard of competence required by the user for the complexity of the technology may be beyond that possessed by the user in the marketplace and users overestimate the technology's capability.

2. Over the life of the product there is a general rise in competence to manage the technology, and the standard of competence increases to beyond that required so that towards the end of the product's life the technology lags the general level of competence in the marketplace and the customer becomes dissatisfied.

In an unpublished study, it was pointed out that the designers of the next generation of Air Traffic Control Systems were now at primary school; that the education system that would enable them to design it was not in place, and therefore the system already has a high probability of failure.

(Source: Education Working Group papers of the Defence Council of the Federation of Electronic Industries (now Intellect))

This leads to early over-excitement regarding the potential of the technology/product, and therefore disillusionment as the competence level rises; and latterly as the competence level rises still further, with grudging satisfaction until the competence level supersedes that required. At that point, customer dissatisfaction takes over.

Adoption of industrial technologies

New is exciting. Change is exciting. Emergent and new technologies offering change are *really* exciting. We live, we are told, in a 24/7 society. Our call centres follow the sun: spaced at 8-hour intervals around the world and linked by computers, we can buy, sell and complain 24 hours a day. Everybody wants it, and everybody wants it now. The Brave New World is here: man has defeated everything. New wonder-drugs arrive almost weekly; new technologies will solve our social problems.

But industrial technologies aren't like that (see Chapter 2): their limitations in providing benefits may not be immediately realized, or their potential may be overestimated. We all know it: 'it's hyped up'. This thinking allowed Gartner (www.Gartner.com) to develop the 'hype cycle' – and the hype cycle has an important role to play in time and industrial technology.

The hype cycle

Gartner defined and catalogued the stages from the introduction to acceptance of an emergent technology, but in fact the hype cycle has wider application than just emergent technologies. It defines five phases (see Figure 10.4, also www.Gartner.com):

1. *Technology trigger*. The technology trigger is the first stage: it begins with a publicized scientific breakthrough, a public technology demonstration, product launch or other event that generates significant press and

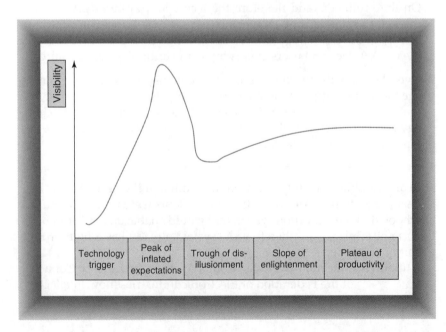

Figure 10.4
The hype cycle
(source: Gartner,
www.Gartner.com)

industry interest and generates speculation as to the technology's potential applications. This lasts for less than 2 years.

2. *Peak of inflated expectations.* As speculation develops, the expectations start to overtake the issues surrounding the development of a new technology. This produces a phase of over-enthusiasm. Unrealistic projections are made, during which a flurry of publicized activity by technology commentators results in some successes but more failures as the technology developed thus far is pushed to its limits. It may be the gap between the technology competence of the developers and the users or the readers of the press speculation; it may be the desire to be (in absolute terms) the 'first to market' a new technology. As Gartner points out, 'The only enterprises making money at this stage are conference organizers and magazine publishers'. The stage is reckoned to last between 2 and 5 years.

3. *Trough of disillusionment.* At this point the technology becomes unfashionable and the press abandons the topic, because the technology did not live up to its (i.e. the press's) over-inflated expectations. This phase lasts between years five and ten of the technology's life.

4. *Slope of enlightenment.* During the absence of press attention, focused experimentation and devoted hard work by an increasingly diverse range of organizations lead to a true understanding of the technology's applicability, risks and benefits. Commercial off-the-shelf methodologies and tools become available to ease the development process. This stage is generally more than 10 years later after the technology trigger.

5. *Plateau of productivity.* The real-world benefits of the technology are demonstrated and accepted. Tools and methodologies are increasingly stable as they enter their second and third generations. The final height of the plateau varies according to whether the technology is broadly applicable or only benefits a niche market.

Table 10.1 lists some sample technologies and their current stage in the hype cycle.

Stage of the hype cycle	Sample technology
On the rise	DNA logic Collective intelligence Augmented reality
At the peak	Speech recognition for mobile devices Social Network Analysis
Sliding into the trough	Grid computing Mobile phone payments Tablet PCs Biometric payments Enterprise instant messaging
Climbing the slope	Smartphone Location aware applications
On the plateau	Net telephony

Table 10.1
Hype cycle for emergent technologies 2006 (source: Gartner)

In the USA, following the close call of the 2000 Presidential Election, nearly $4 billion of funding was allocated to pay for thousands of touch-screen voting machines to be rolled out across the country. Voting touch-screens were adapted from ATM touch-screen technology. In 2000, ATM technology was still relatively new.

In 2002, touch-screen machines made by Sequoia Voting Systems were implicated in a fiasco in a local election in Bernalillo County, New Mexico. The system registered only 36,000 votes out of the 48,000 that had been cast. It turned out that the error occurred after votes were downloaded from individual machine's memory cards to a central tabulator: a software bug told the tabulator to ignore all votes cast above a certain threshold.

> Diebold Election Systems allegedly told California state officials that its Accuvote-TSX machines were federally 'qualified', when they were not, and the machines were used in state elections in four Counties in March 2004.
>
> (*New Scientist*, 16 October 2004)

> A three-month review of Diebold electronic voting machines used in Cuyahoga County during the May primary concluded that the votes recorded electronically and on paper receipts did not always match.
>
> (*Colombus (Ohio) Dispatch*, 16 August 2006)

> Diebold Election Systems provides accurate vote counting, extremely reliable security, and accessibility for voters. Over 130,000 Diebold electronic voting stations are being used in locations across the United States to assist voters in exercising their most fundamental constitutional right: the right to vote.
>
> (Diebold Press Release)

The hype cycle is important to us in establishing which technology we need to adopt to offer our customers' better value: too soon with technology and we will not change the environment; too late and we are behind. If customers expect 24-hour coverage, then we need to provide it. If the market isn't ready for 24-hour coverage, don't do it. Vendors of e-business-related products are only too pleased to highlight the need, and the need is *now*.

In developing advanced industrial technology-based products and bringing them to market, consideration has to be given to a number of other things:

1. The rate at which the market is moving – is the product:
   - an intercept product, or
   - designed against the market definition of best value last time we looked?

2. The company's ability to respond to change: we are all aware (all too often) that change is the only constant, but the rate of change is also critical to any intercept program. More fundamental, however, is the direction of change, and there is scant attention paid to this issue in most companies, which seem to be more concerned with managing the effects of change than trying to control change to their own advantage.

The complexity which the new technology now permits may outstrip that which the ultimate target audience can either manage or desires – for example, mobile phones targeted at the less technical end of the market offer a bewildering array of functions that the less technically-minded find daunting:

> Today's [13 June 2005] launches showcase Nokia's commitment to offer consumers easy-to-use mobile phones in a variety of desirable designs – regardless of cellular technology, whether that features WCDMA, GSM, CDMA internal circuitry, or whether it offers mobile music, mobile photography or 3G services . . .

> The compact Nokia 6280 3G slide phone (WCDMA 21000 and GSM 900/1800/1900) comes with a range of features that enable customers to take full advantage of 3G multimedia. Equipped with both a 2-megapixel and a VGA camera, the Nokia 6280 provides an ideal platform for 3G services such as real time video-sharing and two way video calls . . .

> The Nokia 6280 is expected to begin shipping in the fourth quarter of 2005, at an estimated price of 375 EUR before tax.
>   (Nokia press release – abstract)

Time and workplace technology

In addition to understanding customer competence in technological innovation, the other advantage of understanding time and technology is to manage *workplace technologies* by:

- pacing a company's TIME element to meet market readiness

- exploiting TECHNOLOGY to introduce innovation over complexity.

While this sounds a pretty straightforward task for a marketing manager, the development of it needs to consider two areas of the marketing function:

1. *Strategically*, the development of time and technology as described above is about sustaining competitive advantage; developing improved value chains and networks and the creation of value nodes as hubs for customers and suppliers are examples.

2. *Operationally*, in the development of that strategy, the development of time and technology is based around several things, mainly:

- the 'first-to-market' principle

- the reduction of costs – for example, auctions and electronic bidding; accounting; other Back Office systems

- systems to explore increased customer relationship management options – for example, database management, marketing information systems

- e-business, including e-marketing and e-commerce.

There are time and technology activities that begin as operational activities and are subsequently exploited as strategies, and strategic ideas that result in tactical operations. In the last decade, the building of websites to save on advertising costs has frequently led to a fully fledged e-marketing strategy, which in turn has led to technology usage changes in the business model. Other companies, such as Dell, set out to gain competitive advantage through the use of workplace technologies in a radical business model from the beginning.

Strategic time and technology

Strategy necessitates longer-term planning as well as the concepts of winning and keeping customers: as we have seen in Chapter 1, it lies at the root of marketing thinking. Therefore, we will start by looking at how strategic advantage can be considered, from a time and technology point of view, by looking at the Strategic Advantage Cycle (SAC).

The strategic advantage cycle

The SAC is our business interpretation of the Boyd cycle, or OODA loop. The Boyd cycle was developed by Colonel John R. Boyd, of the US Air Force, during the 1960s and 1970s, but was not widely published until after his death in 1997. In its original form, the Boyd cycle became a cornerstone of US Air Force combat thinking; by understanding its individual components, it became key to the design and development of US fighter aircraft. It has been applied to business activity by such writers as Thompson (1995), but is yet to be widely understood as a competitive business proposition. What we plan to do here is to use it to understand what we need to do in terms of the time and technology commitment of a company to gain – and sustain – competitive advantage.

Boyd defined four phases where combat advantage could be gained:

1. *Observe*, where you watch to see what is going on around you.

2. *Orientate*, where you decide what is important in the environment that you have observed, and why it is important.

3. *Decide*, where you decide what to do about the environment in order to make it more favourable to yourself.

4. *Act*, where you implement the decision taken.

Boyd then went on to point out, through numerous military examples, that the winner is the person who changes the environment in his favour faster than his competitor, so that when the competitor is ready to implement his strategic decisions, the outcome of these decisions is no longer appropriate in the new environment. Combative excellence is therefore the outcome of understanding and applying each of the four stages faster than an opponent. These simple concepts have far-reaching implications, as the warrior needs to understand time at each stage of the loop.

Let us turn this into business thinking. We all agree that:

1. Customers buy what they perceive to be best value.

2. Best value is defined by the environment in which the customer operates.

3. Sustainable competitive advantage is achieved in the long term by continuously offering the customer 'best value' in the changing environment. This means either:

   • waiting for the environment to influence the customer to redefine what is best value, then racing with your competitors to create it, or

   • helping to define best value with the customer so that the customers' new perception of best value disadvantages the competitor.

In other words, if my company can:

• create (or at least identify) the factors that are creating 'best customer value'

• orientate the company to create that value through its strategy

• implement that value through its operations, and

• deliver it through its marketing channel

faster than its competitor can do the same, then the environment that creates the factors for best value and into which the competitor is selling its own 'customer best value' has already moved on by the time that that competitor is ready to go to market.

Competitive advantage is therefore generated through continuous customer value improvement created by:

• observing the environment that defines best value for the customer

• orientating the company towards the changes that are necessary to provide best value

• taking strategic decisions

• implementing these decisions through operational actions to produce that change, and thereby change the environment in which the market operates.

In other words, we can interpret the Boyd cycle from the military OODA cycle to:

1. Environment (or marketplace), where we observe the drivers and manifestations of customers' view of best value.

2. Strategic decisions, where we understand our own competences and other factors which create competitive advantage (see Chapter 2) and where the outcome of the decision acts in a specific way on that environment.

3. Marketing operations, where marketing takes the strategy and interprets it into a go-to-market operation which:

   ● best satisfies the customers' requirements, and

   ● develops the marketplace (environment) in such a way as to change the expectations of customers, discommode the competitor, and strengthen the company competence that created the change in the environment in our favour which we can exploit in further cycles.

4. Marketing implementation, where the go-to-market programme changes the environment and is turned into sales.

The faster we can go around the cycle relative to our competitors, the more the environment is changed against them. After several cycles, we should have moved the environment sufficiently far for the competitor to have inadequate skills to compete effectively. We can summarize this as shown in Figure 10.5.

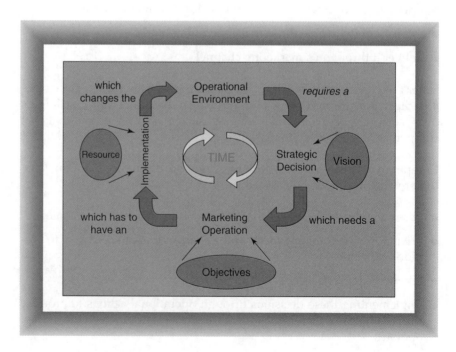

Figure 10.5
The SAC

This cycle then defines sustained advantage, and as such becomes the Strategic Advantage Cycle, defining the importance of time, with its implementation: technology.

The implication is that we need a number of things to take advantage of the SAC. At each of the stages, we have a different requirement that impacts the implementation of marketing.

Environment

First, we need good information about the marketing environment. However, information itself is not really of great value: we need to turn information into knowledge. We do this by evaluating it; deciding on its overall worth and accuracy and the timeliness of the information. Once knowledge has been gained, we can start to build a picture that is useful in making decisions. Intelligence is usually targeted and specific; knowledge is ongoing. We develop this in Chapter 11.

External knowledge

We need knowledge about the marketplace, and we need to gain this knowledge faster than our competitors. Our research must generate the data required faster. What technologies can we use to get data faster? What analysis can we do to make faster information? What information do we need to have faster knowledge? The knowledge must include not only what the customer perceives as best value to satisfy his wants and needs, but also competitive knowledge and knowledge about the macro- and micro-environments.

If the phases of the SAC are to be followed, then environment research is a roadblock if not conducted against time.

Gaining time advantage in the environment phase of the SAC requires the ability to gain time advantage in the time taken in environmental research.

Classical research techniques include:

- studying the literature
- developing primary research plans to complete any missing data
- establishing the sampling frame
- developing and piloting survey questionnaires
- placing and collecting the questionnaires
- checking the returns
- analysing the data
- disseminating the results.

Each phase needs to be completed as fast as possible.

Literature searches

Literature searches online are now common practice. The likes of Emeraldinsight.com offer online journals and excellent search facilities; Mintel and other research agencies place their reports online for a subscription; market research reports can be had from Internet companies; indeed, Google searching on the Internet provides a great deal of secondary research data – the only caution is to make sure you understand the source of the information. A word of warning: there are a number of questions that you should ask before accepting Internet information as being 'true'. O'Dochartaigh (2002), cited in Baker (2003), offers 12 questions:

1. Is it clear who is responsible for the data?

2. Is there any information about the person or organization?

3. Is there a copyright statement?

4. Is there a print counterpart to reinforce the authority?

5. Are sources listed so that they can be verified?

6. Is there editorial input?

7. Are the spelling and grammar correct? (There may, of course, be linguistic issues here in valid sources using translation services, which are not always as accurate as in the native tongue.)

8. Are any biases and affiliations clearly stated?

9. Is advertising clearly differentiated from information?

10. Are opinions labelled as such?

11. Are there dates for when the information was 'published'?

12. Are there dates for the revision of the data?

The first space shuttle was to have been called *Constitution*, but after 400 000 letters to the White House from *Star Trek* fans the name was changed to *Enterprise*.

This information can be found on a number of webpages, but the fact that it is also on the NASA website adds legitimacy to the 'fact'.

(Baker, 2003)

Developing research plans

Research plans need to be made no matter what medium is used to conduct the research, but the guiding factor throughout the development of the plan is that the plan must be implementable as fast as possible and without compromising accuracy.

Setting a sampling scheme

Setting the sampling scheme includes the style of the primary research. This means that the choice of the sample must be such that it is readily accessible by rapid means – for example:

● Do I need to eyeball the sample?

● What is the response rate likely to be, and therefore what sample size do I need to ask in order to meet the completed sample size?

● How can I ask many interviewees in parallel about the same thing?

These questions do not necessarily imply that *only* Internet-based research will meet the time requirements, but it is certainly one answer; it is a classic case of workplace technology substituting for time.

Sampling technique is also affected by the sample required and the collection technique that is most appropriate. It is possible to run online focus groups – set up a chat room for specifically invited participants, for example, or develop an open chat room and guide the discussion, checking the parameters of those who come into the room for segment membership.

Online questionnaires can be sent out to selected respondents, or a pop-up questionnaire can be attached to a willing website, either on arrival to, or more usually, departure from, the website.

Telephone surveys are useful tools, but the rejection rate is high.

The balance here is between costs and speed – but in the SAC race, speed must win.

A study at the University of Goettingen (2001) showed that on-line data collection was better than traditional research for speed or response; cost per respondent; and overall cost. It was worse for sample representation of the total population, quality of answers to open-ended questions, the ability to probe and confidentiality of the topic.
(Cited in Burns and Bush, 2003)

You pays your money and takes your chances.

Questionnaire design

Online questionnaires can be developed with computer-assisted design software. These mainly allow better layout than conventional techniques, but they are designed around web technology and therefore allow posting of the questionnaire on a webpage and inviting respondents to go there. They also allow for automatic data collation, presentation and report writing. Websurveyor is such a software package. The problem is herding the potential respondent onto the site.

Disseminating the results

The results must be sent back to the strategy team as soon as possible. Good dissemination always obtains receipts for data arrived (see Chapter 11).

What type of company are we?

We also need to look at states of readiness of the company to supply the state of the market; to anticipate and move the customer on. To do this, we need to understand what type of company we are; what is our position in the market lifecycle? By understanding this, we will be able to adapt our strategy to the right time in the market.

We need to forecast the environment and decide on an intercept strategy or a leading strategy.

Types of company

As we saw earlier, the 'first in, best dressed' is in fact a myth, based on the expectation of prime-mover advantage.

In every market there are a number of companies, and as the product lifecycle progresses, these different types of company rise to prominence and then decline. We can identify four types of company in a developing marketplace:

1. *Market scopers.* These are the innovators of the product lifecycle; they build the product/service and are seen to have prime-mover advantage; their go-to-market strategy actually scopes the market rather than satisfies it. The lessons learned from market scopers (who often don't realize that what they are doing is setting and identifying certain long-lasting market parameters) are:

   ● the readiness of the market for the product/innovation

   ● how big the market is, both in realized demand and in latent demand

   ● how the market wants to buy the product

   ● what the market considers it will bear in price.

Such companies are generally technology driven, are pioneers in the technology and are content to return to further research and development as soon as the market stiffens.

> A classic example of the market scoper was the BBC computer. First into the market (1982), the BBC Personal (although the term had not yet been coined) Computer was bought by individuals (stocks were sold out on the first day) and educational establishments. However, the manufacturer had not foreseen the development of the market, although it:
>
> ● highlighted that there was a market demand for a small computer among the technically minded and in education (and hence there would be an ongoing demand for recreational computing when the computer-literate children left school)

- identified the likely future major purchasers
- established the pricing points which successors had to use as a base for their own pricing (and therefore profit) strategy.

The BBC computer, developed by Acorn, had left the market by 1985.

2. *Market makers*. Market makers are first into the main market and generally build the largest market share. Market makers can create the 'best value', but as the market begins to segment they are (in general) insufficiently agile to meet the fragmenting segment requirements. Such companies are generally driven by product development rather than the tracking of market activities. They generally come into the market at the early stages of market growth, grab market share, and remain a leader (in BSG terms we would regard them as 'star' companies) until the market starts to enter maturity.

IBM waited to see whether the recreational PC market was really going to happen. When they had waited just long enough, they made their move.

3. *Market exploiters*. Market exploiters are those companies who are fast followers of technologies and can take advantage of fragmenting segments in the market to introduce, develop and provide 'best value' through brand or services. Such companies are able to offer superior value within the segments to the market maker, either through better meeting the customers' expectations of 'best value' or through leverage on some other (segment recognized) brand values. Market exploiters often exist alongside the market maker and take market share. They operate market follower and market challenger strategies.

IBM, however, kept its eyes firmly on the mainframe and services market and didn't adapt to the PC markets when the environment for 'best value' changed and the market segments fragmented. IBM, with original market-leader advantage, had ousted the BBC computer, but in turn lost market share to companies offering better value in areas other than standards and brand.

With the availability of chip technology, national manufacturers (for example ICL in the UK, Bull in France, Olivetti in Italy) began making PCs and challenging IBM for market share.

With the IBM brand meaning excellence in computing, and as market leader having the largest market share and top-of-mind position of the then computer market (still mainly mainframe at this time), IBM fought back using their pole position with the bullish question, 'Is it IBM-compatible?' As it was unclear to the customer what 'IBM-compatible' meant (actually IBM's attempt to retain market advantage through the imposition of specific standards), it was safest to buy IBM-branded machines.

IBM no longer manufactures PCs, having sold the brand name to the Chinese company Lenovo.

4. *Market changers.* Market changers are those who move into the market and redefine the concept of best value. They change the market by forcing the previous competitors to modify their offering. Market changers usually do this through a price/quality analysis or by providing a service unobtainable elsewhere.

The PC market was shattered with the arrival of two market changers – Amstrad and Dell.

Amstrad's analysis showed the main usage of computers at this point in the market was for domestic word processing. The PCW 8256 was born. Selling at less than half the price of any current computer, the PCW was anything but IBM compatible; running a near obsolete operating system, with its own software, disk drive size, green screen and simple operation, the Amstrad PCW was a complete computer (with printer) for simple word processing, and redefined 'best value' by focusing on *price*.

Market entry then allowed Amstrad to develop its own more conventional PC, again focusing on price as the major component of best value in its chosen segments.

Dell entered the market as a B2C mail-order computer manufacturer, allowing customers to specify the components of their computer, which was then bespoke and delivered directly from the factory. Here, Dell offered best value to its segments in terms of technical specification and low(er) price than the IBM clones. To achieve this, Dell invested in significant time-saving workplace technologies.

We can summarize the time element of a market by the graph in Figure 10.6.

Clearly, different types of company need to focus on different timings within the market lifecycle. While it may be true that in each phase there is a prime-mover advantage, it is not true that prime-mover advantage early in the lifecycle is sufficient to ensure a 'cash cow' in its latter stages. Few companies are able to manage all stages; even Microsoft, which is currently still a market maker (through new releases, facilities, etc.), is being challenged by newly arriving competitors (Star Office, for example), which are redefining best value and will therefore change the market and ultimately force Microsoft to follow.

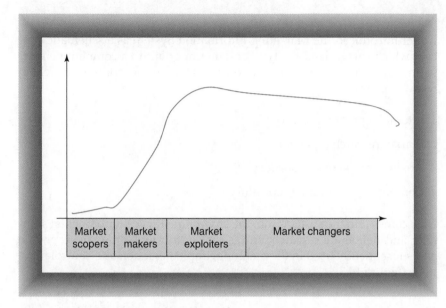

Figure 10.6
Dominance of
companies over a
lifecycle

Time (or perhaps timing) is therefore critical to meet the changing needs of the market. Had the Dell approach been available to the proud owners of the BBC, Dell would certainly NOT have been a successful company.

The factors are, then:

- rate of progress of the market taxonomy (Figure 10.6)
- speed of acceptance of the changing industrial technology by the marketplace
- rate of change of (implicit) definitions of best value as the market segments fragment.

Internal knowledge

To understand our company's capability, we must have a thorough understanding of the company, its finances, the financial constraints, and its manufacturing or service delivery abilities. Internal research is rarely performed well.

Chapter 12 covers measuring marketing, and therefore its contribution to the assessment of the company's internal knowledge.

Between environment and strategy

Between environment and strategy in the SAC comes the transfer of data into knowledge. The data was collected in the environment, but, as we will see in Chapter 11, it needs to be converted into useable information and then into knowledge. We need to transform and transfer this data quickly, as delay between these two stages can be significant.

MkIS

Kotler introduced the *Marketing Information System* as a schematic concept which categorized the type of data important to a competitive marketing function (Kotler, 2006). He considers four areas of data, each held in its own separate repository:

1. Internal reports repository.

2. Market research repository.

3. Analytic marketing repository.

4. Competitive marketing repository.

Data comes into the system from the environment via environmental scanning and deliberate research, and is viewed through an analysis engine and subsequently used in the planning, implementation and control functions (Figure 10.7).

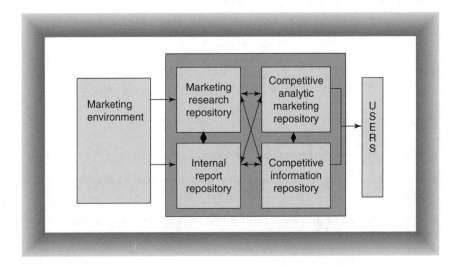

Figure 10.7
Schematic of MkIS
(after Kotler, 2006)

Before we can use the MkIS, we need to address how Figure 10.7 should be interpreted. As we will see in Chapter 11, there are two things we must consider:

1. The cost of data collection and data entry.

2. The time from demand for information to delivery.

In this section, we are most concerned about the time delay in a formal structure.

Kotler's schematic was developed in the late 1960s, before the advent of the ubiquitous computer on every desk – and certainly before the advent of web technology and distributed data systems. By rethinking Kotler's diagram in terms of time and resource instead of ultimate data usage, we can start to see that the old technology (based probably on a card index and filing system and staffed by a trained researcher/librarian) is now too slow.

Strategy development here is throwing up the demands to be satisfied. By the time the research is conducted, analysed and reported, the strategy is in place and the best that the research can contribute is some form of verification. We discussed earlier some techniques to speed up the research.

To place the MkIS in the SAC, it needs to respond faster. Every member of staff is a data collector and every (secondary) research report is available online, whereas in the older structure it was requested from the research agency; an invoice was raised; payment was agreed; and the report was posted, received, read, abstracted, disseminated and stored.

What is needed is not a formalized system, managed according to the schematic, but web technology to which everyone contributes (see Chapter 11 regarding source grading and collection requirements). The data then must be available to all, made available by all; with empowerment comes responsibility – no more silo politics, 'knowledge is power' or 'what do you want it for?' roadblocks. The time saved by decentralizing, local entering of data and network-wide search tools allows us to move from the study of the environment to the decision stage more quickly (Figure 10.8).

The MkIS can now become a reality rather than a concept. While the type of data requirements need to be widely publicized, the interpretation of Kotler's schematic into modern technology speeds up the space between the environment and strategic decision phases (Figure 10.9).

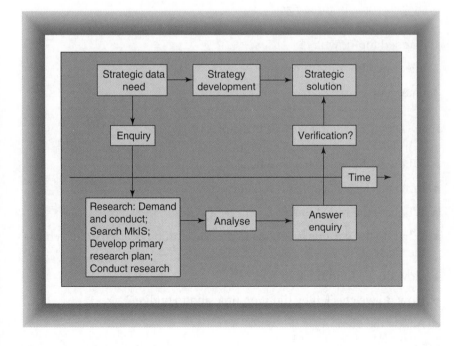

Figure 10.8
MkIS operation overlaid with strategy development time

Figure 10.9
Schematic of data management for MkIS

Strategic decisions

This handbook is not a manual on strategy development, although of course the issue needs to be addressed (see Chapter 1, for example). We are more concerned about the use of technology and time to speed up strategic decisions for competitive advantage through environment change.

Strategies come in three sizes:

1. Planned top-down.

2. Integrated bottom-up.

3. Emergent.

A *top-down strategy* follows the principles of:

- Where do I want to be, by when?
- What strategies enable me to get there?
- What are the road blocks?
- What do the various functions in the corporation need to do to achieve the strategy?
- How do we fund them to do it?
- How do we check they did it on time and to budget?
- Action the plan.

Bottom-up strategies, often followed by companies dominated by large key account management, follow the process of:

- What can be achieved?
- Aggregate the results.
- Are they good enough to meet corporate expectations (see Chapter 12)?
- What contingency do I need to develop?
- What support is needed?
- Approve for action.

To a certain extent these two approaches can be considered as *'outside-in'* strategies: the focus is on the external world, the environment, but the marketer is a passive actor in the change to the environment in which competitors will operate.

Emergent strategies are even less formalized; the process follows something like:

- identify company Strengths and Weaknesses, Opportunities open to it and Threats to it, usually through some auditing procedure
- match SWs against OTs, either with TOWS, SoWOT or other matching tools
- identify target opportunities and write a profile for future targets
- aggregate assessed opportunities for achieving corporate expectations
- identify support requirements
- rank and allocate target opportunities
- continue external environment scanning and auditing for emerging opportunities that fit the profile.

To a certain extent this can be regarded as an *'inside-out'* model; the company's strengths and weaknesses are identified, then matched to known or emerging opportunities.

Most companies use a mix of all of these, but in terms of advancing around the SAC the 'outside-in' strategies are almost blind to the activities of competitors and their impact on the environment in which the plan will operate, except when the plan is first constructed. Any change in the environment for 'best value' is unlikely to be assessed during the life of the plan. If the SAC is active and fast-moving, the delay could be too long.

Strategic decisions about the company and its products are unlikely to have the effect required without a supporting increase in relative timing from the other members of the marketing activity. No company works on its own in a marketplace; there are the suppliers and the distribution channel to consider, and their integration into the SAC is essential.

Strategic integration of the value chain through workplace technologies

Integrating the company and the supply/distributor chain is a major strategic consideration, not just about the marketing but also about the future of the company. Technology and what it allows in terms of speed, cost and precision has changed the way in which companies think about their value chain. In technology terms, this change has been collected into the development of e-commerce and its umbrella, e-business.

Most of the practical activity in e-business has been focused on bringing together the various players in the companies involved in the provision of the product; this is called *convergence*.

Convergence is generally thought to be achieved as the goal of an integration process which creates a value transformation for the companies concerned. If we consider the taking of a product to market, we used to think in terms of supplier – producer – distributor. If we widen this thinking, we can see that the suppliers supply more than one producer and the distributor specializes in presenting goods to a customer, so the distributor will also be offering competitive products. And in many cases, companies are presenting services to their competitors.

E Walters UK provides a manufacturing capacity of over 120 000 garments per week through its owned facilities in the UK, Slovakia and Bulgaria. Its European-wide logistics infrastructure is capable of handling over 60 000 garment movements each day. The company itself handles 120 000 garment movements a week, leaving spare capacity in its logistics and finishing functions.

Its logistics solutions are provided to companies across a wide range of manufacturing and retailing sectors. Walters therefore provides both a competitor and a partner to other members of the clothing industry.

(Source: E W Walters UK Ltd, www.ewalters.co.uk)

As a result, it is probably more sensible to think about networks rather than chains. In this sense, we can now start thinking about *value* as being created at nodes in the network rather than each member adding value to the last member until the customer's best value is reached (Figure 10.10).

Integrating the net is a strategic decision; it is beyond the scope of this book to discuss this in detail, BUT if the SAC is to be followed then the integration of the value chain, with our company as the node, is essential. Such integration should include:

- shared databases
- production scheduling
- delivery scheduling

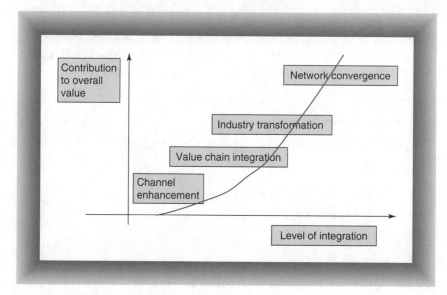

Figure 10.10
Value chain to value net (after Deise *et al.*, 2000)

- shared servicing
- usage rates
- pricing structures.

However, the main driver of the transformed company is to speed up the time element of the operational aspects, although this is a strategic decision by every member of the whole value network.

Between strategic decisions and marketing operations

The translation of strategy into operations is common to all the three planning modes described above, and is usually done on a lowest cost principle (for some ideas on this see Chapter 12). However, this is not the case if we are attempting strategies for sustained competitive advantage; what is critical here is time. How can we achieve what we need to achieve in the right timescale? In other words, the management of time again becomes the driving factor rather than adherence to costs, as it is time that drives our position in the competitive marketplace through the SAC rather than the budget.

In order to understand the time elements, we need to look at forecasts once the strategy has been implemented – not operational forecasts as in, for example, projected sales figures required by the financial department for budget building, or units to be sold as needed by production for scheduling, but strategic forecasts about the impact of our strategy on the environment, which after all is what we are intending to change. Some of the numerical techniques that we are familiar with in classical forecasting are not important in strategic forecasting. Sometimes here we approach the realms of futurology.

Forward projections and forecasting

Time series analysis, for example, is not important in strategic forecasting; neither are some of the modelling methods. What we should be considering are the *qualitative* techniques. These are generally regarded as:

1. Imagination.

2. Standard strategy forecasting:

   - panel techniques (jury of experts, or Delphi approaches).

3. Cross-impact techniques.

4. Building pictures of the future:

   - scenario planning

   - future planning.

Imagination

Imagination is by far the easiest and most uncontrolled of all techniques: it is blue-sky thinking about what the future will look like after the innovation has been accepted. There are several drawbacks here: subconscious influence in belief in the innovation will skew the results favourably; the absence of unconsidered events or unconscious ignorance will also have an impact. Imagination can be extended to include the impact of other companies seeking to change the environment, but on the whole imagination makes an interesting starting point for strategic forecasting although it needs to be supplemented with more controlled techniques.

Standard strategy forecasting

Standard strategy forecasting relies on the combined knowledge of a number of experts, usually assembled into a jury or a panel of some description. A jury need not be 12 good men and true, but any number of specialists. There are several techniques for guiding and recording their output into a useful prediction of the future.

Panel techniques involve assembling a panel of experts and asking the panel to consider the future and then manage the individual member's considerations into a consensus. There are a couple of approaches, each with variants:

1. *Juries of expert opinion.* Juries of expert opinion are just that – panels of experts brought together to discuss the topic and reach a consensus, the approach being a forum for discussion and agreement. These experts are either your own or an assemblage of other people's. The discussion results in a jury view. However, as with all forums, the influence of individuals can cloud the true opinion of the panel.

> When investigating a macro view of the impact of disruption caused by global unrest to the business environment in the UK, a jury of experts was assembled, consisting of experts not only in business but also in religion, population, economics, education, logistics and culture. A number of sessions were run; each started with a different

topic area, led by the relevant expert. The final session was a drawing together of the outputs to create a strategic view of the future environment into which the client's industry was to operate.

(The ComMentor Group)

2. *Delphi systems*. To overcome the forum issues and to generate independence of thought, the Delphi system also obtains a consensus opinion of a group of great experts about likely future developments, but does it iteratively – a series of questionnaires is posted, completed and returned, and an anonymous summary of the thoughts of the great experts is then posted to participants, who prepare a second forecast, and so on until a consensus is achieved. While this has some merits, it does have the drawback of being slow.

In a study into Irish speciality foods, experts from a wide variety of speciality food related areas were invited to participate.

A panel was formed of twenty-seven experts comprising nine speciality food producers, six retailers, four distributors, three restaurateurs, two public servants, two food writers, four buyers from the major multiples, one academic and one regional food cooperative manager. (Some acted as non participative observers.)

A questionnaire on speciality food was constructed and broken down into three sections: one to forecast overall sales growth, one to forecast sales growth in specific product categories and one to forecast sales growth in specific markets. The panellists were requested to make estimates for two points into the future: five and ten years.

Three rounds of the Delphi process were undertaken. With each iteration the panellists were presented with their previous responses and a summary of the arguments used by them to support their forecasts. Then, based on this information, they were asked to reconsider their previous forecasts and make any necessary revisions.

Three iterations were required before a consensus was achieved.

(from Meehan *et al.*, 2001)

Both of these techniques are usually fairly limited by the following:

1. The starting point for the discussion. Experts immediately like complexity, so expert forums can begin in the wrong place, rather than develop the discussion. Experts may have already developed an opinion. To start the discussion in a forum situation, small, single ideas are best. By tackling one area at a time, a picture of the whole environment can be built up.

2. The singlemindedness of jury members. The Delphi system is particularly prone to being very linear in thought processes, as each expert tends only to consider his own specialization – which is not such a problem with discussions in expert juries. Expert juries have their own drawbacks; dominant personalities (since this is a forum) can take over, or a particularly persuasive view can drive the thinking of other members. Both suffer from the fact that there is often little guidance in cross-discipline thinking. This can be overcome by cross-impact analysis.

Cross-impact analysis

Cross-impact analysis logically studies the effects of the interaction of specified events with each other (Figure 10.11). The wide variety of mutual impacts that can occur between potential events are analysed and assessed to determine the overall effect. This can be thought of as a series of two-dimensional matrices, with each key area that could affect the outcome being a dimension. Along each dimension there are a number of trigger events, and in each intersecting cell a starter question is posed – for example, 'if this events occurs, what will be the probability of the other event occurring?' These matrices can be built up from two dimensions into multiple dimensions, the logic in each cell being checked, until a view of the strategic future emerges. Cross-impact analysis produces some excellent views of the future of the environment.

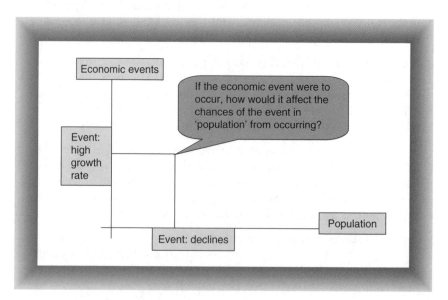

Figure 10.11 Conceptual structure of cross-impact analysis

Non-jury methods can overcome some of the issues above; the primary non-jury methods that are widely used for strategic forecasting are based on building pictures of the future.

Building pictures of the future

There are basically two approaches: scenario planning, where the future is sketched out by considering the motivation behind change in the environment; and future mapping, which looks at connections of events.

Scenario planning, as we saw in Chapter 4, is a forecast (not a prediction) of what the business environment will look like at some point in the future, based on what factors change the environment – for example the underlying drivers. Figure 10.12 shows the basic process: the drivers of an environment are identified and their behaviour is monitored. The state of the driver over the period of interest (the period over which we intend to move around the SAC, for example) is projected, and those projections are supported with evidence. The result will be a number of 'what if?' scenarios predicting the environment into which we will be marketing.

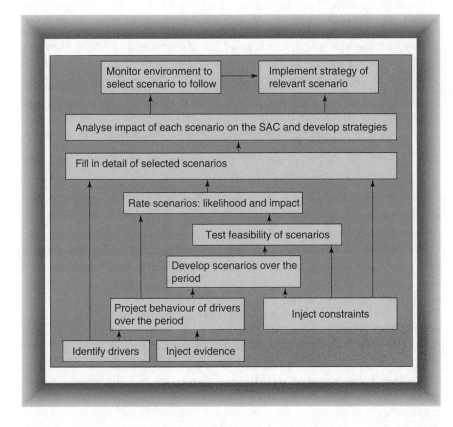

Figure 10.12
Scenario planning process

The scenarios are then ranked; we are strategically predicting the environment so that we can control the marketing in it in accordance with the SAC, so the ranking will be based on the likelihood of the scenario happening and the impact on the environment of its occurrence.

Each scenario that is developed has to be tested for feasibility, from 'highly likely' to 'very unlikely' although, after the terrorist attacks on the USA of 9/11, 'unlikely' needs qualification. The most likely scenarios are selected and fleshed out in some detail. The result is a working package of some four or five scenarios, based on the possible behaviour of the key drivers in the marketplace.

These 'most likely' scenarios can be fleshed out and the details filled in (see imagination and panel methods above). Then this artificial world that we have just developed can be tested and analysed, and our responses to it put in place. Each scenario is often given to a team to work on, with teams coming back together at intervals for peer review.

The next step is to monitor the environment to see how the scenario predictions are holding. You can do this in a number of ways:

1. You can monitor the environment *per se*, although the difficulty here is that changes can be masked by a number of other things – how do you know if something has happened until it actually has? – and again we are behind the SAC.

2. You can monitor the behaviour of the drivers and see how they are moving; this will take out the background noise that clouds the method in (1) above.

3. You can set up a number of indicators that will lead the scenario; you could establish these from cross-impact analysis. These indicators should be both quantitative (economic trends) and qualitative (for example public opinion).

It is possible to set up a series of questions based on indicators and the impact of the drivers into a traffic-light system, and placing each in its scenario so that the progress towards that scenario can easily be seen.

Future mapping is a development of scenario planning, and is intended to speed up the process. It was developed by A.D. Little, the US-based analysis company, for fast-changing environments. Instead of developing the scenarios from an understanding of the driver behaviour, future planning takes a set of events and end-state predictions made from a forum approach or a Delphi approach. The end-state predictions need to be kept up-to-date if the approach is to be used against time.

The future maps therefore are developed rapidly as outputs rather than fleshed-out views of the world, and are based on views of the connections between events rather than drivers – the 'what happens?' approach rather than the 'why does it happen?' approach.

Marketing operations

The marketing strategy now needs to be put in place. Research to understand the environment is in place, the corporate strategy which drives around the SAC is in place, and the data retrieval to manage the data is in place; at this stage we need to develop the marketing strategy; the 'operations' which will turn the strategy into reality for the marketing team to action. We now need to understand what the options are for us to maintain the tempo of the SAC, and our thoughts readily turn to 'E'. During the evolution of a company to a full 'E' commitment, four main areas of 'capital' will change which will have an impact on marketing.

Types of capital

The transformation to being fully E-ed relies on transformation of four capitals:

1. Brand capital.

2. Human capital.

3. Working capital.

4. Physical capital.

Brand capital is transformed from the value of the product as a solution to the customers' wants and needs, where brand is merely a replacement for product, to becoming a significant component of the value of an overall solution. The manufacturing process in terms of 'where' and 'how' ceases to be critical to the user, but remains a subset of the value associated with the solution – in terms of both the physical elements and the psychological elements of the brand. The customer adds 'brand' into the bundle of components of 'best value'. In the product-driven company, brand is merely a label denoting the origin of the product. The increase in brand capital comes from the customer's increasing reliance on brand (see Chapter 9).

Human capital is transformed from a production focus – making goods because the products are the best and highest quality, irrespective of the expectation and the requirements of the customer – to high contribution (to the solution) value-added tasks. During this transformation the company needs to become fully marketing oriented; it is NOT true that a fully marketing-oriented company is ready to be E-ed. Indeed, it could be said that those companies who adopt 'E' and that are not marketing oriented will struggle most over the transformation of human capital. Changing the capital is due in part to realizing that products are mainly an element of service, service being something performed by people with the help of product. For example, shoe polish is the product element of shoe cleaning, the service being DIY. The percentage of product in the developing service should be carefully considered, and it is through increasing the service element that the human capital transformation takes place. The implication is, of course, that the training and education of the value-adding workforce must be anticipatory of the value to be added in both skill and time.

Working capital – oh joy to accountants! – moves from high working capital to low working capital. As the company involves its partners in both the customer and supply sides of the business, so the integration of customer requirements allows not only just-in-time delivery but also just-in-time manufacture and shipping from the outsourcer. Seamlessly.

Physical capital is transformed from high physical capital to low physical capital. If the brand becomes the major part of the customer solution and human capital is transferred away from low-value production tasks towards high contribution value-added tasks, then with the introduction of integrated design to manufacture (where manufacturing can take place remote from the design bureau), outsourcing becomes a major consideration for non-core activities. This in turn frees up or releases manufacturing resource in the manufacturing industry.

Some companies who drive the transformation of all of these capitals can dramatically transform the business.

Whitbread, brewer of excellent ales since before 1750, moved into managing the outlets – i.e. into pub management. The result was that in 2001 the company was able to close the brewing (manufacturing) element of the business, thereby reducing human, working and physical capital. As their skills at hospitality management improved, they moved into managing other hospitality outlets. Recently, Whitbread has moved away from managing the outlets to managing what it sees as the real value-added: brand.

Whitbread now consider itself to be a brand management company, and has set about procuring a stable of brands; it owns Premier Travel Inns; Brewers' Fayre; Beefeater; Costa Coffee; TGI Friday and David Lloyd Leisure, thus moving from low-end manufacturer to high-end value creation through brand, with high brand capital, low human capital, low working capital and low physical capital.

(Source: Whitbread plc, www.whitbread.co.uk)

E-marketing

The role of e-marketing as a workplace technology and as a resource is now seen not just as a cost-saving exercise in sales and procurement, but also as a time-saving exercise. It allows faster implementation, or, in some markets (like tourism), changes the way in which customers perceive 'value'. Those companies without e-business are already behind the SAC; the environment has already changed. This does not mean that everyone wants everything through e-business, but different customer segments want 'E' for different things at different times; the development and purpose of 'E' needs to be followed through to ensure that this happens. We often find management issues here; IT departments often report to the finance function (as in cost-cutting) rather than marketing (as in a driver to the SAC). It is possible to serve both masters, but great understanding of time marketing is necessary in managing the 'E' business. We need 'E' in every stage of the SAC; faster intelligence and knowledge of the environment, in gathering, processing and dissemination; faster 'what if?' analysis of marketing options; faster communications and planning; faster implementation and go-to-market.

Historically, there are several stages that a company goes through on its path to e-marketing:

1. *A presence.* This is usually a single webpage, possibly supported by a local Chamber of Commerce or an online information sheet about the

area: such a presence does little more than announce the existence and contact details of the enterprise. This is the entry level into e-marketing, and tends to be confined to the smallest businesses. The webpage of Castle Vets Pet Health Care Centre (www.castle-vets.co.uk) in Reading, UK, is a good example of presence.

2. *Development of a brochure.* Once the website presence no longer seems adequate an online brochure is usually developed, covering the products or services offered by the company and containing contact details or including a clickthrough email form. There is a significant amount of software for easy development, Dreamweaver and Microsoft Front Page probably being the easiest to use. The bulk of the e-marketing on the web is in this category, or developments thereof. Brochureware can also include simple order forms. Raja Fashions (www.raja-fashions.com) of Hong Kong and The Spanish Guitar Centre (www.spanish-guitar-bristol.co.uk) in Bristol are good examples of simple brochureware websites. There can be extensions to include information relevant to customers – for example, publishing start times of contestants in an equestrian dressage competition saves hours on the phone (Hall Place Equestrian Centre; www.hall-place.com). Amazon's website (www.amazon.co.uk) is a large brochure with an order form.

3. *The e-salesman.* The next stage on from brochureware is the development of the e-salesman, including Frequently Asked Questions, a capability to tailor requirements, and other salesman-related activities. Amazon is moving towards this stage with its readers' reviews and recommendations.

The decision to sell online is based on a number of factors, not least the ability or will to deliver. Is it really sensible for Dulux to offer a sales service, or Kellogg's to offer single packs of cornflakes? Publishers do not sell individual copies of books to Amazon. Therefore, we should tailor what we offer on the web to our market; in the B2B marketplace it may well be very sensible to offer sales (Brassfast (www.brassfast.com) uses an email contact to open a dialogue). The question of intermediaries should be carefully considered at this stage: it can be possible in the integration of the value net to bypass some low-value members who are not nodes, in which case a careful value analysis of every member and node needs to be conducted.

Such an analysis can lead to a change in operational procedures. The ability of technology, especially the introduction of the web, can allow procuring companies to speed up the process of writing to every supplier for a quotation, so by publishing their requirements online and assuming that interested suppliers are scanning the web (either mechanically or through the use of shopping agent crawlers) the contribution of the procurement function to the improvement in creating better value for money can be speeded up. And from there it is a short step to opening online bidding and the development of auctions, for both procurement and unloading superfluous stocks.

The disintermediation of value-adding intermediaries and the shift in pricing structure brought on by auctions, where price is the only value component set against a series of specific requirements, has led to a reinvention of intermediaries in terms of their value. Portals, where similar products are compared for value as well as price, have sprung up, acting as an intermediary – often on a no-charge basis, as they derive their revenue from other sources.

Between marketing operations and marketing implementation

This area of the SAC consists largely of the communications issues, and has been dealt with in Chapter 9 of this book.

So far we have implied that all the above is about establishing the starting point for strategic decisions, while this book is about implementing marketing. The SAC sees implementation as an integral part of strategic choice; choosing an unimplementable strategy is not going to create ongoing best value to a customer. The best strategy in the world is going to fail if the resources and capabilities do not fit the requirements to pace the change in the marketplace.

So we need to understand our own ability internally – to communicate our decisions to ourselves. Easy; the office email system sees to that – it's what management do; they cascade and interpret strategy into tasks. If we are moving to time pacing to drive the SAC, we need more confidence than that!

Marketing implementation

Marketing implementation is about the 4Ps – Product, Place, Price and Promotion. But once we start to think in terms of the SAC, we realize that we need to start thinking about their role in the tempo of strategic marketing. We therefore need to pace the development of products (as we saw above), pace the placing and readying of promotional material, and pace the logistics and payment.

There are two types of pacing:

1. *Event pacing* is where everything in the decision process is adapted to be triggered by events in the external environment. Event pacing is the completion of tasks as a reaction to an event. In product development, this could be the availability of a new technology, or the launch of a product by a competitor. Companies that event-pace follow a plan and deviate from it only when unacceptable change occurs. In markets that are stable (i.e. the SAC is slow), event pacing is an opportunistic and effective way to deal with change. By definition, however, it is also a reactive and often erratic strategy, and is oblivious of the SAC.

2. *Time pacing* is where the process is scheduled against relative time; completing tasks against the clock, not in absolute time but relative time. As we go round the SAC faster and at our pace it is necessary to pace against a time element, and this requires control of the tempo. If we are using the SAC concept to change the environment to gain and sustain competitive

advantage, we have to be time-driven, not event-driven. We need to understand finance well enough to understand what the reciprocal impacts are; time pacing requires a range of different concepts in project management; the impact on resources and capabilities will be likewise adapted. And we need to try to establish a budget for each of these techniques, as well as measure our success in implementing marketing.

Implementing the marketing strategies now needs to be *time paced*, most current marketing activity is usually *event paced*. In the case of the SAC, we need all marketing activities to be based around time. The 4Ps must therefore be based around time, not events. The change in thinking from time pacing to event pacing is critical to the application of relative time and the SAC.

Gillette completes about 20 new-product changes a year. Gillette sees itself as managing a steady flow of products – developing, launching and harvesting products all at the same time. Gillette manages this balanced product pipeline through time pacing. The Sensor razor, for example, was not launched until its successor product, Excel, was in development. In turn, Excel was not launched until its successor product and more than ten candidate products after that were under development. They describe their pacing as 'orchestrating and commanding a business'.

Through repeated learning how to time-pace, Gillette has cut the time it takes to dominate a market. After launching the Sensor line in the domestic market, it took Gillette four years to penetrate all of its markets. With its successor line, Excel, Gillette was able to cut that time to three years. Not only does this hasten the company's revenue flow, but it also prevents competitors from copying Gillette's products in one market and introducing them into another before Gillette does. This is a good example of the SAC in action; dominate a market, and move on before the competition catches up. The competitors are probably event pacing, anyway.

(From Eisenhardt and Brown, 1998)

What we are talking about here is a rhythm within the company regarding controlling the environment rather than a race to capitalize on an event. Once the rhythm is established, it can be sped up or slowed down as required. When the market is not yet ready, or the hype cycle is still in the trough, the tempo must be slowed; on others an *accelerando* is in order.

In marketing implementation this may well interpret, for example, into a product launch not being when the product is ready (event), but when the factors in the SAC are aligned (time). As we have seen, releasing an innovation too early can result in a failed product. The OPD of the earlier ICL case study was an event-paced activity; the technology was available, so the product was launched.

There are three questions you can ask about time *v.* event pacing (Eisenhardt and Brown, 1998):

1. *Performance metrics.* Most companies use performance measures that focus on costs, profit or innovation. Do your current performance metrics also include measures based on time, such as elapsed time, speed, and rate? In product development, for example, consider measures such as the number of products launched per quarter, the average time from concept to commercial launch, and the average downtime between projects. In integrating acquisitions, consider tracking the time until the new organizational structure is finalized, the time it takes for the sales growth rate to turn positive after the acquisition, and the number of acquisitions absorbed per year. Every critical transition process should be tracked with at least some time-based measures.

2. *Transitions.* (Transitions are changes from one activity to another; introducing a new product to market is a transition, withdrawing a product is also a transition.) Review the critical transitions in your business. Among the most important are shifting from one product development project to the next, changing merchandise according to the season, entering new markets, absorbing acquisitions, ramping up to volume production, or launching new strategic alliances. Do you have formal processes for managing each critical transition? Can you simplify or shorten them? Can you accomplish more within a transition than simply getting from A to B?

3. *Rhythms.* List your company's own rhythms, and ask yourself which are really attuned to your business and which are merely habit. Are there important areas with no rhythms at all? For each of your key external relationships – with buyers, suppliers and competitors – list the major rhythms driving their businesses. Would getting in sync. with any of those rhythms create new opportunities for you? What would it take for your organization to exploit those opportunities?

Product

We have already considered how we can innovate against time, or at least have a sporting chance against time. In the manufacturing sector we may well need to understand the limitations of our manufacturing capability, no matter how flexible we think our manufacturing plant to be. In the service sector; how quickly can we develop the service required – skill up for it and develop a corpus of practice?

Event pacing in product development is the classic 'stage-and-gate' procedure, (see Chapter 2), with each stage being completed and the next approved before resources are released. This is exemplified by the Booz Allen and Hamilton approach to new product development (Booz Allen and Hamilton are a US consultancy based in McLean, Virginia).

While this demonstrates an orderly and cost-efficient approach to innovation development, it is slow and open to abuse. However, it does fix design at an early stage, because it has been assessed that change in design is expensive once development and manufacture have started. Early work in the US Department of Defense CALS programme showed that this limitation can be overcome by transformation of the value network. (CALS, Computer Aided Logistics Support, was the exploitation of computer interworking where master databases were used for computer-controlled manufacturing, so that a change at a database could immediately be reflected in manufacture, support and spares. When CALS became a commercial concept, it was renamed Commerce At Light Speed. It is regarded by many as the *urpunkt* of e-business.) While CALS has (almost) entirely been superseded by other more integrating concepts, its basic ideas are still valid (see, for example, the United Kingdom Council for Electronic Business, at www.ukceb.org).

Flexible design and manufacture can speed up the go-to-market process, changing absolute time to give space in relative time. Given that CAD (Computer Aided Design) has left the hype cycle and is now a mature technology, and that database and real-time data sharing is a reality in CAM (Computer Aided Manufacture), the sequential approach of stage-and-gate (Figure 10.13) can be replaced by a faster, more flexible approach (Figure 10.14), where redesign is not such a monster and much work can

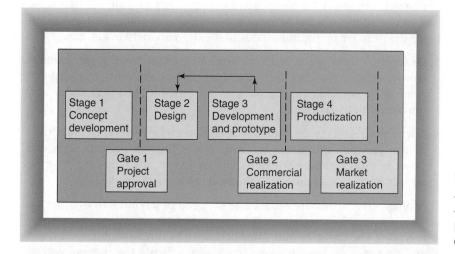

Figure 10.13
Archetypal stage and gate method of product development

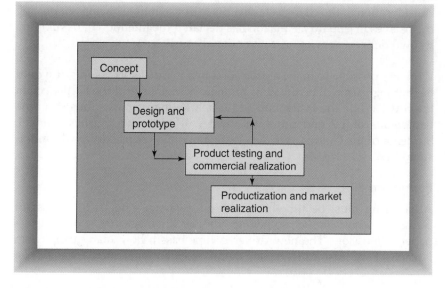

Figure 10.14
Architecture for flexible product development

be conducted in parallel. Integration of key users into the value chain, particularly those at the top of the ladder, can allow post-prototype redesign to take place.

Place

Place is seen not just as an outlet where our goods and services are delivered to the customer, but as being more about all the channel issues in time pacing – and in our SAC race we need to integrate the whole logistics chain and intermediary management. In terms of resource, we should think about four areas:

1. **Delivery** – how and where is the product/service to be delivered? Over the counter in a conventional retail – in pharmacists or electrical spares shops, for example, the resource is a counter assistant; in a supermarket the resource becomes shelf-stacking staff and check-out oper-ators; in an e-business grocery service this needs to be augmented by the delivery service and vehicles. How many vehicles the delivery channel needs depends on how long the customer is prepared to wait. The deliver-ed soggy, cold pizza is evidence of too few delivery staff. The same is true for the number of intermediaries in the delivery network.

2. **Ordering** – how is the order placed? Fast order placing (for example e-ordering) needs more IT resource than counter assistants; mail-ordering even more so. This can be outsourced offshore, but here there is an impact on time to deliver.

3. **Ownership** – this is an issue about legality; who owns the components of the product and therefore who meets the resource to service it? Ownership is a major issue in the integrated supply network. When we tie this into some of the fiscal issues, it ceases to be trivial.

4. **Money** – we will address the issue of speed of payment in Chapter 12.

Integrating the logistics and intermediaries is fundamental. Companies that strip out 'cost' from the resource which satisfies the channel without consideration of the changes taking place through time pacing are placing themselves in jeopardy. Amazon has declared the intention of developing its own delivery service, as conventional couriers are too slow.

If it were possible to make a projection in a manual such as this, it would be that logistics will be the new strategic battlefield and the bottleneck in the SAC. While the last round of the marketing war was fought on the battlefields of TV and press, the next will be in the logistics channel. Students of the Golden Wonder/Walkers potato crisps battle will understand that.

Promotion

Advertising must be time-based; brand awareness needs to be instant across the whole market, so perhaps the weekly magazine or daily newspaper is too slow. The new driver is time-based; how many people can I reach? How fast can I reach them? Conventional media have been supplemented by the acceptance of new industrial technologies which improve the time resource.

Advertising online

Advertising online in 2005 was worth some £19 billion in the UK alone, and is growing at 2.6 percent per annum. So effective and lucrative is well-targeted advertising that Spiral Frog, a music download site, plans to cease charging for its primary product and support itself on its advertising revenues alone. It is likely that many others will follow suit in areas where the charge for purchase is minimal, thus opening a new channel for placed advertising.

'Spiral Frog' is targeting under 35s with free popular music downloads while competitors (for example Napster) charge 79p or seek a subscription for the same service. With 420 million tracks downloaded in 2005, the revenue rejected by Spiral Frog is significant.

The music offered is the back catalogue of Universal Music, the world's largest record label, which includes Bob Marley, ABBA (target market under 35s?), U2 and the Scissor Sisters.

Stickiness to the site is created by news, reviews and gig listings.

Spiral Frog will offer free downloads provided the downloader agrees to watch 90 seconds of advertising for each download. Downloaders also divulge data such as age, postcode and gender to allow accurate targeting of advertising. Research by Spiral Frog suggests that downloaders will endure advertising so long as the brands are relevant.

(*The Times, The Daily Mail*, 30 August 2006)

Napster fails to make a profit and is put up for sale.

(BBC News, 20 September 2006)

Popular advertising methods are:

- SPAM – unsolicited emails and attachments. This is the oldest and most annoying form of Internet advertising; unfortunately (or fortunately, if you are a victim) SPAM filters, which are readily available, can take much SPAM out. However, Eastern-European, Far-Eastern and African SPAM houses are getting quite good at defeating SPAM killers. In the Western world at least, SPAM is frowned upon and its use results in adverse responses to the adverts placed. Legislation (particularly in the UK) controls business-to-consumer unsolicited emails; although at the time of writing no-one has yet been prosecuted, the lobbyists have been active.

- Pop ups (which have spawned the industry of pop-up killers, thus negating the advertising value). These are adverts that pop up and intrude into a website.

- Banners (and their vertical version, skyscrapers). These are either fixed or rotating/changing adverts that remain in the window during viewing on specific webpages. They too have given rise to the development of banner killers.

- Placed 'adverts' to members of Internet communities (for example, viral circulation of humorous adverts, such as by SEAT and Volvo; and 'research' adverts, such as those by Guinness, where breaking adverts are forwarded to known sympathizers, ostensibly seeking feedback for research purposes).

> In the USA, Virgin Mobile gives free minutes of air time to customers who agree to watch its adverts.
>
> (Quoted in Andrews, 2006)

Permissive advertising is becoming the accepted approach to advertising. A taxonomy of advertising over technology could be:

- No choice; company timing – for example, terrestrial main channels (ITV, Channels 4, 5)

- More choice; company timing – for example, digital, cable

- Customer choice; company timing – for example, advent of the Zapper

- Customer choice; customer timing – for example, Internet ads, herding onto websites, video on demand, interactive TV.

Herding onto a website usually takes the form of the integration of TV-presented advertising with website advertising. The usual approach is to show an incomplete advertisement – either physically incomplete, as in SAAB's 'It's A Mystery' adverts of 2004, or psychologically incomplete, which requires the resolution to be found on the website, where more facilities to encourage the customer to engage with the advert are available.

Non-Internet technology is also changing the nature of advertising. Interactive digital TV allows viewers to request details of products placed in programmes, and even the BBC is conscious of the remunerative possibilities of product placement.

Video on demand allows the exact placement of advertising before and during the showing of the video; viewers sign up to on-demand rental companies, and their profile is therefore known. Advertising can thus be carefully targeted.

Viral marketing is where an email containing something of 'value' (a good joke, a cartoon, a heart-rending poem, an offer giving a donation to a charity for every time the data is forwarded [how does the originator know?], a *zeitgeist* analysis of current affairs or subversive commentary) is forwarded requesting further distribution. This self-selecting segmentation is theoretically very rapid: if 64 percent of the UK population of 60 million read their emails every day, then the whole population can be covered by 8 forwardings to 10 people each. Clearly this is a faster version of our childhood chain letter. Viral marketing is at least rapid.

Mobile advertising uses text messages to mobile phones, and is equally rapid but requires knowledge of the database. The WAP and SMS systems are still relatively new, but are they in a hype stage? Is the technology really ready? Is the customer ready? No matter, the worldwide spend on mobile advertising will exceed $11 billion in the next 5 years (Informa Telecomm and Media, quoted in *The Times Business Supplement*, 15 September 2006).

Price

Price in the consumers' mind is still related to costs: technology reduces costs therefore sales using technology rather than humans should be cheaper. ATM transactions were introduced by banks on the grounds that they offered better 'service' (for example 24-hour coverage) to customers. The fact that banks were able to reduce expensive counter transactions may have been incidental. Subsequently, the fact that banks have been tempted to introduce a charge for cash withdrawal from ATMs suggests that the sole purpose was financial.

> While commercial websites offer 24/7 sales ordering at reduced prices, the UK Government DVLA online motor tax renewal costs £2.50 more than over-the-counter renewal at the Post Office with no personal or social interaction.
>
> (Source: DVLA website)

Technology, and specifically 'E', therefore covers two crucial areas:

1. Developing workplace technologies for internally speeding up processes to enable time pacing to take place.
2. Access to better information and intelligence to make faster decisions and to access and associate data to create a predictive knowledge about the impact of our strategy and marketing implementation.

Checklist

We will close this chapter with a checklist of readiness to embrace the benefits of time and technology. For each section, transfer the score on the left to the relevant column on the right. Add up the score in the columns, and plot yourself on the matrix.

Score		X score	Y score

Infrastructure
1 (Y)   Stand-alone computers
2 (Y)   Stand-alones grouped within functional areas
3 (X)   Most computers linked within the organization
4 (X)   Most users have pan-company data access but limited external access
5 (X)   All users have fast, reliable access to information in the company's operational environment

Applications
1 (Y)   Stand-alone applications with incomplete functional coverage in several key areas
2 (X)   Stand-alone applications covering all major functional areas
3 (Y)   Mostly off-the-shelf applications; data sharing limited to within functions
4 (Y)   Data and application sharing by request
5 (X)   Complete business data available from any source and used across applications

Communications
1 (X)   Paper, personal and voice main communications methods
2 (X)   Limited email, fax and telephone still main methods of communication
3 (X)   Basic email, data exchange, limited access to external data
4 (Y)   Most users have limited access to data required for their job
5 (Y)   Comprehensive, highly integrated, accessible and searchable data from anywhere in the company

Performance and outcomes
1 (X)   Financial aspects take priority
2 (X)   Corporate ability creates products
3 (X)   Issues surrounding the market dominate
4 (X)   Time-based activity focuses product development
5 (X)   Variable tempo practiced in product development

Team working
1 (Y)   Team-work limited to functional activities
2 (Y)   Managers work together on specific tasks
3 (Y)   Teams interacting with mutual support
4 (Y)   Integrated project teams form and perform quickly
5 (Y)   Empowered integrated teams work across the extended enterprise

Strategy sophistication
1 (Y)   Boards *do not* have a marketing presence in strategic decision-making
2 (X)   Strategy is based on shorter-term financial requirements
3 (Y)   Strategy is set bottom-up by department
4 (Y)   Strategy is set by an iterative process between departments
5 (X)   Driven by SAC

Management
1 (X)   The first topic on the Agenda for Board meetings is finance
2 (X)   Marketing is a function reporting to Sales
3 (Y)   Departments are empowered to develop their own strategies
4 (Y)   Departments treat other departments as customers
5 (Y)   Departments integrate their activities with other departments

Total	Total X score	Total Y score

Transfer the scores to the matrix in Figure 10.15 – the X score to the cultural attitude towards strategy axis, and the Y score to the strategic implementation sophistication axis.

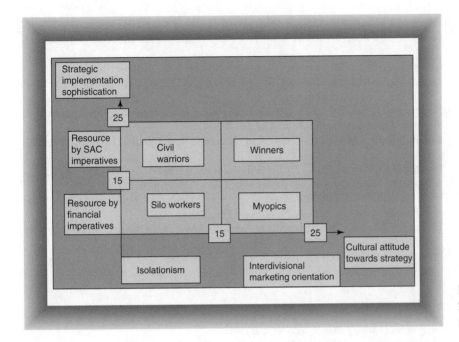

Figure 10.15 Strategy SAC readiness matrix

Winners are companies which have a long-term, whole-company view. They have a strong control of the competitive environment and a good understanding of the value network and their position within it. Individual departments have an understanding and cooperate with fellow departments to create customer value.

Myopics have got a good grip of the integration of the departments needed to create value, but are still hanging on to the tried and tested short-term profit/historical financial analysis for strategic management. The result will be a short-term view (shorter than the SAC, probably) and reluctance to make the step to drive the company through the principles of the SAC.

Civil warriors all agree the goal, but not how to get there. Each department and function has its own approach, and may well be encouraged to do so by a management team reluctant to embrace a true marketing orientation. The result is that these companies often lack the cohesion in time, resulting in delays and lost market opportunities.

Silo workers have little or no linkage between departments; the basis of management is the cost base. This correlates with low innovation and a weak understanding. Survival is usually based on sales, and the company's products/services arrive into the marketplace when the company is ready rather than when the market is ready.

References and further reading

References

Andrews, A. (2006). Operators Relish Future of Mobile Advertising. *The Times*, 15 September.

Baker, M.J. (2003). *Business and Management Research*. Argyll: Westburn Publishers.

Burns, A. and Bush, R. (2003). *Marketing Research*. Upper Saddle River, NJ: Prentice Hall.

Carmichael, H. (1998). *Another ICL Anthology*. London: Laidlaw Hicks.

Deise, M., Nowikow, C., King, P. and Wright, A. (2000). *Executives Guide to E Business*. Chichester: Wiley.

Eisenhardt, K. and Brown, S. (1998). Time pacing in markets that won't stand still. *Harvard Business Review*, **Mar/Apr**, 59–70.

Kotler, P. (2006). *Marketing Management*, 12th edn. Upper Saddle River, NJ: Prentice Hall.

Meehan, H., Murphy, A., O'Reilly, S. and Bogue, S. (2001). *The Market for Speciality Foods in Ireland*. Dublin: Agriculture and Food Development Authority.

Stalk, G. and Hout, T. (2003). *Competing Against Time: How Time-Based Competition Is Reshaping Global Markets*. New York: Free Press.

Thomson, F. (1995). Business strategy and the Boyd cycle. *Journal of Contingencies and Crisis Management*, **3(2)**, 81–91.

Wheelwright, S.C. and Clark, K.B. (1992). *Revolutionizing Product Development*. New York: Free Press.

Further reading

On speeding up the product development cycle:

MacCormack, A., Verganti, R. and Iansiti, M. (2001). Developing products on Internet time: the anatomy of a flexible development process. *Management Science*, **47**, 113–150.

Wheelwright, S.C. and Clark, K. (1994). Accelerating the design–build–test cycle for effective product development. *International Marketing Review*, **11(1)**, 32–46.

On Internet marketing:

Chaffey, D., Mayer, R., Johnston, K. and Ellis-Chadwick, F. (2006). *Internet Marketing*. Harlow: Pearson Prentice Hall.

11 Knowledge, information and intelligence

Introduction

We have already seen in Chapter 9 that there is a need for information to assist us in retaining loyal customers, and in our understanding of the SAC (Chapter 10) we need knowledge to predict the future state of the environment in which we will operate. In this chapter we will look at the difference between *data*, *information*, *intelligence* and *knowledge*, and how we use them differently. Data is worthless until associated with something to become information; information that can be used pre-emptively in some tactical competitive situation leads to intelligence; and relevant, coherent and constant information allows us to build knowledge. Intelligence is tactical: knowledge is strategic (Figure 11.1).

- *Data* is what we collect
- *Information* is what we use
- *Intelligence* is tactical, competitive information, but
- *Knowledge* is what we need.

In implementing marketing in terms of driving the SAC, we need intelligence and knowledge. In fact we also need a way of assessing the *value* or

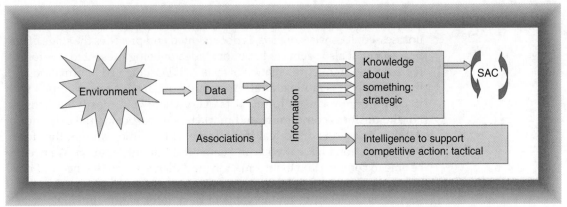

Figure 11.1 The relationship between data, information, intelligence and knowledge

worth of data before we waste time turning data into worthless and therefore useless information.

Marketing was once defined as 'Putting the company resources at risk to make a profit'. Marketing could therefore be thought of as concerning long-term business risk reduction. While financial systems do exist to 'reduce risk', usually by increasing various punitive financial measures, the only real way of reducing risk is to have good knowledge. Good knowledge will support lower-risk decisions that are to be taken in the future. Knowledge comes from intelligence and information; information and intelligence come from data, data associations and processing. Each piece of data has value in this systems approach; some data is more valuable than others: yesterday's paper probably holds little value; today's will be of considerable interest and tomorrow's – well, if you were to get tomorrow's paper today, the bookies would be out of pocket!

But first let us consider *data*.

Data

There are a number of definitions of data. For example, here are some taken from the Internet:

- 'a collection of facts from which conclusions may be drawn' (wordnet. princeton.edu/perl/webwn)

- 'Documented information or evidence of any kind' (www.cdc.gov/ tobacco/evaluation_manual/glossary.html)

- 'A representation of facts, concepts, or instructions in a formalized manner suitable for communication, interpretation, or processing by humans or by automated means' (sam.dgs.ca.gov/TOC/4800/4819. 2.htm)

- 'A formal representation of raw material from which information is constructed via processing or interpretation' (www.florite.com/support/ terminology.htm).

The common thread here is that data is raw material: unfiltered and unassessed. It consists of facts, is documented and precedes the stage of any processing. It also seems to have some idea of being presented (. . . formal representation) (A representation of facts . . .) (Documented information . . .). But critically, it is raw material. We abound in data; we are swamped with it. Data in unprocessed form exists everywhere, and mostly remains so. For the business community and marketers in particular, the existence of data on its own is of no real importance. It has little value in that form. BUT if you don't have it you can't convert it into information. We need to be able to convert data to information (and thence to intelligence and most importantly, knowledge). In the first instance, we need to be able to set some useful measures on the value of data, information, intelligence and knowledge.

Use and value of data

What do we use data for? Most importantly, data is what is collected. It can be a collection of facts (for example our profit was £110 k last year), or it can be a string of numbers. The following are examples of data:

1. 'A competitor will take delivery of cartons. The cartons are of an unusual size and printed with an unusual design.' This is data because it is unprocessed; it is not associated with any particular activity or event. It mainly conveys that a competitor is taking delivery of some cartons. What for? It doesn't say. When? It doesn't tell you. Why? We don't know. It merely tells us *what*. Cartons.

2. A weekly sales return:

	No of units sold		No of units sold
Monday	50	Friday	80
Tuesday	50	Saturday	60
Wednesday	150	Sunday	20
Thursday	100		

This is data because it is unprocessed. We don't know anything except that Product X sold Y amount on Monday, Tuesday, Wednesday, etc. We don't know why there was a change on Wednesday: we don't know whether Sunday sales were down because the shop sold out and the customer bought a competitive product. The data merely tells us how many units were sold on which day.

Collecting data is very expensive; storing it until it is useful is equally so. Data has a shelf-life, as does information and intelligence. The trick is to know when to stop collecting data, or at least to target its collection, and when to delete it, as it will no longer provide useful information and intelligence.

Data is often stored in data banks: high-tech companies use IT systems to sort and retrieve; low-tech equivalents are card files. Both are data banks, and both operate the same way: data is stored for future use.

Retrieval depends on how the data was stored. Not only should the facts themselves be stored, but also some indication of:

● when it was collected

● why it was collected.

Moreover, the source from which it was collected should be stored with it. Here, the word 'source' means the agency, collection method, research tools, who prepared the research report, etc. Collection of data is often outsourced, and the management of quality of data and its fitness for purpose in the outsourced company needs very careful monitoring.

Good databases also record when they were last used (if possible – online database may not have this facility, but you really do need to know how long after collection it was used, if at all) and why. The setting up and structure of an MkIS was discussed in Chapter 10. If a web-based MkIS is used as a repository, automatic software logs of those accessing the data should be included in the database. Analysis of this information may help to reduce the data you collect.

So: data is raw material, it has a shelf-life, and is used to create information and intelligence. There is a cost associated with its collection and storage, which is why you don't want to collect unnecessary data. On its own, it tells little. To be useful in marketing it needs to be converted to information.

Information

What is information? Information is when data is or can be associated with something else – an event, analysis, or other data. Thus it is of more interest than data; in many ways it is the result of the processing that was referred to in the data definitions.

- Information is the result of processing, manipulating and organizing data in a way that adds to the knowledge of the person receiving it (www.orfaq.com/glossary/fagglosi.htm).
- Information is gained when data has been processed to add or create meaning and hopefully knowledge for the person who receives it. Information is the output of information systems (dssresources.com/glossary/dssglossary1999.html).

Information, then, is of more interest and value than data; it is the result of processing the data; that processing being the association of the data with something else – other data, as in a statistical test, or an event. But it is not yet knowledge, despite several attempts to define it as such, because it is still specific. There will always be information that you don't have which will reduce risk and allow more knowledge about a subject. Information itself is non-predictive; it is processed data that links to some other association and is therefore still historical.

There is a concept in information engineering and in economics: the concept of 'perfect information'. Remember, information is still historic; we are talking about 20/20 hindsight. Perfect information is associated with the activity of decision-making. After all, information is only collected to help make a decision less risky. So there are two ideas here:

1. The idea of risk being reduced by perfect information (and risk analysis is a real minefield in its own right), and

2. The idea of decision-making under risk, or imperfect information.

Imperfect information is only imperfect when used in a specific scenario and the information used in that scenario leads to a different outcome to that expected. It stems from wrong data, which has two roots:

1. The data is incorrect because:

- it was wrong in the first place
- correct data was incorrectly recorded or transcribed
- it was right in the first place but is now out of date.

2. The association is inappropriate because:

- the wrong association is applied to correct data
- the right association is applied to wrong data.

We can represent the outcomes as follows:

	Correct data	*Incorrect data*
Appropriate association	We can assume this is accurate information	Data needs to be revisited to identify the source of the inconsistency
Inappropriate association	The associations historically made to the data need to be checked, and the outcomes of previous data associations need to be verified	Both inputs which will create the information are at fault; the danger of using data which falls into this category is serious

The above matrix may help when things go wrong; historical checking of associations against outcomes will give a guide as to whether the associations are still valid; and checking the data sources for accuracy is necessary if the outcome is not what is expected. The other thing to do, of course, is to look for alternative associations which could better explain the results.

Misuse of data, or misexpectations of data sources, leads to the usual list of complaints from company executives about marketing data:

1. *There is too much information of the wrong kind.* The origin of this complaint can usually be traced to one of more of the following:

- The collection plan being wrong.
- The requirements having been changed in the time (a) since implementation of the collection plan; (b) since the verification of the associations; (c) since the dissemination of the information to the executive; and (d) taken for the executive to get around to turning the information into intelligence or assimilating it into knowledge.
- A change in the information requirements not being sent to the collectors.

2. *There is not enough information of the right kind.* The origin of this complaint can usually be traced to one or more of the following:

- The right kind of data being too expensive and the budget not running that far. Data is often assumed to be available from cheap, instant secondary sources (see later), but such data can be inadequate, and primary collection (which can be both costly and time consuming) is required.

- The right kind of data is too hard to collect. Some required data, especially competitive data for intelligence purposes, can be 'company secret' data. If this data is not available, either some espionage work is required (but see later before ringing your local industrial James Bond!). Often the data is implicit elsewhere, and collectors and sources of data are often unaware of the fact that they can provide this data – frequently from open press sources. A company's annual accounts and news releases (especially ones released when their boss is away) can reveal a great deal of 'company confidential' data. In my view, every self-respecting marketer should have a copy of the published accounts of his competitor on his desk. In my experience, few ever have.

- It may be illegal to hold or to use the data (see the US Economic Espionage Act, later in this chapter).

- Information is not being collated in a way in which the executive can use it, and therefore he doesn't realize that he has it.

- The data retrieval system is at fault.

- The data is being held but the 'knowledge is power' game prevents it from being entered into the database and disseminated – a common fault in sales(person)-led companies (see Chapter 10).

- The data retrieval system is inadequate to the demands.

- Data is arriving too late to be useful.

- No time limit has been put on the collection agency for the data.

- The data plan has not been updated.

- Data requirements have changed in the light of new information and the new requirements have not been properly transmitted to the collectors.

- Information accuracy and validity cannot be assessed, and therefore it is worthless. Data collection should be tracked into information, information constantly rated and the sources constantly validated.

We need to verify both the data and the associations. We need to know what the source of the data is and how reliable it is. Did the sales records in our second example come from till receipts; shelf restocking or the manager's opinion, or is it the result of some shopping mall research? Has the data that the cartons have been printed come from an observer or the printer? Or was it overheard in the pub? It is a useful trick to grade data

A–C for likely accuracy (as assessed from other sources), and 1–3 for quality of source (Table 11.1).

Table 11.1 A data quality/source matrix

Source	Assessed data quality		
	A (Good data)	B (Mediocre data)	C (Poor data)
1. Traditionally highly reliable source	Good data, high confidence	Review the reasons that restricted the data quality	Review the outcomes to downgrade source
2. Either source is not focused or is learning on the job	Some confidence, may be worth checking data against other sources	Most data lives here; data needs to be verified and, if it is good, maybe source can be upgraded	Historical analysis is needed here: can the data be used?
3. Traditionally unreliable source; consider switching data provider	One-off or has source improved?	Review the outcomes to confirm data	Why did you collect it?

In our previous example, we might set till receipts as A; manager's opinion as C; information overheard in the pub as 3; information from the printer himself as 1.

As a rule of thumb, the weaker the data source, the more sources we would like to have to corroborate the data before associating it for information. Even reliable sources may need corroboration from other sources; the EPOS system may have gone down in the middle of Saturday and the store lost stocktaking data, but it could carry on taking money (without till receipts!), because till receipts don't measure the intention to buy nor how many units were put back on the shelf. Good data will be supported from at least two sources, preferably more. While till receipts are highly reliable, other sources of corroboration are required and should be used.

> ASDA, the Wal-Mart owned UK supermarket, not only looks at till receipts from its EPOS/stock management system but also at stock movements, measuring stock brought into replace stock 'bought' (or wasted, or stolen or other errors due to shrinkage).

So we need to establish the source of data and how it is corroborated, and the reliability of these sources. There are two concepts to introduce here: validity and reliability. Validity is measuring what you set out to measure; reliability is whether, if you do it again, you will get the same result.

The usual way to do this is to think about the historical accuracy of a data source: has it traditionally been accurate? If so, there is a fair chance that the source will still be accurate – but be aware; it might not be!

What is 'risk' in this context? It is the probability of getting it wrong – or, if you prefer, the chances of getting it right. The more information we have to support a decision, the less risk we put ourselves in or, conversely, the higher the chances are of getting it right. If we knew everything about the customer, the competitor, the macro-environment and the advancement of technology, about the future (and actually about the past too), we could significantly reduce the risk of a marketing decision. In other words, if we had perfect information, we might be able to make perfect decisions. We can rarely afford to do that, in terms of either time or money, so we trade risk off against cost.

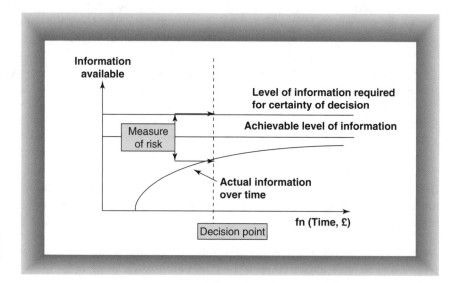

Figure 11.2
Trading risk against cost (source: Millier, 1999)

However:

- perfect data is rarely available; as Figure 11.2 indicates, even the level of achievable information is asymptotic when considered as a joint function of time and money

- Figure 11.2 indicates that the law of diminishing returns starts to apply; the (moveable) vertical line represents when the amount of data is sufficient to form the decision, or the level of information that can be gathered as a result of the budget (as a function of time and money)

- risk will be reduced as data accumulates; the gap between the data at the decision point and the 'perfect information' line is a measure of risk associated with imperfect data.

Since perfect data is not generally available and we have to do the best we can; we need to balance data, data inaccuracies, the increased benefit of better data, cost and (in SAC terms) time.

Even if we did have perfect information, we would have needed perfect associations to go with the perfect data – and, as we have seen, data is expensive. In too many companies data collection is a rump activity; if, as many pundits declare, we live in an information age, information management, assessment and dissemination must take centre stage.

Value and uses of information

Information is now only as valuable as the importance of the outcome of the associations. If the outcome is not important, then the information is not important, and the effort put into collecting it is reduced.

From our earlier example of the cartons, if we are aware that novel package design heralds the release of a new product, then the association we can make is that the competitor is about to launch a new product. This is still information: it is based on an association (novel packaging = new product) and one piece of data: the competitor has novel cartons.

If we look at the second example, the weekly sales return, if we take into account the fact that there was an advertisement on the 10 o'clock news on Tuesday evening, the data starts to become information and on its way to contributing to knowledge. The additional piece of data (that there was an advertisement) allows us to make an association. It now becomes information. It would be a brave marketer that would yet claim knowledge of the impact of advertising on sales from this single piece of information.

Information, then, is about something or with which we can do something. Information is what we need to collect to gain knowledge. Knowledge at each stage of the SAC is what we need to understand how to drive it.

Thinking back to the previous section, we discussed the difficulty of perfect information, and how it required perfect data. Data comes in two types: accurate and sufficient.

How accurate is accurate enough? How much do you want to pay? How long do you want to wait? To a large extent, the answers to these questions hinge on both intelligence and knowledge. What are the gaps in our knowledge that we need to plug? How important is the usage to which we can put the data? This leads us to the concept of intelligence.

Intelligence

Let us again define intelligence:

● Intelligence is the product resulting from the collection, processing, integration, analysis, evaluation and interpretation of available information concerning foreign countries or areas. It is information and knowledge about an adversary obtained through observation, investigation, analysis or understanding (books.nap.edu/html/C4I/ch1_b1.html).

- Intelligence is a prediction or assessment following the analysis of information (Intelligence Corps definition).

- Intelligence is effectively perceiving, interpreting and responding to the environment. It is also taken to mean the ability of an organization to survive and meet desired goals and objectives (www.mountainquestinstitute. com/definitions.htm).

Intelligence (in its information-engineering sense) is information about which we can or want to do something specific. Intelligence is assessed information that enables us to make a specific decision about our activity in the event of a competitor's activity. The carton delivery can be tied into a block booking of advertising time. This second association leads to the assessment that there is a possible launch by the competitor of a new product, coming at or just before the advertising campaign. We may want to take some competitive action – reduce our prices, drive other sales promotions, push products into the channel. The data through associations has become intelligence about a competitor on which we can take action with confidence.

Collecting and maintaining intelligence is an ongoing task. It involves collecting data, associating and processing it to create information, then validating the information to create intelligence.

It can be the interpretation of the information in the light of other associations. Intelligence is something that others may not have.

Independence of sources

This brings me to a cautionary tale – that of circularity, if such a word exists. Data from different research agencies may well not be independent. Anecdotal evidence shows that a number of shopper surveys are based on the same database of respondents. It would not be a surprise, therefore, to expect the market research reports to show a high degree of consistency. Reports produced by one agency may well be based on the same data and associations as that used by another, often unwittingly. The famously 'sexed up' Iraq dossier is a case in point.

In other words, intelligence is to be used. Without an application or a use, intelligence becomes information again.

We have seen where intelligence comes from: let's just take a moment to see where it doesn't come from. It doesn't come from industrial espionage – well, in decent companies it doesn't.

Espionage in intelligence gathering

There has to be fine line drawn between competitive intelligence (the printer telling you that there is a print run coming) and industrial espionage.

In July 2006, an administrative assistant in Coca-Cola tried to sell the rival Pepsi Corporation Coke's marketing plan for a new drink, the plan being full of alleged 'company secret' information.

Under the US 1996 Economic Espionage Act, it is a federal crime to steal or misuse trade secrets. Pepsi informed Coke, and the vendor of the plan was arrested.

In a separate incidents AdAge reports that 'once a year . . . Burger King would receive a full or partial McDonald's marketing plan, and it would be forwarded via legal departments back to McDonalds.'

(Source: McArthur, 2006)

But where is the boundary between espionage and competitive information? Is overhearing something in the pub espionage? Is reading something on someone's laptop at a café hotspot espionage? How about looking at Geosat photography to identify raw-material movements of a competitor, or counting and analysing delivery schedules, or tracking lorries on the road – is this espionage, or intensive intelligence gathering? Should new employers debrief new employees from competitor companies about intentions, operations, plans and so forth? There is no real answer to these questions. A company's behaviour must be an ethical issue for the company itself. Outside legal requirements – and not all countries have legislation similar to the US Economic Espionage Act – the guidance has to be 'do as you would be done by'. It is commonplace for supermarket managers to send employees on mystery shopping expeditions and to use the pricing data gathered for promotional purposes. One reason often given for (and against) outsourcing of material to third-party agencies is the opportunity (or risk) of competitive intelligence. The nearest answer, and one which gives the best definition of espionage in the industrial sense, is that of the Society for Competitive Intelligence Professionals (SCIP), a US-based world-wide association. The SCIP defines espionage as 'the use of illegal sources to gather data'.

Satellite photography is all right, then, as is debriefing new employees, competitive mystery shopping and looking over the laptop terminal in the departure lounge. Bugging the Boardroom is not.

To support best ethical practice in intelligence and data gathering, the SCIP has established a code of conduct.

The 'Code of Conduct' for competitive intelligence gathering is:

- intelligence gatherers must abide by all national and international laws
- gatherers must accurately disclose all relevant information, including their identity and the organization employing them, prior to conducting any primary research interviews
- any conclusions drawn must be honest.

(Adapted from the SCIP Code of Conduct)

Knowledge

- *Knowledge* is the relationships, facts, assumptions, heuristics and models derived through the formal and informal analysis or interpretation of data (www.cordis.lu/ist/ka1/administrations/publications/glossary.htm).

Knowledge is the amalgamation over a period of time of reliable intelligence and information that allows us to build a complete – or as near complete as possible – picture of the environment; most importantly, it allows us to predict changes in the environment – changes resulting from competitive activity; customer activity or macro-environmental activity. We need knowledge to understand the impact we will have on the environment as a result of our actions; it is through knowledge that we can predict what will happen in the SAC, and through knowledge that we retain our competitive advantage.

Government intelligence agencies use a system called the 'intelligence cycle' (Figure 11.3). Since the intelligence agencies are interested in intelligence to build knowledge, we can think of this as a knowledge cycle. In marketing terms, we are interested in the SAC, and therefore the cycle is applicable to us building knowledge from information.

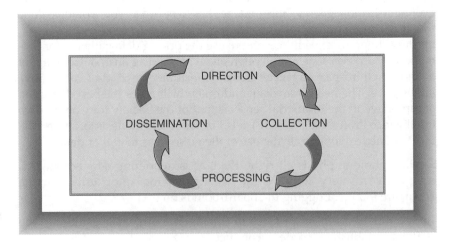

Figure 11.3
The intelligence (knowledge) cycle (source: Intelligence Corps)

- *Direction* is comprehending what information is missing in our understanding of an environment, and assessing the value of including it in our knowledge. Remember that perfect information is unobtainable, and costs increase rapidly as we approach perfection.

- *Collection* is the act of market research to collect the data.

- *Processing* is making the associations with the collected data. These associations will be with previously collected data or with events.

- *Dissemination* is just that – getting the updated knowledge to the right people so that they can take the right action. Knowledge, information and intelligence are useless in the wrong (or no-one's) hands. Look back to the list of grumbles about marketing data; could any be avoided by having a carefully managed dissemination programme?

Dissemination needs to follow some simple guidelines:

Requires	Who requested the data be collected? They certainly need a copy!
Action	Who will take the action on the data and make it useable information? They need a copy too. And check that they have taken some action. I had a shock once when I realized that no-one was using some very expensive data I was collecting on an ongoing basis, because the person who actioned it had left!
Courtesy	Who feels that they should know about the data, but probably will not be instrumental in processing it? They need to be informed, can always request a copy and can be added to the distribution list in the future.
Excluded	Who doesn't need a copy but is on the mailing list? Should they be excluded?
Storage	Where is the data stored until next used or deleted?

RACES is a good mnemonic, and using it is a good habit to get into. Check your standard mailing list, and that it is valid.

If we manage the knowledge cycle properly – and that takes resource – we should be able to avoid the criticisms noted earlier.

Fundamentally, knowledge is the accumulation and interpretation of information to make predictions.

What do we do with data, information and knowledge?

Marketing is all about helping to reduce the risks in business decisions. We know these risks come mainly from three areas:

1. Risk associated with the customer.

2. Risk associated with the marketplace.

3. Risk associated with the company.

The previous sections of this book consider the latter point, and thus we will not dwell on it much here.

So we need to use data, information, intelligence and knowledge for a number of things:

- to predict changes in the environment brought about by the customers' changing view of what is best value, and therefore

- to go around the SAC as fast and as knowledgeably as possible, reducing risk to ourselves but increasing it for competitors.

The problem with marketing is that you sometimes need to challenge received wisdom, especially if it comes from well-established and experienced marketers. In resource terms, we may well need to challenge where resource is being spent, and why. As a result, we may need to think in terms of challenging traditional views and opinions. I have chosen to call these challenges *'heresies'*, because in some marketing circles challenges to tradition are regarded as such.

Heresy 1

If through knowledge we are in control of the SAC, we need to ask, what is the purpose of a customer?

Hopefully, the purpose of a customer is to provide the company with sales. The more customers, the more sales, and the higher the company's profits and the more satisfied the shareholders. However, business is not just about higher profits. If we believe that the real purpose of business is to generate increased shareholder value, as suggested by people such as Rappaport (1988) and, more recently, Doyle (2000), then we need to look at shareholder value. Shareholder value comes from three areas:

1. Dividend payout: how much immediate return is there? This is a function (usually) of profit made – the higher the profit, the greater the dividend.

2. Increasing share value: if there is no potential future profit, once the annual dividend has been paid, a share is worthless until the next annual dividend payout. So an idea of future dividend is what actually gives a share – and therefore a company – its value. And of course, company credit, and hence borrowing potential and investment potential, depends on share stability and value increase.

3. Bluebirds, derived from spontaneous events, and generating self-feeding 'value': these are too difficult to predict and even harder to manage (for example, the dot-com and other bubbles).

Concentrating on the former two points, this means that the long-term survival of a company is critical, and maybe more so than immediate dividends.

It is a small step from there to go back to look at the purpose of customers and consider them in the context of increasing the chances of long-term survival.

About the customer

The value of a customer

The customer is your data source (this phrase should be in large, friendly letters on the front cover of every marketing book!).

Yes, customers spend money with us as well, but if, as many gurus (such as Nonaka, 1991; Palmer, 2004) tell us, marketing and business are knowledge-based activities, then we should be regarding customers as data sources; collating their individual data, associating it, building a wide understanding of it to produce knowledge about each individual. In that sense we can become knowledgeable about the segment we operate in: we can predict its behaviour and its expectations of best value. We are then in a position to create best value for our customers, as well as to predict the future environment of the SAC to see when, where and what the customer is going to see as best value, and to drive our marketing operations around the SAC to achieve it.

As a result, the customer is worth a great deal to us, not just in financial terms but also in information terms – whether we take 'customer' in its narrow form as someone who buys from us; or include the concept of a prospect (a member of the segment who may switch to us at some point in the future). Either way, the customer is primarily a source of data. Once the customer is captured, then economics takes over and we strive to continue to provide best value – that is to say, we move our customer base and ourselves around the SAC. But to capture the customer in the first place, we need knowledge.

> Tesco's loyalty card is not about loyalty but about data collection. By giving rewards for accumulated purchases and ensuring that customer-profile data is gathered at each purchase, Tesco is able to look at the data collected through sales patterns throughout the day and make associations with it. In Reading (Berkshire, UK), for example, the use of postcode associations has allowed Tesco to reschedule its courtesy bus timetables from specific postcodes in order to offer particular segments (such as senior citizens) special prices at defined times of the day. It can also offer meals at specific times that encourage the elderly to eat at Tesco, or make mother and baby offers, and thereby it has gained competitive advantage over its rivals, who do not have such accurate data in both spend and service delivery.

Customer value ladders

In previous sections we have referred to customer retention and customer relationship management as a way of achieving customer value. Other ideas have centred on a so-called 'ladder of advocacy' (Christopher *et al.*, 1991; see Figure 11.4).

But what do we need to do to implement it? Without implementation, there is no data. There have been a number of approaches to this

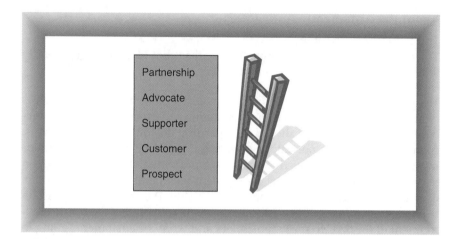

Figure 11.4
The ladder of
advocacy

problem – Peck *et al.* (1999), for example, have established the idea of the relationship programme in marketing thinking. However, in resourcing for the ladder, we need a more pragmatic view.

At each stage in the ladder, we expect something from the customer – repeat purchase or recommendations at the lower levels, referrals and advocacy at the higher levels, and, at the highest level, true partnership and sharing. But this has to be translated into something of benefit for the customer. At each stage we need to see what it is that we need to do to encourage the customer to climb the ladder. And of course, the customer is not only climbing our ladder; he or she is being encouraged up other's ladders too. In the case of a dual-supplier relationship, where the customer is being coaxed up two ladders, we need to ensure that climbing our ladder provides better value.

Cross and Smith (1997) suggest that the company invests in five levels (rungs on the ladder) of relationship, each bonding the customer more tightly to the company, and at each rung a different level of investment activity is required (Figure 11.5). It should be remembered that a relationship is a two-way street; pumping the monthly newsletter into the address

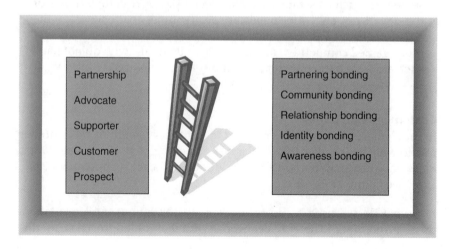

Figure 11.5
The ladder of
bonding

list is *not* creating a relationship, but generating junk mail for the mailing agencies to make a profit. Relationships therefore are reciprocal.

Rung 1 is creating bonding through awareness – building brand awareness (for a discussion of brand awareness, see Chapter 9). In other words, we need to invest in buying *share of mind* in the early stages: if there is no bond with your brand on the part of the customer, then there is no chance of progress up the ladder. Once achieved, though, this bonding must be reinforced and maintained. Once a customer decides that your brand is not what he or she wants any more; this link will be broken and the whole ladder becomes unstable and collapses for that particular customer. In other words, once you have started to teach the customer the changes in the environment that you are proposing for the SAC, the more necessary it is to keep the customer and to build on his or her wants.

Rung 2, identity bonding, is starting to build the relationship beyond the awareness stage. Here, we are building the *share of heart*. It is a bond based on shared values and aspirations. You build this bond through creating a cause, and cause-related marketing has a role to play here.

Berry (1995) defined four types of relationship you can have with a customer:

1. *Legal*, where the relationship is tied in law. A guarantee or maintenance contract is a typical consumer level of relationship bonding, and can form a very useful route to data collection. Do you service your guarantee holders? Once registered, do you use the data in the registration form to develop this level of bonding? Do you use it to revisit and build the relationship with the customer? Do you use it at all?

2. *Fiscal*, where mutual financial links bond the customer. A hire-purchase agreement or deferred-terms payment schedule offers significant opportunity here. However, this will require the company to have a relationship with any outsourcing credit company (for example GE Capital) to maintain the bonding relationship. Credit terms have greater value to you than just being a helpful way of letting the customer pay for a product; they are a method of bonding, particularly in the business-to-business market.

3. *Social*, where there is social bonding to maintain share of heart. In the UK, for example, the Classic-FM radio station runs regular lollipop concerts for listeners, where the different show presenters and their support personalities are on hand to press the flesh.

4. *Organizational*, where the bond is built by integrating the organizations. This is a wide opportunity for the business-to-business market, and especially where strategic alliances and partnerships are concerned. We will remember this when we address the partnership level.

Rung 3, relationship bonding, is where values start to be exchanged and knowledge is built. Ongoing relationships require the relationship to have value at this stage; in other words the very fact that the customer has reached this stage implies that he or she is getting an ongoing 'something' out of the relationship. At a basic level, it could be the status of continued use of the product – for example, a set of Tiger Woods-branded golf clubs would create ongoing value – but that is only a starting point. The ongoing use of a brand, while creating product value, does not create value bonding on its own; however, a Tiger Cubs Club, for example, where score cards are submitted, leader boards produced and maybe a prize is awarded annually, would be a start towards offering an exchange of value. The customer derives value from the relationship, which is now moving away from 'direct mail to our customer base' or 'regular newsletters', both of which ignore feedback communication (see Chapter 9) and therefore do not constitute an exchange of value. The value to the owner of the brand is:

- having knowledge about the segment and the environment (and hence the SAC)

- the share of heart and

- the ability to support the lower and very vulnerable rungs of the ladder.

Loyalty programs (such as frequent-flyer programs and in-store loyalty cards) again offer a starting point for value exchange. Value here can be offered through a variety of media: the correspondence via email offers different value to hard-copy, posted letters, and again a value rather than cost needs to be established. What is the cost (of postage)/value (of receiving) ratio of a posted letter compared with the cost/value ratio of an email? This will not only depend on the technical availability, but also on the recipient's circumstances. There is increased value in opening a valued, personalized letter (not a junkmail flier, though) over 'F5: delete'. Charities could make the significant value of personalized letters work for them.

The World Vision child sponsorship programme includes a number of exchange value ideas – letters from the sponsored child which sit on the sponsor's mantelpiece, regular photographs of the sponsored child, reminders from HQ as to when the sponsored child's birthday or other significant life event is about to occur. This is a constant exchange of value through impulse donations and personalized information.

The Royal National Lifeboat Institute, the charity-supported UK lifeboat provider, could follow this 'exchange of value' approach by linking donations to a specific lifeboat and providing donors with regular updates regarding the success of that lifeboat – thereby moving contributors onto this rung, increasing the bonding and commitment, and thus donations. The opportunities for social bonding through (ticketed) beach barbeques could start to move the value towards the community bonding rung of the ladder.

Rung 4, community bonding, explores the social relationship (see above) required to create communities. This community's focus is a common lifestyle interest. Whether these communities are owners' clubs (for example the MG Owners' Club), user groups or whatever, the bonding comes through a sense of community. Companies then provide support to the community and bonds develop between members – even to the extent of providing a marketplace, or perhaps developing referral markets. It is this community member-to-community member bonding rather than company-to-community member bonding that creates real value. Having said that, communities created through community bonding not only provide a ground for the collection of data, but also are willing participants in developments, communications and new product/product development launches. The values of exchange from Rung 3 need to be carefully analysed; at this stage, Rung 4, information becomes knowledge; we have access to such significant amounts of information and associations that we can start to make predications regarding the behaviour and expectations of the customer and generate a deep understanding of the environment and how it will change, thus giving us a start on assessing the changes and speed of change of the environment in the SAC.

Rung 5, partnering bonding, takes advantage of the community bonding developed at Rung 4 and builds on it. The concept is that the customer feels very deep loyalty to you, so much so that he or she recommends and sells your products for you – the true referral market. In advanced stages the company may reward the partner with some form of proxy authority – maybe the right (through administrative relationship) to investigate stockholdings, or to broker deals. In some companies, a separate department is set up (MCI, now Verizon, for example) to respond to referrals. Here, we do not mean the company-driven '£10 voucher to introduce a friend', but offering valued rewards to Rung 5 customers for successful referrals. The links need not (and probably should not) be obvious or necessarily tied directly to sales, and in these circumstances will probably be bespoke. In the business-to-business markets we may find that Company A would like to be involved in the Integrated Project Team developing the new product, while Company B would like access to the stockholding data or delivery dates, and Company C would like to share a distribution channel.

It is at this stage that true partnering will occur. Once the partnership and mutual respect for the community has been established, the integration of value chains could well become a reality. As we saw in Chapter 10, the transformation of supply chain to an integrated value network is eased by the integration of IT systems.

Necessarily, then, we need to collect different data and make different associations about the customer, and to use that information to provide the steps of the ladder and the rewards the customer will get back from climbing the ladder. At the lower levels, the sort of data we need to convert to information would include:

- the customer's views
- how the customer chooses between suppliers

- how important the rewards are to the customer, and, most importantly,

- how important the rewards are that the customer gets by moving from being a customer (a one-off behaviour) to being a client (regular customer)?

And what knowledge about his future behaviour do we need to move him from client to supporter? Or from supporter to advocate? Moreover (although not included in the ladder and only now coming to prominence in marketing thinking), how do we manage his advocacy? Indeed, there is great scope here to segment a market by satisfaction of CRM rewards and the level of expectation the ladder provides to the customer.

Somerfield, the UK grocery chain, scrapped its loyalty card scheme in March 2006 (and therefore abandoned its loyalty ladder) to offer a wider range of everyday low prices to all. This was a step also taken by Asda following a pilot study on introducing its own loyalty card, which was never rolled out. Clearly, in a competitive market some companies believe that loyalty rewards are so little valued by customers that offering everyone the same benefits will have no impact on loyalty, or that loyalty has no impact on their business. It would be interesting to see the effect on both basket and footfall of Somerfield's decision. However, these traditional measures would not measure the true effect of the removal of a loyalty program on the brand of Somerfield, which is loss of impulse, loyalty-driven purchases.

A data collection programme along the lines described below would therefore make a useful early contribution (see Table 11.2).

Table 11.2 Resource data requirements table

Rung on the ladder	Segment	Data needed on customer	Expectation of reward	Reward which needs to be provided	Resource required to deliver reward
Rung 1 Rung 2 etc.					

Collecting data to make knowledge

Earlier, we mentioned collection agencies and collection plans.

A *collection plan* is an ongoing programme, disseminated to the collection agencies, indicating:

- the collection requirements over the next collection period; and

- ongoing update requirements for data which is in constant need of updating.

These collection requirements come from an analysis of the information required to keep the knowledge (which exists to make less risky decisions) up-to-date.

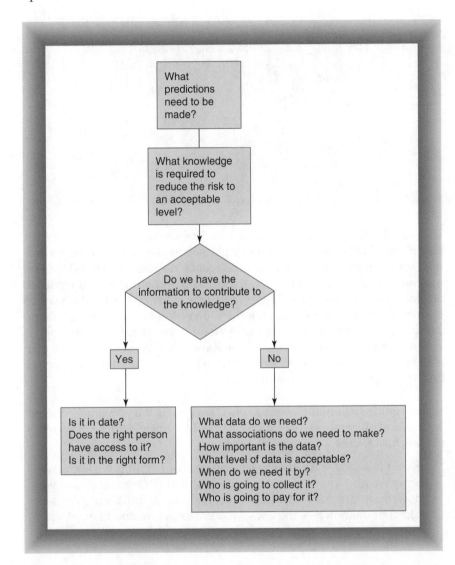

Figure 11.6
Collection
requirements
flow chart

In a well-structured, knowledge-based company, collection plans are continuous and everyone must be involved (Figure 11.6). Everyone's commitment, both in collecting against the plan and entering the data into a databank on which everyone can draw, is a fundamental requirement of the knowledge-valuing company. Since everyone can collect data and should be urged to do so, so everyone should have a role in a collection plan. Indeed, some authorities (for example Kotler and Lilien, 1983) take the rather draconian view that 'sales managers should review the intelligence {they mean information gathering} performance of their {sales} representatives and make it a factor in their pay rises'. Twenty-three years ago they advocated that, and I still feel, 'if only . . . '.

A plan could look something like Table 11.3.

Table 11.3 Suggested data collection plan

Requirement	Requested by	Date requested	Date required	Which agency will collect it?	Date collected	Date disseminated	Executives to whom disseminated	Acknowledged?

The plan should be monitored and reviewed regularly; old requirements that haven't been collected and are no longer needed should be removed (see my caution in dissemination), and the agency responsible for collecting it informed. Progress should be chased on outstanding data, and feedback on data quality, collecting agency and use requested from the user to upgrade/downgrade the rating of the source. A collection plan is a living document, and needs to be kept up-to-date to be useful. If knowledge is vital to a company (and I hope we have shown that it is), the collection plan is as fundamental to the company as the marketing plan. Indeed, there is a case to suggest that it is more so.

A good guide to thinking about a collection plan is the previously quoted, famous and often mocked assertion by Donald Rumsfeld, then US Secretary of State for Defense, that in intelligence:

> 'as we know, there are known knowns; there are things we know we know. We also know there are known unknowns; that is to say we know there are some things we do not know. But there are also unknown unknowns – the ones we don't know we don't know'.

Yup, I'll go with that.

The sources of data

Data comes into the system through two channels:

1. Targeted through the collection plan – market research is an example.

2. *Ad hoc* data collected on an opportunity basis – conversations overheard in the pub and casual comments in the press are examples of data collected as an adjunct to targeted data.

While most data generally comes through the first channel, *ad hoc* data can have a very important place. Provided the sources are graded, there is no difference in the value of the possible information that it results in.

> Government intelligence agencies have a variety of code words attached to intelligence material: Top Secret, Secret, Confidential, etc. Contrary to popular opinion, these code words are about dissemination of the data – not the quality of the data itself.

When collecting new data to turn into information to compile and help plug the knowledge gap in the knowledge/intelligence cycle, agencies have two sources: primary and secondary.

Primary sources are when data is from the horse's mouth, so to speak. The data must therefore address the specific gap: data can come from questionnaires administered in all their different ways, from observations and from focus group discussions. It can be qualitative, dealing with emotions, insights and feelings, or it can be quantitative, dealing numerically with how many; how big, how much and so on. The key difference between qualitative and quantitative data is that qualitative data doesn't easily lend itself to statistical or other numerical analysis, while quantitative data is collected specifically so that it does. A word of caution here: always know how you are going to analyse your data before you settle on its collection. If you don't know how to analyse it, or are not sure what the associations that you want to make to it are; don't collect it – if you do, don't be disappointed if you have to go back tomorrow and ask the customer again!

As a result, it can take a long time to collect and process primary data into information, but on the plus side, it will be data that you know you can use; accurately targeted and timely.

Secondary sources are when data is collected for other purposes, by someone else and at some other time. It tends therefore to be lower cost, but is often inadequate and its existence may not be well known or readily available. Secondary data often comes from:

- within the company (internal secondary data), from such things as invoice lists, order quantities and production runs

- outside the company (external secondary data), from, for example, government sources, World Bank data, UN, UNESCO, trade associations and research agencies. Websites (for example http://company.news-record. com/advertising/advertising/ratio.html) are becoming a source for such data, and can be found in the most unusual places, but website data needs to be very carefully assessed for value and quality.

Figure 11.7 summarizes data sources.

Primary data, being expensive and time-consuming to collect, is not normally perfect; taking a *census* (that is, talking to everybody in the population) is expensive and usually slow. Remember, in this context, population means the total number of people that are the subject of our enquiry. If we were

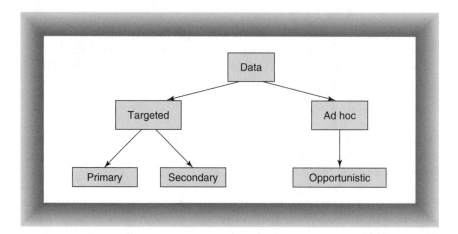

Figure 11.7
Research data
structure

enquiring into the potential uptake of a new grocery outlet, the population would probably be the number of people within a certain radius of the proposed shop who would have need of it.

In the same way as a chef doesn't drink all the *jus* but only gives a good stir to make sure the flavours are evenly distributed and then sips a bit, so we believe that the data we require is evenly distributed throughout a population and that we too can therefore take a sample. There are basically two ways of sampling from a population:

1. *Random sampling*, where each member of the population has an *equal chance* of being selected for sampling. This process is called 'simple random sampling'. It usually involves a complete list of the population and a computer to do the selection.

2. *Non-random sampling*, this is a generic name for all the other types of sampling. Because this is non-random selection, there has to be some judgement made about sections of the population being excluded from the sample. The non-randomness of the selection can occur in a number of ways; the easiest is to choose who is conveniently around (a convenience sample). This excludes everyone who is not around – so sampling a population on a convenience sample to enquire about charitable giving, for example, may produce biased results if done outside a church on a Sunday. The most common form of non-random sampling is *quota sampling*. In quota sampling, the characteristics that you are interested in among the population are noted – for example, the divisions in terms of age and job type – and the sample aims to include similar proportions of people with these characteristics. The assumption is that if a population contains known proportions of particular identifiable characteristics, and the sample is representative in these proportions, the data will be representative of the population. Random sampling may well take place once the quotas have been established. In quota sampling, it is therefore important that the characteristics on which the quotas are based are easily identified in the population. We can summarize this as shown in Figure 11.8.

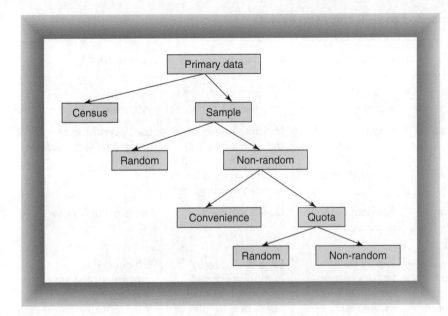

Figure 11.8
Sample structure

Suppose we are about to collect data about the market's view of brand (see Chapter 9). We could develop four ways of seeking the population's attitude to the brand (see Table 11.4).

Table 11.4 highlights some of the issues attendant on collecting good data. For in depth details of market research techniques and methodologies, see a good text on the subject – for example, Crouch and Housden (1996).

Collecting data about the marketplace

If knowledge is to enable us to move around the SAC faster than our competitor, then we need to understand what sort of knowledge we require. Many of us hoard data (which we think of as knowledge) – great for the pub quiz, but not much help for the focus required to build information and market knowledge. So we need to go back to the knowledge/intelligence cycle to identify holes in the knowledge and assess the value of filling the hole. What sort of data, then, do we need to collect?

This question leads us to a new set of challenges – so on to Heresy 2.

Heresy 2

Going back to our basic marketing theory, one of the early matrices we are taught is the GE matrix family with its orthogonal axes being (x) segment attractiveness and (y) business strengths needed to respond to segment wants and needs, either now or in the future. Matrix analysis is part of that processing which turns data into information; what it can't do is turn data into knowledge. That which we think that we know is often what we have

Table 11.4 Four approached to collecting survey data

Elements	Approach 1	Approach 2	Approach 3	Approach 4
Survey method	Telephone interview	Postal interview	Personal interview	Personal interview
Method	A few factual questions	Short (no more than two-page) questionnaire	Multiple questions; many sections and options depending on answers. Could be computer supported	Uses psychological projection techniques[1]
Sample	Random from the whole population	Random from population	Quota sampled	Focus group of users
Comment	Should produce a good result if the questions are well structured and the sample is large enough. There may be a high rejection rate due to 'SUGGING'[2]	Expect low (<10%) return. Bias may result as the respondents (because they have responded) may not be representative	Expensive due to manpower costs; response bias may result due to 'please the interviewer' responses	Effectively a convenience sample; may not be representative

[1] Psychological projection techniques are well discussed in specialist texts on market research (for example Crouch and Housden, 1996); in short, they use self-administered psychoanalytic test techniques and analysis to probe into unconscious attitudes (story telling, cartoon development, sentence completion and psychodrama are common tools).

[2] SUGGING is Selling Under the Guise of research and is prohibited under Market Research Society regulations. It doesn't stop unscrupulous companies tainting the honest researcher.

been told – hence the source of folklore, fairy stories and much corporate mythology.

In the case of the GE matrix, we need data of segment attractiveness. These data requirements were explored by Simkin and Dibb (1998). In their study, they showed that there is a mismatch between what data academic debate suggests is important and what practicing marketing directors believe they need to have.

Practice suggests that the key data collection areas are those listed in Table 11.5.

This research suggests that *in practice* we will most likely be asked to research the top five rows in Table 11.5 in terms of the SAC, though we need to be measuring other factors as well (actually in the enlightened company, instead).

Ranked importance to industry	Criteria
1	Profitability
2	Market growth potential
3	Current market size
4	Likely customer satisfaction
5	Potential sales volume
6	Likelihood of sustainable competitive advantage
7	Ease of access for the business
8	Other opportunities in the market
9	Freedom for product differentiation
10	Competitive rivalry

Table 11.5
Key data collection areas (adapted from Simkin and Dibb, 1998)

This leads to a number of data issues:

- How do we measure the potential profitability of a market?

- How can we predict likely customer satisfaction? It is worrying that this comes fourth in the practitioner's requirements.

- How and what do we need to measure to meet the requirements of the SAC?

Potential profitability of a market

First, we need to establish how much market share we will get. We can use market research to try to establish this. Good market research will give us data about what percentage of the market thinks our product offers best value and therefore will buy it in preference to a competitor's product. Before we accept this information – and we need to convince ourselves it is information not data – perhaps we need to understand how the market has been divided in order to establish market share.

Breakdown of markets

We saw in Chapter 2 that *market* is really a rather loose term, particularly if we are trying to define its value both now and in the future. We need to break markets down into smaller groups of customers. The usual way of doing this is as shown in Figure 11.9 (Kotler, 2006 and previous editions).

The potential market consists of the total number of consumers who have expressed an interest in the market offer that we are making. However, there may well be conditions which preclude all those people with an interest in our market offering from buying our product; it may be that the price is too high or it may be some other qualification – perhaps age, or proximity to a suitable sales outlet. So the available market is that group of consumers who have an interest in our products and meet other conditions – for example, income or access. There may also be conditions associated, perhaps by law, with our product – for example, cigarettes and alcohol both

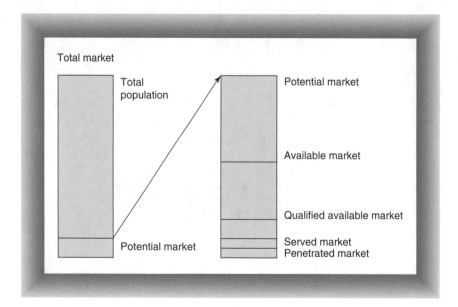

Figure 11.9
Breakdown of
markets (after
Kotler and others)

have age restrictions on their purchase. Therefore, while the available market may include them, they are not qualified for our particular market offer. The result is that we are left with a qualified available market. It is the qualified available market that requires segmentation, and the selection of that segment then becomes the target or served market. Once the market has been targeted and the product offer has been made, the penetrated market then consists of the number of consumers who have already purchased the product.

We can therefore think of markets as groups of customers; if we can be confident of our market share and we can be confident of the long-term value of a customer (see Chapter 1), then remove our associated marketing costs, we will then be able to calculate the potential market profitability, and hence order the market segments. Here we have taken data and turned it into information; the association in this case is numerical analysis.

Through-life customer values and how to calculate them

Irrespective of our view about customers as data sources, economically we should understand who our most profitable customers are. We can do this by looking at what they have bought in the recent past, calculating the net profit and assuming they will continue in the future. This may work in some closed environments, particularly where pure competition exists at every purchase opportunity. There are some markets, for example military markets, where this does not happen and the historical purchasing pattern is no predictor of the future. It would be worth reviewing the section in Chapter 1 about customer value, to refresh your memory about the material presented there.

What we need is a method of calculating the future income from a customer. We started to look at this in Chapter 1, but now it becomes a data and resource issue. What data do we need? How could we collect it?

Simple methods

Consider the value of a customer buying a motor vehicle. We need to consider:

- the purchase price of the initial vehicle
- vehicle servicing fees
- the vehicle replacement price.

If we assume that the vehicle purchase generates £15 000 revenue and there is an annual servicing bill of £2000, with the vehicle being replaced every 3 years for half the purchase price (balance from trade-in), we can calculate the customer value. Let us take a 7-year customer value on these prices (Table 11.6).

Table 11.6 Example through-life customer revenue

Year 1	Year 2	Year 3	New vehicle Year 4	Year 5	Year 6	New vehicle Year 7	Total value
Initial purchase	Service	Service	Trade-in	Service	Service	Trade-in	
15 000	2000	2000	7500	2000	2000	7500	38 000

This example uses revenue rather than profit, simply as a device. We can, of course, complicate this with various assumptions about the time value of money and discounting to obtain a net present value.

We could say that customer value is therefore £38 000. We could now calculate the profit given the margins in use; given a required ROI figure, we could calculate the allowed marketing spend on acquiring the customer. If it costs less to acquire a customer, well done marketing; if it costs more, the marketing targets will not be met.

Given our marketing budget, we can calculate how many customers we can afford to acquire and hence calculate corporate profits (Table 11.7).

Conversely, if we know the cost of acquiring a customer, we can then calculate how many customers we can acquire. If we have revenue or profit targets, we can then calculate how much each customer must be worth and hence the prices the customer must pay – and therefore the value of the benefit of the service/product we will supply – for each of the items in

Table **11.7** Calculating corporate profit

Factor	Value	Source	Notes
Customer spend Overall margin	£38 000 10%	Calculated above Given	Margins on selling the car and on servicing it will be different; an overall average figure should be used
Profit	£3800	Spend × 10%	
Marketing's ROI (corporate)	98%	Given	This is an expected figure and usually historically calculated
Allowance for acquisition	£760	2% of 3800	
Marketing budget	£38 000	Assumed	
No of customers	50	Budget/acquisition allowance	
Corporate profit	£190 000	Profit × customers	

his or her portfolio. From this resource calculation flows our total marketing strategy.

Probability trees

There is, of course, no guarantee that the customer will spend anything in the future, so all predictions must have a probability associated with them – a probability that spend will occur against the probability that it might not. This leads us into a consideration of probability trees and expectation.

A probability tree looks at the probability that a customer will spend and how much. In other words, if we can assume that there are three brands on the market and each is equally likely to be chosen for purchase, the probability is 0.3. If the value of the purchase is £10, then the expected spend of the customer is 0.3 × £10 = £3.33 if we look at this over a period of purchase decisions (see Figure 11.10a).

Going back to our example; the customer may choose to go elsewhere when choosing to update his or her car. If there are two other dealerships, and all things being equal, we can assume that there is a one chance in three that the customer will return to us. Therefore, at the end of the second period the customer value is reduced to 0.1 (i.e. 0.3 × 0.3).

Our customer's value, taking into account the fact that he may not return to replace the car, is now £7600 (see Figure 11.10b).

This is about resource requirements for acquiring a customer. However, there is also the cost of servicing a customer – how much will we pay for a

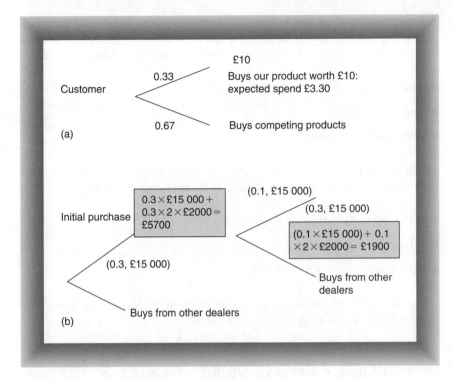

Figure 11.10
Probability tree

customer to climb the relationship ladder? Again, we can do some calculations to calculate how many customers we can afford to have on our marketing budget, and how many new customers we can afford to buy with our resource. We return to budgets in Chapter 12.

First of all, we need to collect data. There are some interesting interactions here – not only what will the customer spend, but also what will he be responsible for in terms of climbing the ladder?

We know from diffusion theory and our own experience that the majority look to the early adopters or opinion leaders for their lead. We also assume that 12 percent of the segment is made up of opinion leaders and 64 percent constitute the majority, so *a priori* we can assume that each of the opinion leaders will bring in five of the majority, if they themselves are sufficiently enamoured of the value we offer.

Perhaps, then, we can then assess the value of a customer as:

Customer's lifetime value + 5 (others lifetime values) = value of an opinion leader

We can play other games along these lines, but the bottom line is that we don't have anything until we have data and associations – and lots of it – to make knowledge. We can't assess whether a change in an environment due to our proceeding round the SAC is worthwhile until we have assessed the marketplace, and we can't work out whether we can go rapidly around the SAC until we have investigated ourselves. And to do that we need:

- timely data
- good data, and
- relevant associations.

To get that we need a collection plan, and to get a collection plan we need to understand the knowledge cycle (intelligence cycle) and also know:

- what the gaps in our knowledge are
- who can plug them, and
- how much it is worth to do so.

We need to disseminate the information as often as required, to those who need to build knowledge or make decisions.

Do you Collect, Review, Update, Delete (CRUD)? Are you a squirrel?

We have seen that data contains time value – once data passes its sell-by date, it becomes worthless. It is of little intrinsic value (other things may be of value to someone – the paper an ancient will is written on may be of value to a student of textile development; the original document may be of value to scholars of calligraphy). In this day and age of computer storage, where retrieval is fast and memory storage cheap, it is easy to hold data.

Again, we have a balancing act here. How many times have we all wanted something just after we have thrown it out? With data, we must balance the likelihood of wanting it in the future against the cost of re-collection, and the cost of deleting it against the cost of storage and retrieval. Anyway, most data comes from a dynamic environment where the data itself becomes out of date and is therefore reduced in worth.

Good CRUD

I am told that the word CRUD came from the nuclear industry; it was the residue of unknown impurities found in the primary coolant (then water) pipework of early nuclear reactors, and stands for Chalk River Unidentified Deposits. Well, here it stands for Collect, Review, Update, Delete.

Data needs to collected and, as we have seen, it needs some tag as to its worth – that means its date of collection, reason for collection, date of use, source and source assessment. It should carry any associations with it. We also need to know who else knows, so that when the data changes, becomes useless or loses its value, we can all keep in step. The same goes for information. And when you delete, please distribute details of deletion.

A *data flowchart* may therefore look something like Figure 11.11.

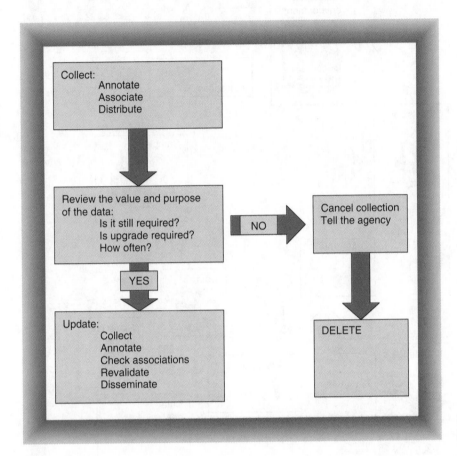

Figure 11.11
Flow for CRUD

Squirrels, like me, never delete information; we squirrel it away. Why? Well, think of all that invested effort – the cost of collection, the mental gymnastics of the associations, the sheer brilliance of the analysis. You never know, you may not be able to get it again, and surely anything, even if it is a bit out of date and no longer valid, must be better than nothing, mustn't it?

So, to summarize: Figure 11.12 looks at what happens to data on its journey through life, where it comes from, how it is collected; the path to information and intelligence, the key areas of knowledge for decision-making and, finally, back to the marketing environment in accordance with the SAC. And in the knowledge-led company, data and associations are some of our most important resources.

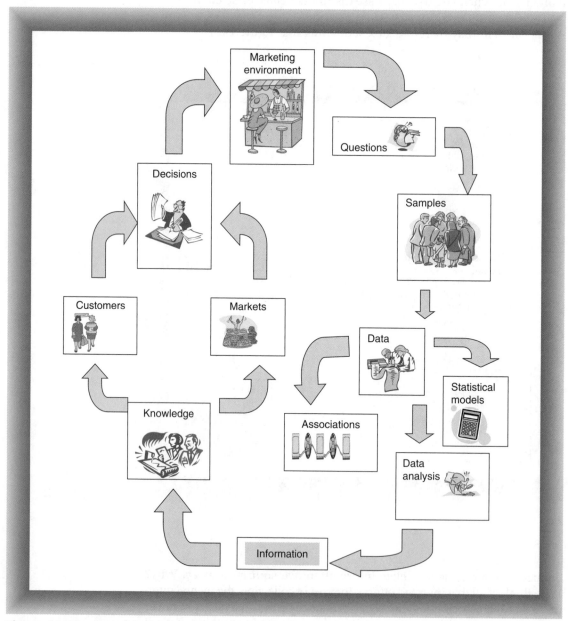

Figure 11.12   Data's journey

References and further reading

References

Christopher, M., Payne, A. and Ballantyne, D. (1991). *Relationship Marketing*. Oxford: Butterworth-Heinemann.

Berry, L.L. (1995). *Marketing Service: Competing Through Quality*. New York: Wiley.

Cross, R. and Smith, J. (1997). The customer value chain. *Marketing Tools*, **Jan/Feb**, 16–18.

Crouch, S. and Housden, M. (1996). *Marketing Research for Managers*, 2nd edn. Oxford: Butterworth-Heinemann.

Doyle, P. (2000). *Value Based Marketing*. Chichester: Wiley.

Kotler, P. and Lilien, G. (1983). *Marketing Decision Making: A Model Building Approach*. New York: Harper and Row.

McArthur, K. (2006). Industrial spying and the marketing business: are you safe? Ad Age.com, 9 July.

Millier, P. (1999). *Marketing the Unknown*. Chichester: J Wiley & Sons.

Nonaka, I. (1991). The knowledge creating company. *Harvard Business Review*, **69**, 96–104.

Palmer, A. (2004). *Introduction to Marketing*. Oxford: Oxford University Press.

Peck, H., Payne, A., Christopher, M. and Clark, M. (1999). *Relationship Marketing Strategy and Implementation*. Oxford: Butterworth-Heinemann.

Rappaport, A. (1986). *Creating Shareholder Value*, 2nd edn. New York: Free Press.

Simkin, L. and Dibb, S. (1998). Prioritising target markets. *Marketing Intelligence & Planning*, **16(7)**, 407–417.

Further reading

Davidson, H. (2005). *The Committed Enterprise*, 2nd edn. Oxford: Butterworth-Heinemann.

Dibb, S., Simkin, L., Pride, W. and Ferrell, O.C. (2000). *Marketing: Concepts and Strategies*. Boston, MA: Houghton Mifflin. (*Originally by Dibb and Simkin, this book is really the European edition of Pride and Ferrell's text. In my opinion, it is one of the best introductions to marketing concepts around.*)

Kotler, P. (2006). *Marketing Management*, 12th edn. Upper Saddle River, NJ: Prentice Hall. (*Note: 'Kotler' is a standard text and is now in its 12th edition. This edition has been updated and co-authored by Kevin Keller.*)

12 Money, measures and outcomes

Introduction

So far we have looked at the resources needed to implement marketing success, and at how we can use them to implement our marketing strategy. We have done this in terms of:

- using the resource of time to beat the competitor and leave the environment changed against him and in our favour
- technology, where we have investigated the issues of using technology to create tempo
- data, which we need to convert into information and intelligence, so that we become a knowledgeable organization.

In this closing chapter, we investigate how we resource to measure marketing, in terms of finances (money), the measures of being marketing orientated as an organization, and what outcomes we should measure. In other words, what resources do we need to measure marketing success? We will do this by looking at *how* we measure marketing success.

Measuring marketing success

Preparing for success

How do we prepare for marketing success?

First, we must go back to the mission and goals of the company. Each department in the company will be contributing to these goals; but the importance of the requirements in each may not be clearly understood. We also need to make sure that the whole company understands that the future profits of the company are in the customers' pockets – in other words, a *marketing orientation* is adopted by the whole company, and to be successful we will need to measure the progress towards its adoption. Marketing orientation was introduced in Chapter 3.

Mission and goals

Missions and goals have also been discussed in Chapter 3 in terms of focus for the whole company and a guide to marketing outcomes. In this section, we will cover how mission and goals can be used to help to measure the success of marketing and, as a result, to guide their resource requirements.

Mission statements are much debated; some commentators (for example Piercy, 2002) believe that they are essential and feel that they are the critical factor in directing a company's outcome. Others regard them as bland. However, they do give direction to a company, and can be used to resolve interdepartmental conflicts in achieving a purpose. To measure mission success, or progress towards it via goals, we need to deconstruct missions into functional responsibilities and use these to help identify the conflicting demands.

One approach to destructuring the mission for this purpose is that developed by Hastings (1996). Hastings deconstructs a company's missions and goals, believing that the ultimate objective is to achieve these rather than purely financial outcomes. If we are to accept that qualitative assessment is needed as much as quantitative, then we need a model to help. In this day and age, where things like corporate responsibility, ethical behaviour, and the many qualitative measures of government, pressure groups and the public are used to measure a company's performance, we cannot ignore qualitative assessments. And it is these qualitative assessments which can be the primary cause of conflict, both in acceptance of responsibility (and hence budget) and implementation (and therefore allocation of resources), and in the acceptance of credit when success is achieved.

Hastings proposes a hierarchical structuring of mission and goals, and from this hierarchical structuring the sub-goals in each of the relevant areas can be recognized and a corporate strategy subsequently developed and measured. The mission of a firm could be something like 'the maximization of shareholder value through the provision of quality goods and services to customers'. Hastings gives a example of an extraction (mining) company which has a number of strategic areas, functional departments and geographical areas. The mission of his example firm is to:

> engage safely, efficiently, profitably and responsibly in the oil, gas, chemicals and coal businesses. The firm seeks a high standard of performance and aims to maintain a long-term position in these business sectors.

The company in question therefore has a number of areas which it can use to achieve its purpose.

This mission statement deconstructs as shown in Figure 12.1.

Objectives are then set, based on internal and external environments, and strategies are developed to achieve those objectives. The strategies derived from the mission are ranked for importance, usually through paired comparisons.

Once this has been achieved, objectives can be set for individual departments and functions within the company, and measurements placed on

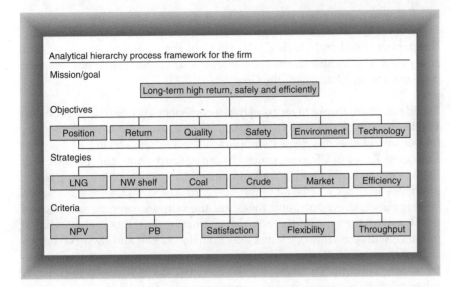

Analytical hierarchy process framework for the firm

Mission/goal

Long-term high return, safely and efficiently

Objectives: Position | Return | Quality | Safety | Environment | Technology

Strategies: LNG | NW shelf | Coal | Crude | Market | Efficiency

Criteria: NPV | PB | Satisfaction | Flexibility | Throughput

Figure 12.1
Deconstructed
mission statement
(from Hastings,
1996)

the objectives. The advantage of this approach is that a data collection policy (Chapter 11) can be set up which will give greatest importance to the highest in the hierarchy – that is, the data budget can be apportioned to meet the most important objectives.

The *data budget* is the list of the data to be collected in order to take measurements of each of the strategic options. At this point, costs of collection can be calculated and collection agencies allocated. These costs, along with the 'real' marketing budget, form the backbone of measuring marketing success. It could be argued that the functional departments are themselves responsible for achieving the deconstructed missions; but should there be a high-profile failure in one of the key mission areas in which the media shows more interest than in the financial success of the company – say through an oil leak or mine-shaft collapse – then we can be fairly confident that the marketing department's PR machine will be called in to mop up the media-created mess. A marketing orientation in each area is therefore fairly important, and marketing's involvement in each area is critical.

Having established the deconstructed mission and goals and identified the need for marketing's interest in other functions within the company, the success of marketing needs to be established in concrete terms.

Why we measure marketing

Why do we need to measure marketing?

Measurement is a national pastime. Witness the proliferation of statistics with which we are confronted in even the most unstatistical of sports – no longer is the score line sufficient; we are also told, for example, the number of fumbles on the cricket outfield, of shots at goal or successful challenges for possession in soccer, of successful wins in the scrum. We, and our followers, judge our success and our progress by looking at statistics far beyond the bottom line and measuring our progress against them. If Rappaport (1986) and Doyle (2000) are right that shareholder value is the sole purpose of business, the spectators in our case are shareholders, and our fans are the Gnomes of the City.

Davidson (2005) thinks in terms of measurement being one of his Seven Best Practices of Business. In UK companies, measurement was adopted by 65 percent of the businesses sampled – the highest scoring of his Best Practices. Among US companies, it came third from the bottom. For Davidson, measurement is about measuring the success of the company as a whole – in other words, he (almost) regards the company as a black box with inputs and outputs, and measures the outputs, probing only lightly into the workings inside the box. To a certain extent, this is somewhat at variance with the view of Hamel and Prahalad (1994) and their consideration of the organization as a learning organism, learning to improve performance. This implies, then, that there are two areas we need to consider when talking about measuring our performance as a whole:

1. *Macro-level measurements* – where the outputs of the black box are measured – these outputs being external measures without too much consideration of what is going on inside the black box.

2. *Internal expectations* – in other words, how we measure what goes in inside the black box:

   ● first, to make sure that the whole company is aligned, and

   ● secondly, to make sure that lessons are learned so that the next revolution of the strategic advantage cycle benefits from the experiences of the previous one.

However, the measurement of marketing as one of the functions within the black box has a number of issues connected with it. We need to measure marketing in a number of scenarios.

First, going back to the SAC, we need to know:

1. How well have we got round the cycle?

2. What we have learned about how to get round faster next time, and therefore, as a result:

   ● what progress we have made towards become a learning organization?

   ● a deeper understanding of what to learn than any macro-analysis can produce?

   ● an understanding of what advantages we can gain from being a learning organization?

Second, although the principles of marketing should be the lead concept for all departments, not all departments have themselves adopted an understanding of a marketing orientation. As a result, if we believe that best practice is to adopt a marketing orientation, then we need to measure our colleagues' progress towards adopting a marketing orientation both at the corporate level and in their dealings within the company.

Thirdly, marketing should understand what interactions are required with other departments in order to achieve the strategic business plan, which itself should be the wellhead of their own departmental plans. Table 12.1 shows that different departments have different views of what they expect of marketing (both the department and the function), and what marketing (both the department and the business function) expects of them. You will notice that there is a mismatch here, so one of the things marketing must measure is the progress being made towards a common understanding.

Internal success

Consider first the internal issues: how do we measure marketing's success at integrating the activities of the company towards a marketing orientation?

Marketing as a function has a number of expectations of other departments, as indeed other departments within an organization have of the marketing function. In many cases marketing is still relegated to the promotions role, and so one of the first tasks is to enter into dialogue with the departments to establish a true role for marketing. Table 12.1 shows some typical responses to a marketing functions query: 'What do you expect of marketing?'

There are a couple of things that emerge from this study:

1. The responses will differ depending on the level of commitment that the company has to a marketing orientation, and how far that orientation has permeated the other departments; and

2. A common ground must be established which both the marketing function and the other departments in the company agree to achieve as they move towards a marketing orientation.

Harris (1998) augmented McDonald's earlier work on why companies don't achieve, or can't even reach a common ground for a marketing orientation. His list, based on shop-floor attitudes to implementation was as follows:

- employee apathy
- lack of personalized incentive to change
- perceived limited power from the bottom to influence management
- lack of long-term employment commitment (both from company and from the employee)
- task compartmentalization
- ignorance
- weak management support.

Table 12.1   Expectations of and by marketing

What marketing expects of:

Management	Sales	Finance	Operations	HR	R&D
Marketing orientation, supporting creation and ongoing delivery of customer defined best value	Dedication to defined segments; regular customer feedback	Long-term view of market development; ring-fencing marketing (especially promotional) budgets	Rapid response time to changes: short demand to production scheduling; capability for frequent customization	On-demand skilled manpower; high customer consciousness among staff	Fast development of technologies to meet anticipated customer requirements

What is expected of marketing by:

Management	Sales	Finance	Operations	HR	R&D
Long-term sustained profits; strong brand image	Promotional support on time to meet sales–customer deadline; lead development, maybe some missionary sales work	Reducing budgets: sustained margins, tight credit conditions, short debtor periods	Ability to sell spare capacity; ability to convince customer of incremental product change/accept productized service	Long notice of changes to HR requirements	Delay market entry until technology fully proven

This table is based on our own data of the most frequent responses collected over a two-year period (2004 and 2005) from about 20 UK service and manufacturing companies.

McDonald's original study found the following list of 10 things which hindered a marketing orientation:

1. Confusion of tactics and strategy.

2. Isolation of marketing from the business.

3. Misunderstanding of the role of marketing (i.e. as more than sales and advertising).

4. Lack of clarity in organizational reporting structure.

5. Inability to conduct marketing analysis.

6. Confusion between process and output.

7. Lack of skills in marketing.

8. Lack of systematic approach to management issues.

9. Failure to be able to prioritize.

10. Hostility due to ignorance (or, more likely, loss of political power).

The original study was completed in 1988, and the results are sadly as valid in 2007 as they were then.

In order to establish the common ground needed at management level, before conversion into reality by the workforce, one approach is to follow the principle of Porter's value chain within the company (Figure 12.2). Porter's value chain was discussed in Chapter 4, but in this case we will use it as handy tool and a model to look at the value that each departmental function contributes to a marketing orientation. The conventional usage of the value chain is beyond the scope of this book, but here the structure is of interest as is its use to measure the common ground in developing a marketing orientation and its subsequent measurement.

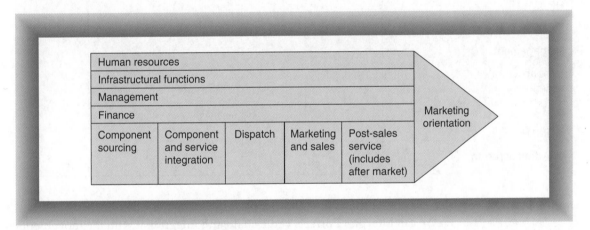

Figure 12.2 Porter's value chain (adapted)

For each function, the questions must be asked about:

● the contribution to the strategy components of the disaggregated mission and goals

● the impact of not achieving a marketing orientation on the company.

In other words, we can use the tool to look at the value each function has in contributing to a marketing orientation.

We will not use the original terminology of Porter, as it is very manufacturing-orientated, but we will translate the terms into something more meaningful. And where Porter, the economist, saw 'margin' as the end result (thereby making it clear that in his view this model saw value as cost-driven), we see the end result as 'market orientation'.

Table 12.2 Marketing orientation worksheet

	Expectations of marketing function	*Marketing's expectation of ......*	*Common ground*	*Barriers to implementing common ground*	*Measures of success in achieving common ground*	*Data to collect to measure success*
Component sourcing						
Operations						
Dispatch						
Marketing and sales						
Post-sales services						
HR						
Finance						
Management						
Infrastructural functions: ● IT ● R&D ● Administration						

We can interpret Porter's value chain and integrate it with the movements towards a marketing orientation, and hence the measures of marketing success. Something along the lines of Table 12.2 will help to generate the right approach.

We can now measure marketing success to a better degree, as we are able to understand the role other business functions play in marketing success, and can measure our progress towards it. Planning practice suggests that objectives are set and, as such, can be measured. If objectives are SMART, we have already built in the measurement.

Further inside the black box

So far we have looked at the internal issues within the company, to see how we are handling our learning as an organization and what have we learned about getting ourselves in trim to move more quickly around the SAC.

We now need to look at the external measures of marketing: how do our investors (and their investors) measure our performance?

Financial measures of marketing

Why do marketers need to understand financial data? After all, there is a whole department, led by the Financial Wizard, beavering away doing financial stuff.

Whatever anyone thinks marketing does, it is the ONLY function in a company that brings in revenue. Therefore, whatever we do as part of the marketing function, we will have some impact – hopefully positive – on the work of the Financial Wizard. We, almost by definition, are responsible for profit, and the Financial Wizard manages the money.

Marketing is the management function that identifies, anticipates and satisfies customer needs profitably.

(Chartered Institute of Marketing)

Also, financial analysis and accounting are the *lingua franca* of business, and measure the accountability of the company to its owners. If business is about making shareholders richer, or putting funds at risk to make a profit, it is only reasonable to expect someone to ask for accountability. Because marketing has to be accountable for the money it spends, we need to look at the whole bigger picture of business to see where it fits, and that bigger picture is painted in financial terms.

As marketing moves around the SAC, we have seen that there is a significant call upon marketing's resource and marketing's resourcefulness. We have seen how marketing is responsible for integrating into, and the integration of the whole of, a company's activities; we have looked at how culture and other management priorities support integration of marketing.

We need, therefore, to understand precisely how these resources are allowed for – where budget comes from and where it goes to; the impact of our marketing activity, its successes and its failures on the overall picture of business. If the purpose of business is to make shareholders richer, then we have to consider the whole of marketing's activities in terms of cost of marketing, the allocation of marketing resource, and the return in financial terms that can be expected as a consequence of this activity. In other words, to develop long-term strategies and even to maintain the very basics of marketing's 4Ps (Product, Price, Place and Promotion) we need to understand funding, sources of funding, and whether that funding could be better spent elsewhere.

So if marketing is about giving best value to the customer in order for the customer to choose to buy our product in preference to that of a competitor, then it is not unreasonable to expect marketing to be best value in comparison to other ways of increasing corporate funds. In other words, we are thinking here in terms of treating marketing budgets as opportunity costs. Where else could we place the marketing budget and give ourselves a better return than spending it on marketing activity? If such a course of action were available, then the purpose of marketing would be brought into question. And the people to whom marketing must therefore respond are the shareholders.

Let us look at these in more detail.

Macro-measurements involve looking largely at the black box. Traditional business measures make up the usual method of measuring the output of the black box; these are the famous financial ratios or results of financial analysis that marketers need to understand so that they can infer how these measures affect their role, and *vice versa*.

Shareholder value

Before we start looking at many of the traditional measures that the Financial Wizard embroils himself with, we ought to see whether we can short-circuit these measures by going straight to shareholders' value. How do we evaluate shareholders' investment to ensure that we give them best value?

Doyle (2000) thinks that this is the dividends and potential dividends to be generated through a company's strategy. The true picture is actually wider than this. Consider Figure 12.3.

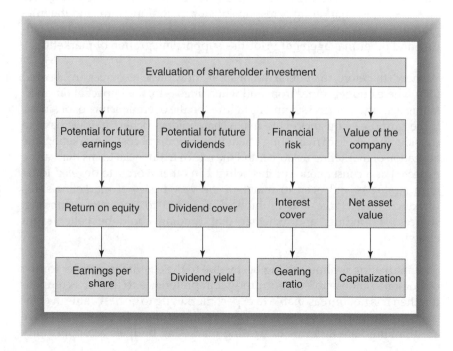

Figure 12.3
Evaluating
shareholder
investment

Table 12.3   Shareholder evaluation, deconstructed

Area	Key ratios	Components	Affected by marketing	Marketing activity affecting the measure
Earning potential	Return on equity	Profit available to pay dividends (profit attributable to shareholders)	Yes	Profit: based on price the customer will pay for a product or service; sustainable market share
Shareholders' funds[1]	Yes Earnings per share	Historic profits Profit attributable to shareholders	As above	As above
		Number of ordinary shares issued	No	N/A
Income potential	Dividend cover	Profit attributable to shareholders	As above	As above
		Dividend paid	Indirectly: based on reserves less estimated future costs	
	Dividend yield	Dividend paid out	No	N/A
		Cost of share	No	N/A
Risk	Interest cover	Profit from trading	YES!	All marketing activity
		Interest on long-term borrowings	No	N/A
	Gearing ratio	Amount borrowed to finance company	No	N/A
		Shareholders' funds	Yes	Historic profits
Value	Net asset value	Net assets	Yes	Marketing should include brand value as an asset
		Number of ordinary shares	No	N/A
	Capitalization	P/E ratio[2]	No	N/A
		Earnings per share	Indirectly	

N/A, not applicable.

[1] The total interest the shareholders have in the company: all the assets and all the reserves once the debts have been paid.

[2] A measure of how willing the company has been historically to pay dividends compared to the profits earned; a ratio of the profits to how much the dividend was.

We can now make a list of the key areas to which marketing must respond. Each of the areas of concern in Figure 12.3 and the deconstruction (Table 12.3) is a measure of the ongoing success of the company and the value it contributes to its owners – the shareholders. Each box can be looked at to see where and how marketing fits into the analysis. Each analysis is dependent on some financial data.

Marketing, then, should really be interested in how it contributes to these key financial factors, and from Table 12.3 we can see that the key ones are:

- sustainable market share
- sustainable brand value
- profit.

Reduced to these terms, marketing must be pretty simple! Keep your customers, increase the brand value and increase the profit – i.e. find ways to keep on raising the price. And keep on doing it into the future. How far into the future?

The Financial Wizard will *discount* future monies to make them comparable to today's prices. *Discounting* is a sort of inverse interest, where the money in the future shrinks rather than grows. And like interest, it depends on the *discount factor*. Over time, the discounted money stabilizes – i.e. it doesn't seem to shrink much any more – and this happens around years 5–7, so we ought to look out as far as 5–7 years ahead. In many companies this is the rationale behind the planning horizon and defines the length of a strategic plan, when probably that timeframe should be determined by the volatility of the industrial technologies in the marketplace.

Starting financial analysis

Profit

The Financial Wizard may well think of 'profit' as that which is found from the profit and loss account, and in that case would talk in terms of profits, costs, margins, mark up, etc., as coming from the profit and loss account and financial analyses. We are more interested in knowing how it got there in the first place, and we all know that profit comes from the following equation:

Price − Costs = Profit

The implication here is that we take the price the customer will pay – i.e. how much the customer measures the value of our offering to be – and subtract the costs associated with getting that value to the customer; the remainder is profit.

However, being mathematically adept, the Financial Wizard will rearrange this equation to read:

Profit + Costs = Price

This implies that price is set by working out the profit desired (in this case, based on something like:

Profit required = Tax + Restructuring costs + Dividend + Reserves

and adding costs. Once the price is set, we can revert to the first of these three equations and increase profits by reducing costs. The implication here is that the job of the marketing function is to keep the price up. And to make lots of profit, all we need to do is sell lots – i.e. have a high market share. Marketing at this level is simple. Flawed, but simple.

By knowing how many units we will sell, we can work out each sold unit's total costs and the share of profit it has to carry, and Bingo! The price is set. But how do we know how many units we will sell? If we get the number too small (i.e. we don't sell enough), then the costs *apportioned* to each unit of sale will be wrong and we will be undercontributing, and subsequently we will make a loss – and go bust.

As a first step, we can calculate how many we will sell through a *cost–volume–profit* analysis. This really is a first cut; it makes a lot of assumptions that are generally good enough if we use the outputs as guides.

Think about profit and costs as much the same thing – costs are negative profit, and therefore making a required profit is equivalent to making costs bigger.

But what are costs? The Financial Wizard will talk in terms of two types of cost: fixed and variable.

Fixed costs are those we stump up whether we make anything or not, and tend to be related to the whole business rather than being related to a specific product. Rent, electricity, infrastructure and the boss's wages are examples here. These costs remain *fixed* no matter how many units we make.

Variable costs are those that change every time we make a unit for sale – for example, raw materials, wear and tear on the machine that makes them, license fees for patents not owned by us, that sort of thing. The Financial Wizard will talk in terms of *marginal costs* rather than variable costs, because he thinks in terms of what happens in the overall picture – what happens if we need to take on more sales staff to service a significant increase in market share, buy a new machine, take on more administrative staff to do the invoicing, or recruit call centre staff to manage the after-sales services. We will incur an extra cost once we get above a certain market share; this clearly requires a change in variable costs, so the Financial Wizard rolls this all together to make a *marginal cost* – that is, the cost of making just one more unit. This in our terms is a nicety we can gloss over; we are going to assume that there is a cost-stable band while growing market share (which after all is only volume sold) in which we will operate, and we will call this stable period *the relevant range*.

If we think of costs (now incurred costs plus profit) as a hole in the ground, when the ground is flat we have made no loss and no excess profit – we *break even* (Figure 12.4).

At each sale, the price is made up of two things: a variable cost and a little bit of profit. This little bit of profit, what is left after we have taken off the variable cost from the selling price, is called *contribution*. What it is, is a

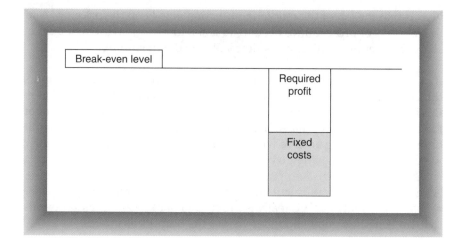

Figure 12.4
The break-even level

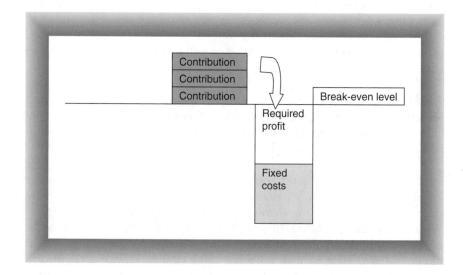

Figure 12.5
Calculating the contributions needed to break even

contribution to the fixed costs (or on our case, fixed costs + required profit). To break even, how many contributions do we need to fill up the hole (Figure 12.5)?

We divide the (fixed costs + profit required) by contribution (sales price − variable costs) and this tells us how many units we are going to have to sell to break even.

Mathematically, to achieve at least the required profit target:

$$\text{Number of units we need to sell} = \frac{\text{(Fixed costs} + \text{Required profit)}}{\text{(Selling price} - \text{Variable costs)}}$$

If we sell more, we make an even bigger profit and declare profits to be 'above expectation' – and the Gnomes love us!

In other words, what the latter equation tells us is that if we know the selling price, we can calculate the market share. It also tells us that if we can predict the market share, then we can calculate the necessary selling price. So now we know the number of units we are going to sell.

We can see that the selling price is going to be the share of the (fixed costs + required profit) that each unit we sell carries, plus its variable cost:

$$\text{Selling price} = \frac{(\text{Fixed costs} + \text{Required profit})}{\text{Number we are going to sell}} + (\text{Variable cost per unit})$$

This calculation is actually more interesting, as it actually asks the question: 'Will the customer assess our product's value as the selling price (i.e. will he pay what we need to charge for it)?' If not, we won't sell the number required and we are bust again. If he will, we are in business.

There is many a company out there that does not do these simple calculations to make sure that the new profit targets (i.e. required profit) set by the Financial Wizard and the Gnomes can achieve a realistic price and a sensible market share – or if they do, then don't interpret them into the impact in the marketplace.

The critical question now is, what is a sensible market share? Can we ever have too much market share? There are several studies (for example, Buzzell and Gale, 1987) that show that market share is directly related to return on investment – the more market share, the higher the return on investment. So we want to capture as much market share as we can have, then – don't we?

Market share and the Law of Diminishing Returns

Rather than thinking in terms of market share that we have already captured, let us think in terms of market share that we haven't captured, and how much effort we are going to have to put into capturing it. We need to think about:

- distribution costs to get the next bit of market share – if we think of a distribution channel in terms of a tube with limited diameter (i.e. limited bandwidth), we need to fight for our space in the pipe (bandwidth) with our competitors, or buy a bigger pipe (more bandwidth to market)

- competitive activity – markets are not infinite – we saw the relationship between served markets (through qualified and available markets) and populations in Chapter 11 – so the value of a market is going to be pretty well fixed, and my profit is my competitor's loss. The competitor will therefore fight back with the full force of the marketing mix, though usually with a pricing tactic.

What we see is illustrated in Figure 12.6: to be in business incurs a cost even though we have no market share, and this cost needs to be made up with profits from sales. Once the sales have achieved a *critical mass*, we move into profit; until then, we make a loss. If you superimpose a product lifecycle

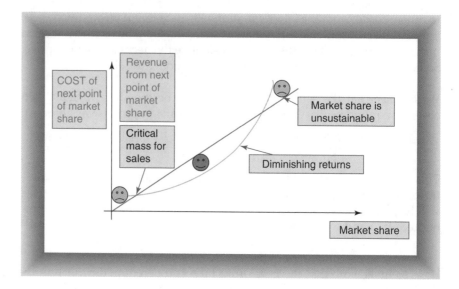

Figure 12.6
How increasing market share limits profits

onto the graph in Figure 12.6, and consider the demands of the Boston Square, it is easy to see why we need so many feeder products – why we, if we are dominant in the marketplace, need to 'kill off growth as fast as possible', and what happens to products if they don't make critical mass.

So we need to understand when we start paying too much for the market share, and when, therefore, our costs will increase to the point where the profit isn't worth the effort we are putting in.

Calculating the value of market share

We have assumed, and will continue to do so, that over the relevant range we can calculate the value (to us) of a point of market share. It will be a function of:

- the contribution (price − variable costs)
- the market size remaining.

As a first approximation, in the growth stage

> Value of the next point of market share (VMS) = (Contribution × market remaining)/100

Thus we could get a rough idea about how we compare the costs of buying more market share against the value to us of owning it.

So while ROI and market share are linked, we don't want as much market share as there is; we want what we can afford.

What market share can we afford?

At this point, we need to think about how much market share we can afford. Buying market share is a function of budget, and budget is a function of the amount of market share that we need to meet the required profit targets. We saw in Chapter 11 that we could think about budget as being a function of:

- the cost of keeping a customer, which will be related to the Rung on the relationship ladder which the customer is on
- the cost of acquiring a new customer
- the number of customers on each Rung of the ladder and the lifetime value of a customer
- how many new customers we need to acquire.

From here, we can calculate the market share that we can afford. This level of thinking is really leading-edge stuff, and a more classical approach is to look at how we can budget for market share by using the 4Ps. From the mathematical developments, we can then play all sorts of mathematical games – as we saw above.

How to start setting a budget

Doyle identified two types of company – those he called right-handed and those he called left-handed. Right-handed companies are those whose business models and strategies are defined by the market, and therefore marketing has the major say in strategy and budget; left-handed companies are those driven entirely by financial ratios and financial considerations, so strategies and budgets are almost entirely set in the light of fiscal considerations. There then arise two questions about setting marketing budget:

1. What constitutes a marketing budget?

2. Who sets it?

What constitutes a marketing budget?

This is a fundamental question that concerns the measuring of marketing success: if marketing is to be measured on the impact of all 4Ps, then we should have some say in the resource allocated – the funding of new product development (NPD), for example. Not only should NPD be managerially under direct marketing control, but so also should the funding, as should logistics strategy. If marketing is only to be measured in terms of an advertising budget, then marketing is not responsible as a function for the other elements of the marketing mix, and cannot be measured on them. Similarly, a company which is not yet a marketing orientated, tempo-driven (see Chapter 10) company will not succeed as well as one that is, and the measure of marketing success will depend on non-marketing orientated departments within the company – for the performance of which marketing cannot be held responsible when the marketing function is being measured.

Who sets a marketing budget?

There are two approaches to budget setting. In left-handed companies, the budget is set by fiscal considerations.

The finance department's approach

The finance department's approach is usually a mixture of the following:

- How much can I afford to give you? Crudely speaking, this is:

  Profit after income and tax − Reserves − Dividend − All other expenditures = What is left for budgets

While it may be fiscally prudent, it implies that there is no relationship between marketing spend and market share. If there is, this approach accepts that the market will give us what we deserve. And if there is no relationship between marketing spend and market share (and therefore return on investment), we may as well have no budget at all, and go and dust off the CV.

- How much did you have last year? (This year will be the same plus or minus a bit.) The implication here is again that there is no relationship between increased marketing spend on brand building, channel development and new value creation, and increased market share, or the implication is that we are satisfied with last year's market share.

Bulmer's (of Hereford), part of the Scottish and Newcastle group, increased marketing spend on its Strongbow cider brand to £27 m in 2005/2006. Strongbow was already Britain's best-selling cider brand. The strategy hinged on a major advertising campaign and on introducing two new products – Strongbow Sirrus and Bulmer's Original.

'This double strategy is paying rich dividends with sales growth in all areas of the cider market.' said David Jones, a Bulmer's spokesman.

Strongbow increased sales by 11 percent.

(Source: Kibbler, 2006)

- Rule of thumb. This usually gives a budget as a percentage of revenue or profit. This percentage varies from industry to industry; fmcg seem to have a greater faith in marketing budgets than business-to-business enterprises.

Table 12.4 highlights some typical A/S and A/P ratios in the USA.

The assumption here is that some marketing activity, usually thought of as advertising spend, is essential to put the product into the public mind, but that there is no relationship between marketing spend and purchase.

If we look at what marketing spends its budget on, we can see that there is at least a clear indication that spend on brand is worthwhile (Table 12.5).

Industry	Ad. spend as % sales	Ad. spend as % margin	Annual ad. growth rate
Health insurance	1.1	8.6	1.0
Preserves (jams, etc.)	1.7	5.8	11.3
Soft toys	12.1	23.2	−8.7
Footwear	4.5	10.6	7.0
Direct mail	25.3	67.5	29.3
Car accessories	0.4	2.6	−9.9
Cosmetics	8.2	17.3	0
Poultry products	4.9	42.3	9.4
Wines and spirits	10.6	27.5	10.2

Table 12.4
Typical advertising ratios (US data from Schonfeld and Associates, www.saibooks.com)

	Blind-tested	Open-tested
Prefer Pepsi (%)	51	23
Prefer Coke (%)	44	65
Don't know (%)	5	12

Table 12.5
Blind-testing preference for brand (cited in de Chernatony and McDonald, 2003)

In other words, Pepsi is marginally preferred when the product is devoid of its brand, but Coke hugely so when the brand is seen. Such is the impact of brand. If advertising spend was just in line with industry averages on both sides (about 6.3 percent of sales in the US market), we wouldn't expect this massive shift. So advertising, particularly brand advertising, really does have an impact on preference, and thus on market share and thus on return on investment – and so these left-hand driven budget-setting methods are highly flawed in terms of long-term growth.

The operational department's approach
The operational (in our case marketing) department's approach is usually: What do I need to do the job?

● Mission requirements are broken down into marketing components (as seen in right-handed companies and following Hastings (see Chapter 11), for example), and each is costed

● What strategic actions must I take to ensure that the objectives are set? Indeed, how do I set objectives to meet the strategic aims and link them to budget?

● What data, information and knowledge do I need to set a budget?

A rational approach to setting a budget
Setting a budget is one of the most knowledge-intensive activities in which a marketer can be involved, and is the wellhead of resource. While this is

not a book about strategies in marketing, we have to have a strategy to implement, and the strategy must be able to be assessed both at the black-box and at the sub-box level. The approach to budgeting offered here is based on an assumption that data is available.

As a basic idea, we can assume that profit is a growth function of market share, even if it does slow down as we buy more market share, as we saw in Figure 12.6.

We will start with a basic Share of Voice model. Share of Voice (SoV) models are quite good for stable consumer markets. This SoV model has been developed much further in differential resource analysis, giving in essence a weighted SoV model, and we can have a look at how to make these improvements later. As an example, we will start to set objectives and resource them with a budget for our company, which markets bottled water.

In our world, the market for bottled water consists of sparkling water and still water sold in two sizes – handy and half-litre bottles. Calcium-enriched water, which we don't sell, comes in handy sizes only. For the sake of simplicity, we are going to assume that we service a single segment with still and sparkling water in both half-litre and handy sizes.

The basic model SoV as enunciated by the American consultancy Frank-Lynn is:

Product cover × Channel cover × Brand selection = Market share

This model assumes an equal value in the sales exchange for all products in the market, which is why price is not a factor at this stage.

Product cover is a measure of how many different versions of the product there are on the market. Suppose that bottled water comes in two sizes (half-litre and handy quarter-litre sized bottles) and in two types – still (available in fresh and calcium-enriched styles) and sparkling – both types being readily available in each size apart from calcium-enriched, which is only available in the smaller bottle. If we only make handy-sized bottles of still water, our product cover is 20 percent, or 0.2. This assumes that the market size and demand for each of the five products in the market are equal. It may not be true, but as a first approximation, it isn't too bad. If we don't make a particular product type – for example, we don't make calcium-enriched water – we automatically lose its share of the market (see Table 12.6).

We have assumed that half-litre bottles of still water sell twice the volume of handy-sized bottles, and half-litre bottles of sparkling sell half that volume, etc. The weighting is a simple proportional calculation. From the data, our product cover is 0.85.

Channel cover is a measure of our product's saturation in the marketplace. Suppose bottled water is only sold in multiple forecourts (garages), supermarkets, and convenience multiples (corner shops). Suppose also that we

Table 12.6 Product cover calculations on SoV model

A	B	C	D	E	F
Products in the market (by type) (*n* = number of product types)	Initial probability (1/*n*)	Relative importance in the market (based on proportion of total sales)	Relative probability (must add to 1), calculated by B × C	Do we manufacture it? (Yes = 1, no = 0)	Product cover, calculated by D × E
Half-litre still	0.2	2	0.4	1	0.4
Half-litre sparkling	0.2	0.5	0.1	1	0.1
Handy-sized still	0.2	1	0.2	1	0.2
Handy-sized sparkling	0.2	0.75	0.15	1	0.15
Handy-sized calcium-enriched	0.2	0.75	0.15	0	0
Total	1		1		0.85

only sell our bottled water through garages. Therefore, our channel cover is 33 percent, or 0.33. Again, this presupposes that each channel is of equal penetration in the marketplace and that we sell water in every garage. You can make a correction for this assumption by looking at the importance to the market of each channel, and repeating the sort of calculations we have just done in the example above.

Our unweighted channel cover is 0.33.

Brand selection is about that proportion of the served market that prefers our brand to that of our competitors. It is going to consist of two parts:

1. Brand awareness (BA) – the percentage of the served segment who have heard of our brand

2. Brand preference (BP) – that percentage of the served segment who have heard of our brand and who prefer it over the competitor's.

Brand selection, then, is

BS = BA × BP

So if 80 percent of the served market has heard of our brand, BA = 0.80; if 60 percent of those who have heard of our brand actually prefer it over the competitor, then BP = 0.6. Thus

BS = 0.80 × 0.6 = 0.48

Our brand selection cover is 0.48.

Our market share of bottled water, according to the SoV model, will therefore be:

$$0.85 \times 0.33 \times 0.48 = 0.13$$

(i.e. 13 percent of the market). If we know the value of the bottled water market (it happens to be around £900 m), our expected revenue will be £117 m; if we know how many litres the market is (around 1000 million), we need access to 13 percent of 1000 million = 130 million litres. Now we can calculate how many units we will sell – i.e. if a handy-sized bottle holds a quarter of a litre, we will sell 520 million bottles. We could now feed these results into a cost–volume–profit analysis.

Is that what the Financial Wizard is basing his calculations on? Close enough? How is he calculating next year's performance? We can now go back to the earlier equations and do some calculations. We can also look at the supply of raw materials (130 million litres is the water availability of the State of Georgia each day) and its impact.

This simple SoV model also gives us a rough idea of where we need to put our marketing resource to increase the market share to meet the expected income on which the financial state of the company is going to be based.

Now we understand where we need to apply our resources to increase market share: strategically.

- Will we get best value from providing calcium-enriched water (i.e. increase the coverage to 1 and SoV market share to 16 percent)?

- Will we get better value from the budget by moving into corner shops as well as retaining the garage outlets (i.e. increase channel cover to 0.66, so SoV then becomes $0.85 \times 0.66 \times 0.48 = 27$ percent)?

- Should we increase brand selection; either by (a) increasing our brand awareness (say to 0.9, so BS becomes 0.54; the SoV model then becomes $0.85 \times 0.33 \times 0.54 = 0.15$, or 15 percent); or (b) increasing brand prefer-ence (by increasing trials or building further brand equity for the pur-chaser) to 80 percent, when BS becomes 0.64 and the SoV model is $0.85 \times 0.33 \times 0.64 = 0.18$, or 18 percent?

We are now starting to develop a foundation for our marketing budget by looking rationally at what marketing objectives we need to set up. Of course we can't afford to enter every corner shop, but by looking at a pro-portion we can start to understand the outcomes, and hence start to be able to look inside the black box as we approach measuring marketing success.

Therefore we can set ourselves a good budget, rationally based on an out-come, tied to logical measures of marketing success, but we have only really looked at understanding what goes into the black box and what comes out. We have tried to understand a little about the workings of the black box – what we put into marketing and what we get out. We have had a glimpse of a way of getting the company to share responsibility for the output of the company, but we still need to investigate further what goes on inside the black box. To do that, we really have to bite the bullet and get on with the numbers' games.

How finance impacts marketing

We as marketers need to understand what the Financial Wizard is talking about, how what he thinks and does affects marketing, and how we can measure our return for marketing investment, thereby showing that marketing activities give best value for the budget allocated. The purpose of being in business, after all, is to make a profit on the investments – in fact, to make a bigger profit on the investment than other investment opportunities; why would someone invest in my company if they could get a better return on that investment by putting it on deposit in the bank or, in the case of a company making a loss, putting it under the bed?

The Financial Wizard uses *accounts* to collect the data and *financial analysis* to create and make the associations to turn the data into information. It is the use of this information which marketers need to understand to help them to build the common ground that we saw in Table 12.2 between the financial function and the marketing function, so here we will:

- start with a look at the data in financial accounts
- then see how associations are made and
- look at how the resulting information affects how marketing is perceived and measured.

Financial accounts

The financial accounts only talk about three things:

1. Where the money came from (the balance sheet: this is only data).

2. Where the money is now (the profit and loss account: still data).

3. Whether things are good, bad, getting better or getting worse (financial analysis: associations).

Where the money came from (which we find on the balance sheet) is three places:

1. *Share capital* – the original investment as made by the original shareholders.

2. *Long-term loans* – how much was borrowed and still needs to be repaid; this turns up in Figure 12.3, in the gearing section, as risk; if the interest rate goes up we pay more interest out of our profits so there is less money available for dividend payout, thus increasing the investment risk of the business by giving worse returns than some other opportunity.

3. How much *profit we squirreled away* to help run the business in the future – this retained money is called, rather misleadingly, Reserves.

Some of the reserves become converted into assets:

- *Fixed assets* are things we intend to keep and use to run the business, such as machinery, IT equipment and so forth. When these are bought out of retained profits they too come under Reserves.

- *Current assets* are things we are using to sell – raw materials, half-finished goods and so on. This, because it is money set to work, comes out of *working capital*.

It is worth remembering that modern accounting grew while the primary economic driver was manufacturing; sometimes the terms fit very uncomfortably with a service industry.

Liquidity, or can we pay our debts?

If we want to know how much money there is to contribute to marketing resources, then we need to know how much money there is sloshing around in the company – or how liquid the company is. Absolute figures don't actually tell us very much, so we need to take a bigger picture. We need to consider what we own and what we owe – and, of course, what we are owed.

Companies all have debts (payable to those people who have extended credit to us: they are called our 'creditors'), and these debts we call liabilities. Hopefully our assets are greater than our liabilities! To test this, the Financial Wizard in his analysis takes the ratio of

Current assets/Current liabilities

as a measure of how much more money we have for the business over the money we owe. This ratio is called the current ratio, and as far as marketers are concerned is a measure of:

- how much money is going to be available to spend on building the brand value that the customer will exchange for money, and

- how much money we will have to spend on developing our customers and progressing them up the ladder, both of which will contribute to *future* profit.

The Financial Wizard is conservative; he often believes that the stock which we hold, and half-finished goods and raw materials, are of no value, yet he has included them in current assets. He therefore often uses a ratio called the *quick ratio*. It isn't quick to do, but suggests how quick(ly) the current assets can be turned into cash to pay the liabilities. The calculation for this is:

(Current assets − Stock)/Current liabilities

Traditionally, Financial Wizards suggest that the current ratio figure should be 2 and the quick ratio should be 1 or greater. However, in reality there is

Table 12.7 Ratios other than textbook values

Industry	Current ratio	Quick ratio	Comment
Banks	1.1	0	All the assets are stock; there are no assets other than stock, so the real estate is not an asset and may be held on a leaseback basis
Used-car dealers	1.2	0.3	Almost all the assets are stock, as you would expect from a used-car dealer; cash flow will be important
Hotels	0.4	0.2	
Advertising	1.0	0.9	There is very little stock in advertising, hence these ratios are not a comfortable fit with service industries
Social service companies	1.4	1.0	Again, little stock but good assets
Metal forging and stamping	1.2	0.9	Little stock, possibly due to a just-in-time manufacturing process or a high level of bespoke manufacture leaving little speculative stock
'Great Britain plc'	1.1	0.7	Should be compared with other G7 countries

a 'benchmark' figure that will be different for the demands and general operational effectiveness of different industries. Look at Table 12.7.

The other thing we need to consider is the cyclic behaviour of the industry, and when the financial year (i.e. preparation of accounts) takes place in the cycle. A fireworks manufacturer, for example, will have a lower stock holding on 6 November than on 1 November (or in the USA, on 5 July than on 3 July), and this may well reflect in the stockholding ratio.

So we should expect The Financial Wizard to look at our own company's ratios in comparison to those of other companies in our industry. Look at Table 12.8, relating to the confectionary trade.

Company	Current ratio	Quick ratio
Cadbury	0.62	0.46
Mars	0.63	0.42
Wrigley	3.25	2.84
Kraft	0.8	0.63

Table 12.8
Company's ratios in the confectionary trade (source: Keynote 2002)

The current ratio and the quick ratio are the main measures of liquidity. They allow marketers to understand how much money is available for marketing activities, and why there isn't much.

It is clear from Table 12.7 that different industries carry different amounts of stock, or that work in progress (taken as stock in these equations) is higher because manufacturing takes longer. One might ask what there is in Wrigley's business model (see Table 12.8) that needs such a high ratio compared to the other industry members.

Looking at a cotton shirt, it takes one year from the cotton plant flowering to the shirt being admired in the office; on the other hand, a pint of milk takes only three or four days from cow to teacup. This is an instance where one blanket does not cover all. It is therefore best if marketers make the effort to learn the benchmark ratios for their industry. These can be obtained from Dunn and Bradstreet's annual publication, *Key Financial Ratios*.

Stock turn, or, is it flying off the shelf?

Managing the conversion of raw materials into finished goods, the warehousing of the stock and the logistics of getting it onto the shop counter, provides a measure of how quickly marketing can turn the raw materials into profit. As this will affect the ratios, we want as little money tied up in stock as possible. It is also a measure of a company's efficiency at operations – in other words, the effectiveness of their just-in-time manufacturing. Stock turnover is a number – how many times in a certain period (usually a year) the company turns raw materials into profit. There are two ways to approach this:

1. The stock turnover, measured as (Sales/Total stock), which looks at the *number of times* stock turned into profit, and

2. An adaptation of this (Stock/(Sales/365)), which gives an indication of the length of time in days that stock is held on the shelves. This is useful for marketers to see how eagerly the customer pulls the product off the shelf. If it is too long, marketing needs to do something about it; a sales promotion perhaps, or another promotional campaign.

Related to selling is the speed with which customers pay for their goods and services. If they take too long, we could be lending them interest-free money – especially if we pay our suppliers before they pay us. On the other hand, we need to balance the attractiveness of credit terms (as part of the value of our market offering) against those of our competitors.

> On 13 August 2006, Nissan and Vauxhall both offered 0% APR interest for three to five years on new car sales. Are they really not paying their suppliers for five years?
>
> (Source: *The Sunday Times*, 13 August 2006)

Thus we need a measure of how long we lend money to our customer for, and for how long we borrow it from our suppliers. The ratio (Debtors/ (Sales on credit/365)) gives a value in days which tells us how long it takes the Financial Wizard to collect the money that we are owed for goods and services already delivered to a customer.

Similarly, (Creditors/(Purchases on credit/365)) gives a value in days of how long we take to pay our suppliers.

Current account financing

Ideally, we want to pay out after we receive, so one of the measures of a successful company is that the debtor days are fewer than the creditor days. Either way, what is affected is the cash flow through the company. Many companies regard their cash flow as if it was a current bank account – when and how much do I pay in, and when and how often do I write cheques? If the cash balance is too far into the black, maybe we can transfer some of it into a high-interest deposit account; if we are close to our overdraft, we have to stop spending – and rest assured, that advertising campaign that you have just spent weeks planning is likely to be a casualty!

Marketers are rarely responsible for deciding how long we will take to pay our suppliers, and anyway there are government guidelines and requirements (especially in UK) about this. So if marketing makes a decision which will lengthen the debtor days, maybe through some promotional activity (such as buy now, pay in January), the impact of the cash flow through the company MUST be a consideration.

DFS, the UK furniture showroom, ran the following advert for their 'Haines' three-seater leather sofa on 24 September 2004:

Regular price	£895
Offer price	£595
Finance	0% (0%APR) for four years
Payment schedule	Nothing to pay for one year

(Source: abstract from *The Sunday Times Magazine*, 24 September 2006)

Marketers therefore have a vested interest in cash flow, in creditor days and in debtor days, and in the relationship between them. Chaotic movements in financial ratios and these four crucial measures can indicate crisis and recovery in a company. Table 12.9 shows these key ratios for Marks and Spencer between 2000 and 2005. The current/liquidity ratios show considerable volatility; when converted to shareholder funds per employee, we can see a dramatic drop. Look also at the creditor days and the debtor days.

Table 12.9
Key ratios for Marks and Spencer between 2000 and 2005

Year	2005	2004	2003	2002	2001	2000
Current ratio	0.65	3.04	3.03	3.13	1.77	1.72
Liquidity ratio	0.39	2.84	2.83	2.95	1.54	1.5
Shareholder funds per employee (£)	7396	64 575	75 036	68 897	60 731	64 836
Gearing (%)	565.54	74.75	52.31	62.66	44.95	43.15

Source: *The Mercurial Marks and Spencer Data*, from FAME.

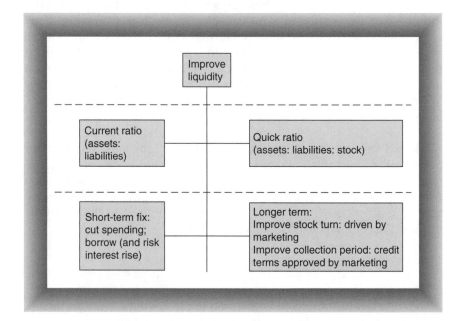

Figure 12.7
Liquidity summary

The Financial Wizard would summarize the use of ratios and their meanings as shown in Figure 12.7.

While the liquidity ratios looked at the availability of money in the company, so we need to look at profitability.

Profitability

If liquidity is about surplus money that we have got now, profitability is about where we got it from. Profitability is all about the ability of a company to generate profit from its assets. In other words, it's about what marketing added to the raw product, how it made the product available to the customer, how it sold it in the channel, what value it added through building a brand – and as such, profitability is *the* measure of marketing performance.

As a tool for our external measures, profit looks at:

- how much money we made selling what we made
- the cost of making it, which is made up of 'cost of sales' (materials, wages, royalties, license fees and other things directly attributable to making the product/delivering the service and overheads), costs we can't avoid having because we are in business, office rent, distribution costs, costs that we share because we make a number of different items.

Profitability is about the company's ability:

- to generate profits from a given level of sales, a marketing responsibility
- to generate sales from a given budget, or resource level.

Putting these two ideas together, we come up with: profitability is about profit and resource levels (capital employed) linked through sales.

The Financial Wizard would write this mathematically as:

Profit/Capital employed

And if we link this through sales,

(Profit/Capital employed) = (Profit/Sales) = (Sales/Capital employed)

- Profit/Capital employed is called 'Return on Capital Employed' (ROCE), or sometimes 'Return on Net Assets' (RONA), because, for practical and certainly our purposes, they are the same: we employ our net assets to make a profit
- Profit/Sales is our old friend margin
- Sales/Capital employed is called capital turnover, or more often, asset turnover (i.e. how many times we turned our capital (assets) into sales).

We can now look at each of the areas in which we deploy capital, be it in wages, product lines, advertising as components of the assets.

It is analysis of the Profit and Loss account – seeing where each component came from, understanding where each was spent – that allows us to resource the business. However, at this macro-level it doesn't tell us anything about what we do as marketers; merely what the outputs look like and how to interpret them. So as a measuring tool, the external financial levels are not the most useful data in the world; indeed, even with associations they only lead to information. Much more interpretation is needed, and some of that at a qualitative level, in order to measure the real success of marketing.

Increasing profitability

If we want to increase profitability (as opposed to increasing profit), we therefore need to investigate the efficient usage of assets. If we tabulate

Table 12.10 Common approaches to increasing profitability – margin

What	How	Method	Examples	Marketing involvement?
Increase margin	Improve profit			
		Reduce costs and other overheads		
			Reduce production overheads (increases sales/production costs ratio)	Yes; quality of product supports brand positioning
			Reduce distribution overheads (increases sales/distribution costs ratio)	Yes; fewer deliveries, fewer outlets, longer shelf-life, multiple deliveries, shared logistics
			Reduce administrative overheads; outsource some functions	Yes; outsourcing some functions; impact of outsourcing
			Reduce ground rent; offshore facilities	Yes; availability of skills in new location?

some of the more common actions, we can investigate marketing's involvement. To increase profitability, we must:

● increase the margin (Profit/Sales); see Table 12.10

● increase asset turnover (increase sales, or decrease capital employed); see Table 12.11.

Once again, we have deconstructed the task of measuring marketing's performance and can now compile the list of tasks that marketing measurements need to do in order to:

1. Progress towards a marketing orientation within the company

   ● measure multiple progress towards the mission

   ● measure internal progress

   ● measure individual functions' commitment to the company.

2. Measure marketing's macro outputs and benchmark them

   ● build a rational approach to strategic budgeting

   ● measure the outputs of the budgets as contribution to marketing success.

We can summarize this activity in our progress towards a measured and accountably successful marketing function.

Table 12.11   Common approaches to increasing profitability – asset turn

What	How	Method	Examples	Marketing involvement?
Improve capital/ asset turnover				
	Improve sales	Generate more sales		Yes; increase market share; develop new markets
	Improve productivity		Reduce fixed assets/capital employed	
			Reduce wages bill	
			Reduce spare capacity	Yes; sell spare capacity (caution: cannibalization; brand impact); increase sales
	Improve efficiency	Develop quality programme	Reduce reworking	Yes; quality issues impact on brand
			Reduce returns	Quality issues impact brand
	Minimize stock holdings	Reduces stock	Improve JIT manufacture	Yes; customer relationships

Trends and changes

We do not just look at other companies' performance; we also look at trends and attempt to understand them. Trends compare this year with previous years: in other words, we use the steady march of history to predict the future. The problem arises when the present deviates from that trend. Is the cause of the deviation us? Or is everyone in the industry affected? The ongoing energy crisis affects all companies in the transportation business, so a comparison of trends and with our competitors will be required.

Trends, movement in the ratios and sudden crises in our own ratios are indicative of change. We should, of course, compare our results with those of our competitors – did their ratios change as well, are they the same or worse than ours? If competitors' ratios didn't change, then it was not an industry-wide factor that caused the change. If they did change, were we better or worse?

We need then to seek explanations in the external environment. When developing the marketing plan in the first instance we will have constructed the SWOT, and from that conducted a SWOT analysis of strengths against opportunities and threats, and weaknesses against opportunities and threats, to identify key strategic areas in order to plan the way ahead by matching corporate competences. We should now compare the results to see whether they can explain any problems.

We need to consider changes that could be a result of the SAC – either because we drove it or because our competitors drove it. Is our value offering still relevant; have sales declined with a corresponding rise in stock holdings or increase in spare capacity?

Ongoing management and monitoring of marketing's outputs in all aspects is therefore required. One of the most popular and effective ways of gathering this to assist management that is in common use is the Balanced Score Card (BSC).

The balanced scorecard

The balanced score card (BSC) – which has strong similarities to *hoshin kanri*, the Japanese organization-wide strategic planning system developed in the late 1970s and early 1980s – was developed by Kaplan and Norton (*cf.* Kaplan and Norton, 1992, 1993, 2004). It is a management system rather than a measurement system, and as such it uses both lead and lag indicators to supplement metrics that assess management progress. It is an excellent tool to gather target areas on which resources have been spent and the results into one place.

A survey by Bain and Co (www.Bainco.com) in 2003 suggested that about 50 percent of the US Fortune 1000 companies used a Balanced Score Card.

The benefits of using the score card are that it:

- focuses the whole organization on the few things that will create breakthrough performance
- will help to integrate the various functions' separate programmes and bring the various different contributory programs into a single initiative
- reduces strategic measures to actions so that the functional managers and their staff can identify their role in producing the corporate mission.

How the scorecard contributes to measuring marketing

The BSC considers the company as being measured on four dimensions:

1. Financial measures.
2. Customer perception.
3. Internal business processes.
4. Growth and learning.

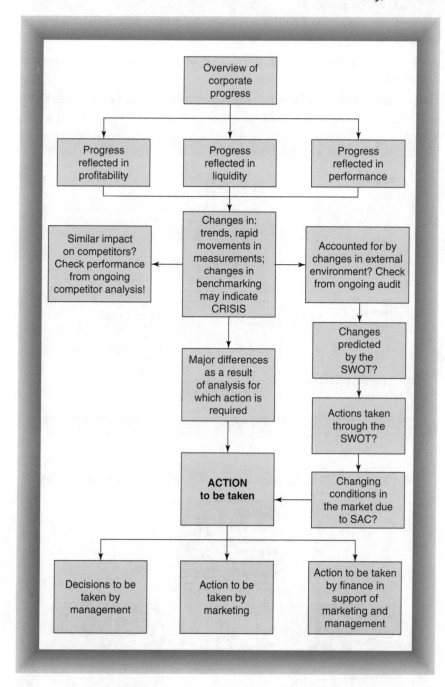

Figure 12.8
The management of ratio information

Each dimension discusses:

- objectives
- metrics
- targets
- initiatives (i.e. actions to achieve them).

In each case a metrics owner is appointed, in practice outside the line of the functional unit or department. One of the reasons for this is that it was deemed too easy to fudge the results if departments marked their own homework.

An example of the logical development of the score card is shown in Figure 12.9.

Diagrammatically, the BSC is usually represented as shown in Figure 12.10.

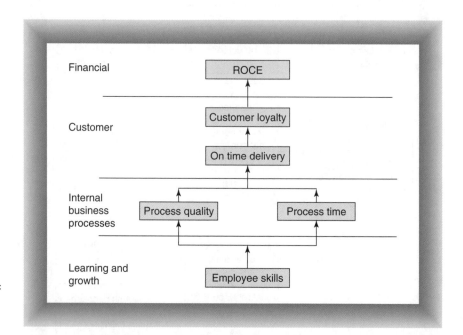

Figure 12.9
Logical structure of BSC (after Meek *et al.*, 2004)

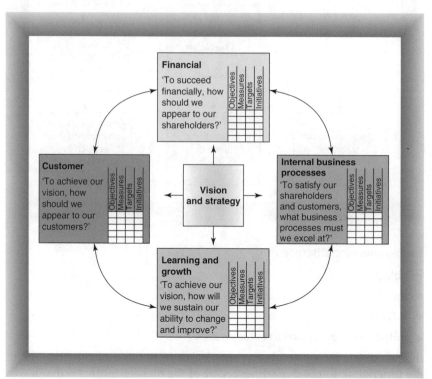

Figure 12.10
Schematic of balanced scorecard (from Kaplan and Norton, various dates)

We can now see how we are going to build into the scorecard the measures of successful marketing.

There are some flaws in accepting BSC as it stands – for example, while we consider that customers purchase best value for money, the concept of *best* needs to be carefully defined so that it can be interpreted and understood by the customer; time to market has its drawbacks as we saw in Chapter 10; a high index may well reflect elsewhere on a low revenue from pioneer products if the innovation is not accepted. And, of course, customer perceptions of best value and margins are linked. So BSC is a good tool, but it needs to be adapted for different conditions. Some measures and indices may well drop out and others be brought in.

Table 12.12 offers ideas on what is being measured.

However, as in all things, getting it right first time reduces the continuing cost of running the card as an ongoing activity. Collecting too much of the wrong data leads to the baby and bathwater syndrome; it also takes too long. Within each area we need a hierarchy of what data to collect, based on what knowledge of ourselves we want. Setting up a hierarchy can create a problem in itself.

Table 12.12   What is being measured

	Objectives	Measures
Financial	F1 Return on investment F2 Cash flow F3 Profitability F4 Profitable growth F5 Corporate reliability F6 Shareholder value	ROCE Funds available Margins Volume growth *v.* industry average Profit forecast reliability; order book Profit after tax; debt; equity; time.
Customer	C1 Value for money C2 Competitive price C3 Customer satisfaction	Customer survey data Price comparisons Customer survey data

Internal	I1 Marketing
	  • Product and service
	    development
	  • Brand strength
	I2 Operations
	  • Lowering operational costs
	  • Improved quality
	I4 Quality, etc.
		
		Percentage of product portfolio made
		  up of pioneer products
		Survey data
		
		Working capital
		Amount of reworking

Innovation and learning	L1 Innovation rate
	L2 Time to market
	L3 Influence of strategic
	  information
		% revenue from pioneer products
		Cycle time *v.* industry average time
		No. of management decisions based on
		  strategic information

Adapted from Kaplan and Norton (1993 and others).

Table 12.13   The steps to measurement

Score card area	Strategy supported	Aspect	Objective	Measure	Data to be collected
Internal	Cost reduction	Increase productivity	Reduce reworking by 5% over 3 months	Time devoted to reworking; scrap and replace	Cumulative hours; units scrapped and replaced
Customer perception	Improve margin through price elasticity	Improve brand position	Decrease adverse perception of product quality among target audience by 3 points over 6 months	Brand value; perceived value against nearest competitor	
Financial	Improve shareholder value	Increase profits	Improve margin by 3% over 6 months	Net profit (£)	Revenue, costs
Innovation	Retain market presence	Test market readiness for application of new technologies	Place three technologically new products on the market over 1 year	Uptake of product's market share	units; £, product lifecycle data; %,£

We can see four steps to measurement:

1. Set a measurable description for the objective to be measured.

2. Get commitment from the agent who will deliver the objective.

3. After the activity, measure according to the description.

4. If there is an adverse mismatch, set actions to improve next time (or adjust the objective's aspirations – it might not be possible to reach the moon in an air balloon).

It is useful to turn these steps into a form, for example as in Table 12.13.

We can summarize measuring marketing success and its financial outcomes into a simple table, assessing the direct/indirect input to the BSC of each contributor to marketing success (see Table 12.14).

Resourcing

We have seen how resource is a crucial factor in implementing marketing. It affects time and the deployment of technology to support time, both in terms of the technology available and ready to meet product introduction and production as well as in terms of supporting the workplace to assist in

Table 12.14   Contributing to marketing success and the BSC

	Deconstructed mission and goals	Pan-corporation marketing orientation	Strategy interpretation	Marketing outcomes
Financial	Indirect	Indirect	Direct	Direct
Internal	Direct	Direct	Indirect	Direct
Customer	Indirect	Indirect	Direct	Direct
Innovation	Indirect	Direct	Direct	Direct

the tempo of marketing. The resource of time needs the most careful managing. In Chapter 10 we considered absolute time and relative time, and looked at how time pacing and event pacing contributed to the resource requirements and using the right resource to meet the conditions for sustained competitive advantage. We also investigated the resource of time as the critical factor in combative marketing to generate best value for the customer and to discommode the competitor; by adapting to and then changing the operating environment into which we market we have started the process of creating sustained advantage. We discussed the tools for prediction, and hence the future requirements for resource, and the resources required to fit into marketing's tempo and, in doing so, how we need to build knowledge of the operational environment.

Developing knowledge requires us to fit market research and data gathering into the tempo of marketing activity which is driving the sustained advantage cycle. The acquisition of data resource was discussed, as was how to generate knowledge. We looked at how the customer can be useful in developing that knowledge base, and how we need to develop him in terms of bonding. We discussed setting up standing data collection requirements and how we might disseminate the results rapidly, again in support of the tempo of marketing.

Lastly, we investigated the measurement of our success in marketing from two directions: first, setting up the conditions before implementation so that we can start the process of ruling out unsuccessful implementations before they start; and secondly, looking at the mission of the company and developing a whole-company approach to support the introduction of a marketing orientation within the whole company. We looked at approaches to understanding the true role of marketing within a company, and discussed resource requirements in terms of analysing the marketplace and strategies before budget-setting. We looked at ways in which we could assess and deploy budgets through the use of Share of Voice models and cost–volume–profit analysis, and investigated the links between these two to verify resourcing. We looked at financial measures of corporate activity and how marketing will affect them and therefore the business at large, and also considered the impact of the business measures and their relevance to the operational environment. Lastly, we turned our attention to selecting a measured whole-company management system which allowed us to inquire of the whole company how it is moving towards the mission. We did this through the concept of a balanced score card, integrating the mission, financial, marketing and intracorporate activities.

This section has discussed the implications and implementation of resource by looking at their contribution to that fundamental of resources, time.

References and further reading

References

Buzzell, R.D. and Gale, B.T. (1987). *The PIMS Principle*. New York: Free Press.

Davidson, H. (2005). *The Committed Enterprise*, 2nd edn. Oxford: Elsevier.

de Chernatony, L. and McDonald, M. (2003). *Creating Powerful Brands*, 3rd edn. Oxford: Elsevier.

Doyle, P. (2000). *Value Based Marketing*. Chichester: Wiley.

Hamel, G. and Prahalad, C.K. (1994). *Competing for the Future*. Boston, MA: Harvard Business School Press.

Harris, L. (1998). Barriers to market orientation: the view from the shop floor. *Marketing Intelligence and Planning*, **16(1)**, 221–228.

Hastings, S. (1996). A strategy evaluation model for management. *Management Decision*, **34(1)**, 25–34.

Kaplan, R.S. and Norton, D.P. (2004). *Alignment: How to Apply the Balanced Scorecard to Corporate Strategy*. Boston, MA: Harvard Business School Press.

Kaplan, R.S. and Norton, D.P. (1993). Putting the balanced scorecard to work. *Harvard Business Review*, **71(5)**, 134–147.

Kaplan, R.S. and Norton, D.P. (1992). The Balanced Scorecard; measures that drive performance. *Harvard Business Review*, **70(1)**, 71–79.

Kibbler, A. (2006). Cheers to Sparkling Cider Sales. *Hereford Times*, 10 August.

Meek, H., Meek, R., Palmer, R. and Parkinson, L. (2004). *Managing Marketing Performance*. Oxford: Butterworth-Heinemann.

Piercy, N.F. (2002). *Marketing-led Strategic Change*, 3rd edn. Oxford: Elsevier.

Rappaport, A. (1986). *Creating Shareholder Value: The New Standard for Business Performance*. New York: Free Press.

Further reading

Kaplan, R.S. and Norton, D.P. (2000). *The Strategy-focused Organization: How Balanced Scorecard Companies Thrive in the New Business Environment*. Boston, MA: Harvard Business School Press.

Kaplan, R.S. and Norton, D.P. (1996). *Balanced Scorecard: Translating Strategy into Action*. Boston, MA: Harvard Business School Press.

Kotler, P. and Lilien, G. (1983). *Marketing Decision Making: A Model Building Approach*. New York: Harper and Row.

Taylor, A. and Steward, K. (1990). *Financial Handbook for Sales and Marketing Managers*. London: Cassell.

Index